Love to Love You Bradys

the bizarre story of The Brady Bunch Variety Hour

Written by
TED NICHELSON

Commentary and Special Features by
SUSAN OLSEN

Art Direction and Design by
LISA SUTTON

This book is lovingly dedicated to all those who helped bring *The Brady Bunch Variety Hour* to life ...and lived to tell about it

Published by ECW PRESS
2120 Queen Street East, Suite 200, Toronto, Ontario, Canada M4E 1E2
416.694.3348 / info@ecwpress.com

LIBRARY AND ARCHIVES OF CANADA CATALOGUING IN PUBLICATION

Nichelson, Ted
Love to love you Bradys : the bizarre story of the Brady bunch variety hour
Ted Nichelson, Susan Olsen, and Lisa Sutton.

ISBN-13: 978-1-55022-888-5

1. Brady Bunch Variety Hour (Television program).
i. Olsen, Susan, 1961– ii. Sutton, Lisa iii. Title.

PN1992.8.V3N53 2009   791.45'72   C2009-902529-9

Editors: Emily Schultz, David Caron
Design and typesetting: Lisa Sutton
Printing: Transcontinental

PRINTED AND BOUND IN CANADA

First printing, 2009

ECW PRESS
ecwpress.com

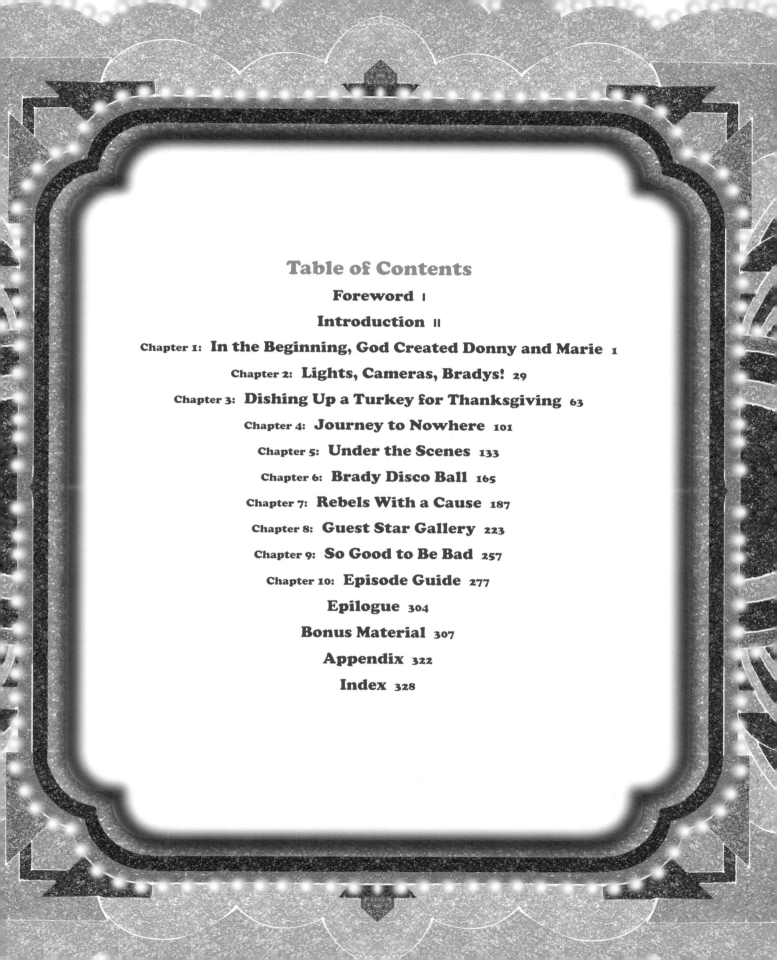

Table of Contents

Foreword

Ever since ending its brief run on television in 1976–77, *The Brady Bunch Variety Hour* has somehow managed to establish itself as one of the eminently infamous, yet mysterious, programs ever produced. Although the Bradys are among the most beloved and recognizable of all sitcom families, this particular outgrowth of the 1969–74 series remains surprisingly unknown. For over three decades it has been largely withheld from the public with the expectation it would quietly fade into obscurity and never be seen again. But this show sank to such depths of lunacy, and was so incredibly bizarre, that it cries out from the grave to be memorialized and preserved for future generations.

When I first met with Susan Olsen and Lisa Sutton to propose this book, we were blissfully unaware of the incredible challenge that lay before us. We couldn't help but love to love the Bradys singing and dancing their way through the disco era with legendary '70s icons such as Tina Turner, Farrah Fawcett, and Redd Foxx. However, we were disappointed when we discovered that almost all materials related to the show had completely disappeared. Was *The Brady Bunch Variety Hour* the victim of a secret Hollywood conspiracy? Much of the supporting cast and crew had seemingly vanished into thin air. When I ultimately located everyone, their reactions ran the gamut. Some people were respectfully polite, yet suspicious, while others were completely shocked by my interest. A few were consumed by uncontrollable laughter, and then there were individuals who fostered palpable hostility at dredging up past events. The emotions coming from people when asked about *The Brady Bunch Variety Hour* were often very strong. I can only say that I endured the experience of interviewing over 100 individuals and, with only a few exceptions, everyone involved with the show was encouraging, helpful, and eventually came to develop a feeling of pride for having been a part of it.

I am grateful to Sid and Marty Krofft and Sherwood and Lloyd Schwartz for being especially supportive of this endeavor. This book also would not have been possible without the assistance of David Caron from ECW Press and our editor, Emily Schultz. There are also dozens other people who so willingly gave of their time, and please accept my eternal thanks. Your spirit of friendship has inspired me when I needed it the most.

This remarkable and compelling story can finally be told for the very first time. Until now *Brady Bunch* fans have unfortunately been denied such an opportunity. It is my sincere hope that our efforts will bring some sense of understanding to *The Brady Bunch Variety Hour,* and that it can be enjoyed and seen in a new light.

Indeed, it's a sunshine day.

— Ted Nichelson
September 2009
Hollywood, California

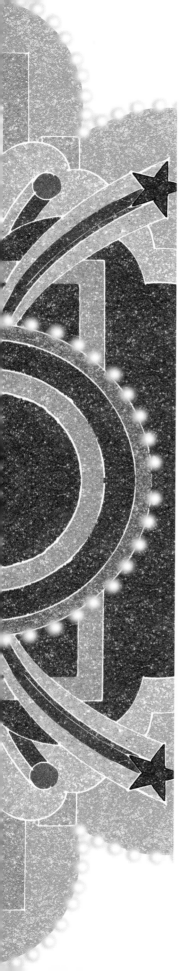

Introduction
by Susan Olsen

How does television's favorite family end up in history's worst show? This begs for some explanation. Having been the youngest member of *The Brady Bunch* for almost all of my life, my inside view may provide some explanation, but alas, there are no excuses.

It is difficult to comprehend how *The Brady Bunch Variety Hour* could ever come to be. This endeavor was the brainchild of Sid and Marty Krofft, who must have been puffin' a little too much stuff when, in 1976, they came up with the idea of making a musical version of *The Brady Bunch*. Alright, it wasn't just a sudden hallucination. The Kroffts had four *Brady Bunch* cast members guest star on *The Donny and Marie Show* and the ratings were so good that the network responded with the typical "more will be better!" — which is rarely the case.

That might explain the insanity of the creators and network, but what about ours? Why did we cast members, with the exception of a very fortunate Eve Plumb, go along with it all so willingly? I believe that the main driving force behind our doing this show was the same factor that may have made *The Brady Bunch*, in its original flavor, an enduring success: we *really* liked each other! The genuine affection that helped grant eternal life to our situation comedy was not enough to surmount the variety hour format, especially not a production so bereft of subtlety. However, an odd sense of family must have played a role in all of us signing our contracts.

To say that we blindly went along with things in the hopes that it all would turn out well is correct. To say that we really believed that we were doing something that had any kind of merit could have varying truth among individual cast members. During the production we had different views of what the show was and was not. This had a lot to do with the fact that we were each given a different description of the show by its creators, Sid and Marty Krofft. Each description was fabricated to appeal to the individual so that they would agree to do the show. Barry Williams was told that the show would be very musical and he would be the star. The show would revolve around him, giving him a wide variety of musical numbers to display his talents. Chris Knight was told that the music was not a big part of the show and he would only have to appear in the opening and closing production numbers. The rest of the *Variety Hour* would be based in sketch comedy featuring, of course, Chris. I'm sure we all had our moments of realizing that this wasn't going to be something we would want to be remembered for.

At this point I can only speak for myself as to my hopes for the show. I knew there was something wrong with this production early on, but it wasn't anything worse than a lot of what was already happening on TV during the 1970s and I wanted to do it. I grew up worshipping *The Carol Burnett Show*. While the musical numbers were never anything

I would have been too interested in, the eye candy of Bob Mackie's costumes made them wonderful. I was content to appreciate the visuals while I waited for more comedy sketches featuring Tim Conway and Harvey Korman. When we made our appearance on *The Donny and Marie Show*, I had nothing but admiration and love for Donny and Marie as people. I was very impressed with their hard work and what they were doing really looked like fun. I really enjoyed our time with them so when the opportunity to do more came along, I was all over it.

It's easy to say, "Hey, that was the '70s, *everything* was bad," but that isn't necessarily so. True, the decade had more than its fair share of bad taste. We think of Afros, platform shoes, and disco music, but there were other things going on at the same time. Bob Marley was touring, Led Zeppelin still had a drummer, and rednecks were throwing beer bottles at the Sex Pistols during their only American tour. The underground American punk movement was gaining steam in New York at Max's and CBGB's. *This* was where I wanted to be, that's where my artistic tastes were. This made doing the Hustle that much more painful. I faithfully bought my issues of *Creem*, *Circus*, and *Rock Scene* as soon as they came out. I carried them with me to the set of our variety show hoping that reading Lester Bangs might serve to protect me from the "artless crap" I was ashamed to be a part of but oddly, enjoyed performing.

The Bradys always find a way to have a good time together and our set was a pretty fun one. An opportunity to be a little older and working again with my second family was very hard to resist. My musical tastes aside, I figured we were all rehearsing so much and working so hard this thing just *had* to be good. I suppose the first reality of what *The Brady Bunch Variety Hour* really was became suddenly evident the day I stumbled upon the stage for our opening number. I was excited about the pool. While Donny and Marie had an ice-skating rink, we would have a swimming pool. Oh, how great that seemed!

I was eagerly anticipating seeing the set. I had hoped that it would be some wonderful spectacle, a sort of Busby Berkeley, Esther Williams extravaganza! …And then I saw it.

I saw the set as it was getting its final coat of glitter before being mounted on the pool. This set was about as far away from what I'd hoped for as anything could be. I couldn't even believe that somebody would make something so tacky (although after our pilot episode, substantial improvements were made). This was like the stage setting for a high-school talent show. While executed with a bit more finesse, the aesthetic was every bit as juvenile: huge, gaudy images cut from plywood braced to stand with two-by-fours painted in a color scheme from art hell. Purple! Chartreuse! Hot pink! All of these colliding in a *loud* color cacophony. I gazed upon this atrocity in disbelief. I am a fairly strong and resilient person.

©1977 Krofft Pictures

I don't cry easily. But seeing this set for our new show made me weep. For the first time I thought, "Wow…This thing could be embarrassing!"

Regardless of the end result, to me the most amazing part of this story is how many really *good* people were involved. There was no lack of great effort and talent, yet the fruit of these efforts was rotten before it even fell off the tree.

While *The Brady Bunch* has been loved and studied for years, the *Variety Hour* is not well known nor has it really been seen. Most people believe that it was just a one-time special and are shocked to find out there were nine episodes. It has been mentioned in documentaries like the *E! True Hollywood Story* and my own *Brady Bunch Home Movies*, but it has never really been examined. We cast members have always tried to underplay the show and sort of pretend that it never happened. I believe that this is a mistake. I believe this show's time has arrived! With the nostalgic love for the horror that was the '70s aesthetic, there is no more garish a Technicolor display than *The Brady Bunch Variety Hour.*

Bring it out to the light of day! We mustn't forget it happened. For we who survived, and for future generations, *The Brady Bunch Variety Hour* must be seen and rediscovered. The memory should be kept alive to assure that this will *never happen again.*

chapter 1
In the Beginning, God Created Donny and Marie
A Little Bit Country, a Little Bit Rock 'n' Roll, and a Whole Bunch of Brady

The Brady Bunch in 1970: (l to r) Susan Olsen, Mike Lookinland, Eve Plumb, Christopher Knight, Maureen McCormick, Barry Williams

The Brady Bunch

Over forty years after it first aired on television, *The Brady Bunch* continues to entertain, fascinate, and fill the hearts of people around the world with genuine happiness. But what exactly is the secret to its enduring appeal? While there have been other shows that ran longer, rated higher, and were critically acclaimed, the Bradys comprise the harmonious, loving family everyone fatansizes about and wishes for. Creator Sherwood Schwartz explains, "The most important thing in the world, I believe, is that people who come from different places need to get along. The Bradys were two different families who were brought together, and it struck a chord because everyone can identify with the problems of a blended family. They became a regular family with regular problems."

"Bradyisms" have infiltrated every aspect of our popular culture. More Americans know the words to *The Brady Bunch* theme than can correctly sing their own national anthem, and few people hear the name "Marcia" without spontaneously saying, "Marcia, Marcia, Marcia!" "Sunshine Day" and "Time to Change" are songs everyone recognizes and, by the way, what ever happened to Tiger? Those of an older generation may find this phenomenon perplexing, but for anyone who grew up with the show there is a universal language and understanding. According to "Bradyologist" Lisa Sutton, "Clearly it's from watching *The Brady Bunch* over and over again. It has the perfect balance of generic plotline and unchallenging sweetness with moments of arcane humor that everyone can relate to, no matter how trite or corny. It was part of a time and place where things were truly kinder and gentler. It was our last gasp of innocence."

It may come as a surprise that *The Brady Bunch* was not considered a successful show by television critics and it never placed in the top twenty-five programs during the five years it aired (1969–1974). Sherwood Schwartz came up with the idea for a new sitcom in 1966 when he read a newspaper article stating that at least twenty to thirty percent of all families had at least one child from a previous marriage. All three television networks rejected Schwartz when he pitched his concept, but ABC reconsidered when a movie about two blended families entitled *Yours, Mine, and Ours*, starring Lucille Ball and Henry Fonda, was a box-office hit. Schwartz rushed the pilot into production and on October 4, 1968, *The Bradley Brood* (the original title) officially began shooting on Stage 2 at the Paramount Ranch Lot in Culver City, California.

Sid Krofft

Marty Krofft

Schwartz remained uncertain if the show would ever reach the airwaves but it was unexpectedly picked up by ABC as a series for the 1969–70 season and premiered on September 26, 1969. It suffered from low ratings and was not renewed by the network for a second year, but at the last minute ABC reconsidered and gave the show another chance. Ann B. Davis, who played Alice Nelson, recalls, "I think there was only one year the whole time that we got renewed for a whole season. Every other time, it was thirteen-week orders. That part of it was nerve-racking. But it's something actors get used to."[1]

The Brady Bunch survived and went on to become one of the most successful shows in television history. Sid Krofft, a longtime friend of the cast, explains, "*The Brady Bunch*, the whole series, wasn't really a huge success. They never took their time period, but years later they became a symbol of America. When you mention them, everyone always has a smile on their face! Everyone always refers to *The Brady Bunch* when it comes to family, don't they?"

Subsequent series reincarnations include *The Brady Kids*, *The Brady Bunch Hour*, *The Brady Brides*, and *The Bradys*. There were also three television movies, *A Very Brady Christmas*, *Growing Up Brady*, *The Brady Bunch in the White House*; two theatrical releases, *The Brady Bunch Movie*, *A Very Brady Sequel*; two stage shows, *The Real Live Brady Bunch*, *A Very Brady Musical*; and a reality show, *My Fair Brady*.

Sid and Marty Krofft

At the very same time *The Brady Bunch* began production in 1969 on Stage 5 at Paramount Studios, two brothers by the name of Sid and Marty Krofft were right across the street on Stage 4 preparing to start filming their first television series, *H.R. Pufnstuf*. Little did anyone know that the two groups would someday become forever connected with producing what *TV Guide* proclaimed in 2002 the "4th Worst Show of All-Time": *The Brady Bunch Variety Hour*.

Sid and Marty Krofft were born in Montreal, Canada, and claim to come from five generations of puppeteers. Sid, who is eight years older than Marty, was encouraged by their father to follow in the family tradition and at the age of seven was already putting on puppet shows for neighbors. He was soon on tour performing in carnivals, and when the Krofft family moved to the Bronx in the 1940s Sid began working with his puppets at New Jersey nightclubs. The Ringling Bros. Circus soon took notice of Sid's talent and over the next two years paid him $75 a week to take his act on the road.

The Kroffts were devastated when their father died suddenly of a heart attack in 1949, and Sid moved to Paris where he staged performances at the famous Lido Burlesque Club. Back in the Bronx, Marty became a used car salesman after finishing high school in 1954. One year later Marty gave up everything and moved west to help Sid, who was performing the opening act for Judy Garland in Las Vegas.

By 1960, the brothers were an established team living in Hollywood when Sid came up with the idea for an adults-only extravaganza featuring topless marionette puppets as showgirls. They called their production *Les Poupées de Paris* and it played to sold-out audiences in Los Angeles. In 1962, they took the show to the Seattle World's Fair where it was a smash hit. Dean Martin took notice of the Krofft puppets and they became a regular feature on *The Dean Martin Show*, but after only eight episodes the Kroffts were let go because Martin felt he was being upstaged.

The Kroffts scored a major break in 1968 when William Hanna and Joseph Barbera approached them to design the animal costumes for their upcoming children's television show, *The Banana Splits*. NBC was impressed by the Kroffts' talent and asked the two brothers to develop a proposal for a live-action program to air on Saturday mornings. Sid and Marty were ecstatic when the network ordered seventeen installments of *H.R. Pufnstuf*, which was based on their puppet theater production *Kaleidoscope*. They then set up production at Paramount Studios and began work on their new show.

During production of *H.R. Pufnstuf* the Brady kids would sometimes drop in at Stage 4 to watch filming. Susan Olsen recalls, "When my best friend from school came over to visit me at Paramount, I requested that we could go in and watch *Pufnstuf*. They let us and the director was really nice about letting me get a good spot to watch. That's when I first met the Kroffts. When I requested to go there it was Marty who would come get me. I just remember looking way up at him, and he said, 'Do you want to come to the set?' and I said, 'Yeah!' I think all of us went over at different times because it was so neat. It was so colorful." In the weeks that followed, the Brady kids, along with their parents, all became friends of Sid and Marty. Although *H.R. Pufnstuf* was cancelled after its first season, the Kroffts never forgot *The Brady Bunch* and the time they spent together.

The Brady Kids in their first stage performance together at Caesars Palace in Las Vegas

The Hollywood Bowl

Several years after Sid and Marty Krofft left Paramount, the *Brady Bunch* kids started recording record albums — a move to keep in step with other family acts such as the Osmonds, the Jacksons, the Cowsills, and the Partridge Family. Their musical talents did not result in any top-ten hits, but the albums did end up producing a profit and in 1972 they hired Las Vegas producers Joe Seiter and Ray Reese to organize a concert tour. They premiered their act at Caesars Palace in Las Vegas on a TV awards show hosted by Ed Sullivan that featured Sonny and Cher, Lily Tomlin, and Danny Thomas. This success was followed by an appearance with Dick Clark on *American Bandstand*. In the summer of 1973 *The Brady Bunch Kids* went on a national tour where they sang all over the United States at arenas, amphitheaters, and state fairs. They performed on the same bill as the Fifth Dimension and Tony Orlando and Dawn. After a series of performances at Knott's Berry Farm, their agent booked them to perform with the Kroffts, who were producing *The World of Sid and Marty Krofft: Live at the Hollywood Bowl* for television.

"When we were filming the original *Brady Bunch* on Stage 5 at Paramount, *H.R. Pufnstuf* was in production right across the street," says Mike Lookinland. "We were filming right next to each other years before the Hollywood Bowl show. The Hollywood Bowl deal came about just as an offshoot of our stage act, and we had been doing that for a while."

Joe Seiter recalls that particular concert was a big challenge for the Brady kids. "The band made the opening number too fast. The second problem is that there were no stage monitors, so the kids could not really hear what the band was doing.

sid & marty krofft present

The
H.R. Pufnstuf
Show

Due to the chaos backstage with H.R. Pufnstuf, the Brady Kids are forced to warm up at the Hollywood Bowl while the audience came in.

The Carol Burnett Show **(1968–1978)**

All that was needed was a host to make introductions saying, "And now for something completely different…"

Tony Orlando and Dawn **(1974–1976)**

I'm amazed that they got as far as they did, and did as competent of a job as they did. They were really under pressure because they had no audio to listen to." Seiter also laments how disorganized the production was. They were forced into doing their sound check as the audience was coming in. Sid and Marty kept rehearsing *H.R. Pufnstuf* right up until the house was open, and only then did they let the Brady kids go out to warm up. Seiter and Reese were unhappy about how things turned out. "I wasn't too crazy about it, but what are you going to do?" Seiter says. "I don't even know why the program took place because all the Kroffts were interested in doing was promoting *H.R. Pufnstuf.* I never would have booked them on a show with puppets." But as a result of the production, *The Brady Bunch* cast renewed their prior relationship with the Kroffts and the kids were allowed an opportunity to demonstrate their musical abilities. The Kroffts had no idea that their entry into variety show television was just around the corner, and that *The Brady Bunch* would follow them there.

Variety Show Television

Variety shows were as much a part of the 1970s television landscape as reality shows are a part of the early twenty-first century. The variety genre originated from burlesque, minstrel, and vaudeville traditions in early nineteenth century America. At one moment an audience might have seen a juggler, followed by a Shakespearean monologue, and then a baggy-pants comedian. After intermission, there could be a magician, an animal trainer, and an opera singer. It was one thing after another and it didn't really matter if it held together. All that was needed was a host to make introductions saying, "And now for something completely different…"

In the early days of live television, variety shows were among the most popular of all programs. The genre saw vaudeville performers transporting their familiar stage and radio acts to a new broadcast medium. Stores and restaurants would often close early so that everyone could be home to watch series such as *Texaco Star Theater*, *Your Show of Shows*, or *Ted Mack's Original Amateur Hour*. With seventy-five percent of all Americans glued to the "boob tube" at any given moment, municipal authorities noticed that water usage would plummet during these hours.

Clearly, variety shows had become an American obsession.

The genre continued to thrive in the 1950s and 1960s with musical programs such as *The Lawrence Welk Show*, *The Liberace Show*, *The Dinah Shore Show*, and *Your Hit Parade*. Comedy-driven programs like *The Carol Burnett Show*, *The Colgate Comedy Hour*, *The Jack Benny Show*, and *The Smothers Brothers* were equally popular. *The Ed Sullivan Show* was a staple of variety television for over twenty years, and helped introduce America to both Elvis Presley and the Beatles.

By the 1970s, the American public was very familiar with the idea of television variety shows. According to radio talk show personality Frank DeCaro, "If there was a show and suddenly there was a swimming pool on the set we thought that made sense. If they had an ice-skating rink, that made sense. If it looked like a fashion runway, as it did on *Sonny and Cher*, it made sense. I think we were very open to any format and quite used to performers who could do a little comedy, could do a little singing, could do a bit of serious acting; it was whatever they could throw at you." Following the *Sonny and Cher* phenomenon in 1971, the networks stopped developing variety shows primarily around comedians and began looking to the record charts for the next generation of musical-variety stars. They included the Carpenters, the Jacksons, Mac Davis, Helen Reddy, Bobby Darrin, Jerry Reed, Glenn Campbell, Tony Orlando and Dawn, and the Captain and Tennille, among many others. DeCaro adds, "I think tremendous amounts of drugs propelled a lot of these shows, because you watch them now and they seem so completely deranged! They seem like they were created in a fever dream."

The Donny and Marie Show

The Osmonds were discovered in 1962 by talent scout Tommy Walker, and got their big break at Disneyland, where brothers Allan, Wayne, Merrill, and Jay premiered their barber shop quartet. This was quickly followed by television appearances on *The Andy Williams Show*, and a national tour that lasted for nearly two years. The Osmond Brothers signed a recording contract with MGM in 1971 and produced nine gold records in a single year, more than either Elvis or the Beatles achieved in such a short amount of time.

During the early 1970s Sid and Marty Krofft were equally busy, producing Saturday morning television shows such as *The Bugaloos*, *Lidsville*, *Sigmund and the Sea Monsters*, *Land of the Lost*, *Far Out Space Nuts*, and *The Lost Saucer*. In late 1975, ABC Television President Fred Silverman took notice of Donny and Marie Osmond when they recorded a series of popular remakes of oldies, such as "I'm Leaving It (All) Up to You," "Morning Side of the Mountain,"

and "Make the World Go Away." Silverman approached Sid and Marty to produce a variety show featuring the duo because, according to Donny Osmond, "We were very young and I had a teenybopper following and the Kroffts knew how to get the kids. It was a perfect tie-in."[2]

The Donny and Marie Show premiered on January 23, 1976, and was an instant success. "That was a big break for us. Because that wound up being a top-ten show. We

Florence, Susan, and Mike are reunited on
***Donny and Marie* in 1976**

Musical finale, "Renaissance Fair," from
Donny and Marie

went on at 8:00 on Friday with that and it was the first time ABC won the nights on Friday," recalls Marty Krofft.[3] The brother and sister act not only sang but also performed in a bizarre array of comedy sketches, usually dreamt up by Sid Krofft. Donny was usually the fall guy and the brunt of nearly all the jokes. "People still talk to me about the time I was thrown into a 96-gallon cream pie," recalls Donny.[4]

At the beginning of the second season, Silverman came up with the idea to reunite *The Brady Bunch* on *The Donny and Marie Show*. After some phone calls, the network managed to book Florence Henderson, Maureen McCormick, Mike Lookinland, and Susan Olsen as guest stars. This was the first time that many Bradys had been together in one room since their sitcom ended two years earlier. "When *The Brady Bunch* ended production we all went different directions and it wasn't until we got together again that we realized how much we missed each other," says Florence.[5] Susan remembers, "When I was called to be on *Donny and Marie* my first thought was, 'Oh no, I don't want to be on that awful show.' To me that was completely uncool, but it's hard to turn down work. But when I got there I loved it! I came away from it with total respect for Donny and Marie. It was like how I can't stand Broadway musicals but I would love to be in one. I watched Marie wearing all these different, neat costumes and doing all this stuff. I just thought, 'Wow!'"

Production #0205 of *The Donny and Marie Show* went into rehearsal on Monday, September 20, 1976. In the episode Florence performed a medley of country folk songs with Donny and Marie, and then the Brady kids performed in a comedy sketch spoofing the soap opera *Mary Hartman, Mary Hartman* and sang in the grand finale, "Renaissance Fair."

A Second Chance for *The Brady Bunch*

After *The Donny and Marie Show* aired on October 8, 1976, Susan Olsen recalls she was approached by a producer who said, "We've got something lined up for you guys, but we can't say anything just now." Fred Silverman was already hatching his scheme to revive the *Brady Bunch* franchise. Television writer Bruce Vilanch explains, "Fred was the guy who pioneered strange combinations in variety show hosts like *Tony Orlando and Dawn* and *Pink Lady and Jeff*. These were all things he'd green-lighted. He was desperate to come up with a show that would appeal to a youthful market. The first thing he tried was *The Partridge Family Variety Show* but they wouldn't do it. That didn't happen, and so he came up with *The Brady Bunch*."

Fred Silverman

Silverman put ABC programming executive Michael Eisner up to the task of making the first call. Eisner had been responsible for getting ABC out of last place in the ratings and was instrumental in getting *Donny and Marie* on the air. "Michael Eisner called me up and said, 'Hey, I have a new show for you. Let *Donny and Marie* go to Provo, you'll stay here. I want you to do *The Brady Bunch Variety Hour*.' So I said yes. That was the first mistake I made. That's how it all started," remembers Marty Krofft. "We also had been involved with *The Brady Bunch* years earlier. So we had a connection with them in the early '70s, and had a good relationship with all the kids and their parents," he adds.[6]

Eisner skipped calling Sherwood Schwartz, who created *The Brady Bunch* and co-owned the rights with Paramount Studios. Sherwood has never forgotten the shock of finding out his property had been given to someone else without his permission. "I didn't hear about it until it was all accomplished, without my knowledge and without Paramount's knowledge. They didn't ask anybody," he says. "The Krofft brothers figured if they said no, they couldn't get the rights, the rights would be Paramount and Sherwood Schwartz, and then Eisner would call us. So they said, 'Sure, we can get the rights.' The first thing we knew, it was already scheduled to go on the air. Paramount thought I gave the rights and I thought Paramount had given the rights because both of us control it. That's the story, and Sid and Marty answered the question with a yes, and they had no right to. It made me angry because when you work hard, which I did, to get the show on the air, it took me four years to get *The Brady Bunch* on the air to begin with, and suddenly these other guys say they have the rights to it and sold our show, which is quite a bit of money," Sherwood adds.

Michael Eisner

Susan Olsen points out, "Never underestimate the brothers Krofft. They're just like a child who will go ahead and take something right from under your face and because they're so brazen about it you don't stop them."

Sherwood's son, Lloyd Schwartz, recalls that they first found out about the new show when they saw it announced in *TV Guide*. "I said, 'Hey dad, *The Brady Bunch* is going to

Brady Love

If I had a nickel for every time I've been asked why *The Brady Bunch* has lasted so long it might be like getting paid for reruns. (No, we don't make residuals and I get asked that question a lot too.) This is a valid inquiry and if anybody really knew the answer we would all be able to make long lasting hit shows.

I think a lot of it was the honesty. Sherwood Schwartz avoided the contrived idea the networks had of making each kid in the cast a certain "type," such as a fat kid, a smart kid, etc. What Sherwood wanted to do was to find six kids who were interesting and build a show around them. He wanted real kids, and, in my opinion, he got them. This reality extends to the adults of the show as well. Ann B. Davis is a pro like no other, well-versed in comedy and capable of pulling almost anything off. A scene almost can't go wrong if she's in it. Florence's genuine love for us and ability to be a great mother in her own right shined through in the way she played Carol. Bob hated the show but loved us as his own children. He also brought believability to every script, no matter how unbelievable it might be, that made it real.

Another thing is that you have representation for every member of the family. Three ages of children in both sexes means that if you're a kid watching *The Brady Bunch*, you have somebody to relate to. In reruns, kids start out identifying with the youngest characters and move up until they are finally relating to the parents. The story lines are timeless. We didn't deal with too many issues of the day so the scripts are largely based on problems that have existed and will exist

be on television,' and he said 'What?!' because it totally surprised him. He was of the belief they couldn't do that, but then, of course, networks and studios do what they want and they did it. His attitude was rather magnanimous. He'd say, 'Look, if they're making some money, that's okay, let them do it.' He always was in favor of that, but we certainly weren't in favor of the show," Lloyd says.

Neither Paramount nor Sherwood Schwartz gave much consideration to putting a stop to *The Brady Bunch Variety Hour*. Paramount was doing a lot of business with ABC, and they were afraid to start anything against the network. Sherwood says, "Fred Silverman was an extremely important man at that time. They didn't want to buck Fred or ABC, so they didn't make a move, I didn't make a move, and so the show proceeded. The only thing we did, Paramount said we should get some kind of a royalty, and so we divided a very small royalty just not to deal with it. But I thought it was a bad idea."

Florence Henderson adds, "I don't think Sherwood was too happy because he was not involved in it. I don't think he was asked to be. I can understand his not feeling too overjoyed about it."[7]

"What would be a smooth, seamless fold for *The Brady Bunch* as a variety show?" Barry Williams asks. "What would you do? Anything, I think, would probably be bizarre."

According to Marty Krofft, the premise for *The Brady Bunch Variety Hour* was modeled after the "show within a show" concept of *Jack Benny*. They would not appear as themselves (Bob, Florence, and Ann B.) like other variety shows of the 1970s but rather as Mike, Carol, Alice, and family. "We were still the same characters but now we were performing. It was a unique concept, actually, that Sid and Marty came up with, I thought," says Florence Henderson.[8] But Mike Lookinland, who played Bobby Brady, was among several confused by what was being proposed. "I had a hard time grasping what they were actually saying to me. You're going to what? You're going to say the Bradys have done *what*? They have their own singing, dancing variety show as a family?" says Mike. In a 1976 interview, Marty Krofft told *Hollywood Reporter* columnist Richard Hack, "The unique thing here is that they never come out of character. They won't be Florence and Robert. They'll be Carol and

Mickey Rooney and Paul Shaffer in the sitcom
A Year at the Top

Mike Brady, plus six. The Bradys have moved to a new house and they are putting on a variety show. The father, of course, is an architect. He goes along with the idea but is not overjoyed."[9] Many years later Florence laughed remembering how it all turned out, "It's kind of weird, isn't it?" she said.[10]

Paul Shaffer, music director of *The Late Show with David Letterman*, was working on the same studio lot at KTLA Hollywood in 1976 when he first learned that the Bradys were scheduled to start production on a new variety special. He was there writing a summer series for Norman Lear called *A Year at the Top* with Greg Evigan. "While we were on a

through generations: sibling rivalry, losing a favorite toy, a first crush, etc. Also important is that these stories are told from a child's point of view. What little girl wouldn't want to have the whole household upset and looking for her missing doll?

But above all I think what really works with *The Brady Bunch* is a mutual respect between kids and grown-ups. This was written in the scripts and it was a reality among us cast members. Florence, Bob, and Ann always treated us

as colleagues and because of that we always tried to live up to their expectations of our professionalism. As the gap between children and adults faded as we grew older, that mutual respect was ultimately challenged for the first time on our *Variety Hour*. But one thing is clear to me. After forty years of friendship, our love for one another is stronger than ever and that will *never* change.   —Susan break from that show I also worked with Chevy Chase on his television special," he explains. Shaffer recalls everyone on the lot was buzzing with anticipation about *The Brady Bunch* coming back to network television. "*The Brady Bunch* sitcom itself was a very influential show, a very important show of its time. It's iconic — the theme song, the opening with the checker board. These things are very strong in television history. When *The Brady Bunch* gets together and does a variety show, because of how strong the sitcom was, it made it even more noteworthy that they were doing a variety show. You didn't expect to be seeing that family of a man named Brady doing a musical," Paul adds.

Jerry McPhie

The Producers

Marty Krofft knew that his first task would be to assemble a production staff so that the show could go into development quickly. He began by appointing his friend Jerry McPhie — who had over twenty-five years of experience, and an Emmy Award — to be the head of production. McPhie recalls that he basically served as a general manager for the Kroffts and dealt with any kind of problem that could possibly arise. "Neither Sid nor Marty on their own could possibly handle a production such as *The Brady Bunch* and control it. I believe in non-interference. I say you hire good, you look good. Once you hire someone you'd better let them do their job, that's what they're there for. I had to hire all the guys to produce and direct. I had to supervise them and keep track of things," he says.

For the position of line producer, Marty and Jerry decided to go with someone they had not worked with in the past. Lee Miller had a stellar resume and came highly recommended to them because of his extensive background in directing and producing television variety specials for stars such as Goldie Hawn, Mitzi Gaynor, Pearl Bailey, Duke Ellington, Cass Elliot, Raquel Welch, Cher, the Everly Brothers, Zero Mostel, Jimmy Durante, and the Lennon Sisters. He also had worked on the Tony Awards, the Academy Awards, and the Emmy Awards programs, as well as *The Kraft Music Hall*. He seemed to be exactly the person they were looking for. When *The Brady Bunch Variety Hour* came up, Miller had been away from Los Angeles for a year and living in Nashville, Tennessee, where he

Lee Miller

produced a country music series called *Music Hall America*. "As it ended and I was coming back to Los Angeles, my manager George Shapiro called me and mentioned the *Brady* series pilot and asked if I'd be interested. I didn't know the Kroffts, and had never met them in fact. But I took the meeting and that's how we joined forces," Miller says.

Now that the Kroffts had secured a support team for *The Brady Bunch Variety Hour*, all they needed was to convince each of the former *Brady Bunch* cast members to agree to be a part of the project and reenlist. It was easier said than done.

Bringing the Bunch Back Together

Marty Krofft is adamant when he insists he should go down in the *Guinness Book of World Records* for reassembling the actors from *The Brady Bunch*. "It wasn't easy!" he proclaims. Surprisingly, it was Robert Reed who was the most excited about the opportunity to have his own television variety show. Reed's distaste for the role of Mike Brady, along with five seasons of bickering with creator Sherwood Schwartz, culminated in him refusing to appear in the final episode of the sitcom filmed in December 1973. However, his negative opinion of *The Brady Bunch* seemed to have softened and the absence of Schwartz from the new production could only have made it more attractive than it otherwise would have been. In 1977, Reed explained why he wanted to be a part of the *Variety Hour* by simply stating, "I've always wanted to do something I've never done as an actor. Here was an opportunity to do a little singing and dancing."[11] His musical experience was limited to an amateur production of *On the Town* in college and then a two-week run in Richard Rodgers' *Avanti!* on Broadway in 1968. In an interview with reporter Charles Witibeck, Bob said, "I'm a frustrated singer. I took dance lessons along with the piano in the beginning, expecting to be the well-rounded actor."[12] Because he had just completed three ABC Movies of the Week, including a role in the miniseries *Roots*, Reed welcomed the change in direction. "I really did want to do it. I've studied voice and dancing. I'm terrible at both, and proved it to be true, but when Sid and Marty met with me, they described the whole thing in very positive terms, and I thought, 'What fun! This'll be a hoot.'"[13]

Robert Reed on Broadway in
Avanti! **(1968)**

Robert Reed, seen here at the Hollywood Bowl, attended nearly every performance of the Brady Kids.

Courtesy of the Rodgers and Hammerstein Organization

Florence Henderson in the 1961 stage production of *The Sound of Music*

Susan Olsen feels she should have been shocked that Bob wanted to do *The Brady Bunch Variety Hour* but suspects that he probably just missed everyone. When the Brady Kids were performing at Knott's Berry Farm, Reed would come to every single performance, every night, for an entire week. He would even come out and watch them rehearse, so they all felt he had some interest in music. Both Barry Williams and Florence Henderson point out that Robert Reed was a classical pianist and in reality he was very musical. He studied music for almost all of his life, says Barry, "but kind of privately for himself, and of course being the perfectionist that he was, he was never satisfied and never a happy guy. He had toyed with doing musicals, so I think this seemed a natural fit with his aspirations of musical theater."

On the opposite end of the spectrum, Florence was the seasoned professional when it came to musical theater; everybody knew she could sing and dance in addition to being an accomplished actress. Florence was selected early in her career by Richard Rodgers to star in the first touring production of *Oklahoma!*, and in subsequent years she starred onstage in *The Sound of Music*, *The King and I*, *South Pacific*, and *Annie Get Your Gun*. She also was the first female host of *The Tonight Show* and starred in the movie musical *Song of Norway*. So there was no question in anyone's mind that Florence could make up for any lack of experience Robert Reed had with singing. The question was if she was available and willing to reprise her role as Carol Brady. Florence had remained very busy since *The Brady Bunch* ended, and was the television spokesperson for both Tang powdered drinks and Wesson cooking oil. She had been active onstage and had made guest appearances on *The Love Boat* and with Robert Reed on *Medical Center*, in which he portrayed a transsexual. Florence definitely had doubts about the ideas proposed to her by Marty Krofft and the show's format. "Frankly, I was a little dubious. I just couldn't see how they could take the Brady family and turn them into variety artists. After all, I knew that none of the children could sing or dance," said

Florence.[14] "The second life for the show really came as a surprise. But the power and popularity of the original half-hour situation comedy is fantastic. When it was suggested as a variety hour special, I was prepared because of my background. Maybe it was time for a reunion."[15] Florence and Bob both signed on the dotted line, and the show had its two stars.

After *The Brady Bunch* ended in 1974, Barry Williams auditioned for Bob Fosse and landed a starring role in *Pippin* both on Broadway and in the national touring company. He also continued work on television — in commercials and on an episode of *Police Woman*. When his manager informed him of plans to reunite the Bradys he immediately declined to be a part of the variety special. "I said no, I wasn't interested, and I was going down a different road. Marty got on the phone and he talked me into it, basically," says Barry. By the time they had finished their conversation Marty convinced him that it was going to essentially be the *Barry Williams Variety Hour* with *The Brady Bunch*. "He recognized that Florence and I were the only two that had any talent [in music], and so he's going to really push that up. I had solos on every episode, the dance routines would be pretty much built around me. I had this whole idea of what to expect when I got back, and it was television. That was before I realized that Marty was doing what a good producer would do, telling me what I want to hear," Barry adds. Writer Bruce Vilanch says, "Barry, he was the one who kept saying, 'Hey, I'm the one who can sing and dance. I'm trained. These other kids aren't.' I think he viewed the show as a way to showcase himself." To Barry, this was the return of Johnny Bravo.

Barry Williams in the 1976 production of *Pippin*

Of all *The Brady Bunch* cast members, Maureen McCormick was the one who wanted to be a serious actress, and segue into films from the sitcom world. As she was trying to launch that aspect of her career, she was informed of an ABC variety show that Sid and Marty Krofft wanted her to star in. Maureen had been somewhat idle since *The Brady Bunch* ended and was enjoying life on her own for the first time. She had recently appeared in the movie *Pony Express Rider*, and television shows such as *Happy Days* and *The Streets of San Francisco*, but was still waiting for the big break that would take her to the next level. Because Maureen enjoyed working with the Kroffts on *The Donny and Marie Show*, she had little objection to being a part of the variety special. "I never thought *The Brady Bunch* would come back. I was shocked," Maureen explains. "I was guest starring on television shows, and doing independent films. When they called me to do the *Variety Hour*, my reaction was mixed. One part of me thought, how great and

Pony Express Rider

wonderful, and another part of me thought do I really want to do this? But I decided to do it because it sounded like it was going to be so much fun, I mean, to be able to work with Sid and Marty Krofft, they were the kings of variety television at the time. I remember Marty saying, 'It would be a great way to showcase your singing talents.' It was something I wanted to do — singing has always been something I loved."

Contrary to popular belief, Eve Plumb agreed to reprise her role as Jan Brady in *The Brady Bunch Variety Hour* "for old time's sake."[16] She had a good relationship with the Kroffts and had worked with them on both the Hollywood Bowl concert and in a guest appearance on *Sigmund and the Sea Monsters*. Eve was active with music and in 1975 she had plans to form a singing group called *The Brady Bunch Three* with Susan Olsen and Mike Lookinland. So, everyone expected she would be interested in being a part of the new show. That all changed when Eve's recording executive father and manager, Neely Plumb, raised objections when details of the contract were proposed. Eve recalls, "I enjoyed doing *The Brady Bunch* series and I wanted to do the special but there was a built in option for thirteen more shows and possibly five years."[17] Marty Krofft explains that Eve was not willing to do the series because at the time she felt her career was in films, and his brother, Sid, adds, "She just didn't want to disgrace herself because she couldn't sing." Eve had just starred in the NBC TV movie *Dawn: Portrait of a Teenage Runaway,* which received glowing reviews and was a ratings winner for the network. There was also the possibility of a sequel and other opportunities on the horizon for the young actress. "I feel for Eve because I know she wanted to do the show. Finally it came down to the fact that she agreed to do five of the initial thirteen series episodes, but then that would have caused contractual problems with all the rest," recalls Marty. [18] When ABC insisted that Eve do all or nothing, she had no other choice but to turn down the offer.

Eve Plumb as *Dawn*

Years later Eve recalled, "I remember it was a very emphatic 'no thank you' and we're doing other things now, and, no, it really doesn't [interest us], because everybody wants us to 'come on, do one for the team, it'll be fun, let's get everybody back together and be a team' and that doesn't seem to be the argument that's going to get me there."[19]

Eve wasn't Marty's only problem. Chris Knight didn't want to be a part of the *Variety Hour* either. "I had difficulty signing up for the show and very easily could have passed like Eve. Imagine a fake Peter too, a *Brady Hour* with a fake center! They could have made it a running gag. Peter and Jan can't sing or dance so they get left at home," Chris laughs. Only two years earlier Chris suddenly quit the *Brady Kids* singing group because of his growing hatred of performing music and the trauma it was causing him physiologically and psychologically. Chris explains, "Singing and dancing were anathema to me. I never had talent in this area. It's very strange, but music is not in me. I can't hear it. I can't feel it, not really, not like others. It's like a foreign language."

In the fall of 1976, Chris had just started at UCLA and turned away from the entertainment industry. "What I realized is that I was learning disabled but hadn't been diagnosed," Chris says. "School was probably going to be impossible and I didn't know why. Now I look back and I realize I was pretty much hiding this ADD thing that I had. I was internally recognizing how long and dark the tunnel was that I was in," he adds. When the opportunity to be a part of *The Brady Bunch* variety special came along, it presented the dilemma of getting back into an industry that he thought he wanted to leave. "When I was at UCLA, I was in a fraternity and a lot of the guys I knew were in cinema and movies, wanting a career in the entertainment industry. Here I was, burying myself in geology, wanting to investigate rocks, running away from the very industry they were working hard to be successful in. I realized then that maybe I was squandering an opportunity. Maybe I should look at it again. I loved the work in the entertainment industry, I just hated the life," Chris says. Chris remembers when the concept for the variety special was presented by Marty Krofft, "I thought it was stupid, it wasn't something I wanted to do." Apparently with Eve out, the show would not move forward if they lost another Brady. Marty made all kinds of promises to Chris. They finally got his buy in by assuring him his singing and dancing would be limited to the opening and closing numbers only, and that he would be given a larger chunk of the sketch comedy work. Chris laments, "It didn't work out that way and I learned one of life's lessons — always get it in writing! When *The Brady Hour* came up

it was a relief, I could withdraw from school and commit to life as an actor. Only I had to go through the door marked 'Singing and Dancing.'"

Susan Olsen was a sophomore in high school and just having a regular life. She was certain she wouldn't do any more acting because child labor laws were such that casting agents tend to pick eighteen-year-olds who look young so they don't have to deal with social workers. Then the call came to be on *The Donny and Marie Show*. When the next call came about doing *The Brady Bunch* variety special, it started out with just one episode. Everyone was waiting to see if they would get to do more. Susan recalls, "I was thrilled. Even though I thought the show was horrible I was thrilled to do it." It was very difficult for those in the cast to turn down anything that was Brady at the time because it was a chance to work with friends. Susan was very excited about it in the beginning and hoped to get into sketch comedy. *Saturday Night Live* had just started and she was obsessed with it. "I wanted to do comedy although I knew that we couldn't do very cool material considering the time slot and our images," Susan says. But she figured that because she was young, there would be plenty of time to do other things that she believed in.

"This was before I was bludgeoned with all the various, embarrassing reincarnations of *The Brady Bunch*. Now when they talk about getting us together for something it is a very frightening thought! Sometimes it's hard for me to understand, why was I happy to be there? I *hated* the music, the sets, the costumes, the material... Artistically it was like my worst nightmare, but I loved these people so much! I suppose I would have done anything with them. It had been a few years and I really missed them all. It was great to be working together. That's my other family," Susan says. "For all of us, it was money. There's always been a bit of a feeling that the power of Brady compels you. It hadn't really occurred to us to jump ship, and then Eve was looking pretty cool for having done it," she adds.

After working steadily in show business for most of his life — first in commercials, then *The Brady Bunch*, and Irwin Allen's epic disaster movie *The Towering Inferno* — Mike Lookinland was ready for a vacation. In 1975 he was offered a leading role in the television series *Swiss Family Robinson* and turned it down so he could finally have some time off. (Ironically, the role then went to Willie Aames who later starred in another sitcom about a large family, *Eight Is Enough*.) Mike enjoyed being a guest star on *The Donny and Marie Show* but was very reluctant to be a part of a variety special with *The Brady Bunch*. "I was desperately trying to figure ways out of it. How in the world could I get away with *not* doing this show?" he says. Mike had one clever idea. "I was on my skateboard down below my house when my mom pulled up in the car and said, 'Mike, they've called, here's the offer,' and I thought, 'Okay, how do I tactfully but definitely get out of doing this?' I said, 'Tell them I'll do it for *twice* that much, there's no way I'll do it for less than twice that much.' My mother went home, called them, and came back ten minutes later and said, 'The deal's on! We're good to go!' and I just thought, '*Oh no!*' So, I have the job that I didn't want but at least I was getting a lot more money. Everybody got more money because of me. I figured I'd get out of it by *doubling* it, but within seconds they said, 'Okay!' That's how I got the job," Mike explains. His mother Karen adds, "Michael didn't want to do it. He's a real good musician, piano player, guitarist, and singer. But he's not a dancer and he knew there would be a lot of dancing. It's hard to dance when you're not good at it."

The Brady Bunch just wouldn't be the same without Ann B. Davis, who played Alice Nelson, the maid to the Brady household. But the actress had disappeared from the Hollywood scene. She left California in 1974 for Denver, Colorado, with little intention of ever returning. "I was tired of show business — tired of running around with my head cut off," she said.[20] However, Ann is quick to point out, "I never heard a voice from the clouds saying, 'get out of show business.'"[21] She was happily working as a volunteer at a vicarage of the Episcopal Diocese, under the leadership of Bishop William C. Frey, giving lectures, leading worship, and performing daily chores on the property. "I decided to sell my house in L.A. and yield control to the Lord," Ann explained.[22] Initially, there was no plan to have the character of Alice in *The Brady Bunch Variety Hour*. Ann recalls, "They had already started it, given out [the cast and crew commemorative] T-shirts and all that, and somebody insisted that my agent call me, just to come in and do a cameo 'cause they didn't feel it was complete without me."[23] Ultimately Ann signed on to appear in the entire series and was soon back in her familiar blue dress and white apron saying, "I'm holding the Bunch together like I always do!"

Susan Olsen adds, "Ann B. was an old pro and still wanted to work. She had done a lot of stage work and it was up her alley. I think part of her thing was that she wasn't going to cloister herself, if she was having this religious experience, from the real world."

So, the Bradys were a "Bunch" again — almost. One of the squares remained empty. The cast began to wonder how Sid and Marty were going to work around the absence of Eve Plumb. Producer Lee Miller recalls the difficulty of dealing with that situation. "We

had everyone else booked and Eve Plumb was hanging us up. We couldn't go forward. There was a point in time where it became a very practical matter where we said, 'She's either got to say yes by Friday or we've got to move on and find somebody else.' It was never a feeling that we didn't want her. It was a feeling that she didn't want us. As a result, we were going to absolutely go into the tank if we didn't move forward. We set a deadline, the deadline came and went, and we turned away and moved on." After meeting to discuss the problem, the Kroffts decided to tear a page from the playbook of *Bewitched* director William Asher. If he could replace Dick York with Dick Seargent as Darrin Stephens, then they could just as easily find a new Jan. But the Kroffts decided that, unlike Eve Plumb, they wanted a Jan who could sing and then work that to their advantage. Lee Miller says, "I thought Eve Plumb made a big mistake by not participating. The negotiation was very difficult and I do believe she or her representatives thought they could prevent this from happening or that it could have been much more lucrative to her than it ended up being. I think the end result was, and the conclusion we all made was that *nobody* in this business is irreplaceable and we'll find a new Jan — and we did."

Finding Fake Jan

In late October 1976 a casting call was put out for a blonde female teenager who could sing, dance, and act. The posting attracted over 1,500 girls who came to KTLA in Hollywood, from as far away as New York, all of them wanting to be the new Jan Brady. By comparison, approximately 1,200 children auditioned in 1968 for all six roles in the original *Brady Bunch* series at Paramount Studios. Sid Krofft vividly recalls the chaos, "There were tons of girls auditioning because that was a very sensitive casting job — to replace an icon, Eve Plumb. We were trying to copy her. We weren't really searching for a look-alike, but we wanted the same kind of structure. I know it was a huge call, and we had to hire an agency to help us cast it." Everything was happening quickly because production was set to begin in less than two weeks. "We didn't have a lot of time. There were a lot of girls, a whole gangbang of them. They auditioned as actors, they auditioned as singers, and the casting agency was good at bringing in a good cross segment of young ladies who physically fit the part and the age and could do the things we needed," says Lee Miller. "We auditioned a lot of people because we wanted somebody who was not unlike Eve physically. It also had to be somebody with some gumption because she had to be stepping into an established role that was played by somebody else. She not only had to be cute and charming, and attractive as Eve was, she also had to be able to sing and dance and hold her own. So, she was going to be judged on that basis," he adds.

Among the hopefuls was sixteen-year-old Geri Reischl, of Lakewood, California, a veteran of over forty television commercials, and series such as *Gunsmoke*, *The Interns*, *The Bold Ones*, and *Apple's Way*. She had starred in two feature films, *The Brotherhood of Satan*, and *I Dismember Mama*, and headlined her own country music band. Geri had been a favorite model at Mattel toys as a child, and had just spent the summer as a backup singer for Canadian teen heartthrob René Simard. She had more experience in show busi-

ness than almost all the other Brady kids combined, and was an immediate favorite for the role of Jan when she first met the Kroffts. It all started when her agent, Toni Kelman, called saying she wanted to send Geri out on an interview. "She would say what the part was for, what it was about, where it was going to be, what time, what I should wear, how I should look — try to look younger or older, do your hair a certain way. My audition for *The Brady Bunch* started out like any other interview," Geri recalls. "I didn't watch TV all that much. I knew of *The Brady Bunch*, I knew who was in *The Brady Bunch*. I'd flipped through and seen it, but I didn't watch it on a regular basis," she adds. Geri had doubts, but her best friend Barbara was confident she would get the role. "When Geri went to the audition I kept telling her how perfect she was for it," Barbara recalls. "She kept laughing because she was a western singer, so she said, 'Oh, they'll never want me.' But I said, 'You look just like Eve Plumb.'"

Geri Reischl in *The Brotherhood of Satan*, filmed in 1969

Geri Reischl onstage with pop idol René Simard

According to Geri's mother, Wanda Reischl, there were five auditions. "Each time they acted like they really loved her, I really felt she had it from the first one. They had different girls at different times and were always auditioning people. Then there were fewer coming back each time and they were keeping Geri longer, which was a good sign. Sid and Marty were both talking to me and having a fit over Geri, they loved her so much." Only 300 girls remained by the second audition. "I think her personality, her singing, and her dancing won her the part. It couldn't have happened at a better time because she had recently finished touring in Canada with René Simard's show and had very good dance training," Wanda adds.

Geri felt completely comfortable in her auditions and was enjoying herself. "When I walked into the room, we just talked for a little while. Each time they had different people,

Sid and Marty didn't want to have just their own opinion. They wanted to have someone else's opinion of me, and any other girl probably. Then they would hand me a one-page script, like with Jan and Bobby. Marty would read the part of Bobby with me. He would read the lines and I would do them back. He would sit in his chair and look at me, and then we would do it again, I guess to hear it differently. I'd go in there and sing, and then they'd ask me to sing something else. I usually never completed a song because they only wanted to hear my voice and my style. Then they would ask if I had a dance number they could see and I would do one to 'Attitude Dancing.' I didn't have music to others but I would show them the dance steps that I knew from other songs I had done with René Simard. I would say I was in there twenty to twenty-five minutes each time," Geri recalls.

Also present at the auditions was seventeen-year-old Kathy Richards, who had appeared in commercials from an early age and made a guest appearance on the television series *Family Affair*. In later years, Kathy gained notoriety for her marriage to hotel heir Rick Hilton and their extravagant lifestyle with children Paris, Nicki, Barron, and Conrad. "We went on several interviews with her for commercials. Kathy and Geri liked one another although they were competing against each other for a lot of things. But every time it was singing, Geri always got it," says Wanda Reischl.

Geri Reischl

The final audition was held in the Presidential Suite of the Century Plaza Hotel in Century City, and included only three finalists — Geri, Kathy, and one other girl. "I thought Kathy was gorgeous and really pretty," Geri says. "She'd always pull up in a very expensive car with her mother. She was very classy. Everything was absolutely perfect on her from head to toe. I don't think she could really sing very well, that was one of my strong selling points to Sid and Marty. I was the right age and had very long, blonde hair. Kathy did not have the long hair. A lot of girls by that time did not have the long hair still," Geri adds. This time representatives from the ABC network were there to observe, and the girls had to do everything for the executives. Geri recalls, "I had to think of something sad and cry. I played my guitar and I sang to my cassette player, and we would talk about school and the things I like — to find out about me personally to see what kind of temperament I had or how outgoing I was. Sometimes they would throw something out to me, like a scenario, and ask me to ad lib.

Paris Hilton's mother, Kathy Richards, as Jan Brady? Almost!

Marty would say a couple of things to me and I would say a few things back without a script just to see how quick-witted I was." At the end of the evening Sid went downstairs to meet with Geri's parents and confidentially told them that everybody really liked her and that she was perfect for the part of Jan. Then everyone was sent home to wait for the decision.

The next day at school Geri was called to a meeting with her guidance counselor, Mr. Abrams, by his secretary, Mrs. Haygood. Geri recalls, "I thought, 'Wait a minute, I've never done anything in school. I've never even ditched a day in my life, why am I being called into the office?' I thought, 'Oh no, maybe somebody found something on me.' I went in there, and I would always go in his office and visit him anyways, and he said, 'Well, Geri, it looks like you're not going to be a student here for a while,' and I said, 'Why?' He said, 'Tomorrow, you need to be on the set starting your show, *The Brady Bunch Variety Hour*,' and I said, 'What?! I got it? You're kidding?!' I was so excited. I was flying up and down, jumping up and down. It must have looked goofy, but I was so ecstatic, I was so happy. He told me he was going to contact all my teachers then, so I could get all my schoolwork and have it ready for me starting the next day. I was just so happy, I couldn't believe it. I almost started crying because I knew I was going to get to go sing and dance and have fun, work, and be a Brady!"

```
JAN SCENE

(JAN AND BOBBY)
                JAN
     My life is over! Oh, why can't
     I be dead!
                BOBBY
     I don't know, Jan, why can't you
     be dead?
                JAN
     I wasn't talking to you, Bobby. I
     was talking to mother!
                BOBBY
     Then you're a little late. She
     left the room ten minutes ago.
                JAN
     She did! Even my own mother
     hates me! Now my life's really
     over! Oh, I could just curl up
     in a little ball and die!
                BOBBY
     You want me to help you curl up
     in a little ball?
                JAN
     I'd expect you to say something like
     that. Of all my brothers and sisters,
     you hate me the most.
```

Producer Lee Miller was relieved to have the casting decision accomplished and seemed pleased overall with the results. "The girl we finally chose was a little more of a country singer than I would have liked

Lakewood girl new Brady family 'Jan

Geri Reischl gets role in TV series

By KRIS SHERMAN
Staff Writer

There's a new face among the grown-up youngsters of Mike and Carol Brady, whose fictional family formed "The Brady Bunch" situation comedy on television a few years ago and recently has returned to the airwaves in "The Brady Bunch Hour."

The face belongs to Lakewood teen-ager Geri Reischl, who was chosen over 300 other girls to portray the Brady's middle daughter, Jan.

The original Jan, Eve Plumb, opted out of the new series to pursue an acting and singing career on her own.

So Geri, a veteran of 28 television commercials, four guest appearances on television series and two movies at the age of 17, is now one of the six singing, dancing Brady children.

Their show, an hour-long variety series, has been broadcast several times and is scheduled to run on six consecutive Mondays (8 p.m., Channel 7) beginning March 1.

Geri, a vibrant girl with long hair and an infectious smile, says she's "thrilled" about being a television star who is recognized in public and asked for autographs.

But her mother, Wanda, adds with a sense of practicality:

"Show business has been rewarding for Geri. And for us, too. But it's maybe not as glamorous as a lot of people might think. It takes all of your time, and you and you can't keep up with your friends."

Nevertheless, Geri says show business is her life, adding that her goal is to become a successful country-western singer.

"I really don't think show business has affected me too much," she explains, flipping a strand of hair back into place. "This is my profession, and I love it."

Since "The Brady Bunch Hour" first appeared on television early this year, Geri has been deluged with phone calls and fan mail from "all over the United States and Canada."

"My friends at school are all really excited for me," she says with a smile. "They're always asking my girlfriend, Barbara, 'When's Geri coming back to school? What's Geri doing?'"

(Geri is a junior at Mayfair High School but is attending classes at the studio while the show is in production.)

Before she signed a contract with ABC to do the show, she had made guest appearances on "Apple's Way," "Gunsmoke," "The Bold Ones" and "The Interns" and appeared in movies titled "The Brotherhood of Satan" and "Poor Albert and Little Annie."

She also sang with a group of youngsters backing up Sammy Davis Jr. at Harrah's Club in Lake Tahoe, led her own band, The Sand Dabs, for 2½ years and toured Canada with French-Canadian rock star Rene Simard.

Ironically, Geri's parents, Herbert and Wanda, never really intended for their daughter to get into show business. And once she got in, they meant to make her get out when she entered junior high school.

According to Mrs. Reischl, Geri's theatrical career began when she was 6 with an understudy roll in "The Sound of Music" at Melodyland Theater in Anaheim.

"I was always shy in school, and I didn't want Geri to be that way, so we put her in an acting workshop," the mother recalled. "She was pretty outgoing, and she had a big, booming voice even at that age."

An agent noticed Geri sitting in the wings during one of the shows and launched her into an acting career doing television commercials.

Since then, she's done commercials for a variety of products including hair cream, pudding, sewing machines, hamburger, corn flakes, toys, department stores and fruit punch.

"Commercials are really where the money is," her mother explains. "You get paid for the commercial, then you get residuals every time the commercial is shown. Geri did one Hawaiian Punch commercial that we didn't think would be any good, and it was so successful they showed it for four years."

Recalling the commercial, Geri adds: "They fed me a big hamburger and pop and everything, then, right after lunch, we began filming and they just kept giving me glass after glass of Hawaiian Punch."

"And they wanted her to just guzzle it down," her mother interjects.

Geri also remembers a similar experience filming a cornflakes commercial. "By the end of the day, I was just one big cornflake," she says.

As Jan on "The Brady Bunch Hour," Geri clowns with the family and often sings solo, something she says she especially enjoys, adding that she wants "to have my own sound" and not imitate other singers.

(Turn to Page B-5, Col. 7)

Geri Reischl of Lakewood Is Jan on New Brady Show
—Staff Photo by BOB SHUMWAY

because I felt that was a little bit off the mark. But she was so adorable, and such a good performer that we decided to work around that. She also seemed a good fit with Susan and Maureen."

After three weeks of phone calls, meetings, contract negotiations, and auditions, Marty Krofft had done what most had predicted to be impossible — he reassembled the Brady Bunch. It couldn't have happened a moment too soon and there was literally no time to spare. Production on *The Brady Bunch Variety Hour* was scheduled to begin the next morning. Susan Olsen explains, "That is so typical of productions to wait until the very last minute to get something done!"

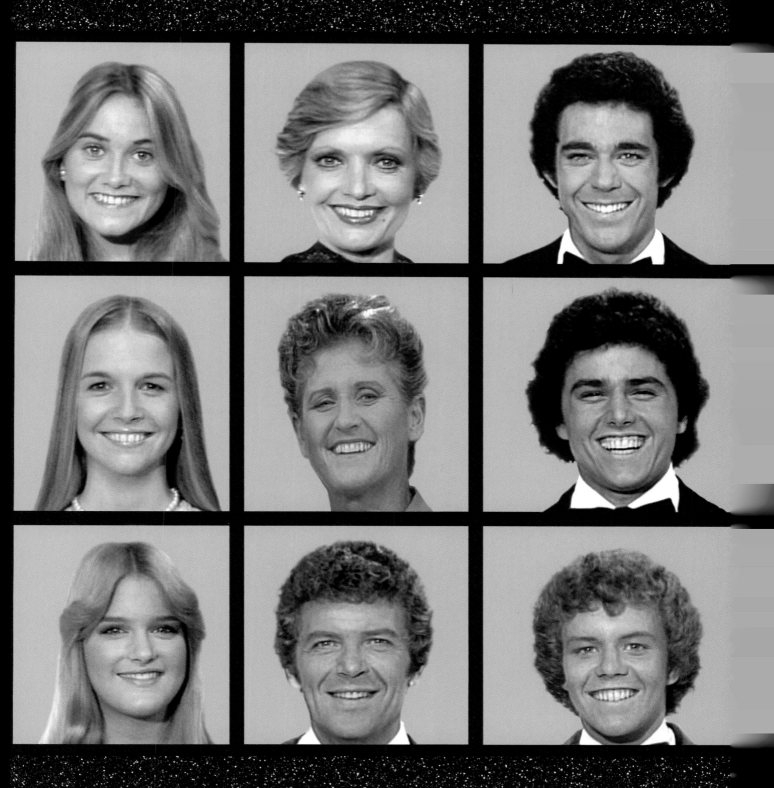

KTLA Golden West Studios

During the 1970s, Sid and Marty Krofft maintained a huge staff of loyal and skilled employees for all of their various projects: their theme park in Atlanta, Georgia; their many Saturday morning children's television programs; and their prime-time network variety shows. The Kroffts had an established relationship with KTLA studios in Hollywood and over the years they filmed most of their elaborate productions on the lot. KTLA is the original site of Warner Bros. Pictures, which was built in 1920 as one of the first large-scale studios in Hollywood. Landmark productions produced there include *The Sea Beast* (1926) starring John Barrymore, *The Jazz Singer* (1927) starring Al Jolson (the first major motion picture to include sound), a series of dog thrillers featuring Rin Tin Tin, and the *Gold Diggers of Broadway* (1929). In 1933, Warner Bros. acquired First National Pictures and moved production to their present day location in Burbank, California, but continued to use the old studio as a rental lot until 1954 when it was sold to Paramount Pictures. In 1958 it was renamed Paramount Sunset Studios and it provided the headquarters for its television station, KTLA. In 1965 retired cowboy actor Gene Autry purchased the lot for $12 million and renamed it Golden West Studios. KTLA television continued its operations on the site, and the stages were leased to independent producers, such as Sid and Marty Krofft. Because KTLA had its own scenic department to build sets, a prop department, costume shop, and office space, it was an ideal location for network television shows to do business.

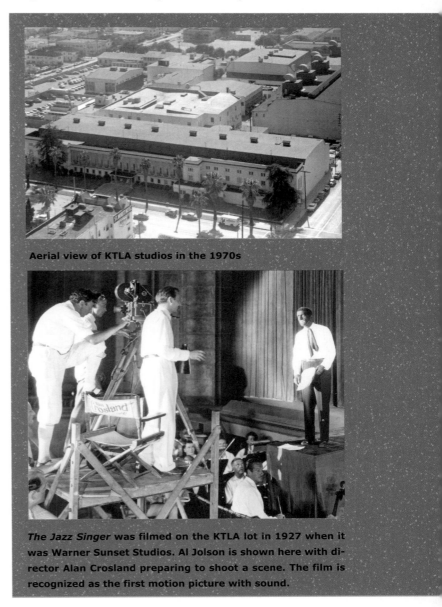

Aerial view of KTLA studios in the 1970s

The Jazz Singer was filmed on the KTLA lot in 1927 when it was Warner Sunset Studios. Al Jolson is shown here with director Alan Crosland preparing to shoot a scene. The film is recognized as the first motion picture with sound.

But by the 1970s KTLA was an aging facility that was sadly in need of renovation. Producer Lee Miller recalls, "It was kind of a hellhole. It was just an old studio that had been converted over for television." The Kroffts ended up at KTLA because it was the right price and they also had high fly lofts on the soundstages. Former ABC network executive Bonny

The World of Sid and Marty Krofft

What is it about those Krofft shows? On a personal level I have absolutely nothing but love for these men. I'd be an idiot to say that what they did wasn't good because I would obviously be wrong — they've been enormously successful. I can complain that their work is an assault on my artistic sensibilities, but the fact remains that they are the ones who took their creative inspiration and actually did something with it.

My first encounter with the world of Sid and Marty Krofft was on the Paramount lot. I had the enormous privilege of watching them film the opening credits for *H.R. Pufnstuf*. It was a closed set because the working conditions for the people in the puppet suits were such that they couldn't afford any bad takes. I think they had a time limit where they could shoot for a while then the costume heads would come off and the people in the suits would grab these hoses that were attached to large fans. Like performing underwater, when these guys would surface they needed air — air conditioning. Each take was followed with the removal of the puppet head and you could see the very sweaty face of the performer inside the suit. My mother made me very aware of these performers' difficult conditions so when I visited the set I was afraid of even breathing too loudly. This was the set of Living

Dore explains, "That seems unimportant, but it's very important because when you're doing an old-fashioned variety show like the Kroffts were, you needed as much space above you as you possibly could. Marty knew you had to have big stages with a very high fly loft because you're flying things in and out. KTLA was a dump. But it was cheap."

The environment around the studio was also less than attractive and Hollywood had been in a state of decline for a number of years. One of the main drawbacks at KTLA was a lack of a commis-

Sid Krofft

Marty Krofft

sary facility so the studio improvised by bringing in something known as "The Lunch Coach" to feed everyone on the lot during meal times. Bonny Dore recalls, "We had the 'Roach Coach' and you sat by a bunch of garbage cans to eat. It was just fabulous. The fast food place next door was horrifying. Anybody who ate there took their life in their hands. The 'Roach Coach' was better than that. Norman Lear was across the street with his shows at KTTV and he literally invested with Denny's to build a restaurant on the corner so we'd have somewhere to eat."

Although the Kroffts had been working at KTLA for several years, *Donny and Marie* was a new experience for everyone involved when they started production in late 1975. According to unit manager Jim Zrake, at the very beginning the

Osmond show was tough for the Kroffts because they had never done anything quite so large. It was a show encompassing two stages, with an ice rink on one and the sketches and dance numbers on the other. "To have two stages tied up with one show, at first, was difficult, but we learned how to do that," he says. Because of the many challenges of producing *Donny and Marie*, KTLA made some major improvements to the soundstages. For example, pulley systems were installed, whereas before everything was dead hung from stationary pipes. "Once we had done the Osmond show, we already had a way figured out to do *The Brady Bunch*," Zrake adds.

Checking up on the Bradys

With November quickly approaching, the ABC network sent Bonny Dore to KTLA so that she could check on the progress of the production. Dore was no stranger to the Kroffts and had already been working with them for several years as ABC's head of the West Coast in children's programming. "I was the executive in charge of their shows.

Bonny Dore

Essentially on the set, I am the network, I'm the boss. I make decisions on the set about what's okay and what's not going to go," she says. However, Dore had been away for several weeks supervising *The Paul Lynde Halloween Special* when she was suddenly promoted to head of variety on the West Coast for ABC television. "I came in late and *The Brady Bunch* was already in motion. Obviously because I worked with Sid and Marty so much, I had

Island; they were filming Jimmy washing on the shore and being fished out of the water by Kling and Klang. It was really like being in another world. I wanted to stay on that set all day. It was magical. We arranged for me to go again when my best friend, Moya, was on our set for a visit. She was blown away as well. We couldn't wait for the show to be finished and to be able to watch it.

That day arrived and I was pretty much driven to tears. What did I find wrong with it? Visually it was all that I had hoped for and witnessed, but the humor was silly rather than funny and the laugh track overbearing. I was aghast to find that several of my friends at school actually liked it. I even tried to get the kids at school to boycott these shows because I thought they were such an insult to our intelligence. This was kind of hard to do with kids who weren't feeling insulted but rather felt entertained. They liked the shows. Then we did an ABC Saturday morning special showing off the new children's programming season. My character, Cindy, was supposed to love *Lidsville*. When I saw *Lidsville*, it was a typical Krofft show and I was mortified that people might think I really liked it in real life. I found it quite fitting that Cindy would like it and that added to my belief that Cindy was an idiot.

If the *Harry Potter* series had been around then, I would have been overwhelmed with joy. That was my aesthetic and still is. I like subtlety, darkness, and mystery in my fantasy. There is nothing subtle about a Krofft production. It is in your face like one of those little gnats that are bold enough to fly right up your nose. I say this to be honest and to make

done *Donny and Marie* and had been to the set and met everybody. So I knew I was going to be taking over that show as part of my responsibilities. But *The Brady Bunch* thing was new to me and it happened very quickly. It seemed like I got my promotion, I showed up at the lot and walked in and said, 'Hi.' Okay, new job, new plan, new show, tell me about it, and the first thing I said was, 'Where's Lloyd and Sherwood?' That was my very first sentence because I couldn't imagine they weren't around. Marty said, 'No, no, no, that didn't work out,' and I said, 'Oh, okay.' So, we started from there," Dore recalls.

Lloyd Schwartz says he has never understood why the Kroffts didn't want the creators of *The Brady Bunch* to have any involvement in the *Variety Hour*. "I don't know why anybody wouldn't want input from people who really know the show. That didn't make any sense. It would have been free advice. We're not the kind of people where it's our way or no way, but we certainly don't enjoy being disregarded and especially

Sid and Marty Krofft

about something that was near and dear to us," Schwartz says.

The biggest problem Bonny Dore was facing as the network executive was that so many decisions had been made before she came into the picture. "My job was to just make it work however I could. I kind of had to play catch-up. There weren't a lot of real preproduction decisions that I could make," she says. Dore was also worried about the airdate — November 28, 1976 — which was less than two weeks away and during Thanksgiving weekend. She felt that such an ambitious production schedule was not realistic. "I said to Fred Silverman, 'How can you do a pilot on such short time with these kids who've never done this before, and with Bob Reed, who's never done this before? Then you put it on during the one time in America when the most people are going to be watching? It's just too much pressure and you're not giving yourself a chance,'" Dore says.

Marty Krofft begged the network to push the show back to a later airdate so they could do it right. Sid and Marty desperately wanted the show to work because with *The Donny and Marie Show* they were partners with the Osmonds. *The Brady Bunch Variety Hour* was going to be their show. Dore recalls, "I told Marty, 'I don't think we're going to make it.' Marty said, 'Yeah, we'll make it, we'll make it.' I said, 'Okay, sweetie, everyone's going to have to heave-ho here. You've got an airdate. I double-checked that with the boys in New York and it's not moving so we have to be there. If we can't do it, I have to know right now.' Well, Sid and Marty and I went in the back room and hashed it over, and Marty said, 'I really think we can make it,' and I said, 'Okay, alright, let's go.' I was there a lot because I had to be to figure out what we were doing." Dore explains further, "When I got there and I found out how little preproduction time they had, I realized we were going to be shooting

the point that in spite of hating their shows, I loved them. They were wonderful guys! Sid with his eyes alight dreaming of more glitter and large sea mammals, and Marty being so tall and intimidating but having the largest heart in the world — there was no way to not love them!

I just can't get past the silliness. Maybe I could with enough substances. Now I can see how their shows could be far more entertaining if one actually has a lid and is puffing stuff. I never tried combining mind-altering substances and Krofft entertainment; I'm afraid the laugh track would send me on a bad trip.

I think that the Krofft aesthetic in all its glory is part of the charm. Never subtle, never less is more, always in your face and choking you to death. It is the very essence of the '70s and it's everything about the '70s that makes me ill. I love to hate it.

— Susan

Marty and I are still friends today.

practically until it aired. There are a lot of changes to any variety show, but when you add to it that it's a pilot, you add to it the airdate it got, which was a huge audience in those days because there were only three things to watch. Thanksgiving weekend was a time of huge, huge ratings in television. The levels were gigantic and we knew it. It was going into a prime spot, there was going to be lots of publicity. You've got to deliver. Of course, *The Brady Bunch* was a pre-sold commodity. The pressure, it's hard to describe how much there was — the pressure on me from my bosses, and pressure on Sid and Marty from me, on themselves and the actors — there was no choice except to say 'we'll make it.'"

"I was really worried because I didn't think we would have enough time. I had certainly done a lot of shows with the Kroffts, and knew the staff very well, and knew what they were capable of, and under pressure they were capable of a great deal. This is taking a bunch of actors who, except for Florence, weren't song and dance people. It was panic time, truly panic time," Dore says.

Sid and Marty Krofft with Governor Jimmy Carter in 1976 at the grand opening of their Atlanta, GA, theme park

Oil and Water

Many people who have worked with brothers Sid and Marty Krofft over the years are quick to remark that they couldn't be more different from one another in almost every way, aside from sharing the same lineage. "They're like oil and water. It is just incredible," says assistant director Rick Locke. Marty stands over six feet tall, with the build and intimidating nature of a football player, while Sid is diminutive, quiet, and introspective. Marty is the moneyman of the family, but Sid is the creative genius. Stage manager Steve Dichter notes, "Sid has a wry sense of humor. He could come up with some zingers, for a guy who was not too communicative with people. He wasn't as outgoing as Marty was, not nearly. You could almost see it. It was almost a 'Mutt and Jeff' kind of thing. Marty is a big guy, and loud, and Sid, to me, was kind of just in the background making suggestions."

Krofft writer Mike Kagan fondly refers to Marty as the "garment district guy." "Every sentence I remember him uttering to me started with 'Goddamn it…' I would say, 'Marty, how are we looking for next week?' 'Goddamn it, the script is too long, we've got to make the cuts and, Goddamn it, the wardrobe is not right, and, Goddamn it, the guest star pulled out, and Goddamn it…' Then you'd go talk to Sid, and Sid said, 'This week I see all silver and blue…silver and blue…with doves…yes…if we could have doves fly across the pool…' You had to pinch yourself to see if you were awake. We'd have a creative meeting and then Sid would go into a long diatribe. We'd sit there and look at each other and think, 'Does anyone know what the hell he's talking about, because I don't have a clue,'" Kagan says.

Often times the two brothers would be at odds with one other, especially when Sid would come up with an idea that Marty felt was not realistic. Assistant director Rick Locke recalls, "We were doing a show called *Bobby Vinton's Rock-n-Rollers* and Sid decided he wanted a bunch of roller skaters skating around with television sets on their heads instead of hats. He wanted live pictures fed into the television sets and so now we're trying to imagine, first of all, someone being able to skate with a television set on their head, and then how to feed these pictures into the sets wirelessly. We had meeting after meeting after meeting on it, and finally Marty just said, 'It's a dumb idea!' It was like a breath of fresh air; everybody thought, 'Thank goodness!' That's what Sid and Marty would do, they really balanced one another," Locke says.

Donny and Marie scenic designer Bill Bohnert explains that Sid didn't want to hear any reason why you couldn't do something. "He always wanted you just to do it. But that was part of his style, and his charm actually. I enjoyed Sid a great deal because he did have that energy."

Bonny Dore adds, "It was hard not to like Sid and Marty. With all the craziness they were a lot of fun. They were the only people I know where I could be at work until three in the morning and still be having a good time. There's a lot to be said for that."

With only a year of experience in variety television behind them, the Kroffts were well aware that to pull off the monumental task of reincarnating *The Brady Bunch* in a musical format would require the expertise and experience of the best people that Hollywood had to offer. According to Barry Williams, "The caliber of people that were working on *The Brady Bunch Variety Hour* was very high. The writers and choreographers were all excellent. The musicians who came in to do the sessions, we had the cream of the crop, there was a lot of talent behind it." Sid and Marty were determined to make it work, and set out to assemble a creative staff that could make their vision for the Bradys a reality.

Art Fisher — Sharp Shooter

To direct the *Brady Bunch Variety Hour* pilot, Marty recruited Art Fisher, who was the top director in variety television during the early 1970s. He was serving in the same capacity for the Kroffts on *The Donny and Marie Show* and had won an Emmy Award for his work on *The Sonny and Cher Comedy Hour* in 1971. "Art was an innovator, that's the most important thing to know about him," says Bonny Dore. "I can't even enumerate all of the things he invented, in what we would call now comedy and reality television, that we take for granted. If I were to show you a program before what Art was doing and after, the difference is breathtaking." Among Fisher's contributions was his groundbreaking use of the handheld camera in television cinematography.

Fisher liked to shoot from many different angles, which he felt was crucial. He didn't like static shots and was always experimenting to get a bigger, more epic feel, or to get in closer to make things more fluid by mounting cameras on rolling dollies or jib arms. The Kroffts couldn't do a show on a small stage with Fisher because he wanted to get the camera up in the air, but even that wasn't enough fluid movement for him. Fisher found a smaller video camera and asked the studio carpenters to create a shoulder mount for one of the first handheld cameras in television. Dore recalls, "This was a very big deal. I think he first used it on *Donny and Marie*. I see this guy, and he's got lamb's wool underneath the wood, so that his shoulders don't break. The camera's huge. Art has the cameraman on his knees, and he's rolling around. I said, 'What are you doing? You're going to kill him.' Art said, 'No, no, he's strong, he can do it.' Of course the cameramen loved Art because they saw what an incredible innovator he was and they wanted to be a part of it. The cameramen worshipped him, anything Art wanted them to do, they would do, they never complained, never. It was an extraordinary experience to work with him for the cameramen and the crew. He expected perfection, demanded it, and technically he always got it." As far as Sid and Marty were concerned, Fisher was gold.

However, Art Fisher's passion and love for cinematography would sometimes overshadow his primary responsibility as a director. Producer Lee Miller recalls, "He didn't know how to

Art Fisher was just famous for tantrums and rages, throwing headsets and pencils and things across the control room. You didn't want to be in the way when he was upset.
— Rick Locke

deal with people and he couldn't deal with people. He'd never been trained as a director, as a theatrical director, and one of the problems with many variety directors who are good shooters is that they know how to take fabulous pictures and move cameras, but when an actor says, 'What's my motivation?' they don't know what to say. They don't know how to answer that question. They don't even know how to truly block a scene in terms of the actors. They only block to how they're going to shoot it. So you end up having people standing in straight lines because it's easier for them to shoot. That was Arthur. To Cher, Art would say, 'You just stand there, I'll do the rest.' That's not a direction."

There was also the issue of Fisher's temper and tyrannical outbursts that would occur when problems developed during production. Stage manager Steve Dichter recalls, "Art had very little patience with any technical, staging, or wardrobe glitches during the day. These would bring on an almost childlike tantrum followed by a 180 degree turn and then he would be completely sullen and silent. Thus, he realized he had no control over the problem or its solution. All I could hear was the drumming of his fingers on the console over the headset."

Art Fisher was an imposing presence on the set. He was fiercely loyal and put together a team he could count on. He knew that he would get his show done and it would be as good as it could be. Fisher was like a military general and when he would sit down at the editing console he would say, "Okay, team, let's take the field!" Everyone was like a well-oiled machine. They knew exactly what they were supposed to do. "Art read books about power through intimidation," says his assistant director Rick Locke. "He was just famous for tantrums and rages, throwing headsets and pencils and things across the control room. You didn't want to be in the way when he was upset."

Jerry McPhie recalls that on occasion Fisher's tantrums could become so intense that they evolved into physical violence. "He would get angry, stand up, pick up the old console telephone — that was a heavy piece of equipment — and he'd throw it. They finally screwed the thing down to the console so he couldn't do it, which made him even angrier. I know one time on the overhead system Art heard a video man make a disparaging comment. He left the booth, went down to the set, picked up the video man and hit him." Camera operator Ken Dahlquist explains, "When working for Art, you didn't want to mess up. He would take care of things right then and there, and not let it linger on."

In spite of his quirks people truly respected and admired Art Fisher. "Even when we didn't work with him he always came to our office, I loved Art Fisher," says Sid Krofft. Off the set, Fisher was known to be somewhat eccentric, and would arrive at the KTLA lot on his red, white, and blue Harley-Davidson dressed in a matching leather outfit. "He used to ride a big Honda motorcycle that he had just an incredible paint job on," recalls Rick Locke. "It had American flags on it. He was just a passionate American. He was so enamored with our way of life and just dedicated to the proposition that America was the greatest country in the world." Bonny Dore adds, "He had a Captain America helmet! That was always a crack-up. He'd say, 'B.D., are you sure you don't want to get on the back of the motor bike?'"

Jerry McPhie is certain Fisher patterned himself after Evel Knievel because he would wear the same kind of jackets related to car or motorcycle racing. "Even when he did an audience warm-up for us at the Mormon Tabernacle in Salt Lake City for *Donny and Marie* he wore that kind of a jacket and leather pants. It just boggled everybody's mind. We had never seen him do a warm-up and he did this in front of a really stale, white-bread audience."

Fisher was also a loyal friend. When Bonny Dore got married, he was there to congratulate her. Dore recalls, "We called it the Krofft wedding. Marty said, 'I kept waiting for Art to stand up and say 'Okay, everyone, let's do that again.'"

The wedding of Bonny Dore. Krofft production staff pictured (L to R): Duane Poole (writer), Madeline Graneto (costume designer), Mickey McMeel (Kaptain Kool and the Kongs), Tom Swale (production/writer), Dick Robbins (writer) and his wife, James Metz (groom), Bonny Dore (bride and ABC network executive)

Ronny Graham

Carl Kleinschmitt

Terry Hart

Bruce Vilanch

Leaders of the Pack

A staff of five writers was hired to write the pilot script for *The Brady Bunch Variety Hour*. The team included veterans Ronny Graham, Carl Kleinschmitt, Terry Hart, and newcomers Bruce Vilanch and Steve Bluestein. Graham, who is referred to by Vilanch as "a genius, an absolute genius," was best known at the time as a comedic actor on Broadway and in television commercials. Jerry McPhie recalls, "Ronny Graham was brilliant and was in the most successful revue on Broadway called *New Faces of '52*. He wrote, directed, and acted in it. Out of that show came Paul Lynde, Eartha Kitt, Alice Ghostley, and Carol Lawrence, among others. He was a great jazz pianist as well. I can't say enough for him." The Kroffts also wanted Graham because he was a good friend of Florence Henderson, had been a writer for Johnny Carson and Bill Cosby, and was closely associated with comedy films by Mel Brooks.

Kleinschmitt, who had been a writer on *The Dick Van Dyke Show, M*A*S*H,* and *The Odd Couple,* was not very interested in writing for *The Brady Bunch.* He remembers, "My agent said, 'Sid Krofft wants to find somebody to give voice to an idea he has, a variety show that has sitcom elements in it.' I said, 'That's a stupid idea,' but was told to go meet Sid anyway. I met Sid and was appalled by the idea, and said thanks, but no thanks, and then Marty got into the act. Marty Krofft is like a bulldog, he will not let you go if he thinks it will help him some way. I eventually caved in to money and took the job as the so-called head writer. I had never paid much attention to *The Brady Bunch.* Sherwood Schwartz had a genius for doing shows that weren't terribly good, but lasted forever, and that people liked. We in the business may not have admired them, but people flocked to them. This idea of putting *The Brady Bunch* back on television was a smart marketing idea at the time since their run as a sitcom was over. But the results, as you can see, are a little questionable."

Terry Hart was the wild card of all the writers and was only there to assist in writing the pilot episode. He was already gainfully employed as a writer with *The Tonight Show,* in addition to *Happy Days,* so his involvement was going to be temporary at best. Hart reflects on his contribution by saying, "Nobody went into show business saying, 'I want to write for *The Brady Bunch Variety Hour.*' We all wanted to be doing movies and independent films. I never went into a bar or cocktail party and bragged about it."

Vilanch had come from Chicago where he was a TV critic, but found success in Los Angeles writing for personalities such as Lily Tomlin, Richard Pryor, and Flip Wilson. Vilanch recalls, "I remember going into a meeting where the guy was producing the Captain and Tennille who had a variety show that was coming up. He said, 'We'd love to have you, but you're really just too hip for this show.' I called my agent and I said, 'I'm too hip. I just have to find something to do that will show people that I can work both sides of the street.' So my agent proposed *The Brady Bunch Variety Hour* and said, 'Here's a perfect marriage, because it's a really square subject matter.'"

Bonny Dore had just worked with Vilanch on *The Paul Lynde Halloween Special* and also felt he would be a perfect addition as a writer for *The Brady Bunch*. "It was my idea to put him on *The Brady Bunch* and *Donny and Marie* because what was missing from all of that was the sting of a Paul Lynde kind of writer, which is what Bruce was. He was always going to go counter to what the other writers would do," Dore says.

Compared to the others, Steve Bluestein had the least experience writing for television and was primarily a stand-up comedian before *The Brady Bunch* came along. He was sent to fill the position because he and Florence Henderson were both signed to the same management company, and they knew that he was funny. "While I was being interviewed they said, 'Do you know what the show is?' and I said, 'No, I don't.' They said, 'Well, it's *The Brady Bunch Variety Hour*,' and as they said that a little tiny gnat flew in front of me and I grabbed for it, you know, to kill it. I just grabbed in the air. They thought that was so funny that they hired me on the spot, because they thought I was making fun of the show," Bluestein says.

For choreography, Marty Krofft turned to longtime family friend Joe Cassini. "I met Marty Krofft in the 1960s before he had his company," Cassini recalls. "I met him through my friend who was a dancer. He and his wife had one daughter, Deanna, she was seven or eight months old at the time, and she took her first walking steps with me." Cassini, who is highly respected as a choreographer, had worked with the best dancers and Hollywood celebrities. Cassini trained and worked with the New York Metropolitan Opera, the Boston Ballet Company, the Philadelphia Ballet, the New York Ballet Theater, the Pennsylvania Ballet Company, and the American School, where he danced under the guidance of George Balanchine. He also studied with Martha Graham and José Limón. Prior to his work with *The Brady Bunch*, Cassini's television experience included choreographing for Dean Martin, Perry Como, Ann-Margret, and Raquel Welch. Joe Cassini quickly recognized the challenges he would face working with a cast of primarily non-dancers with little experience. He knew that he would have to find a suitable assistant and dance coach for the Bradys.

Casey Cole recalls how she ended up filling the void. "Joe Cassini came over while we

Steve Bluestein

Joe Cassini early in his dancing career

Casey Cole

were filming one of the finales for *The Donny and Marie Show*. He knew I was the assistant to the choreographer and during one of the breaks he asked me if I would like to assist him on *The Brady Bunch Variety Hour*. I said of course I would and it was a real honor and pleasure to be working with him," Cole says. "I knew we could do it because I had a lot of experience. I'd choreographed ever since I was nine years old and knew that Joe and I could put together a variety show for these folks. It was a piece of cake for me. It really was."

Sid and Marty Krofft made use of other trusted friends for the art and musical direction. Bill Bohnert had been busy for many years in New York City as a designer on Broadway and also for *The Ed Sullivan Show*, where he is most remembered for creating the set for the Beatles' first appearance on American television. His other experience included serving as art director on variety shows for Perry Como, the Doobie Brothers, and with children's programs such as *The Electric Company* on PBS, making him a perfect match for the Kroffts. "I got involved with Sid and Marty Krofft originally with *Donny and Marie*, their variety show, early on. I think their manager had worked with me on *The Ed Sullivan Show*, so he knew me from there. Then they hired me to do this special with *The Brady Bunch*."

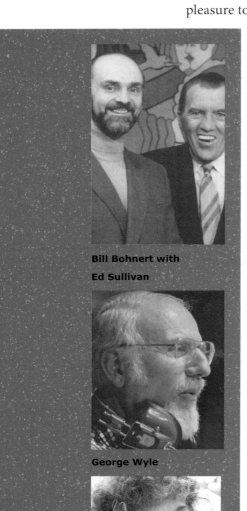

Bill Bohnert with Ed Sullivan

George Wyle

Madeline Graneto

For musical director, Marty Krofft was fortunate to secure the talent of George Wyle, who had a long and distinguished career and was most famous for writing the television theme to *Gilligan's Island* and the perennial holiday favorite, "The Most Wonderful Time of the Year." He began his musical career in 1933 as a pianist and arranger, and began conducting in 1944 for radio programs such as *Serenade to America* and *The Alan Young Show*. He also conducted and arranged music for big names such as Kate Smith, Andy Williams, Doris Day, Flip Wilson, the Lennon Sisters, Dinah Shore, and Jerry Lewis. Among Wyle's other 400-plus popular-song compositions are "Wasn't It Wonderful?" "I Said My Pajamas and Put on My Prayers," "I Didn't Slip, I Wasn't Pushed, I Fell," "Quicksilver," "I Love the Way You Say Goodnight," "Give Me Your Word," and "Santa Claus Party."

When it came to the costume design, Marty knew that for *The Brady Bunch* they needed to work with someone young, with a mastery of modern 1970s fashion trends who could adjust to the emerging disco style that was becoming increasingly popular. That person was Madeline Graneto, a recent transplant to Hollywood from Massachusetts and New Jersey, where she had been designing costumes for dozens of productions at Holy Cross College, Burlington County Theater, and Glassboro College. Graneto had just moved to Los Angeles when fate intervened. Her friend, art director Anthony Sabatino, introduced her to Duane Poole, who was a writer for the Kroffts. Graneto recalls, "Anthony said to Duane,

'This is my best friend Madeline and she's the greatest costume designer in the whole world.' So I went home, and as soon as I walked in the door Duane Poole called and said, 'Are you the greatest costume designer in the whole world?' and I said, 'YES.' What was I going to say — 'No, he lied?'"

Graneto almost immediately went to work with the Kroffts on *Dr. Shrinker* and *ElectraWoman and DynaGirl*. Then during production, one of their producers called Graneto and asked her to come over to KTLA for a meeting. "I thought I was getting fired. I went there and they said would you like to do *The Donny and Marie Show*, and I said yes. I was only a couple of months into *Donny and Marie* when they decided to do *The Brady Bunch*," Graneto recalls. "*Donny and Marie* was my first job and in the middle of all that they wanted

me to do *The Brady Bunch*. I had a hard enough time putting out 400 costumes a week for the Osmonds. It was a huge undertaking," she adds. Sid Krofft was amazed by what Madeline Graneto accomplished for them. "She was fantastic and a hot costume designer at that time. I really respected her talent," he says.

The Krofft Water Follies

As a child, Sid Krofft was mesmerized by the spectacular 1930s Busby Berkeley movies, which featured musical production numbers with dazzling props, showgirls, and complex, kaleidoscopic cinematography. This influence was evident when Sid created the Ice Vanities troupe that skated on *The Donny and Marie Show*, but even more so when he decided to have water ballet and synchronized swimmers for *The Brady Bunch*. Art director Bill Bohnert recalls, "The giant swimming pool was one of Sid's many ideas. He was trying to emulate Esther Williams, and that's why he did the pool. He wanted to get that feel and that size. He liked big things, and that certainly was a big statement. He had used an ice-skating rink on *Donny*

Busby Berkeley's *Footlight Parade* **(1933)**

Esther Williams in *Million Dollar Mermaid* **(1952)**

AUDITION

Beautiful Female Dancers Needed. Age 18-28 for TV Special. Also must be able to swim well.

MONDAY, OCTOBER 25, 1976 — 9 A.M.

ABC-TV
Rehearsal Hall 2
1313 N. Vine St., Hollywood

Advertisement from *Daily Variety*

Home of ABC Television in the 1970s at 1313 N. Vine, Hollywood. It is now occupied by the Academy of Motion Picture Arts and Sciences

Fort Lauderdale swimming champion and water ballet choreographer, Charkie Phillips

and Marie, and so he didn't want to do that so the next best thing in his mind was a big swimming pool."

Writer Bruce Vilanch adds, "Sid had the ice for the Osmonds but then he came up with the water ballet for *The Brady Bunch,* inspired from the same pipe." Vilanch remembers running over to meet Sid and Marty for the first production meeting to hash out ideas. "They were just hysterical together. Sid just sat there and said, 'I see a waterfall…and thirty-six mermaids coming over the waterfall…doing lovely water ballet…' and Marty quipped, 'Eighteen mermaids.' All of that was stuff Sid came up with while he was stoned, and, in fact, where do you think they got the mermaids from?!" Vilanch laughs.

Producer Lee Miller was not happy about Sid's swimming pool idea because it was going to be a burden on the production. First, he had to figure out how to build and maintain it. Then they had to find a stage they could dedicate to it because the pool was so large. "None of us had ever done anything like that before so it was a lot of experimenting with it until we got it right. It was not something I would want to do again," Miller says. In addition, head writer Carl Kleinschmitt had some serious concerns about the swimming pool idea and the complications it would present for writing scripts. "It appalled me when I first heard it because it just seemed so incongruous that on top of all the other craziness there would be someone in the water! It's just a classic example of what happens when things go wrong," he complains.

A casting call that went out to all female dancers in Hollywood for the upcoming "Brady Bunch Variety Special" attracted hundreds of applicants. Auditions were held on Monday, October 25, 1976, in Studio 2, at ABC's Hollywood studios at 1313 N. Vine. A group of dancers were initially chosen by choreographer Joe Cassini as potential "Krofftettes" but the final qualification came from finding professional dancers who were also professional swimmers, or could at least learn quickly. Marty was unsure if he would ultimately be able to fulfill Sid's dream of having synchronized swimmers for two reasons — they didn't have a swimming pool on the KTLA lot or a choreographer with experience staging numbers underwater. Enter Charlotte "Charkie" (pronounced Sharkie) Phillips, from Fort Lauderdale, Florida, who had been working in Hollywood for several years as a dancer on programs such as *The Mac Davis Show* and *Ray Anthony's Bookend Revue*. She caught everyone's attention when in her resume she listed water choreography, synchronized swimming, and water ballet. "They asked me to come forward, Sid and Marty did, and probably Joe Cassini, I remember them sitting at a table, and they said, 'So, I see here that you do synchronized swimming and have choreographed it. Do you think you could take these girls, find the best swimmers out of the ones we've chosen, teach them how to do synchronized swimming, and put something together?' and I said, 'Absolutely.' That's how that happened," recalls Charkie.

For her assistant, Cassini selected Christine Wallace, who was an established Hollywood dancer and had been a competitive swimmer in high school. Wallace recalls, "With water ballet, if you're a dancer and you're a strong swimmer it's not that big of a leap. Charkie and I ended up trying out different dancers who could swim, and watched everyone to see who could do certain basic things. It takes a lot of stomach control, whether you're lifting one leg up or down, you do

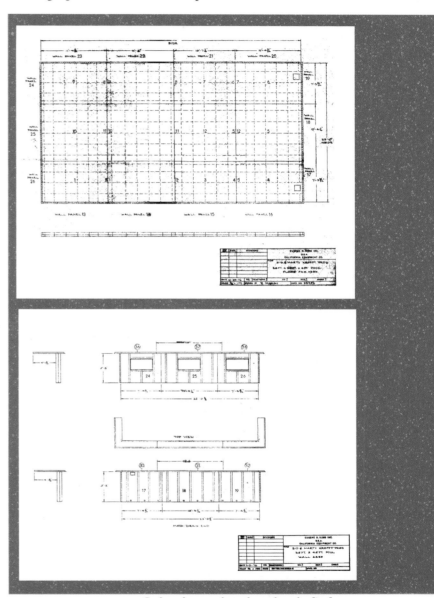

Swimming pool engineering drafts for
The Brady Bunch Variety Hour

have to be in good shape. We ended up with just a small group of women. It was hard to find people who could do both, dance and swim. It was very difficult."

Florence Henderson was more than a little surprised when she learned that a swimming pool was proposed for *The Brady Bunch Variety Hour*. "Well, I think Sid and Marty Krofft, you know, they're a little insane. They said, 'This show needs a swimming pool,' and so on the soundstage at KTLA in Los Angeles they built this huge swimming pool, and it was amazing!" Henderson said.[24] But the swimming pool itself did not just appear one day. The staff and crew at KTLA put forth a heroic effort to pull off the monumental task. Art director Bill Bohnert recalls, "A swimming pool is very difficult to deal with simply because it weighs so much. The soundstage they put it on is so small, and this pool very nearly filled it." Unit manager Jim Zrake remembers the concern that the weight of the pool might be too heavy for the structure of the floor. He had to bring in structural experts, engineers, and get special construction permits. "It was a big pool, that's a lot of water, that's a lot of weight. I remember before we had done that, we had put in an ice rink next door for *Donny and Marie*, and that was pretty cool, but a lot less water and a lot less weight, there wasn't a problem. When we started looking at the swimming pool, we knew, obviously water is very, very heavy when you put it in that magnitude. You've got to make sure you don't have the floor collapse. Can you imagine the panic that would have occurred and the damage?"

An engineering draft for the swimming pool was submitted by Eugene D. King Inc., in association with the California Equipment Company, and was finalized on November 3, 1976. KTLA obtained the services of a professional pool company, and the pool arrived in sections that were bolted together and sealed. They had to get clearance from the City of Los Angeles that the substructure of building itself would hold it up, and because the water weight distributed itself evenly over the floor, the pounds per inch was given approval. Bonny Dore recalls that structural concerns about the pool nearly shut down production. "I thought Marty was going to have a nervous breakdown. The pool, when they built it, didn't quite fit right. It looked like the pool was going to go through the floor. Marty was pretty hysterical as I remember. He didn't know what he was going to do. At that point he looked at me and said, 'Do you think this pool was a good idea?' and I said, 'We'll see. If it doesn't flood we'll be fine.'" The swimming pool was forty-five feet long, twenty-five feet across, and sixty-eight inches deep, and was constructed on Stage 2 at KTLA above the stage floor. It contained 47,756 gallons of water complemented by spiral staircases, psychedelic lights, steep water slides, rushing water jets, and overhead runways. Seven porthole windows along the sides of the tank and underwater cameras allowed crew members to film the swimmers performing "aquabatics."

Assistant director Rick Locke remembers their disappointment when they filled the pool for the first time. "We filled it up with regular water and it looked like milk. We had a window on the side of the pool that we would shoot through outside for the cameras and you couldn't see anything," Locke says. Production manager Pat Davis explains that Marty ended up having to put 50,000 gallons of Sparkletts bottled water in the pool to clear things up. Then the crew at KTLA had to put in chlorine to purify the water, and recycle it with a Swimquip Vertical DE filter, which required pumping facilities outside the stage entrance. Writer Steve Bluestein says, "I just remember thinking 'amazement.' I don't think there had ever been a television show with a swimming pool. During that era, Sid and Marty were in their heyday. They were the Disney of their time. They were doing things. Sid's imagination was incredible. They would take risks. They would go out on a limb."

The Script

Writing a script for *The Brady Bunch Variety Hour* became difficult because of all the diverse elements involved. "The challenge was the sitcom combined with the variety show. You know, to combine the two elements," says writer Steve Bluestein. "So, some of us wrote the variety stuff and some of us wrote the sitcom, and some of us wrote just the jokes for what we called the 'Octologue,' which was the eight people up in front during the opening," he adds. Jack Benny's "show within a show" concept was already in place when the writers were hired. Bruce Vilanch elaborates, "I don't know if it was Sid who came up with it or somebody from the network. *Jack Benny* is the prototype for that kind of thing but *Burns and Allen* did it, and Bob Cummings did it too on his show." The premise was to have the writers depict a behind-the-scenes Hollywood story about an American family, the Bradys, who were, as a unit, moved from Los Angeles to a beach house in Malibu to do a television variety hour. In 1973, PBS ran a show called *An American Family* about the Louds, the prototype for what became reality TV. It was a documentary that ran for thirteen weeks with cameras following the family

The Louds — *An American Family* (PBS, 1973)

around in their ordinary, everyday lives. Vilanch says, "Nothing like that had ever been done before. I think the rationale was the Bradys are a network version of that family, everything we had seen on *The Brady Bunch* series was actually stuff that was filmed for a documentary. Now the Bradys had become stars the way the Louds had become media stars. So the Bradys had been given a variety show to do, and they move to California — from wherever they were living — to Malibu and they were now doing a variety show with guest stars. That was the tortured rationale to explain how it happened," Vilanch adds. "You just have to get stoned and watch it because it all makes sense when you're stoned."

(AS THE OTHERS STEP UP TO THE
MACHINE AND TAKE A NUMBER, MRS.
BRADY CONTINUES, <u>TO CAMERA</u>)

                    MRS. BRADY (CONT'D)

With eight Bradys, this is the only

fair way to decide who talks first,

who eats first... or, in the

morning, who gets the bathroom.

                    JAN

(THROWS HANDS OVER FACE
IN EMBARRASSMENT)

    Mother! How could you! Now everybody

<u>knows</u>!

                    BOBBY

(TO CAMERA)
    My sister Jan doesn't want anybody

    to know we even <u>have</u> a bathroom.

                    GREG

(TO CAMERA)
    Actually, in our old house, we <u>didn't</u>.

                    JAN

(HUMILIATED)
    Oh, I wish I was dead!

                    MRS. BRADY

Come on now, they're waiting for us

to say something. Who's got twenty-

seven?

(ALL CONSULT THEIR NUMBERS, SHRUG.
NOBODY HAS IT. MR. BRADY GETS
IMPATIENT, ASSERTS HIS FATHERLY
AUTHORITY)

There was not much effort made by the writers for the characters to be consistent with the original series. In fact none of them had seen the sitcom more than a few times. Because Vilanch, Bluestein, and Hart were generally unfamiliar with *The Brady Bunch* they relied on Kleinschmitt and Graham, who had more knowledge of the characters, to guide them through the process. "We would be writing jokes and Carl Kelinschmitt would say, 'That's not Brady,'" Bluestein says. Kleinschmitt laments that there wasn't enough "funny" to go around. "That was probably our fault. It was just an awkward format. Plus we had the further restriction of trying to weave a guest star into the story. So, we would take ludicrous leaps of logic to work them into the episode. It was like taking a bunch of disparate elements and throwing them at a Velcro target and seeing if they would stick. It was nuts," he says.

The Kroffts had already adopted a standard variety show format for *Donny and Marie* that they then adapted for *The Brady Bunch*. Every script began with an opening song and "Octologue," and after a commercial break a "Family Production Number" would introduce a "House Sketch" depicting a behind-the-scenes sitcom in the Brady living room. A solo musical number ended the first half of the show, and after a second commercial break the audience witnessed the conclusion to the "House Sketch." This was followed by a performance by the special guest star, another musical solo (usually sung by Florence Henderson), and then the big musical finale. The first draft of the script for the pilot involved guest stars Donny and Marie Osmond (a convenient choice for the Kroffts) and Tony Randall. Sid came up with a spectacular opening entitled "The Best Disco in Town," which was a musical medley complete with "Fountains, Fire Jets, and Swimmers," according to the first draft.

Bill Bohnert's original sketch for "The Fraidy Bunch" set, which was later cut from the script

The script also featured a Halloween-theme skit, later removed, entitled "The Fraidy Bunch" (see previous two pages) which was described as "Our lovable Bradys made-up in light green tint and dressed not unlike the *Addams Family*…your average American family of vampires or ghouls." Among other things, it involved Marcia feeding McDonald's cheeseburgers to a live plant named Waldo, and a dead corpse seated at a harp as the Bradys sing "The Monster Mash" with the Osmonds. Bruce Vilanch still laughs to this day at how campy the scripts were. "We tried to do the best with it we could. In a bizarre way it was entertaining but we knew we weren't coming up with something that was going to live for the ages," he admits.

The final draft of the script eliminated "The Fraidy Bunch" and added songs from *A Chorus Line, Pippin,* and an additional series of disco songs for the finale. "What I remember is that everybody worked very hard and the results were not as wonderful as many of us would have liked," says Carl Kleinschmitt.

Scenic Design

Sid Krofft's elaborate vision for *The Brady Bunch Variety Hour* required ten major sets for art director Bill Bohnert to design. Stage 6 was one of the largest on the KTLA lot, so there were not many limitations on scenic design for the production numbers. But Stage 2 was very small, with only 7,000 square feet of space (a hundred feet by seventy feet) and thirty-five foot high ceilings. This presented some limitations for the swimming pool idea. To complement the front end of the pool stage, Bohnert created a large proscenium archway that stood twenty-two feet high and fifty-eight feet across, and sprayed from top to bottom with glitter. "Sid liked everything big and he liked it strong in every regard in terms of color," Bohnert says. Bill also designed a large blue screen to cover the front of the stage, which folded open spontaneously to reveal the Bradys standing on a giant staircase. Susan Olsen recalls, "When I saw the set for the pool I cried. I couldn't believe how tacky it was, how lame and ugly. But we were on a Krofft production. I never agreed with their aesthetics."

Barry Williams immediately recognized the swimming pool as a spectacular kind of prop. "I envisioned all kinds of stuff going on. I saw people coming down from the ceiling on ropes, they're going to be pulled out of the water, there's a bunch of slapstick stuff you can do with that because people get pushed in, and so I thought it was a versatile kind of centerpiece for a certain part of the show. I am a swimmer so I felt

comfortable around the water. My biggest memory is that the water was clean and that it was warm. I was appreciative of that," Barry says. Sid decided that he was also going to have the Bradys dance on a small, round platform surrounded on all sides by water. Carl Kleinschmitt says, "Some of us still laugh about poor Bob Reed standing out on this round island in the middle of the pool that looked like a Necco wafer." How did the Bradys make their way onto the island? Steve Dichter recalls, "They put a board out and they just walked across it. The island wasn't particularly stable because of the water and there was some buoyancy to the platform. We tried every which way to make it secure for them because most of the cast was pretty insecure about it."

Also on Stage 2, Bohnert created a "Fire Copter Trapeze and Burning House" for something Sid entitled the "Comedy Water Circus" featuring the Bradys in the swimming pool as clowns frolicking to the nineteenth century folk tune "Hot Time in the Old Town." Two large living rooms were proposed, one for the *Brady Bunch* family and one for the previously mentioned "Fraidy Bunch," which was later cut from the script. Bohnert also designed a roller-skating rink for a "Ratsie's Rollerama" skit, and a ballroom with hanging chandeliers for the "Family Portrait" song to be sung by Florence Henderson.

Stage backing elevations were built as the setting for other musical scenes: Tony Randall's production number and the grand finale "Young and Old Songs." The sets were constructed on-site at KTLA, where they ran a large workshop headed by Cal McWhorter and Ray Brannigan. "There were very capable people working at KTLA at the time," Bohnert says.

Costume Design

Prior to coming to Hollywood, Madeline Graneto's experience was on the East Coast in live theater, so her theory of costume design was somewhat different from other people in television who had a background in fashion. "My things were individually designed for each Brady character. In the theater costume design is about one thing — character, character, character," Graneto says. "My professional actors who come from theater are in a lot of instances easier to deal with than people [in television] who don't have theater training. That is because they cannot separate themselves from their character. They want to be themselves. I have to answer two questions — who are these people and where do they come from? You have to answer that the minute a person walks onstage or into the television camera or film camera screen. When James Bond walks onto the screen he is James Bond. When each one of the Bradys walks onto the set, even though it's *The Brady Bunch Variety Hour,* they are still Greg, Marcia, Peter, Jan, Bobby, and Cindy. They still have to be themselves even though you lump them together and call them the Brady Bunch. The people who were not characters were the chorus line girls who jumped into the swimming pool. They were chorus and it doesn't matter who they are as individuals, that's not their role. What they are is sexy, fun, and cute. That's my theory, which comes from the theater and not from fashion," she adds.

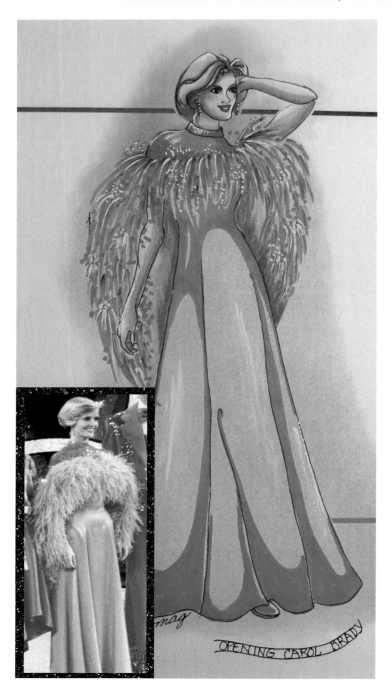

OPENING CAROL BRADY

Bonny Dore had many concerns about costume design for the pilot and what Graneto was being asked to do. "Madeline got blindsided on the pilot. She wasn't getting paid for it and Marty was hustling her saying, 'Oh please do this for us because you've done so many other things and we love you.' They have to have this now, it's got to be overnight, and they were changing their minds every thirty seconds about what they wanted. Eventually it was Sid, Sid, Sid, more glitter, more glitter, more glitter. It was so much glitter you couldn't get past it. Sid would drive her crazy. She'd design things and Sid would say, 'More glitter,' more this, more that. Madeline would say, 'No,' and he'd say, 'I'm the executive producer. Do it.' Time was so short, by the time you're there you can't take it off. I was nervous, because I was worried that there was going to be too much of everything. The sets got over glittered, the outfits got over glittered, and there was no time to change it," Dore says.

By the time everything was put together the production was ready to shoot. Dore continues, "I remember when Madeline came to me and she said, 'Sid made me put extra glitter on everything,' and I said, 'Oh my God…' Then I asked, 'Did you have time to check with the set designer?' and she said, 'No, because he didn't tell me that Sid said to over glitter the background,' which of course they did. By the time you got to the number with the opening staircase, it was like, 'OH MY

GOD.' Marty came over to me and said, 'So how much trouble am I in?' and I said, 'Well, let's hope everyone performs well. I think we're going to scale it back later.' But there was no time to change it. When you're that close, you can't say, 'Oh, you know what, you have to redo those costumes,' you just have to hope to God you can get through it."

Madeline Graneto was called into a production meeting with Sid and Marty, which Dore attended and issued a stern warning to the Kroffts about her disapproval. "I warned Sid. I said, 'Sid, you're over glittering this thing, we're going to hate ourselves in the morning.' Madeline just gave me a look like, 'I love you.' Then Marty told Madeline he had changed his mind and wanted something completely different. It involved a lot of people, and then he just left the room. Madeline looked at me and said, 'Does he think I have gremlins that come in the night?' She was just stressed to the max. She was just at the end of her rope and she had every right to be. Madeline wanted to make sure I understood. I was the network. I did understand. I was one of those people who would actually go in the back where wardrobe was and see the miracles she pulled off on a daily basis. Madeline and I worked together a lot and I have great respect for her," Dore says.

Graneto says that despite the constant stress she was subjected to

while working for the Kroffts, she always felt grateful to have a job and was excited to be given the opportunity. "I just thought everything was great, because it was my big chance. I always have been really on the positive side. I never had any bad feelings. I look at things

The Bradys dance down the staircase in their opening number

really well. It's interesting that people think I was abused but I was as happy as a clam. They always asked for too much but I always took it in stride," she says.

An Odd Couple

Although the Kroffts had Donny and Marie Osmond booked as the guest stars for *The Brady Bunch Variety Hour* pilot, they felt the Bradys needed some kind of comic foil to play against. Paul Lynde was a big hit with audiences on *Donny and Marie* and provided exactly the kind of element they were looking for. Sid suggested Tony Randall. "In many ways, Tony Randall was their Paul Lynde. It worked on *Donny and Marie* and they hoped it would work here. There was a thought, only a thought, that if it worked out with Tony then maybe Tony would come back," says Bonny Dore. Head writer Carl Kleinschmitt accompanied Marty Krofft to meet with Randall to discuss the idea, and was left with an everlasting impression. "I had worked with Tony Randall on *The Odd Couple*. Marty Krofft and I went to visit Tony at the Chateau Marmont on Sunset Boulevard in Hollywood. Tony had one of those bungalows and he came out to greet us in his bikini underwear, and he laid down on his chaise lounge and talked to us for an hour. I always thought that was one of the strangest interviews I'd ever had with an actor — with a man lying in his bikini underwear — and he was agreeing to come on *The Brady Bunch Variety Hour*," Kleinschmitt recalls.

Matching Tony Randall with *The Brady Bunch* seemed like its own odd couple because he didn't enjoy being around children. "Tony, of course, could do comedy in his sleeve," says Bonny Dore. "I remember in the run through he was looking around, and I knew what he was thinking, 'I'm here with children.' Tony liked adults who were brilliant actors. That's who he liked to hang out with. But children who had to be accommodated, that's not Tony's thing. He expected everybody to be perfect or they shouldn't be there." When Tony arrived on the set of the *Variety Hour* the production staff wanted to make sure the Brady kids didn't get on his nerves. Wanda Reischl remembers, "They told all of us mothers in the room to talk to your kids and to not let them make a nuisance of themselves around him because he didn't really care for children."

Tony Randall

Susan Olsen feels that Tony never really had a problem with the Bradys because they knew each other already from their days working in proximity to each other on the Paramount lot. "The thing I remember about Tony Randall on the *Variety Hour* is that I was sitting on the edge of the couch, he kept walking over, they're busy lighting the set or whatever, and he'd walk over and push me over. I'd fall back on the couch, and I would get back up, and wait for him to come by and do it again. We kept this up. We never said a word about it, and then do the scene. The scene's over, and then they're fussing around waiting to do another take, he'd come over and push me again! I don't think Tony ever had a problem with us. That was the production being ignorant because we were great kids. We didn't annoy anybody," Susan says.

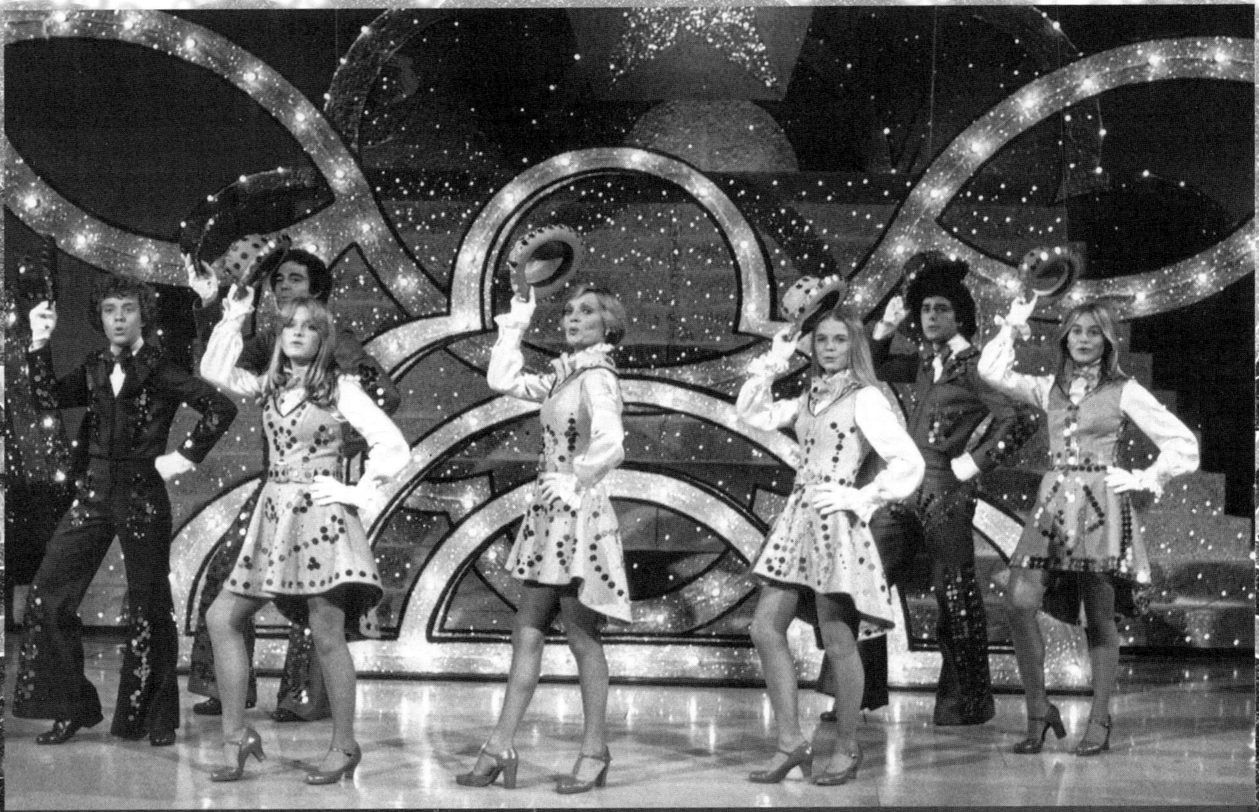

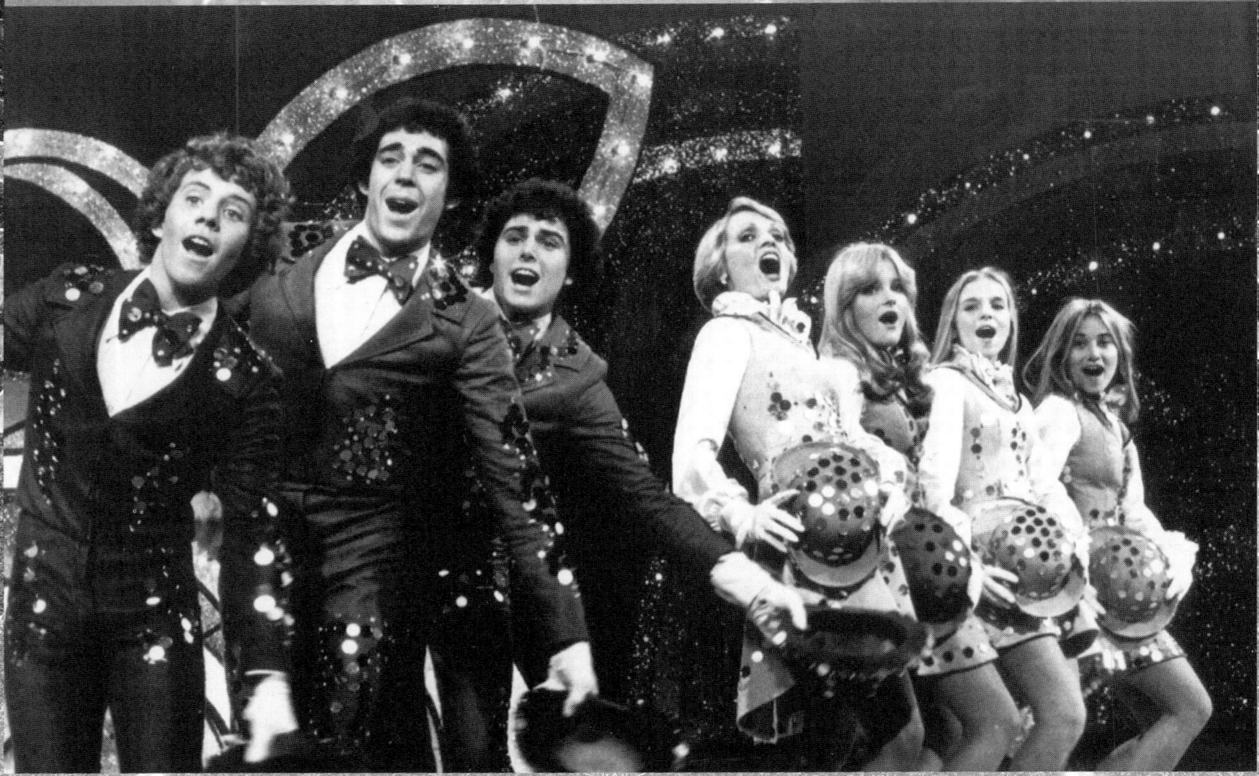

Do It Like a Brady

During production delays related to building the swimming pool and recasting the role of Jan, the Kroffts sent the Bradys to North Hollywood, where they participated in dance classes with Joe Cassini at a small studio on Chandler Avenue. Susan Olsen says, "We took workshops with Joe where we weren't learning choreography for any specific number, we were just learning to dance better." Cassini's first task was to assess the capability of the Brady actors by putting them through a simple dance routine. "I would say, 'Let me see you do some fun walks, let me see you do some sexy walks, let me see you move around to this piece of music,' then I would choreograph the piece around their capabilities," Cassini says. He recalls that a lot of the pieces that were developed for *The Brady Bunch Variety Hour* were fun pieces. It wasn't easy to choreograph for them, but he tried to use movements that would make them all look good. "Some of them had a more natural feeling for movement and dance than the others. Using props and having them do things always added to the production. That's something I learned years ago about when you're working with people who are not trained and yet getting the best out of them you could get, you have to make it fun," he adds.

Bob Reed was ecstatic when Cassini proposed featuring him in "One" from *A Chorus Line* and eagerly participated in learning the production number. "It was so great seeing how happy he was, how much fun he was having, and that he realized he could do it,"

Cassini says. The dance workshops proved instrumental in getting the Brady actors in step with one another, both on and off stage, and prepared them for the challenges of a weekly variety show. "Joe Cassini took chicken shit and turned it into chicken salad," says Bruce Vilanch.

Some of them had a more natural feeling for movement and dance than the others.
— Choreographer Joe Cassini

"He took nine people who couldn't dance, he choreographed it, he got it done, and it looked decent. As far as he was concerned, it was serious work for him and he was very proud of it," Vilanch adds.

Brady, Set, Go

After three weeks of preparation, rehearsals for *The Brady Bunch Variety Hour* finally began on Tuesday, November 16, 1976. The first thing on the schedule was a photo shoot for new publicity pictures. Geri Reischl, who was selected to play Jan only the day before production began, arrived with her mother at KTLA early that morning and was introduced to the other cast members — all except Maureen McCormick who was inexplicably absent. Bonny Dore was not the only one annoyed by Maureen's lack of punctuality. "Marty wasn't used to people who didn't show up on time. I can't say it enough — there was tremendous pressure to get things done immediately. There was a lot of push

Official photo of the new Jan Brady

and a lot of tension because there was so little time to do it. When somebody doesn't show up on the first day, it's kind of a bell weather of what's coming. Believe me, as a producer, you look for bell weathers," says Dore. The cast sat around and waited for Maureen who finally strolled in nearly an hour late. Geri's mother, Wanda Reischl, recalls what happened next. "Sid and Marty threatened Maureen on the very first day of rehearsal. They weren't yelling at her, but talking very strongly. It wasn't like they were shouting but it was definitely reprimanding in front of us."

Following the photo shoot, the Bradys went right to work and began by reading through the script. Then they immediately went into dance rehearsals with Joe Cassini. The Bradys worked extremely hard and rehearsals ran an average of fourteen hours each day for four days. Chris Knight recalls, "They were long days, fourteen-hour days. To be honest with you, that's a regular day. Fourteen hour days are regular. The rehearsals were a drag because we didn't pick it up very easily, but believe me I needed every last minute of it!"

Geri Reischl was not a stranger to everyone involved with *The Brady Bunch*. She and Susan Olsen had done a commercial together in 1967 for the doll Skediddle Kiddles by Mattel toys. Geri had also been on casting calls with Maureen before. Susan Olsen recalls her reaction when she first saw Geri come to rehearsal, "I was like, 'Oh yeah, she's that girl.' We would see each other. You kind of know all of the kids around your age group that are working because you see each other on auditions."

Geri's presence on *The Brady Bunch* set that first day was met with a little bit of reservation.

Barry Williams says, "I'm a purist. I was never happy when we didn't have the original group together. That is the family, and so it's tough for anybody to move into someone else's shoes. Geri Reischl was like a triple threat. She was very, very pretty. She was a great singer. She was the best singer, I think, of all of us. A most naturally, gifted singer, a country kind of singer, so she wasn't really threatening Florence or me, for that matter, because it was a completely different style. She was really selected for her talent and her ability, and she was really good," he says. Maureen McCormick explains that while it was great to be back with everyone, she found it strange that Eve Plumb was not there and having Geri in her place. "I had never met Geri, never seen her. Geri was really sweet, but she wasn't Eve. It was like there was always something missing to the show. Geri couldn't have been a nicer person, but if you do *The Brady Bunch* and you don't have everyone it's just not complete. Part of me thought Eve was smart for bowing out, yet it was an offer I couldn't refuse," Maureen says.

Best friend Barbara Evans recalls that Geri was somewhat intimidated but received a warm reception from the Bradys. "She just loved Florence Henderson and she was so excited she could hardly talk to her. She'd even

> **Geri Reischl was like a triple threat. She was very, very pretty. — Barry Williams**

stutter she'd be so excited. All the kids were so astonished with how good a singer she was, and how friendly she was. Geri got along well with everybody. There was no problem with her fitting in whatsoever. I think she felt she was beneath them but she wasn't," Evans says.

When Eve Plumb didn't come back, the writers made a conscious decision to minimize Jan's character. "We never addressed it. We never mentioned this was a new Jan, this is just *The Brady Bunch,* and quite frankly I think eighty-five percent of the viewing public never knew the difference," says writer Steve Bluestein. "She looked quite a bit like her, and because of the age difference people thought she was older, maybe she grew," he adds. Bonny Dore says that the situation was definitely the subject of conversation at the network, "When it wasn't going to happen with Eve we knew we had to have a replacement. The network was concerned about if she would be accepted by the public or not. The question was: will America accept a replacement no matter how good she is?"

Look-alikes Maureen ~~~ Reischl, and Susan Ols~~~ punch to be back with ~~~ Geri replaces Eve Plumb~~~

"The Brady Bunch~~~ Whooping It Up Aga~~~

Eve Plumb

Why She Left The Brady Bunch

It wasn't an easy decision. Eve Plumb will tell you that upfront, but when the time came to choose between rejoining *The Brady Bunch* on their variety series and pursuing an acting career she decided on the latter. And she has no regrets.

"Originally," Eve told TEEN BEAT, "they wanted me to just do the special, which was the pilot for the series. Then they wanted me to do like five shows in adition to the pilot, and finally they wanted me to do all or nothing: the special and the whole series."

With that choice, and having just received good reviews for her portrayal in the television movie, *Dawn: Portrait of a Teen-Age Runaway*, Eve decided she didn't want to add to her already established identity with *The Brady Bunch*.

Since *Dawn* was so well received by the public and critics alike, Eve and her agent and press representative advised her to remain available for other dramatic

as well as comedy roles, rather than being obligated to the Brady Bunch show.

"There's been a lot of indications that there'll be a sequel to *Dawn*, and that's exciting," Eve says, "but I'm not going to say it's anything definite yet because you never know what's going to happen. But it is in the works, so perhaps!"

"*Dawn* was a very good experience for me," she explains. "It matured me as an actress, and also, I hadn't really thought of runaways so it made me aware of how many there are. I think statistics show that like a million kids will run away from their homes this year and of those something like 65 — or 70% are girls. That's incredible. I like having the opportunity to do other roles that might have a lesson in them for young girls to learn from. I find myself being considered for a lot of roles now th~~~ for girls in the 1~~~ range. A l~~~ would~~~

with ~~~ of a Teenage ~~~ unaway."

The Bunch That Bounced Back

~~~
separated from first-~~~
years, the Brady ~~~
series of var~~~
that pl~~~
~~~
~~~on its
~~~will be seen
~~~, replacing "The
~~~nother test to see if audi-~~~variety show. The
~~~by the suc-~~~

BACK!

~~~"~~~ Bunch" is back on TV ~~~d, a midsea-
~~~with the same group, save ~~~drawing good
~~~e, Florence Henderson and
Robert Reed, Susan Olsen, Geri
Reichel (she's new), Maureen ~~~al background
McCormick, Barry Williams, Chris ~~~usicals and is
Knight and Mike Lookinland. ~~~usical theaters
~~~ound the country~~~ ~~~enced the net-
~~~ork's decision to produce a Brady variety show.
~~~arry Williams, who played Greg in the Brady
~~~unch's situation-comedy series, is the only other
~~~person in the show with substantial musical credits;

The Brady's are Back!...

REGROUPING EASY

Regrouping "The Brady Bunch" turned out to be easier than it appears. Robert Reed had finished a three-week run on ABC Movies of the Week and welcomed a change of duty. He could be e~~~

~~~up
~~~the
~~~ie-
~~~er

s~~~
sh~~~
Su~~~
rati~~~
Broth~~~
the B~~~
Chris ~~~
Maureen ~~~
(Cindy).~~~
the group~~~

Continued o~~~

Left to right are Mike Lookinland, Chris Knight, and Barry Williams, all single guys looking for the right girl to fall in love with. Could you be the one?

chapter 3
Dishing Up a Turkey
for Thanksgiving
A Smorgasbord of Glitz That Was Hard to Swallow

Bradys Rock, Cameras Roll

Taping of *The Brady Bunch Variety Hour* began on Monday, November 22, 1976, and once again demanded fourteen-hour days for three consecutive days. Lee Miller explains that the production was always under enormous pressure because it was a major variety show that was doing something new. "It was taking a plotted situation comedy that had been highly successful and recreating it into a new form using music. That was the first problem. The second problem was the Kroffts had a concept they wanted it to conform to and include the other things they did, which some people loved and some people didn't. They were involved in children's shows and puppetry, and they were trying to blend those into a sophisticated situation comedy with music. So, we had some differences of opinion. Thirdly, we had the production problems that we were never far ahead. We had a small staff, because we were short on money compared to other shows that were on the air," Miller says.

The Bradys were accustomed to a little more coddling from Sherwood and Lloyd, and had a family on the set for a long time.
— Bonny Dore

Bonny Dore wholeheartedly trusted director Art Fisher who was as good as it gets in terms of being able to function under pressure. "I said to him, 'Hey Art, do you think you can do this? Are we going to make it? I don't want to go dark air Thanksgiving weekend.'" Once cameras began to roll, Dore was relieved and held out hope that the show was going to air as scheduled, but she was worried what condition it would be in considering the circumstances. "They were working until one in the morning. Everybody was trying to get there. The Kroffts knew that because it was *The Brady Bunch* franchise, everyone was involved — all the way to the top of the ABC network," she says.

In addition to the other problems behind the scenes, it became increasingly apparent that director Art Fisher was not as well suited to work with young, inexperienced performers as the Kroffts first expected. "The Bradys were accustomed to a little more coddling from Sherwood and Lloyd, and had a family on the set for a long time. Art was used to people being Vegas performers, and it wasn't like that with the Bradys, and it wasn't fair. Two things collided all at once and Art took the heat for it. We're working with variety writers, not sitcom writers. Then you've got the Brady kids — with the exception of Barry — who are really not

©1976 Krofft Pictures

variety performers, who don't have the experience to go into rehearsal and to change up a combination in five minutes. They were going to need a lot of time and a lot of nurturing. The kids were trying, they were really trying. They were stressed, and they were scared. Art would deal with the Bradys the way he dealt with Tony Orlando: *'You fucked up! What's the matter with you?! Let's go back and do it again!'* What a disaster," laments Dore.

Conflict with the Bradys was inevitable because Art Fisher expected everybody to be as much of a perfectionist as he was. He prepared all day and all night. "Art would make it look easy," Dore says. "He came in prepared. He always knew where he was going. He always had thought it through. When someone's that good, when they've prepared so brilliantly and throw improvisation on top of that, they're amazing. But when it came time to go onstage and deal with the actors — that was his weakness. He loved to talk to them from his microphone in the booth. It sounded like the big, booming voice of God. We use to call him 'Art the God.' Even in rehearsal, he was charming, but he needed to be a little bit more charming to the actors."

Although Fisher was considered a brilliant variety director, comedy was not his strength. Being down on the floor with the actors and getting comedy out of them was not what he did well. Dore recalls, "If it was there, Art knew how to shoot it. Art wasn't going to come out of the booth and go down on the floor, and lay out the comedy scene, and make it work. That's not what he did. Art longed to be good in comedy, he really thought he was. He didn't get the comedy gene, it just didn't happen. He certainly had a good sense of humor as a person. Believe me, he made a lot of jokes in the booth at the right time. Things can be very tense in the booth and Art always tried to loosen it up, when he wasn't throwing something. But even after that, he would tell a joke, he would say something funny, usually about himself."

The Kroffts decided to have different people come in and block some of the floor

Tele-Visions
RICHARD HACK

JUST AS WE ARE SOUNDING the death knell for variety shows, doesn't someone come along with still another variation on the theme by Milton Berle. Actually, there are several new looks in the area, one being "3 Girls 3" for NBC from Kenny Solms and Gail Parent, and the other "The Brady Bunch Special" pilot from Sid and Marty Krofft for ABC. The former makes news by taking three unknowns and starring them in musical-comedy. The "Brady" project is unique in several arenas. "The show will star the original cast from the Paramount series — Florence Henderson, Robert Reed, Ann B. Davis, and the Brady kids," says executive producer Marty Krofft. "The unique thing here is that they will never come out of character. They won't be Florence and Robert. They'll be Carol and Mike Brady, plus six. And what we do is the old Jack Benny thing, a show within a show. The Bradys have moved to a new house and they are putting on a variety show. The father, of course, is an architect. He goes along with the idea, but is never overjoyed." And small wonder. The show's big feature is dancers-swimmers who cavort in a 400,000 gallon pool. ("The biggest thing since Esther Williams.") And like Mike Brady says, "At $10.00 a five-gallon bottle, I should be smiling?"

comedy with the Bradys, but it was variety comedy, not the situation comedy they were accustomed to. "You're dealing with sitcom actors who'd been very, very successful at it," Dore explains. "Sherwood and Lloyd were the producers through all of those years, and Lloyd was very close to the kids. So they were really thrown for a loop at the beginning. Florence wasn't, but everyone else was because it was so different. Now they'd have three minutes to rehearse the comedy, and then you have to go to pre-record. Of course we had a replacement Brady and that was difficult. Then there was some question as to what was going on with Marcia, Marcia, Marcia. They weren't like Florence, who had spent her life in musical comedy. It's even hard for people like Florence to do a variety show, from start to finish, in five days. For people who are not use to it, it is overwhelming. They're doing

Good Seeds, Rotten Fruit

The road to hell is paved with good intentions. The one thing that impresses me most about *The Brady Bunch Variety Hour* is how many talented people were involved with the production. There was some really good work and effort put into this show. How could it all turn out so wrong?

It's easy to place all the blame directly on us, the cast. Let's face it, the material wasn't any worse than *Donny and Marie* and that show was a success. But, hey, take a look at it, is it really much better? I don't think so, but Donny and Marie Osmond are. Is it really because some of us are so bad at singing and dancing? Frankly I think we did pretty well for people who were not singers and dancers (those of us who weren't), but we were miscast. It's a fish out of water thing. You can't watch the Brady Bunch doing "Shake Your Booty" without your mind screaming "WHY?!" It's just so out of character. Why are these people singing and dancing? It's like watching Lassie hump someone's leg. You just want to say "No! Stop that!"

Time to break out my handy dandy Band-Aid that covers all of our crimes against art: it was the '70s. That's honestly the best excuse we have. While good designers designed sets, and good musicians played their instruments well, the content of what was being presented was as flimsy as

the comedy, the singing, the dancing, the sitcom, and they do it live in front of an audience. It's a lot. Even really skilled variety people have to work at it. It's an amazing weight," Dore says.

The next challenge the production faced was that they didn't have any promotional material prepared other than some publicity pictures. As they were shooting, Bonny Dore was literally cutting videotape off the reels and rushing it back to the network where she stayed up all night cutting a trailer so they could get it on the air immediately. "It was total insanity. I managed it over a day and a night. I kept calling Marty and telling him what I was cutting to get them on-air promos because we desperately needed them long before we ever had anything edited. They were thrilled because at least we would have some real promos airing for seventy-two hours before the show came on," recalls Dore. Since there wasn't much time to spread the word about the upcoming *Brady Bunch* Thanksgiving special, Marty Krofft enlisted the help of newspapers and magazines across the country to generate viewer interest. He described his vision of the show to the *Hollywood Reporter* this way: "We open very high energy — with a big kick line. It looks like you're at the Roxy Theater. The dancers turn into swimmers, and then the Bradys come over the swimming pool, and then the whole thing ends on a disco beat. It's easier to watch then explain." [25]

Few people not directly involved with the production had any idea of the chaos going on behind the scenes. Paul Shaffer and others that were working for Chevy Chase on the KTLA lot decided to stop by the soundstages out of curiosity to see how the Bradys were faring in their new environment. Shaffer recalls, "There we are on the KTLA lot and we were fun-loving guys and guys with an ironic sense of humor already. Here was this wonderful show taping on the same lot, *The Brady Bunch Variety Hour*. It was really something. Sid and Marty, of course, were huge with *The Donny and Marie Show* at the time. It was so funny, bizarre, and strange to see the *Brady Bunch* kids,

Sid & Marty Krofft Prods.
5800 Sunset Blvd. — 469-3181
THE BRADY BUNCH VARIETY SPECIAL (ABC)
Cast: Florence Henderson, Robert Reed, Barry Williams, Maureen McCormick, Chris Knight, Michael Lookinland, Susan Olsen, Geri Reischl, Ann B. Davis, Tony Randall, Donny & Marie Osmond, The Krofftettes.
Exec. Prods., Sid & Marty Krofft; Prods., Lee Miller, Jerry McPhie; Dir., Art Fisher; Prod. Exec., Toby Martin; Pub., Solters & Roskin.

all but Eve Plumb of course, singing and dancing, and obviously they weren't known as singers and dancers. But by God they were going to sing and dance in this, including Robert Reed and Ann B. Davis. To see them poolside, singing and dancing, was hilarious. Some of us writers spent more time on the set of *The Brady Bunch* watching them shoot these numbers than we did working for Chevy," he adds.

A Very Brady Nightmare

Taping of *The Brady Bunch Variety Hour* was finally completed on November 24, 1976, the day before Thanksgiving. The airdate on Sunday was quickly approaching and not a single scene in the

the Mylar used to make glitter. There actually was plenty of good stuff happening at that time. We just weren't doing any of it. The choices made for our show were of vapid commercial nature. Disco existed and was a successful music form. Did it endure as art? I would say that with a few exceptions, it does not hold up. It is now looked at as "what were we thinking?" the way all bad choices are looked at in time. The way we look at how we did our hair for our prom. We were young, we

didn't know any better. Disco music is a good example of the product of the day. It fit a cultural need that suffices for people who want to be entertained but just don't have the time for art. This is a category known as "pop culture." It is the fast food of creative endeavor. Quick and easy, the result of an immature and impatient society that just can't wait for things to be done right, they want them done now. The Britneys and Mileys of today will age as well. They too will be seen as a laughable fad that no longer holds any of the allure that ever made it popular. It will be kitsch, it will be nostalgic, maybe comforting and poignant, but it will never be deemed as art.

As trite as *The Brady Bunch* might seem to the uninitiated, people loved (and still love) us with a depth. Kids grew up feeling genuine comfort from the Bradys as an extended family. There was a core of love and respect that was real and is why the show has a soul. A soul is immortality; this is why *The Brady Bunch* endures. To see this family engaging in the most commercial and soulless art

forms is unsettling. It is difficult to see Mike Brady dancing in a Carmen Miranda dress without feeling some level of an urge to spoon one's eyes out. The writing of the comedic sketches was well done by great people, but it was missing an adherence to the characters that were already established in people's minds. Bad choices made this production a loser before the race started, but the fact remains that many people gave it their all and did their jobs well, very well. But nobody notices a lovely sweater on a hunchback.

— Susan

show had been edited. "That's where the real crisis came. After the crisis with the pool and the crisis with Bob-can't-dance-and-sing, and the crisis when I got there and saw that Sid had gone crazy and everything was glittered to death…" says Dore. Art Fisher, Lee Miller, Bill Breshears, and Bonny Dore all went to the editing room, but before they walked in they made a pact with one another that nobody would leave until they were finished.

Dore recalls, "Bill sat at the desk and did not sleep for three days because we still hadn't sweetened it with applause and sound effects — that's another whole process. Then you have to lay it in for the commercials. It's a long process and we didn't have enough time. I remember we had real matching problems with editing because they shot it so fast. We did our very best. I knew we were screwed. You're dealing with kids who are not professional singers and dancers so there are going to be mistakes. If you don't have anything to cut away to, you don't have anything to cut away to. Art had shot four cameras, sometimes five. That meant he had to do what we call keypunch editing. He had to sit there and punch as we go. I had to stay there so I could approve the edits as we went because there was no time to show them to anyone but me. How could we? I'm on the phone with my bosses from the network telling them what I'm looking at and they have to go with me, they have no choice."

Lee Miller adds, "Part of the problem was it was slowed down by too many people with opinions. However late it gets, my feeling is that I know how to get it done and edited. I never had a feeling we wouldn't make an airdate."

When the sun came up on Thanksgiving morning they were still editing. Bill Breshears refused to sleep but Fisher would go and lay down for an hour or two for a catnap while Breshears put pieces together. "Then Bill would look at me and say, 'Is it okay?' and I'd say, 'Yes,' and we'd go to the next section," Dore remembers. "That's the only way we could do it. There was no time to do it the way we normally do it." Then they started receiving phone calls checking in on their progress — from Fred Silverman and others from the network, who were all having Thanksgiving at home with their families. "I missed having Thanksgiving with my family. As I recall, we all did," says Lee Miller. Dore didn't think

that it was fair and had an idea. "I called the Beverly Hills Hotel — I could have only done this then — and I ordered the entire menu and had it brought by cab. We had Thanksgiving while we were finishing editing the show," she says.

"Thanksgiving was a nightmare, we had to get it out of editing, out of sweetening, over to ABC, and it had to be rolled in for the commercials which was, in those days, another whole process. We made it, just barely. It was so close. Of course it was my responsibility to make sure that it was done right. It was done the way they wanted and it was there on time or we would have gone to dark air," Dore adds.

Thanksgiving Miracle

The Brady Bunch Variety Hour was a huge ratings winner, beating out all the competition when it premiered during Thanksgiving weekend on November 28, 1976. Nielsen

©1976 American Broadcasting Companies, Inc.

projected that the show was watched by an astounding 15,789,600 people, and by 31 percent of all households in America. But creator Sherwood Schwartz, who was excluded from the *Variety Hour,* was not impressed by what he saw. "I tried to watch it, but Mr. Brady looked like a fool on the show. This is my opinion. Florence is a good singer and an adequate dancer and she came off okay. The others were okay, [but] they were out of their field, and they were out of their depth," he says. Lloyd Schwartz adds, "I only saw half of one episode. I despised it. I thought it was ridiculous. It made no sense. I don't know what that was about — people all in garish outfits and they were supposed to be a regular American family. So suddenly American families do variety? It was the pain of what I thought it was doing to a good show, that's what was most troubling to me."

Leonard Goldenson, founder and chairman of ABC, was also not happy and made sure that Bonny Dore knew it. "He loved *The Brady Bunch* and that's why he wanted the show," Dore says. "Normally he would never get involved, but this was something he particularly liked and I knew that from Fred Silverman, whom I reported to directly. My colleague Marcy Carsey would say, 'It will all be fine. Just get it done!' She wasn't worried about the details and Fred wanted to make sure that the audience who loved *The Brady Bunch* would be happy with it — a very real concern. But when Leonard saw it — and he didn't see it until it was on the air — he felt that it was a little over glittered, and of course he was right. He wanted more excitement out of Bob Reed, he loved Florence of course, and he thought the kids were cute, they just needed more help," Dore adds.

Producer Sid Krofft had the same impression. "I knew that we didn't have a hit," he says. "We were hoping we were going to get picked up but we knew it wasn't *Donny and Marie*."

Lee Miller, however, was very happy with the results. "I thought it was a good special — that's what it was. Yes, it was a 'backdoor pilot,' but it was a guaranteed air whether it went to series or not. It was elaborate, it was glitzy. It was very much the style of musical variety that was current at the time. It had some funny moments, it had some very good sitcom moments, and it had some good writing."

Some actors in *The Brady Bunch* cast were ambivalent about their experience with the *Variety Hour* special. Chris Knight says, "I didn't tell anybody about it, and then I tried not to watch it. People would see it, and I said, 'Yeah, well, it's tough to turn down.' It wasn't something I maintained at a high profile." Barry Williams didn't have any problem with how things turned out but remained realistic about the future. "I thought our show was certainly the same quality as *Donny and Marie* and they were having a success with it," says Barry. "It certainly was no less corny than that. There was more variety because of the personalities that we had. So, I thought there might be an audience that really would gravitate. I knew it wasn't for everybody, and I knew it wasn't some of the markets it would play to because it was corny."

The Brady's are Back!....

THE BRADYS are a family once again! Left to right: Sue, Geri, Maureen, Barry, Chris, Mike—and of course Florence and Robert.

and aren't you glad?

Yes, it really is the Brady Bunch, back as a big family once more! Their TV special was a big hit, and maybe they'll have another TV series as "The Brady Bunch" once more!

BRADYS RETURN!

If any group of people ever returned "by popular request," it's The Brady Bunch! ABC is hoping that the "Brady Bunch Variety Hour" will become a regular thing, since so many people watched the special on November 28! The only Brady missing was Eve Plumb, who had so many other commitments that she couldn't make way for it in her schedules. Donny Osmond (Donny & Marie were guests) was *particularly* sad to see that Eve couldn't make it, since he'd already gotten to know her from waaay back when they both guested on "The Lucy Show"!

Choreographer Joe Cassini recalls receiving a glowing letter from Florence Henderson after her family watched the show, "Her husband at that time was in the big theater business and said he loved it," Cassini says.

Maureen McCormick's family couldn't have been happier to see the Bradys back together. "My parents were thrilled about it. They were thrilled we were doing music and comedy, and working with the Kroffts. So they were really excited about it," Maureen says. Susan Olsen recalls her family also liked the new show. "My mother would defend it. My mother would say, 'Oh, it isn't that bad, Susan, stop it. We can't do material like what you want to do, it's not appropriate for the Bradys.' Mom loved anything that we did."

Of course, many people wondered about Eve Plumb's reaction to the *Variety Hour*. According to Susan Olsen, her mother Dee and Eve's mother Flora spoke on the phone shortly after the pilot episode aired. Apparently, Flora confided in Dee that Eve was devastated when she saw another girl playing Jan and that she just sat there quietly watching the television, crying at times, tears streaming down her face.

Mike Lookinland, on the other hand, was more philosophical about the entire situation. He says, "I have a pretty high threshold for embarrassing behavior anyway. Especially with my own behavior, I have a very high tolerance for embarrassment." It was difficult for everyone to imagine what was yet to come. A feeling of uncertainty enveloped *The Brady Bunch* cast, but they had no other choice than to put forth their highest effort and hope for the best.

Marching Orders

Following the ratings success of *The Brady Bunch Variety Hour* during Thanksgiving weekend, ABC decided to pick up the show as a series and rushed eight new episodes into production to begin airing in January 1977. "When we came back I brought a whole new set of marching orders to everybody, because I had to," says Bonny Dore. "Fred Silverman said, 'You have to work with Bob.' We also had to pull back on the sets and the wardrobe, and he was right. They wanted the wardrobe to be much simpler, scaled back, and more 'Bradyish' in a variety sense. They wanted the sets to be far less glittery — less *Donny and Marie*, more Brady. They wanted more interaction with the family. They were good notes, they were the right notes," Dore adds. The name of the show was truncated to *The Brady Bunch Hour*, and then decisions had to be made about production staff. Art Fisher, director, and Bill Bohnert, art director, were both sent back to *The Donny and Marie Show*. The writing staff stayed intact with the exception of Terry Hart, who was already busy with the *Tonight Show* and had never intended to stay on past the pilot. He was replaced by Mike Kagan, who had recently written for *Laugh-In* and Bob Hope. George Wyle, music director, and Joe Cassini, choreographer, were also retained by the Kroffts for the series.

Madeline Graneto, costume designer, was relieved when she was sent back to *Donny and Marie*. Dore recalls that almost didn't happen. "Madeline got blamed for all the problems and it wasn't fair. I really argued with Fred Silverman because I knew what a good designer Madeline was, and I knew what she was capable of when she wasn't being browbeat. Had either the costumes or the set design in *The Brady Bunch Variety Hour* been one glitter, one not, it would have been okay, but they were both way over-the-top. So the decision was made to change everybody. They were all on loan anyway from *Donny and Marie*. Nobody got fired."

The original *Brady Bunch* sitcom and *The Brady Bunch Hour* had very little in common other than the title and the characters. Both the Kroffts and ABC were intent on making the new version a completely different production. "We're talking a cast of thousands on the *Variety Hour* because of all the swimmers, dancers, guests, and you're literally talking about twenty-five cast members," says Chris Knight. "It was more of a vaudeville circus/Vegas spectacle than it was a television show. It was happenstance to have cameras there because most of the time it wasn't cameras, it was rehearsal. Whereas in the original *Brady Bunch* we had no rehearsals whatsoever," he adds. In the past the Brady actors were accustomed to working with a single camera, performing in street clothes, and completing an episode in as little as three days. Now the time demand was double and the environment foreign. "It was a completely different kind of show," Sherwood Schwartz says. "I didn't feel that could hurt me or my use of *The Brady Bunch* in syndication. It was all song and dance and a couple of very bad comedians, in my opinion. It was not my show, so I had no right to an opinion. I said okay, and took whatever royalty there was, which was really minimal, and I stayed out of it. I had my own things to worry about," he adds.

Prince of Pandemonium

A main concern the Kroffts had with *The Brady Bunch Variety Hour* pilot was an overall lack of comedy. The Bradys were neither a cast of dramatic nor comedic actors, but somewhere in between. They needed a unique element for audiences to want to come back and see them again. Sid and Marty felt that adding a comedian to the show would create some of the spark that was missing. Their most obvious choice seemed to be Rip Taylor, who they enjoyed working with on *Sigmund and the Sea Monsters*. He was affectionately known in Hollywood as "The Prince of Pandemonium," and the "King of Camp and Confetti." Sid explains, "Rip Taylor was a star and a huge, well-liked comedian at that time. He was pretty versatile. He wasn't just the stand-up, he was outrageous. The Bradys weren't very funny." Rip recalls his reaction when he was approached for the role of Jack Merrill, the Bradys' new meddling neighbor. "I love the fact that they asked me. They asked me to be an

'irregular' and a love interest to Ann B. Davis." But Rip had doubts that such a beloved sitcom could be transformed into a variety show musical. "I figured, what are they going to do next? They stretched it to death! That rubber band is going to break! How much can you pull? Please! That rabbit died in the hat but they keep pulling it out," he says.

Not only was Rip someone Sid and Marty admired, but he was a close friend of choreographer Joe Cassini. Cassini's assistant Casey Cole recalls, "The three of us used to go to the same hair dresser together. The man is brilliant, I just love Rip. He was nuts! With Florence Henderson you can see how serious she was. Everything was the right lighting, the right dress, and this and that. With Rip coming on, they needed that versatility in the show. That's exactly what he gave it."

Rip Taylor quickly became a welcome addition to the Brady family, and found the cast to be some of the most pleasant actors he had ever worked with. "When they said 'cut' the Bradys were still nice people, which was even more surprising as opposed to snotty Hollywood kids that I've known, and we all know," Rip says. "I had trouble memorizing lines and they'd help me, which was wonderful. It was a very happy set. I can't imagine anything more fun to do than that show because there wasn't one sour puss among them. It was just a lot of fun," he adds. Although the Bradys privately questioned Rip's presence when he first came to rehearsal, they quickly warmed up to him. Chris Knight says, "At the beginning I thought it was really strange they brought him in and then was very happy that they had, because he's really an over-the-top odd duck but a very sweet guy and quite capable."

While everyone on the set appreciated Rip's comedic talents, they were also struck by his genuine kindness and positive attitude. Writer Steve Bluestein remembers Rip coming to work with boxes of donuts for the entire cast and crew, or boxes of chicken thighs. According to Bluestein, Rip was always bringing food, or thanking the writers for a wonderful script. "He would tear a page out of the telephone book and on it he would write 'We all thank you!' or he would take a huge piece of paper, maybe four feet by four feet, to each writer and would write: A BIG THANK YOU, RIP TAYLOR. He was very sweet, very funny, and easy to get along with," Bluestein says. The only thing that irritated the crew was Rip's love of confetti, and at the end of every show it was his trademark to grab a huge bag and throw it up into the air until it came raining down all over the stage. "He would toss that damn confetti around and what a mess that was," says stage manager Steve Dichter. "They were constantly vacuuming and cleaning up, take after take."

> **At the beginning I thought it was really strange they brought Rip Taylor in and then was very happy that they had, because he's really an over-the-top odd duck but a very sweet guy and quite capable.**
> — Chris Knight

When Rip Taylor was added to the cast of *The Brady Bunch Hour*, writer Mike Kagan brought his seven-year-old son to the taping of the first episode. The little boy quickly became Rip's biggest fan and wanted to meet him after the show. Kagan will never forget what happened next. "So, I pick up my son, and take him over to Rip's dressing room, and knock on the door, and he says, 'Oh, come on in…come on in…' I walk in and the first thing Rip does is take off his toupee. My son starts crying his eyes out, my son got hysterical! He meets one of his favorite funny men, and he thought the guy ripped his head off. He had no idea. He had never seen a toupee before," he says. "Rip's standing there saying, 'I thought he wanted to meet me! I thought he likes me!' I said, 'Well, he didn't expect you to rip your head off!'" Kagan laughs.

Rip Taylor also showed his sense of humor when presenting gifts to the female half of *The Brady Bunch*. He had dimes glued onto individual safety pins and tried to pass them off as diamond pins ("dime-on-pins") to each of them. They had a mixed reaction. "Sorry, it's not my kind of humor, but I still treasure the 'dime-on-pin' he gave me and wear it on special occasions," says Susan Olsen. "When he gave me the dime-on-pin, he'd always call me 'baby.' He invited me into his dressing room with his pretty boyfriend and he had all this food. I've got home movies of all this disgusting food that's left over. He's like, 'Little Cindy, Cindy, Cindy, come in here. We want to hang out with you.' I felt really honored."

Regal Regas

To direct the new *Brady Bunch* series, Sid and Marty hired their trusted friend Jack Regas. He was a well-established actor, dancer, choreographer, and director with over thirty years of experience working with the best of Hollywood royalty. Regas made his debut on Broadway at the age of seventeen and was soon put under contract as a stock dancer for MGM where he appeared in such classic films as *Meet Me in St. Louis, Ziegfield Follies, The Harvey Girls,* and *Easter Parade.* After breaking out as a freelance dancer Regas appeared in dozens of other movies, including *Royal Wedding* and *Annie Get Your Gun.* He was featured partnering Marilyn Monroe in the iconic musical number "Diamonds Are a Girl's Best Friend" in *Gentlemen Prefer Blondes.* Regas also toured in stage acts with Judy Garland and Betty Hutton. He had his first big job on television in 1957 as choreographer for *The Loretta Young Show,* and the following year he staged dance numbers on *The Jack Benny Show.* His other credits in this capacity included working with Dinah Shore, Andy Williams, Bob Hope, Perry Como, Elvis Presley, and many more showbiz luminaries, as well as appearing in *The Flip Wilson Show* in 1970 with his very own Jack Regas Dancers.

Regas recalls how he got involved with Sid and Marty, "I started directing in 1972, but before that I had worked with the Kroffts," he says. "I was a choreographer, and we did a night club act with a puppet designed by Sid. Then I started doing their Saturday morning kids' shows." In addition to Krofft shows, such as *ElectraWoman and DynaGirl, The Lost Saucer,* and *Dr. Shrinker,* Regas also directed an *ABC Afterschool Special.* For his assistant director on *The Brady Bunch Hour,* he appointed Rick Locke, who had started out as a stage manager with

Director Jack Regas

Jack Regas working with Elvis Presley

Assistant Director Rick Locke

the Kroffts in the early 1970s and had assisted Regas on other projects. Locke says, "Jack Regas, the director, is so competent. I watched him work with people who had absolutely what I consider no musical talent, and just whip them into shape, and even work with choreographers who were well known. Jack had these little secrets from way back in the old movie days that he would share with us. It was great fun working with him."

Jack Regas was the antithesis of Art Fisher and was specifically brought in to direct the series because the Kroffts had a lot of problems on the pilot with Fisher and the Brady kids. Bonny Dore explains, "Art and Florence were no problem because she'd just tell him off. Bob Reed and Art were not a combination. There were many tiffs with Bob stomping off mainly because Bob knew he couldn't sing and dance. When Art would push him he'd just get pissed. Art was 'Mr. Macho' so that was also a problem. When Jack came in, Jack was like everybody's grandpa. Jack loved the kids and he came up as an MGM chorus boy. Art came from a completely different place. It's a completely different lifestyle, point of view, everything. Jack loved fluid motion but he wanted to be down on the floor with the dancers and the actors. He wanted to dance with them and he wanted to hang out with them. Jack had a sense of humor, and his forte was doing great production numbers, and he did those brilliantly. Jack had his hands full because it had been a very stressful time with Art. There had been a lot of to do about the pilot, too much of this and too much of that, not enough comedy, and this didn't work, and that didn't work. It was like, 'Hello Jack, now it's your problem!' I love Jack because he got it done. Jack rarely ever lost his temper, it just wasn't his style. He'd get cranky, but he was never like Art. He'd never blow up. He was very good at giving the kids a hug, or telling them to try it again, or taking them over to the side to try to work with them if he could."

Refurbishing the Formica

The Kroffts settled on Rene Lagler to take over designing the sets when Bill Bohnert went back to *The Donny and Marie Show*. Lagler had just won an Emmy Award, and also impressed Sid and Marty with his designs for their Atlanta, Georgia, theme park. In addition, he had assisted with designing a huge typewriter for chorus girls to dance on in *The Donny and Marie Show* and seemed to be just the right person to handle any challenges *The Brady Bunch Hour* would present. Lagler says, "Sid and I got along real well because Marty comes totally from the dollar side, Sid comes totally from the creative side and doesn't care about what things cost. He just always wants, and then when you give it to him, he wants more. He's a terrific person to work for because he is so creative and lets you go with things. Our job, on a weekly basis, was to pump out sets for all the wishes and wants of Sid."

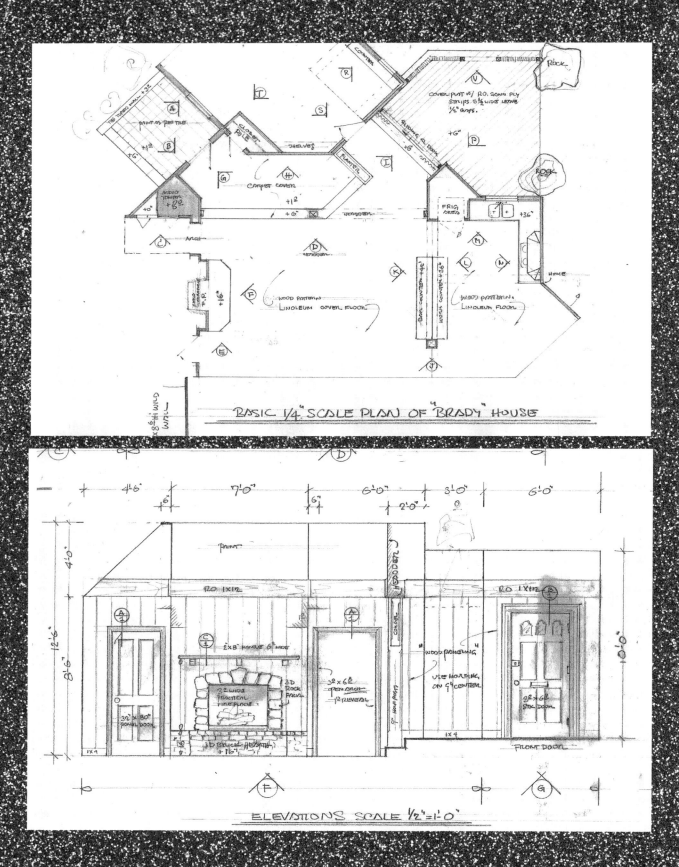

BASIC 1/4" SCALE PLAN OF "BRADY" HOUSE

ELEVATIONS SCALE 1/2"=1'-0"

When Lagler arrived at KTLA to begin work on *The Brady Bunch Hour*, there was scenery from the pilot episode in the scene shop so he refurbished and redid everything. The pool stage proscenium, which originally featured bright fluorescent colors, was substantially toned down to a silver, blue, and beige motif, and was accentuated by 160 clear lamps along the perimeter. Lagler also reevaluated the design of the pool itself. The deck panels were given an overhaul. During this process, the water slides were removed and discarded. He also wanted to be more creative with the water ballet scenic design since it was a main feature in the show. "I had this brilliant idea with some new fabric that

The new Brady living room

was very reflective, so we put it at the end of the pool in hopes of having that reflect back to give us more depth," Lagler recalls. "Everyone was thrilled because it looked like the whole pool had no end. It just pushed it back. It worked really well," he adds. Unfortunately, the next morning they couldn't see three feet into the pool — it had turned milky. The backdrop was some kind of Mylar-coated material that had dissipated into the water. "The best part of all, that I remember, you would think that the producers would go ballistic on me and of all things Sid and Marty, mostly Sid, said, 'You know what, we'll just do something else first and let the filters work it out and we'll do it this afternoon.' That was all that was said, it wasn't 'you dumb so-and-so.' It was a nice moment for me because I was scared to death that was it, I was fired and everything else. No, they were just very kind about it," Lagler says.

Lagler was also asked to design a new house set for the Brady family, which was proposed as a beachfront home in Malibu. "I usually design things to look like what I think — or what America thinks — something should look like, and inflict a bit of good taste. In this case, I recall the *Brady Bunch* house being a lot like where I was living at the time in the Hollywood Hills, with a view overlooking Los Angeles instead of the beach," Lagler says. The house set would require additional space at KTLA, but assigning an extra soundstage to the Kroffts was not a viable option. The Kroffts already had four stages in use between *The Brady Bunch Hour* and *Donny and Marie.* Other major productions, such as *Mary Hartman, Mary Hartman* and *Liar's Club*, were taking up space on the lot as well. Stage 6 was assigned to the Kroffts for the large musical production numbers, so Sid and Marty improvised by assigning space for the Brady house in a corner behind the audience seating. There, Lagler designed a 2,400 square foot set (sixty feet by forty feet) with a small living room in typical '70s rustic colors. It included wooden beams, high ceilings, a fireplace, a kitchen, and a side porch with French doors. Behind the living room he also designed a set for Mike Brady's den. No bedrooms were ever seen. Because the house set was to appear in every episode, a larger budget was allowed for its construction.

Rene Lagler

Pete Menefee

In addition to expenses for the swimming pool and house sets, there were a variety of production numbers in each episode that required scenic design and construction. For the series premiere of *The Brady Bunch Hour* on January 23, 1977, the Kroffts spent $37,722 on all the sets, which adjusted for inflation today would be approximately $130,000. That total did not include the amount spent on building the swimming pool set for the pilot, the wardrobe, or the payroll for cast and crew. It was a massive financial investment for the Kroffts. Marty says, "We put every dime we had into that show."

Producing sets for *The Brady Bunch Hour* was a huge undertaking, and Lagler ended up reusing a lot of the set pieces in other episodes to keep everything within a budget. For example, he built two enormous half circle flats made out of mirrors that served as background for many of the introductions and incidental scenes. These mirrors could easily be rolled around wherever they were needed. For the weekly "Family Production Number," Lagler designed a portable stage with a large apron that appeared to extend into the audience, lit by a row of light bulbs along the front. To give the illusion of depth and height, the flat stage was mounted on a black tarp. Some of the other sets were recycled or traded with *Donny and Marie.* "Money was one of those limitations, so you build a certain amount of basic units that you can rearrange. The way that you're looking at the show today nobody looked at it that way in 1977; it was from week to week," Lagler explains. "You could get by with reusing something by either repainting it, or redoing it, or adding something to it, or just by the virtue of setting it up in a different way. That's how you prolong the cost of an item over a period of eight shows. In all fairness to what we did, in those days on shows like that, recycling things was not that uncommon. Just look at the motion picture industry, how many times has Universal's main street been on different movies? It's the same street. It's just redressed for different productions," he adds.

Brady Buttons and Bell-Bottoms

From the earliest days of motion pictures, Hollywood studios produced some of the most dazzling and elaborate costumes ever seen for their big-budget musicals. By the 1970s movie musicals were an endangered species. Deborah Landis, president of the Costume Designers Guild, says, "Look at the incredible creativity that was going on at that time in television, it certainly wasn't happening in costuming in the movies. It was happening in television, and every single week they were putting on incredible costumes…couture-level costumes done instantly, almost magically." Sid and Marty were very aware of the importance of costume design and it was an especially important trademark for Krofft productions, which were always colorful, outlandish, and innovative. When *The Brady Bunch Hour* was picked up as a series the Kroffts brought

Tom Swale, Pete Menefee, Gordon Brockway on the set of *The Brady Bunch Hour*

back their old friend Pete Menefee, whose creativity they admired and with whom they had worked before. Landis notes, "Pete Menefee has always been so obviously just a shining talent. Even as a young up-and-comer I looked at Pete's work and I knew then that he had a huge amount of style and a tremendous amount of talent, and his contribution really helped to make *The Brady Bunch Hour* memorable. How much of what's successful about the show can be attributed right back to his sense of humor, his sense of style, and his sense of color."

Menefee had worked with the Kroffts almost from the very beginning of his career. He got into working as a sketch artist through Tony Urbano, who had designed *Les*

Poupées de Paris for Sid and Marty. "I was really working as a dancer then," Menefee recalls. "I sketched for a weekend and got paid very, very well for it. Tony looked at the stuff, and I was very pushy about colors and things. He asked if I would like to help codesign a show that Sid and Marty were doing at Six Flags Over Texas. That was the first time I had any contact with them." Later Menefee became a designer, also through Tony Urbano. "Bob Mackie had drawn for Tony and when he saw what my work looked like he said I should really go to the Chouinard Art Institute like Bob did, because I didn't sew, all I did was draw. I did, I took his advice," Menefee states.

Dore recalls her first meeting with Menefee when he was approved by the network to begin work on *The Brady Bunch Hour*, "My comment to Pete was: simple…simple…simple. NO glitter!" After viewing a videotape of the show, he immediately came away with many ideas on changes that he wanted to make. "I didn't like the way the pilot looked," he says. "I thought the costumes were overdesigned. I thought they had to look a little more acceptable, more like real people, more like the characters they were in the show. I just tried to clean the look of the family up a little bit, and then when we did production numbers you could go pretty much wherever you wanted. I always kept in my mind that they were this unit, an American family that was clean-cut. In opening and closing productions, they had to be a little more mainstream than they were done originally."

Polyester Pants, Please

The actors who wore costumes on variety show television in the 1970s fondly remember it as a charmed process during which stunning gowns, suits, and character outfits seemed to appear out of thin air. But in reality the work behind the scenes was tedious and only the result of exceptional talent and determination. Pete Menefee worked on a very tight schedule with *The Brady Bunch Hour* and in only a matter of days an entire set of costumes was conceived, designed, and ready to be worn. "We were always working on the next show that we'd be doing a week before it went into production. We'd have meetings where everybody would sit down and say something like, 'This week we're going to do a spring show, and next week we have so-and-so as a guest,'" Menefee recalls. "Sid would tell me what the music was and I was pretty much given free rein on the design. If I was going to do something early, I would go to Sid and Rene [the set designer] and say, 'I would love for the finale to be red. Can we avoid red in anything else?'" The template for the show was pretty much the same week in and week out. Everyone knew there would be the opening with the Bradys by the pool, and at the end a musical finale. The interior numbers were always slightly different. Menefee says, "I'd sit down, and sometimes I'd do a rough sketch and show people, and say this is the direction I want to go with it. Most of the time I would draw that whole day and do some fabric shopping and then try to get it drawn by the next day so that everything could be okayed."

Menefee did most of his design work in his office at Elizabeth Courtney Costumes, where some of Florence Henderson's gowns were made. The men's suits came from Joe Cotroneo in Hollywood. They had a set of jump suits with

jackets over them, and the colors would change from week to week. "Joe did all of the men's tailoring, and he worked with me until he died. He was just really one of the most fabulous tailors," Menefee says. All of the ladies' clothes and specialty costumes were made by the NBC Costume Department in Burbank. "When I started working at NBC in 1975 it was the largest costume shop in the United States," says Deborah Landis. Many costumes for variety shows were manufactured there, including *The Captain and Tennille, Flip Wilson,* and *Dean Martin.* The NBC Costume Department also created a lot of what was seen on *Sonny and Cher* and *The Carol Burnett Show.* "It was a huge costume shop and really bustling," Landis adds. "Angie Jones was the head of the department, and she was a visionary. Not only did she have a great passion for the work, but she was also a great business woman. It wasn't accidental that the NBC Costume Department grew they way it did, because it was under her very astute stewardship that it was so filled with talented people — talented people on the interpretation side but also talented designers."

Each week Menefee would visit the costume shops he was working with and meet with the pattern maker. He would explain how he wanted something done. He would do a rough sketch, known as a "croquis," that would show all the seams in dark lines. Then Menefee or one of his assistants would go out and buy the fabric, and in some cases an item would be purchased directly from a store then brought to a costume shop for alterations. Ret Turner, who designed costumes for the Kroffts on *The Donny and Marie Show,* would sometimes help Menefee on *The Brady Bunch Hour* when things got hectic. Turner recalls, "A lot of it we bought. We'd buy something and change it. When you're doing a show like that you can't custom make everything. Quite often we didn't even make patterns. We cut directly into the fabric and made the garment because there was no time to do a pattern fitting. All weekly television is very quick. We had a lot of quick turnaround in those days."

Menefee adds, "I always called it 'Taco Bell' — it's driving through, and ordering, and picking up at the next window."

Once the costume shop came back with a draft for Menefee he would make any ne-cessary changes before approving the final design. Kelly Kimball, who worked in the NBC costume shop, says, "Most of Pete's costumes were in clear, bright colors. There was a lot of polyester double knit that got used. Pete was one of my favorite people to work for." Menefee's good friend Frieda was in charge of su-pervising his costumes at NBC, and Dan Morris at Elizabeth Courtney Costumes would make all the gowns for Florence Henderson. Wardrobe mistress Mari Grimaud remembers, "We'd rush them across town to Andre's Beading. Everyone in Hollywood used Andre for bead-ing. It was a lot of running around. We didn't have cell phones. We did-n't have pagers, so we were on the road all the time. It was now go here, now go there, now get this, now get that."

In the costume shop at NBC, Kelly Kimball sometimes found dealing with variety show sche-dules more than a little frustrating.

"It was a rat race," she says. At one point Kimball started to put her foot down when work orders came in at the last minute. "I said, 'You just can't do this, you have to let me know everything because I have other shows I'm working on and if I have to hire extra people, I will.' At 4:30 p.m. they'd give me something, and I'd be cleaning up getting ready to go home and they said it had to be on the set at 8 a.m. I'm like, 'Oh, thanks,' and they've known about it since Monday. That was typical. The directors and producers did this, it

came from the top. We were always scrambling at the last minute." Mari Grimaud notes that the main difference between *The Brady Bunch Hour* and a lot of the other variety shows was that they weren't doing the work at the same place they were shooting. "NBC did a lot of variety shows and we would just go down the hall to get things done. If you're shooting at KTLA in Hollywood and prepping at NBC in Burbank it's a lot of schlepping back and forth. It was exhausting. By the time Friday would roll around, we'd be like, 'Thank God, that one's over with!' and then we'd start all over again," Grimaud says.

Menefee was also constantly driving back and forth between Burbank and Hollywood, transporting costumes from NBC. But on Thursday, February 17, 1977, he was desperately racing back to KTLA when the Los Angeles Police pulled him over. "We were on such a short, fast timetable on the show. I remember leaving NBC, I had the top down and the car was jammed with clothes from *The Brady Bunch Hour*," he recalls. "I was on my way over to the studio and I had to get there very, very soon and there was a police blockade right around the corner for some reason or another. They were very curious about what everything was and of course on top of everything was a head piece that was a lot of bananas, fruit, and flowers, and stuff," Menefee says. Writer Bruce Vilanch remembers everyone sitting around the stage back at KTLA wondering where Menefee was. Vilanch recalls, "Pete then said, 'I'm in a tremendous rush because I have to get back to the studio because I just have this dress, and I've got to get it in, and if I don't I'm going to get fired,' and all that. Every cop at that time wanted to be an actor, and the cop said, 'Oh really? Who's the dress for?' and Pete said recklessly, 'Robert Reed!' The cop looked at him and said, 'Robert Reed, the dad from *The Brady Bunch*?'" Nobody believed Menefee until he took out the sketches and showed them to the police.

Krofftette Linda Hoxit displays her "Floaters"

Menefee says, "It wasn't about speeding, they were stopping cars, I don't know what the deal was. I never did find out, and they were just outside of NBC, and I thought, oh jeez, I'm going to be so late for taping." Vilanch adds, "The cop looked at him like, 'I don't even want to deal with you, you freak! Go!'"

Dressing the Bradys

Pete Menefee has many happy memories about designing costumes for the actors and dancers involved with *The Brady Bunch Hour*. He particularly enjoyed working with Florence Henderson, who had at least three gowns custom designed for her in each episode. "I knew that Florence almost always had a ballad," he says. "With Florence I might do three or four dresses at once. Sometimes I would fit with muslin because her clothes were very often beaded and you don't want to be ripping beaded clothes apart. So if you fit the muslin, it's almost 98 percent that the dress is going to fit perfectly."

Menefee's other favorites to dress were Ann B. Davis and Rip Taylor, and in one musical finale he dressed Ann as a basket of Easter tulips and Rip as Cupid (see previous page). "She was all over the place. It was a little over-the-top. At that point, she and Rip were our really two comic figures, and you always expected to hit hard with the two of them because you could. I would have never done that with any of the kids, but she was a prime target for stuff like that. She had everything, she was such a good sport about it and so was Rip," he says.

When it came to designing costumes for six kids, Menefee started to run into problems with the budget. "The kids had sets of jumpsuits that were red and a set that was yellow and sometimes, economically, you'd have to take what you had done and revamp it. I remember I never went over budget. It was fairly stringent as most TV variety shows were. It takes a lot of planning."

Chris Knight recalls the jumpsuits vividly. "Everything was just real tight. That was the day of disco. It was tight, tight everything. Tight, tight, tight!" he laughs.

Dressing the Krofftette dancers and Water Follies presented a unique set of challenges for Menefee and Grimaud that further complicated an already frenetic schedule. Although the dancers were easy to fit, it was difficult to get them because they were constantly rehearsing or in the swimming pool. Grimaud and her crew couldn't sit around waiting because they had to be on the road running errands for Menefee and their time at the studio was limited. Grimaud recalls, "It was probably easier to get the talent than it was to get the

Mari Grimaud

dancers. Pete would order the swimsuits. Sometimes we'd get them, other times we'd be sweating bullets thinking we wouldn't get them in time. Then he would have them jeweled and studded with rhinestones." As he did with the cast of Brady kids, Menefee also resorted to re-cycling some of the wardrobe pieces for the Krofftettes to save money. "The floater props for the swimmers when they'd do overhead patterns would sometimes get ripped up and remade. One week they were stars, then sun flowers, then hearts. You'd have to redo stuff," he says. Grimaud also remembers that when the women were on land as dancers they were allowed only one set of shoes because they cost over $100 a pair. "The shoes would always start out nude and then each week we'd spray them whatever color they needed to be for that pro-duction number. At the end of the show on Friday, we'd take them and drop them off at the shoemaker, and they'd strip them over the weekend and we'd start all over again. We'd tell them, 'Strip them, and make them nude!' It was wild," she says.

Krofftette Dee Kaye gets a balloon lift on the set

> **Pete thought it was fitting for our finale about "Places" to design an arrow on my chest that pointed out my recent developments.**
> — Susan

Hit the Ground Running

After days and hours of preparing the costumes, at last the time came for taping the show. Mari Grimaud would hire extra workers for the shoot, which originally took place every Thursday and Friday and then later the schedule changed to Tuesdays and Wednesdays. Everything involving the swimming pool would be shot the first day, along with smaller musical numbers, and then the next day the big musical finale and scenes in the Brady house were taped. Grimaud had to make sure every costume was in the proper dressing room at the right time, and then she and her workers had to double-check to be sure everything fit correctly and solve any last second glitches. "It was hard, it was really hard," Grimaud recalls. "I'd have extra ladies come in to help me. We'd be on our knees spraying shoes and stuff. We would start with a swim number, and then those swimmers would become dancers the next day. My buddies who would come in to help, we would assign them. I'd say, 'Okay, you're going to dress the three girls, you're going to dress the three boys, you're dressing Florence, you're dressing Robert.' They all had to be ready at the same time, it was all really fast." Among her friends were: Tina Hoyser, who made sure Florence was ready to go; Paul Dafelmair, who was in charge of Robert Reed; Paul Lopez, who dressed Rip Taylor, and Michele Neely Puluti, who supervised the Krofftettes. Grimaud recalls that Ann B. Davis dressed herself. "If it was a costume, I usually helped her. Otherwise anyone would hang her blue uniform and shoes in her dressing room. She was self-sufficient, I didn't worry about her."

On several occasions Menefee designed costumes involving balloons and at the taping Grimaud and her crew always made it work. "Pete would come in and say, 'Now we're going to have back frames on the dancers that have balloons!' We'd have to go get a helium tank. Then Pete would come back again and say, 'Now we're going to blow up 5,000 balloons!' We were happy to do it and it was fun, and it was with my buddies. You bond with the people you work with because you're going through it together. We laughed a lot," Grimaud says. "Pete was a taskmaster. He had a photographic memory and would say, 'Now we're going to this, now we're going to do that!' and we'd say 'Okay!' and hit the ground running," she adds.

With all the effort put into designing and sewing the costumes one might assume they were cherished works of art to be saved and worn again. That was not the case with variety shows produced by the Kroffts. "None of the stuff we did was built to last. It was going to be on camera for thirty seconds. The point was the visual impact," says Kelly Kimball. Mark Evanier, who worked for Sid and Marty as a writer, recalls coming across some of the Krofft costumes in the garbage in 1979. "The Kroffts had tons of dancer costumes in their facility at Vineland and Sherman Way when I worked there," he says. "One day, I was wandering through their warehouse factory when I spotted some glittery, satiny wardrobe peeking out of a trash can — outfits that had been worn by dancers on the Kroffts' variety shows. As I was then living with one of those dancers, I asked and received permission to take some of these unwanted costumes home for her. I believe the discarded ones I found came about when someone gave the order to thin the collection out and get rid of the shabbier ones. They weren't throwing all of them out," Evanier adds.

Menefee says that Sid kept all the costumes that were made for *The Brady Bunch Hour*. "He probably still has them," Menefee says. "I remember Florence, I did two beaded gowns for her every week and she wanted them very badly. At that point I was doing Florence's nightclub act and I remember Florence asking Sid for them and he wouldn't give them to her."

Turn the Beat Around

Music plays an important role in the success of any variety show. However, in the case of *The Brady Bunch Hour* it was more of a pivotal element since most of the actors appearing in the production were not exceptional singers. The Kroffts already employed a group of chamber musicians to provide the soundtrack for *The Donny and Marie Show*, and many of those musicians played for *The Brady Bunch Hour* as well. The ensemble included three trumpets, two trombones, two saxophones, two guitars, a synthesizer, a large rhythm and percussion section, and a backup choir. The entire orchestra also played kazoos for *The Brady Bunch Hour* theme song. George Wyle served as the music director and his assistants were Sid Feller and Claude Williamson. "It was a ball working with George Wyle, we really had a riot of a time. It was fun. It was a good show with good musicians on it. The top musicians in the country were on that," recalls lead saxophone player Phil Sobel.

Selecting the music for each show was usually a decision made based upon the preferences of Sid and Marty. Claude Williamson recalls, "They picked a lot of old tunes and did them in a new style. That was the year of disco rock and they wanted to do some of the numbers in a disco feeling. Most of it had to do with the rhythm section. The rhythm section created the disco feel. They couldn't pick whatever they wanted. If they

wanted to do an old standard tune, they had to pay whoever wrote the tune, or if the man was dead they paid his estate." Sid Krofft adds, "I always wanted to begin with an Americana 'get your attention' kind of opening, like 'Yankee Doodle Dandy.'"

Because of the Bradys' average singing ability the music options were somewhat

limited, and to save money the Kroffts relied more on songs in the public domain. "I love music and I knew all the songs that we were constantly forced to sing," says Mike Lookinland. "I saw a list the other day of public domain songs and it's so funny, it's like a list of every song we ever sang on *The Brady Bunch* — 'Home on the Range,' 'Twinkle, Twinkle, Little Star.' I think we were into a lot of public domain there with *The Brady Bunch Hour*," he adds.

John Rosenberg was the music contractor for the Kroffts and it was his job to hire and manage the musicians. All of the music was rehearsed and recorded at Sunwest Studios in Hollywood, just down the street from KTLA on Sunset Boulevard at Western Avenue. "We would come in one day a week to prerecord the music and then we'd go away for the week," Rosenberg says. "Studio musicians are just used to sitting down, reading, rehearsing it once, and then recording it. So it went pretty fast." Alf Clausen, who later went on to serve as music director of *The Simpsons*, worked for the Kroffts on *Donny and Marie*, and recalls, "We would come in at eight o'clock in the morning and start with the opening number. The tape was cut off the reels and zapped over to the stage right away. The schedule was nuts," he says.

On prerecord day the *Brady Bunch* cast would come in a little bit later than the orchestra to hear their songs, and they would rehearse the music in the studio. Then when the musicians left, the Bradys would record their vocals separately. "The reason we did that is that we didn't want the orchestra to sit there and pay for that. Sometimes you get a vocalist that gets it in one or two takes and then you get someone who has to work at it, and it takes quite some time," John Rosenberg says. Claude Williamson recalls, "I ran the vocal rehearsals with the Bradys, and we would rehearse everything in a couple of hours, which is nothing. Then they would have to go in and record it, which was the night before the taping. I had so much else to do, I didn't have enough time to give them a proper rehearsal. I was working with the dancers and Joe Cassini, along with the writing and arranging. I just didn't have the time. So it really wasn't entirely their fault the vocals were weak."

Writer Mike Kagan recalls just how much some of the Bradys struggled with singing. "When it came time to tape the show they'd lip-synch to their own vocals because they were dancing and running around anyway. That way if you took Robert Reed in the studio you got a chance to do twelve takes with him until he got it right, or at least until it sounded pleasant!" Kagan says. Williamson fondly remembers coaching Bob each week on his singing. "I will say that Robert Reed was wonderful to work with. He was a great guy. He was very nervous. I had to calm him down so he would not worry. When you're working with famous people you sometimes have to be a therapist," Williamson says.

Not only were the prerecord sessions a challenge for the Brady cast, but they were yet another requirement on a very full production schedule. "It's hard enough just to do the comedy, and then to learn the dancing, and then they have to go sing, it was bewildering at times for them," says Bonny Dore. Mike Lookinland's mother Karen adds, "Sometimes they would just give them a lead sheet with the words. Michael could read music and

would say, 'Why don't they give us music?'" Susan Olsen recalls that the prerecord sessions were definitely not her favorite part of the job. "A couple of the recording sessions were really very grueling. You've got nine people or eight people gathered around a microphone. It's tough. I don't like singing anyway," she says. In spite of the challenges the kids had great respect for George Wyle. Phil Soebel says, "They adored George, and whatever George told them do by God they did it. He was brilliant at it."

When every recording session was finished each of the Bradys was given a cassette tape of the music so they could continue to rehearse their singing in the car, at home, and any other place they could. The Brady cast were some of the first actors in Hollywood to carry around little Sony tape recorders that played cassette tapes — a novelty in 1977 — to record rehearsals. "They were the first thing you could consider a Walkman," says Mike Lookinland. "It weighed about eight pounds, it was all made of metal, but it was very small and it had all the buttons a cassette deck would have on it. It was the size of a paperback book, but it was heavy. I thought that was the sweetest toy ever." Few of the rehearsal tapes have survived over the years with the exception of those given to Geri Reischl who saved them in her attic. Susan Olsen explains how her tapes were lost. "When we were shooting the *Variety Hour,* Mike Lookinland was driving himself to work in his new Toyota Celica. That summer after production was over I turned sixteen and got my own Celica. One of my first joys of the road was to drive my

Sid Feller

car over the *Brady Bunch Variety Hour* rehearsal tapes I had. These were just recordings of us around a piano singing the horrible songs we were to learn for our musical numbers. I suppose somebody might pay money for those now and maybe I should regret it, but I maintain that destroying any recording of 'Toot, Toot, Tootsie Goodbye' might be considered a job well done. But to destroy a recording of us singing, it was a service to humanity."

According to Claude Williamson, George Wyle assigned much of the musical arranging to Sid Feller. But the music that needed to be arranged in a more rock 'n' roll fashion he handed to Williamson because neither Wyle nor Feller had experience in that style. "There were three or four recording sessions where Sid and Marty were there and they said, 'This isn't the way we wanted it at all,' and George would sit there with his head in his hands," Williamson says. "He said to me, 'Can you do anything with this?' I said, 'I can't rewrite the arrangement while we're waiting, but I might be able to get the rhythm section to do something to help it.' So that's what I did. I'd go up to the rhythm section and say, 'Look — let's make this a disco feel,' and that was about all I could do. The horns played the same things, but rhythm section was totally different so Sid and Marty were happy. That happened quite often. I told Marty, 'If this keeps happening, I want his job.' If he didn't know what Sid and Marty wanted in the very beginning then he shouldn't have taken the job. That was my feeling," Williamson adds of Wyle. Claude Williamson continues, "Thank God I did the musical arrangement for Tina Turner because Sid Feller and George Wyle were still writing arrangements that sounded like they were from 1926 instead of 1976. The Brady kids didn't know 'Toot, Toot, Tootsie, Goodbye,' good lord! That was written in 1919. Disco was huge at that time. Finally on the second show, I said to George, 'If there's any rock arrangements to be done on the show, do you think you could hand them my way?'"

Bickering over the musical arrangements became more intense when George Wyle and Sid Feller began shouting at each other in rehearsals. Williamson recalls, "Sid and George were way out of line and would argue in front of the orchestra about the arrangements. Sid would yell, 'YOU RUINED MY ARRANGEMENT!' and then George would shout, 'JUST SHUT UP!' The Kroffts would also be sitting there listening to all this garbage going on. I have never worked a show where the conductor and arranger would have arguments on every prerecord session and waste time and money." Saxophone player Phil Sobel saw the situation differently and to him it was business as usual. "They were so funny together. Sid Feller had become a producer of records in New York, then he came out to L.A. to do television and he didn't understand the way our business went out here. George and Sid would clash. George would say, 'So why did you write that? It doesn't work!' They were such close friends, it didn't matter what they said. They really loved each other madly," Sobel explains.

Bernie Weissman, who later took the stage name George Wyle, and Sid Feller were like brothers who literally grew up together playing in orchestras on the East Coast during the 1930s. They remained best friends for over sixty years and felt open enough with one another to argue like an old married couple. Sid's daughter Debbie Feller Glassman explains, "I believe if there was any fighting — it was really not fighting but both of these geniuses voicing their opinions. I have never heard anything but total admiration and love that they both shared for each other from the start. I know that when George or my father would speak to anyone — it would be to say that this was the other's dearest, most loved friend. They always walked arm in arm, and hugged and kissed every time they saw each other, even if it were the day before. You have to understand — they were both New York boys, and we are very demonstrative people. To hear each of them speak about the other's gift of music, it was with awe and respect."

Williamson says that they did everything possible to make the Bradys sound good. Chris Knight recalls some of the methods Williamson used to help him deal with being tone-deaf. "I just remember the one Collette the Puppet number, 'Sing a Song,' and that Florence had to sing my part. They had aspirations of just me singing the part but they soon gave up on that. They then played that track back on my headphones so I could sing to it," he says.

Florence Henderson recalls, "Chris Knight would say, 'I can't! I can't carry a tune…' and was very honest about it."[26] Phil Soebel adds, "We'd be leaving and I'd hear some of what would be going on and it was hysterical. They couldn't do half the stuff they were supposed to do without hard work."

Maureen McCormick also couldn't believe the challenges they all faced trying to get the vocal tracks completed for each episode. "It was pretty crazy. We'd all look at each other like, 'Do you really think this is going to work?' I remember looking at everyone and thinking, 'Okay, I guess, here we go…' They were brutal recording sessions because of what we were dealing with," Maureen says.

Best friends Sid Feller and Bernie Weissman (George Wyle) in 1939

Susan Olsen objects to some of the criticism of the Bradys' singing ability. While she agrees the cast had varying degrees of musical talent, she believes that kind of a judgment depends heavily on what one considers music. "I will admit that I was not any good at the type of material that was performed on *The Brady Bunch Hour*. But I would never have any desire to be! Hey, nobody doubts the musical abilities of Florence Henderson, but how well do you suppose she'd do with a Led

Zeppelin medley?" Susan points out. "Frankly, I don't think any of us were that horrible. We're not good, but for a bunch of actors I think we did pretty darn well. Chris always declared that he's somewhat tone-deaf but he's not even as bad as he thinks. Bob couldn't sing, and so they tried to do this kind of talk-singing with him. I don't know, I mean, I suppose I'm not very objective, but I just look at it as 'God bless us, we're all trying so hard,'" she adds.

After the Brady cast completed prerecording each week, Williamson would then bring in a choir of three men and three women to augment the rest. "As long as we got a feeling of their voice on the tape we'd cover it up with the choir, except for Florence's track," he says. "I'd have to sit there with Lee Miller, the producer, and figure out if we could really hear those kids or if we could barely hear them. They could sing, but not professionally. I couldn't sit in judgment of them, because I didn't know if they could sing or not. I figured that if Sid and Marty felt they could do it that was good enough for me. That was about as far as it went. It was a busy nine weeks."

Miller says in the end he was pleased with how the music turned out, "George was a consummate choral director. He did not ever like the idea that he was working with amateurs. He was very short-tempered, except with Florence who was a singer. The fact that the kids weren't such great singers didn't sit well with him. But he had to be able to write so these kids could sing, get through this stuff, and appear plausible. I thought he did a very credible job."

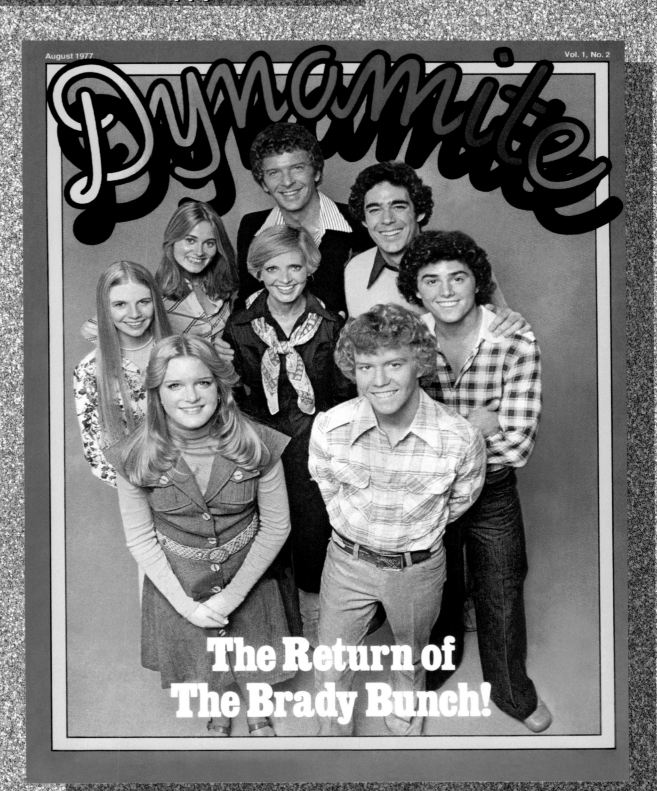

August 1977

Vol. 1, No. 2

Dynamite

The Return of The Brady Bunch!

They Work Hard for the Money

The Bradys were generally upbeat about the challenges of a network variety show and wanted to make it a success — at least for the first few weeks of production. They remained in good spirits and kept open minds about everything. Maureen McCormick recalls that although she definitely had doubts early on, everyone seemed to have blind faith in the Kroffts. "It struck me as very strange, but I thought Sid and Marty must know what they're doing. I kept hoping it would get better. I kept hoping it would become this great show," Maureen explains.

The cast and crew continued to work long days during the early episodes of *The Brady Bunch Hour* before they were finally able to establish a routine. Writer Steve Bluestein recalls, "By the time we got to the ninth show, it was like a machine. So, the days became shorter. But in the beginning everyone was feeling each other out, they were getting their rhythm. There were many nights I didn't get home before 11 p.m. after getting to the studio at nine or ten in the morning."

Florence Henderson recognized she would have to set the standard for this production and was particularly concerned with the show's appeal to the viewing audience. She told the *Chicago Tribune*, "I'm the only one of the *Brady Bunch* with a variety and musical show background so it's very satisfying to see how hard everyone works. We learn our script in two days — we all agreed to memorize our lines to make the scenes more believable — and we only use cue cards for some of the musical numbers. That makes a big difference in the quality of the show."[27] Florence often took the initiative to make sure last-minute details were covered. Assistant director Rick Locke recalls that Florence would arrive early to work with the lighting director so that everyone would look good on camera. "We would walk onstage and the first thing she'd say is, 'Where's my key light?' and she knew where that key light had to be. She knew from years of watching herself on television and in movies where she looked best when that key light was in a specific spot. If it's improperly placed it can make you look almost ghastly. Florence made it a point for herself to know where to put it because she never knew what kind of lighting director she was working with. Florence also came in knowing her parts, she was always on time, and she was just a consummate professional," Locke says.

Even though Mike Lookinland was not thrilled about the revamped version of *The Brady Bunch*, he did recognize two things — that he was working and he was receiving a

Mike Lookinland and a visitor to the set in March 1977

The Return of the Brady Bunch

The new Brady Bunch (left to right): Chris Knight (Peter), Barry Williams (Greg), Maureen McCormick (Marcia), Florence Henderson, Robert Reed, Susan Olson (Cindy), Mike Lookinland (Bobby), Geri Reischl (Jan).

"When I see myself on an old *Brady Bunch* show," 16-year-old Mike Lookinland said, "I sometimes think that I'm watching a completely different person on screen." *Brady Bunch* fans who tune into their new show may get a similar feeling. The faces look familiar, but everything else has changed.

For almost six years the Bradys were one of TV's favorite families. They shared their home and lives with millions of viewers each week. Then the ratings dropped and soon the show was cancelled. Even though the cast went their separate ways, the show stayed alive through the magic of reruns.

Then a little over a year ago, a TV executive noticed that the Bradys' show was still enormously popular, even in reruns. He thought, "What if we could get them all together again in a new show?"

It was easier said than done, but after months of meetings and phone calls, the Bradys were reunited. But this time they're in the middle of a variety show, complete with singing, dancing, flashy costumes, and even water ballet!

Dynamite visited the set, where we spoke to the Brady kids about their new show. The show is a big production, with what seems to be a cast and crew of thousands. A line of dancers and swimmers paraded past, high stepping over the thick wires that snaked across the floor. Camera, sound, and light crews were busy adjusting their equipment for shooting. There were even two camera-

paycheck. Mike understood that almost any actor would gladly trade places with him and that maybe things weren't so bad. "You really have to be careful in the entertainment industry what you wish for because for every person who gets a shot at driving onto that lot and performing, whatever the performance happens to be, for every one of those people who gets that opportunity there's a thousand waiting outside the gate, saying, 'Gosh, I wish I could get in there!' The job you have to do isn't the one you wish you had, it's the one you have today," he says. Mike knew he would never be the star of *The Brady Bunch Hour*, which provided some sense of relief and consolation. "I didn't wish for it, nor was it offered to me, and not in the format they had laid out. The screen time was spread pretty thin because there were nine regulars, and I never really felt like stepping out front, and nobody really suggested it. The funny thing about that, ironically, is that Chris Knight would be the featured spot, because he was the teen heartthrob at the time. They would be much more inclined to give him a lead portion of the show, and he was absolutely stone tone-deaf," Mike says.

A Pleasant Predicament

Having an opportunity to bring an old show back to prime time was almost unheard of in Hollywood, especially considering that the original *Brady Bunch* had not been a ratings winner. However, reruns of the sitcom were playing three times a day in some markets and the show had become wildly popular since its cancellation. News of the reunion was an immediate magnet for the media and one of the first reporters the Bradys hosted on the set at KTLA was Chip Lovitt, who wrote for the children's Scholastic News publication *Dynamite* magazine. Over thirty years later Lovitt still remembers the excitement of his article, "The Return of the Brady Bunch." He says, "What I recall was an atmosphere of camaraderie, like a high school or summer camp reunion. There seemed to be a lot of warm fun vibes between the actors." Lovitt recalls that the Brady kids were genuinely friendly and happy to talk about themselves in his interviews with them, unlike some child actors. "They had retained some of that everyday kid persona that had previously connected with fans of the show. Barry Williams was especially proud of his song and dance work. Chris Knight told me how hanging out at the beach with his friends was more fun than being on a Hollywood set, and Mike Lookinland told me about how he had to dye his hair black to look like a Brady. Susan Olsen struck me as one of those professional, self-assured child actors who was not at all ego-centric or driven like some of the other kid stars I met in my *Dynamite* days."

ABC network supervisor Bonny Dore recalls, "Chris Knight would always come over to me and say, 'Is it okay to talk to the network?' and I'd say, 'I won't bite you.' He was very sweet. He was the only one of the kids who would come and talk to me and had no problem about it. He just wanted to know if I liked everything, and if it was alright. He'd even talk to the crew guys. He was just a kid and he loved to hang out with everybody. We'd break for food and he'd be popping from table to table." Chris was enjoying himself, yet he recognized he was making the best of what he viewed as stressful circumstances. "It was odd, it was slightly odd, but the entire show was so much odder than just that," Chris says. "It drowned out that oddity. On top of it, the fact that we were all swimming in this very strange current, that we were all preoccupied with our own concerns about how to survive it, or how to synthesize it, or how to ignore it, or how to not have it or not affect us," Chris reiterates.

KTLA stage manager Steve Dichter says, "I think they were just scared enough that they would show up on time and get into their costumes. I'd get them through makeup. There were three makeup people so we had to rotate them. Then they'd be anxious to get out on the floor with a 'get it over with' kind of feeling."

Throughout production a steady stream of old friends, relatives, and VIPs were stopping by to visit the set. The kids were especially pleased to see their former studio teacher, Frances Whitfield, who brought her newest student, Philip McKeon. He was playing the

> Every week they did their stuff, they worked hard, and that's not easy. They got into a different world, it was like me taking the professional dancers and throwing them into the pool.
> — Charkie Phillips

Frances Whitfield

**Natalie Wood with daughters Natasha
and Courtney**

role of Tommy on the sitcom *Alice*. Susan Olsen recalls, "Philip allegedly had a crush on me. I remember us talking, he was very sweet. I thought that it must be such a drag to be on a show and be the only kid. He was talking about how nice his costars were and the one that played the ditzy, frazzled one, Vera, that she was especially nice and that she was not like that in real life. I was like, 'Who the hell are you talking about because I never watch the show.' Then later on I did because I had met him."

Perhaps the Bradys' most exciting visitors were Natalie Wood, famous for her roles in *Rebel Without a Cause* and *West Side Story*, and her two daughters, Natasha and Courtney. Sid Krofft recalls, "I definitely remember Natalie Wood. Her daughters were crazy about *The Brady Bunch*. I knew her and we made sure that they met the cast." Geri, Susan, and their mothers, Wanda and Dee, had just finished eating from the lunch truck before a taping was scheduled to begin. Geri recalls, "Dee said to my mom, 'Here comes Natalie Wood!' They were both so excited. My mom has always remembered how Natalie Wood was so nice and sweet to us. You would have never guessed that she was famous. Her little girls went straight to Susan and me. The littlest one, Courtney, wanted me to pick her up and hold her. We hung out in the parking lot for a bit and then we went back in to tape the show and they watched." Wanda Reischl adds, "They sat right behind Dee and me. We mothers always sat together. Natalie Wood, I was surprised because she was just normal, she wasn't all dolled up. She just looked like a normal person, and looked like she was out with her kids for the day like any other mother. You wouldn't have known she was a movie star if you had seen her out on the street. The little girls, you could tell they were crazy about their mom."

Susan Olsen remembers being completely intimidated by Wood's presence. "There's no forgetting her at all, because she scorched my retinas she was so beautiful!" Susan says. "I was so completely flattered that she wanted to be on our set and that she wanted to meet us. Of course, Florence already knew Natalie and sat down next to her," she adds.

Wood's daughter Natasha Wagner fondly recalls their visits with the Bradys: "Courtney and I loved *The Brady Bunch* so much as little girls. It was our favorite program. Our mother would take us to the set to watch tapings of their variety show and they were all really nice."

Every week the Bradys had a large group of visitors when a studio audience was hired to watch the music finale being taped. Bonny Dore recalls, "Having a live audience gave a real charge to the performers." This was the first time they had ever used a live audience, as a laugh track had been used for the complete run of the original *Brady Bunch* series at Paramount. The swimming pool on the *Variety Hour* took up an entire soundstage, leaving no space for spectators. In addition, the Brady's living room set was constructed behind the bleachers in the corner of the soundstage, leaving the finale as the only viable option for a live audience. "That's why we had such a ridiculous laugh track, obviously phony laughter, which is another feature of Krofft shows," Susan

The Bradys filmed their musical finale each week in front of a live audience

Olsen explains. "I remember being eight years old and watching *Pufnstuf* and just thinking, 'Will they get rid of that awful canned laughter?!' The audience was hired. All I know is one time my cousins came to the set. It's like bizarre world to me — they don't blend. They don't mix. You don't put my real life and that life together. It was really embarrassing to me to have my cousins there. The people would have to sit for three hours while you did a five minute number. Well, there were so many camera angles and things to do. We had sets to light and dress, basically you're making a day of it," she adds.

Geri Reischl's best friend, Barbara, who usually came to weekly tapings, recalls, "They would do a little bit of a number and they would redo it again. Then they would do it one more time because one kid stepped out of line — usually Mike Lookinland or sometimes Susan Olsen would mess it up. Geri tried to hold them all together because she was already a performer and dancer, so I remember her really standing out. Robert Reed was especially impressed with Geri."

Although few openly criticized the show at the time production began, this was the calm before the storm. The cast did not receive unfavorable comments from friends and family about *The Brady Bunch Hour* and most remarks had a positive or humorous spin. Mike Lookinland recalls, "I was not set up for ridicule by my close friends. Of course it could be said I have 50 million friends, *Brady* fans, all across the country and the world. So from them, ridicule was expected. You could count on it because of the nature of what we were doing. It was just so fundamentally flawed as a concept. My close friends didn't tease me, and anybody that would have given me any sort of grief, I didn't know them. So it was all pretty much okay."

Geri Reischl says that nobody ever once criticized her for replacing Eve Plumb and she never encountered a hostile fan. "They all loved *The Brady Bunch*. So I was on a show everybody loved already. That helped out a lot. What they would comment on would be our costumes. They would joke about those and because of the colors, and how wild they were, and the guys wearing the jumpsuits. They kind of laughed at that. I never heard any negative comments about the show. Everybody was always really nice about it," Geri says.

Susan shows her true feelings about the *Variety Hour*

Some Fun Now

Lunch hour sometimes saw the Bradys playing football against the Osmonds in the KTLA parking lot. Geri Reischl and Mike Lookinland would join in, but Susan Olsen wasn't very interested. "No, I wasn't very athletic. I'd sit in a chair and stuff my face while they played," she says. On other days, Geri and Susan enjoyed sitting with their moms for some girl talk in the back of Denny's across the street. Eventually their obsessive chitchat ended up causing problems on the set.

Geri recalls, "Of course I always paid attention, except there was a certain number, 'One' from *A Chorus*

Line, where Susan and I were talking. We kept talking, and talking, and talking. My mom said to Susan's mom, 'Dee, just mark my words. That Geri's going to mess up because she's talking and not paying attention. I just know she's going to mess up and ruin the shot.'" In the final moments of the number Geri threw her hat down in the wrong direction and ultimately that take ended up appearing in the episode. "I almost went through my seat trying to hide," Wanda Reischl says. "I could have kicked Geri's butt. I knew she and Susan were not paying attention." Geri was also oblivious when the ribbon on her ponytail slid down in the "Ratsie's Rollerama" roller-skating skit. "When I say, 'I could D-Y-E die!' the ribbon on my ponytail, throughout the whole thing you slowly see it sliding its way down. Then you actually see it fall off onto the floor," Geri recalls.

For unknown reasons the video editors were letting all kinds of ridiculous goofs into the final print of each episode. In another sequence in the "Ratsie's Rollerama" skit, Barry Williams is clearly seen wiping out on his roller skates and crashing into the floor. Susan Olsen left her mark in a later episode of the series when she gestured into the camera with her middle finger (pictured on previous page), which made it past network censors completely unnoticed. Susan explains that because so many things were going wrong with the production, the editors were overwhelmed and merely did the best they could with what footage they had. Clearly there weren't enough hours in the day to remove every last blunder the Bradys made, and it was always a losing battle with one Brady ruining an entire shot for the rest of the cast. Chris Knight had one of the all-time most memorable goofs in the Bradys' opening number, "Yankee Doodle Dandy," when he excitedly threw his arms up in the wrong direction, and gracefully brought them back down again hoping nobody would see. "That's why Chris' horrible mistakes showed up, because they ran out of time," Susan says.

The Bradys also flubbed a sketch with Milton Berle. When he would perform comedy routines on his television show he would whack people with a huge powder puff, which was loaded with powder, and scream, "MAKEUP!" Sid Krofft had Geri dressed in a chicken suit and wanted her to satirize Milton Berle. Geri recalls, "I was supposed to get the powder puff away from Berle and hit Bob Reed with it. Well, I did, but I hit him a little too hard, kind of on the legs, and he fell to the ground. But he died laughing! In the same scene with the powder puff I nailed Chris Knight. So many people loved it because I almost knocked him on his butt too. Then later in the same scene I was up really high on a pedestal in that chicken suit. I had to flap my wings a lot. Well, being light and weighing so little, I actually flew off and almost

Susan and Geri riding in the Pan American Parade in April 1977

Mike Lookinland at home with his new Toyota Celica

landed in the huge pool. Everyone came running to see if I was okay and they were in hysterics." Maureen McCormick, on the other hand, was not very amused, "The sketch with Milton Berle seemed so stupid to me, the thing with the makeup and the powder puff. It seemed so ridiculous when we were doing it."

Geri Reischl and Mike Lookinland were becoming especially good friends during *The Brady Bunch Hour*. "We were very close, like brother and sister, or best friends. We talked a lot on the phone and one time I went over to his house and I met his older sister and younger brother," Geri says. Mike had just received his driver's license and invited Geri to go cruising in his new Toyota Celica GT. They had fun driving around, but when it got dark they ended up getting lost in Compton, sometimes described as one of the most dangerous areas of Los Angeles county. "We didn't know where we were," Geri admits. "Back in those days all the gas stations were closed so you couldn't go and ask directions. They didn't stay open all night. So we ended up finding a telephone booth in the parking lot of the gas station. He called home to tell his mom where the streets were. We ended up getting kind of scared, actually. I remember his mom telling us 'Lock your doors, keep your doors locked,' so we got in and locked our doors. But he ended up getting the right directions and he managed to get me home okay," Geri adds.

For the first time, Mike was driving himself to the studio for *Brady Bunch Hour* rehearsals although his mother was not a big fan of it. Susan Olsen says, "I remember Karen coming to work and saying, 'I have aged ten years riding in the car with Michael driving. I told him if you change lanes one more time, we're taking this car away from you.'"

Geri also had a memorable experience in the car on her way to make a *Brady Bunch Hour* appearance as a celebrity guest, along with Susan, for *The Ice Capades*. Geri and her mother left for the show after lunch and as they drove up Ocean Boulevard in Long Beach there were a bunch of police cars. Wanda recalls, "They were standing looking at the curb, and Geri says, 'Mom, there's a dead man down there.' There had been a shooting."

On another occasion the two girls appeared together in the Pan American parade, riding in a Thunderbird and waving to fans. That evening Susan went to visit Geri at her home and the two Brady girls had an innocent slumber party. "We slept together. Sorry Geri, I just had to let the world know," Susan says.

"But, I faked it," Geri quips.

Be Our Guest...Please?

With an established commodity like *The Brady Bunch* it is logical to assume that celebrities would be lining up to be the spin-off's next guest star. But when it came to the *Variety Hour,* more often than not, guests were reluctant participants. Bonny Dore explains why people hesitated. "It's always a problem to get anyone to do a new show. Everyone wants to wait until it's a hit. Believe me, when you're doing a show like this, and we had some difficulties with the pilot, getting stars to do the show was not so easy." The production schedule was also an issue for some people because a guest star would need to work for the full week and they had to go to all the rehearsals. Ted Knight was one celebrity who bailed on the Bradys at the last second and was replaced by Vincent Price. Dore explains, "Ted couldn't just come part-time. It wasn't like a normal sitcom shooting schedule. He had to go to prerecord, he had to go to dancing rehearsal. It was a lot. Sometimes what would happen is their agents would book them. They took one look at how much work it was and they'd say, 'You know what, I think I'll pass.'" Dore was struggling to book anyone and even had musical guests canceling, so at one point she was forced to bring in H.R. Pufnstuf to fill the void when nobody else would. She recalls, "Yeah, well, we were a little short that week. I remember we said, 'Marty, do you think you can get Pufnstuf in here? Okay. Good.' We had to."

Bonny Dore and Marty Krofft talked and worried constantly about who was going to be the guest star. "Marty had to get them, I had to approve them, I had to make sure Fred Silverman didn't hate them, and we had to get them down to the writers so they could actually write something mildly amusing," Dore says. Head writer Carl Kleinschmitt recalls

Will Anybody Play With Us?

Guest stars! The thought of having guest stars on our show seemed like the most fun of all. I had some wild dreams about who might be on the *Variety Hour*, but quickly realized that most of the people I wanted wouldn't be caught dead on any variety show. Geri was lucky. She got to meet her idol, Lynn Anderson. Lynn was a musical guest on our show and Geri was in seventh heaven. I knew there wasn't a snowball's chance in hell that my idols would be performing with us. Emerson Lake and Palmer certainly had better plans. No chance we'd have a skit where we'd find Roger Daltrey in the kitchen helping Alice make pies.

Looking back, it must have been difficult to get anyone to appear on our show. It had no track record. Nobody had seen it yet. How do you describe it?

"It's a variety show like *Donny and Marie* only with the *Brady Bunch*."

Rich Little takes out his frustrations on me

the routine, "Marty is famous for 'let's get a name' for anything. 'Babe, guess who I got for the show,' he would say. I would reply, 'I don't know,' and he'd say something like, 'Rerun' or 'Epstein.' We would then have to start thinking what the hell would we do with these people?"

Producer Lee Miller adds, "Sometimes it works for you because it gives you a reason to write for somebody. But some of these people had no reason to be there."

To book guest stars, the Kroffts decided to join forces with Michael Ovitz, who was one of the founders of Creative Artists Management. The first show the agency ever "packaged" was *The Brady Bunch Hour*, for which they took a packaging fee. Bonny Dore says, "I was having a terrible time with Michael Ovitz because he wanted to put a lot of the older comedians on the show. The difference from being an agent and being a packaging agent is that an agent sells you an actor, but packaging means that they brought a number of elements to the show. They weren't just taking ten percent of what Sid and Marty got, they were taking ten percent of the whole deal. So, they were deeply involved in booking the show. All of the bookings had to be approved by ABC. I was struggling with Ovitz because there were some people who weren't working that he wanted to put on the show that were 'in their stable.'"

Weaving a guest star into the script was a constant struggle for the writers. Bruce Vilanch says, "So much of what each episode was built upon was who we had on as a guest. We were always handed a star and sometimes you got lucky, like Vincent Price. Right away there are a million things you can do with him. But when you're handed Farrah Fawcett and Lee Majors what do you do? Any of the other people we had to work into the thing. Rich Little is easy because in any situation he can pretend to be somebody else. The Hudson Brothers — not so easy, they just came out and performed, as did our guest Tina Turner. There was one that always had to be in the story line because that's where the plot came from. Otherwise we would just be doing *Brady Bunch* the sitcom."

Mike Kagan also recalls that in addition to guest stars who didn't want to do the show, ABC would pressure them for the cross advertising and publicity. It was a marketing philosophy espoused by production executive Michael Eisner, who envisioned all the stars on the ABC network cross-pollinating one another. "Michael Eisner's favorite word was 'synergy.' If I heard it once, I heard it a

Tina Turner shooting her solo sequence in the musical finale, "Songs About Stars"

thousand times a week. He wanted to 'synergize' *The Brady Bunch Hour* and *Donny and Marie*, and it would all be one large canvas. I would hear the word 'synergy' from Michael about once an hour," says Dore. Steve Bluestein found this mentality from the network frustrating. "As writers, we were saying,

"Oh, the *Brady Bunch* can sing and dance?"

"Well, not exactly…"

Maybe some people said yes just out of curiosity. Some guests made sense. The Hudson Brothers had been successful with their own variety show. Rich Little was great. Paul Williams showed up drunk, but that didn't detract from his charms. One wonders what the Ohio Players' manager was thinking when they booked them on our show.

Then there were guests that didn't make sense, like the kids from *What's Happening*, but they were some of my favorites. I had never heard of their show or seen it. Danielle Spencer and Haywood Nelson were young enough that they had to attend school with Mike, Geri, and me. This was great. We had new friends! Haywood was just adorable and Danielle impressed me so much. While I'd never seen her character, Dee, it was obvious that our writers enjoyed writing for her. She would go into this deadpan persona that was quite different from her true self. She had natural comedic timing. I'm very pleased to say that I'm still in touch with her. Danielle is now a veterinarian who practices near where I live. She has cared for several of my many, many fur babies.

Our moms got new friends too. Danielle and Haywood's parents had to hang out in the greenroom with our mothers. What is funny about this is how much concern it produced in my mom. It wasn't just that someone new would be in their little coffee klatch, but that these new people were black. People don't get too much whiter than DeLoice Olsen and Wanda Reischl. Our mothers were not the least bit prejudiced, it was quite the opposite. They were scared to bits that they might say something that could be racially offensive. When my mother went out to the catering truck to get a sweet snack, she was mortified that she had announced that she was getting a brownie. I told my mother that I was sure that nobody took offense or even noticed what she said unless of course she and Wanda sat there acting uncomfortable about it, which I think they undoubtedly did.

As I've said before, I had some very strong opinions about music. While I knew I wouldn't likely be very thrilled about anyone who appeared on our show, I didn't expect to be sickened. Well, that was pretty naive of me! This is a Sid and Marty Krofft Production. These guys gave the Bay City Rollers a special! When Kaptain Kool and the Kongs were on, I wanted to move to another country. The reason for their appearance was obvious, they were a "band" created by the Kroffts. Either that, or somebody else canceled.

I believe that some musical guests were booked by unknowing agents and once the artists figured out what show they were appearing on, they bowed out. Ted Knight canceled. He came down with laryngitis, that magical disease that suddenly strikes performers who decide they don't want to do the job. I already knew of this trick. On another Krofft production I was in, Charles Nelson Riley declined to appear as his *Lidsville* character Hoo Doo. He was replaced by Charlie Callas, who was supposed to be his brother, Voo Doo. Laryngitis — nobody can argue with that. They say you can still perform when you have the flu, you can vomit in between takes but laryngitis? If you can't talk, you can't work. It's kind of like using diarrhea as an excuse to get out of a date.

I'm sure it had to be a cancellation that was responsible for our lowest point in musical guests: H.R. Pufnstuf. Already the subject of a

'These are the guests we're getting? The *What's Happening* kids?' I think at one point…that was the show where we said, 'Look, we've got to get better guests.' Not to be insulting to those people, but they weren't huge stars and they had promised us huge stars. I think *What's Happening* was on ABC and I think the network insisted that we use them so they would cross," Bluestein says.

While some of the guest stars made an indelible impression on the cast and crew, others fell far short. Lee Majors and Farrah Fawcett made their appearance only because they were told to do it. Bonny Dore says, "I don't think it would have been their choice and it certainly wasn't their strength. It certainly wasn't my choice. It was heavily suggested by my bosses. I remember the writers were tearing their hair out trying to figure out what to do with them. They didn't sing. They didn't dance. They stood there a lot. When you bring in someone from a filmed, one-hour, dramatic show all you can do is make fun of them."

Stage manager Steve Dichter adds, "I was just astounded when Farrah Fawcett came in and the way she looked in the morning, and after she came

Charlie's blonde angel and her *Six Million Dollar Man*

out of makeup it was like two different people, absolutely. I didn't even know it was her when she walked through the door because I had to intercept her as well and get her to her dressing room, and I didn't even know it was her and then magically they transformed her into Farrah Fawcett."

Majors and Fawcett were treated as royalty on the set. When Majors requested a steak dinner, Marty Krofft had production assistant J. Paul Higgins rush to Musso and Franks Grill down the street on Hollywood Boulevard. But things didn't turn out exactly as planned when Higgins returned. "I had the steak on a tray and Marty was so excited that he grabbed the tray from me, and started rushing to Lee Majors' dressing room, and tripped. The steak went flying across the stage floor and he panicked! He ran over to the sink, washed the steak, dried it, and served it to Lee Majors — 'Here Mr. Majors…' It was just a hysterical moment," Higgins recalls.

Carl Kleinschmitt explains that Majors and Fawcett showed up, sort of stumbled through their lines, and left. "They interacted with the cast, and I remember being on the stage to watch it, but it might have been a 'cash in a paper bag' kind of deal

Farrah Fawcett styles her hair on the *Brady Bunch* set between takes

major childhood disappointment, I was horrified to find he was appearing as our musical guest. Adding to my horror was the realization that ol' Puf bears a disturbing resemblance to a penis wearing cowboy boots and he was mutilating a song by somebody I dearly loved: Elton John. His partner in this musical crime was an obnoxious duck creature. It was awful, but I had yet to experience psychedelics. Maybe with enough acid, it was brilliant. Since I no longer partake of such things, I guess I'll never know. Again, as always, underneath it all were good people doing good work. Van Snowden and former Mouseketeer Sharon Baird were wearing the costumes. It is grueling work and they were both pros and right nice folk.

Speaking of right nice folk, I think that everyone who appeared on our show fit that description. Vincent Price was as gracious a man as you could ever meet. He'd been on the original show and actually remembered the real names of all of us kids (that was rare of people). Edgar Bergen was the living definition of sweet. If I had my way, we would have had Charo as a guest every week. She was a hoot! I liked that we showcased her as a serious and very talented guitarist. As a personality, she is just one sharp lady. She is totally aware of her image and how to play it. She used her accent like a master chef would use seasoning: a little more here, a little less there. I was convinced that she could speak with a perfect American accent if she wanted to. Everyone loved her and I loved watching how much people just got such a kick out of her. They were there a lot just to enjoy Charo. She was funny every minute she was with us. The only time she got serious was when she was playing guitar. Stupid me, I didn't know she was a musician. I left the schoolroom and went to the set on a break. They were taping her musical performance. My jaw hit the floor when she started playing, and I didn't go back to school until the teacher came looking for me. I learned that she had studied under Andrés Segovia before she became known as "Charo" (which is a nickname and much easier to pronounce than Maria Rosario Pilar Martinez Molina Baeza). I think the surprise of all this is what made me love her so much. Hers was a musical appearance that even I could enjoy.

Another honor was Tina Turner. This was the year she left Ike, which provides the only possible explanation for why she was doing our show. I didn't get to socialize with her at all but I know everyone liked her and she's the guest star that gets the most reaction today, "WTF is Tina Turner doing on this???" is what most people say. It might be one of the more fun aspects of the *Variety Hour*, to see us with these different personalities. From Redd Foxx to Milton Berle, it all added to the bizarreness. I'm glad to find that some of the guests that I have met since have no regrets. I think Paul Williams was the first to tell me that he thought it was cool to have been a part of such an unusual production. I'm kind of surprised he remembered it.

— Susan

to get them to come out. I can't swear to that, but Marty's good at various things and that's probably one of them," Kleinschmitt says.

One of the more controversial bookings Michael Ovitz proposed was Milton Berle, who was notorious for taking over a production and not allowing anyone else but himself to be in charge. Bonny Dore recalls that she and others resisted. "I worked with Milton many times and he was just crazy. He'd say, 'I do the jokes here, I do the jokes.' We had a story line that he took over the show because we knew he would. There was no question. This was one time when the network called Marty directly and Michael Ovitz got involved. He told me I was taking Milton Berle because he already called Fred Silverman. Then Fred called later and

The cast enjoys a lighthearted moment with Milton Berle between takes

got mad at me because he didn't want Milton. I said, 'Well, you already said yes to it. What am I supposed to do?' By then it was done, so we had him. I felt he was too old for the show but it was a political problem that I couldn't get out of. I could have said no, but they went around me."

Stage manager Dichter explains that Berle could be very overbearing and all anyone could do was try to tolerate him. "'Mr. Television' was 'Mr. Know-it-All.' He would tell the director how to frame the shots, he would always take center stage, he was very difficult to work with, and you really had to walk on eggs with Milton. Right up until the last thing I did with Milton he was still a jerk. His poor brother was his assistant and he would badger this poor guy, who would carry in Milton's wardrobe bags and all this stuff. Milton would always have this huge cigar he'd puff on. What a royal pain. Every time I saw Milton coming in as a guest on a show I'd just cringe."

The writers had a different point of view because as comedians they shared camaraderie with Berle. But they were also quite fascinated by a rather provocative rumor. Steve Bluestein explains: "Milton Berle is supposed to have a huge you-know-what. We're all sitting around the table, the writers and Milton Berle, and we're reading the script and Milton Berle says, 'Excuse me, I have to go to the bathroom.' There was a moment of silence after he left where everybody was thinking the same thing, and the entire room stood up to go to the bathroom to pee next to him. We started laughing hysterically."

Bruce Vilanch adds, "We all wanted to see the largest penis in Hollywood. I subsequently told Milton he had to show it to me, and he said, 'Why? Are you queer?' and I said, 'That's beside the point. You're legendary.' I said, 'Here's how queer I am, Milton. I don't want to see it because it's you. I want to see it because you did Marilyn Monroe. I want to see something Marilyn Monroe saw.' He had a fling with Marilyn Monroe. Everybody had a fling with Marilyn Monroe, unfortunately. It was not that unusual, but he talked about it. But he also pretended they hadn't."

Needless to say, Berle refused to reveal his most famous asset.

Another memorable guest star was Charo, who commanded attention with her domineering presence and was loved dearly by the Bradys for her sparkling personality. Susan Olsen recalls, "Charo was a doll, Charo was so funny. I remember her coming up to me. I was chewing bubblegum, and all of the sudden she yells, 'You!' and points her finger. It was very funny because she would speak and she had an accent, but it wasn't nearly as thick as when she was performing. Whenever she wanted to be cute, she'd turn on the accent. She comes over to me, and goes, 'Oh! Oh! You, you have gum for to make bubbles?' and I was like, sure, yes, I have more. I gave her some gum. Whenever she got excited about something she'd go, 'Jipee! Hoopy!' and that became our catchphrase. From then on whenever anything good happened any one of us would go, 'Jipee! Hoopy!' She was very sweet, very fun, I'm sure the writers and everybody had a great time with her. She was like sunshine."

In addition to her abundant charisma, Charo was undeniably sexy and attracted onlookers wherever she went with her large bustline, exposed cleavage, and tight pants. Costume designer Pete Menefee recalls, "We had a problem with Charo because her sister gets involved in all of her clothes. I wanted some cutoffs when we did *Cinderella*, and I remember her sister came in at the fitting and said, 'Oh, we have a pair of pants that are fine for that, little cutoff jeans and I said, 'Well, bring them.' They must have been designed by a gynecologist because when she bent over you could see Cincinnati. That's very, very true," Menefee states.

Wardrobe mistress Mari Grimaud also remembers that situation well. "She'd wear everything way too tight. She would say, 'Oh, please, tighter, tighter, I promise you I will be losing weight by the time this shoots!' So, Pete would make it really tight, and the day she'd get into it, the seams would pop right open. You'd go running in there two minutes before cameras are ready to roll and you'd be trying to stitch up her crotch. They'd go, 'Five, four, three…' and we'd scream, 'We're not ready yet!' and we're still standing onstage stitching. 'Two, one…' and the tape would roll, we'd go running off the stage, and there'd be a needle and thread hanging off of her! We'd say, 'Do you hear us when we say we're not ready yet?!' It was really and truly crazy all of the time. All the variety shows were like that."

Chris Knight, who played opposite Charo in the parody of *Cinderella*, vividly recalls the moment when she tarnished his tender innocence and threatened his fragile virginity. "At this point I am now nineteen so I'm coming into manhood, if you will. I should have already been there but, okay, I came in late. This was a privileged position that Barry had always maintained, and I was invading his territory. But now I was sort of relishing in it and it was sort of like I got to steal some of his thunder. What was really interesting was this one scene. It was a western thing with Charo and they had Barry in black and me in white. I was the white hat, he was the black hat. So I was the hero and he was the villain. I personally got such a great pleasure out of that. Whatever the subliminal message was, it was there. At one point I jump for her and grab her boot. Then

we've got to hold still and they're going to take her out of her boot, she disappears, and all I have is a boot. Charo was wearing these cutoffs and there wasn't very much left after they cut off the leg. I remember grabbing her boot, and looking up, and I saw her cuchi! All I could do was…I looked at her…and thought, 'Oh my God' and I remember staring straight ahead thinking, I didn't see what I just saw. It took all my energy not to stare back, not to look back. She just had a strap, she had a thong on. She invented, sort of, the denim thong. She seemed quite comfortable. Charo wasn't wearing any underwear."

Susan Olsen says that among her favorite guests were the Hudson Brothers, "They were adorable, naughty boys. I had a crush on Brett. He asked during rehearsal if I could jitterbug. I could so he said, 'Let's.' At the end of the medley we performed, Brett swept me off my feet, literally, bending me back and planting a kiss on my mouth. I was just dumbstruck and overwhelmed. When the episode aired, it was edited so that was never seen. The one time a really cute guy paid attention to me instead of Maureen, and my proof of this miracle was laid to waste on the cutting room floor."

Susan continues, "Our swimming pool was above ground and there were windows for filming underwater sequences. When the Hudson Brothers were doing their segment they each took a porthole window and mooned us!"

Sid Krofft adds, "They should be happy they saw the Hudson Brothers' butts."

Bonny Dore says one of their worst guest star bookings was Redd Foxx, who was yet another example of network-forced cross promotion. The Bradys didn't understand it either. Barry Williams says, "Redd…who's he really going to relate to? He didn't relate to any of us, as I recall. I don't remember having any face time with him in particular, so the scenes were kind of his. I just didn't feel very engaged or involved with it."

Foxx's appearance on *The Brady Bunch Hour* really had nothing to do with the Kroffts or the Bradys. At the time Fred Silverman had sent Bonny Dore and Marcy Carsey to Vegas to see Redd Foxx in his stage act. Dore recalls, "We were with Redd for hours and he was just horrible. The next morning Marcy and I met, and I said, 'What in the world does Fred want to do with Redd Foxx? It's ridiculous. This is not going to work.' Marcy said, 'I know, what are we going to do?' and I said, 'I don't know, but I hear Fred wants to book him on *The Brady Bunch*' — at which point Marcy just sat down and said, 'You're kidding?!' I came back to Fred and said, 'I don't know what to do with Redd, he's crazy.' At that point he was a big cocaine addict,

and I'm not telling you anything everyone didn't know. Fred insisted we were going to do the show with him. It's not that I didn't think Redd was talented. I just didn't think he was a talented variety performer. We had just gone through trying to take sitcom people into variety, and it didn't work, and I didn't want to do it again."

There were several guest stars that everyone felt were an excellent choice. For example, Bonny Dore and Marty Krofft agreed that Rich Little was the best of anyone who came on the show because he could do anything. "There is no Rich Little, but there's hundreds of other people there, as the writers found out when they met him," Dore says. "Rich was a real talent. He was coming from Vegas to do our show, which was terrific because you could literally ask him to do anything and he would do it. He would do it in two seconds. He could improv with the writers, and he could improv with his moves onstage. Jack Regas loved Rich because when he asked him to do something he actually did it right the first time," she adds.

Rick Dees poses with Dee Kaye and Susan Buckner while filming "Dis-Gorilla"

Another favorite guest star was Rick Dees, who had recently topped the record charts with "Disco Duck" and was a very popular performer at the time. Dees' primary recollection of being on *The Brady Bunch Hour* was his fascination with the swimming pool. "The swimming pool was incredible. The production value of that show was off the chart. I walked into this soundstage and they had a swimming pool! It was phenomenal. It was a space in time when you could get away with that and today it's all reality and all budgets," he says. Dees also never forgot *The Brady Bunch Hour* appearance because it gave him an opportunity to make a second impression on a very special young lady. Dees recalls, "I met a girl named Julie McWhorter about two weeks before when I did another television show. I had asked her out and she had forgotten what I looked like totally. So she had a Betamax video recorder and she taped *The Brady Bunch Hour* so she could see what I looked like. There I was onstage with these huge gorilla arms swinging back and forth singing 'Dis-Gorilla.' 'Disco Duck' had just come out, and *King Kong* was being rereleased, and I thought it would be a perfect time to do 'Dis-Gorilla.' It was a moderate success, certainly not the 6 million copies 'Disco Duck' sold. But *The Brady Bunch Hour* was really a very vital part of my life because my wife decided if she would go out with me by watching the show. She actually still has the white suit and orange shirt that she first saw me wear and decided, 'Yeah, I'll go out with him one more time even though he's jumping around stage like a gorilla.' She was an absolute beauty. The check from *The Brady Bunch Hour* came in faster than any show I ever did. It was terrific! A week later I had a check. It wasn't for a lot, but it certainly was a check, and the show was responsible for my wife saying, 'Yes, I'll go out with him again.' We've been married for over thirty years."

A Show Within a Show

According to Mike Kagan, ambivalence permeated the set when he arrived at KTLA to replace Terry Hart as a writer in January of 1977 after *The Brady Bunch Hour* was picked up as a series. "The Bradys were all being pushed into this, which did not come naturally to any of them except Florence," Kagan says. "Nobody was too sure this was going to work. This was a lark. Everybody was waiting for the other shoe to drop. Nobody expected it to go on the next week," he adds.

Writer Mike Kagan

When Bonny Dore came in to meet with the writers she explained that the new scripts needed a greater reflection of who the Bradys were as people. Dore says, "Finding that family element with the writers, who were variety writers and not sitcom writers, was a little more difficult than Sid and Marty anticipated. If it had been my choice I might have suggested than they do an inside out show. You start in a sitcom and it evolves into the other side of the show. They're putting on a variety show. That would have been my instinct if I had the opportunity to work in development with them. Variety was a very big deal at that point and there were whole hoards of A-writers who only wrote variety, they didn't write sitcoms. It's a different way of writing and I think they struggled with that. It was something that they were starting to get their feet in the right place as we got three or four shows into it. By then it was too late."

The first thing the writers had to do was to find a way for the Bradys to appear in musical numbers every week, determine what role they were going to play in that, and decide how they were going to relate to the guests. Steve Bluestein says, "Everyone on the show would say, 'Just write it, it's a job, just go on.' No one was there writing art. We were writing, 'Hey honey, I'm home.' We did the best we could with insurmountable odds. You had a variety show with a lead character who couldn't sing or dance, we had secondary characters who couldn't sing or dance, you had the Kroffts who were like, 'We're going to fly in a cow and the girls are going to dance on its back,' and we're like, 'What are you talking about?!' It was stuff like that. It was *The Brady Bunch,* it was not hip. There was a reason why it became the worst show in the history of television. All of the elements just weren't there."

Another problem was that the Bradys' clean-cut images restricted what could be written, and all the writers, Ronny Graham in particular, had a very adult sense of humor. "It was acceptable with Florence because Florence knew how to look like everybody's mom and deliver a slightly salacious line and no one would question it. But with the kids, you can't put those kinds of lines in kids' mouths and have it come out right," says Bonny Dore.

Marty Krofft asked Ronny Graham to come in and help director Jack Regas work with the Bradys on comedy. Steve Bluestein explains, "Ronny was working with the actors showing them where the jokes are and working with them on timing. He was more like an acting coach than a physical director." Dore says that Regas didn't mind at all when Ronny

Comedy director Ronny Graham as "Mr. Dirt" in commercials for Mobil Oil in the early 1970s

Graham came in to assist. "Jack and Ronny got along okay. You have to remember in five days there is a lot that has to be done in a variety show and the director can't just work with the cast. He has too many other things to do, which is why they brought Ronny in. You have to know that they did that on *Donny and Marie* too, they also had a floor director for Art Fisher to work on comedy. It wasn't unusual if you were on a very tight schedule."

Regas recalls that Florence couldn't understand why Graham had taken over directing the comedy skits because he had worked with her many times before that. "It didn't matter and it all worked out, I just sat in watching," Regas says.

Almost all of the writing was done in the offices at KTLA, then the script would be passed down for a review. When the writers met at the beginning of the new series they didn't know what kind of show to come up with. The first bit of writing they put together was trial and error, and even Sid and Marty Krofft didn't have a firm idea of what the content should be. "We would go to rehearsal to the read through and see what needed to be changed," says Steve Bluestein. "Obviously, there would always be changes made. When it came to the actual shooting we would wander down to the set, we weren't required to be there. For me it was like a big holiday. I would go down there as much as I could," he adds.

With ratings hits such as *Donny and Marie* and *The Carol Burnett Show* on the air, having the Bradys doing variety was hardly earth-shattering and it certainly didn't break a form for the writers. "The only innovation really was this stupid swimming pool, which only ended up presenting enormous problems," says Mike Kagan. "When we first walked onto that soundstage and saw this mammoth swimming pool, we all said, 'Oh, wow, this is fantastic, I've never seen anything on television like this, and it's going to look completely different than any other show.' That was the first week. Two weeks in we were sorry we ever had a swimming pool. What a pain in the ass that was. To write for it and keep coming up with stuff, throwing people in the pool, and sketches around the pool, and written pieces that involved swimming and learning to swim, it was just a pain," he adds.

The writers eventually came up with a running gag in which one of the Bradys gets pushed in the pool. The female half of the cast pretty much refused to go along with the idea. Florence was a good sport and tried it once with the "Comedy Water Circus" in the pilot, and Susan was willing to bump heads underwater with Rich Little so he could lose his memory. But neither Maureen nor Geri was thrilled to be thrown in a pool on national television. Geri recalls, "My mother told them, 'No, you're not going to have my daughter do anything in the pool,' so they had me sit by the side wearing my bathing suit. I didn't even get in. They said, 'Okay, Geri, you can just dangle your legs in the water and then after a little bit you can leave.' That was just one of my things. I don't like deep water!" In the pilot, the writers had Greg push Peter in the pool and because Chris Knight actually enjoyed it he was elected to take the plunge for each show, always screaming, "Mom!"

Chris says, "Well, you know, it's slapstick. Someone's gotta take the cream pie and I took it as a privilege. I was looking at it as vaudeville. You've got to take the fall. Dick Van Dyke was always falling down. He was the one taking it on the chin. He was the one who was the butt of the joke. He was the one who was compromised. In comedy, I took it as flattering." Barry also ended up being thrown in the pool on several occasions, and in one episode Chris and Barry ganged up on Robert Reed and threw him in the water. Instead of screaming for his mom, however, Bob predictably yelled, "Carol!"

Geri and Maureen stood by feeling a bit uncomfortable yet entertained. "I was just hoping I would never have to have a scene with Barry and Chris where one of them pushes the other in the water. That was not going to be me!" Geri exclaims.

Rip Taylor was also not a big fan of the swimming pool, and always feared it would explode because of how it was built. He says, "I was scared to death! I just saw black plastic underneath this something or other, which was a pool. It wasn't a pool. It was water in black plastic, and then weights to hold it together. It looked like it was going to blow up! We were very scared of that. It was slippery, I almost fell, but they didn't care. It was silly, I just said, 'Now, my imitation of Esther Williams…'"

Rewriting the Bradys

In the pilot for *The Brady Bunch Variety Hour*, little priority was given to keeping the Brady characters consistent with the original sitcom created and written by Sherwood Schwartz. When the pilot became a new series there wasn't enough time for the writers to thoroughly analyze Mike, Carol, and the kids, so they improvised. In the first few episodes, Carol was no longer the docile and obedient "Hello, dear!" housewife America remembered and

A production assistant stands in for Florence Henderson during dress rehearsal

recognized. In this series, she dominated the Brady household with her strong personality while husband Mike was acquiescent. The network was not very happy about it.

Mike Kagan recalls, "They were telling us whatever you do we have to keep Robert Reed's character as macho as possible. We couldn't allude to the fact that Bob was gay because there were rumblings about that. They wanted us to just quash any thought of that at all, but then we came in the next week they've got him in a pink suit with rhinestones and it's like, 'What are you doing?!'"

Bonny Dore explains how the issue was viewed by ABC. "The network was terrified of anyone finding out that Robert Reed was gay because he's Dad Brady. Dad Brady cannot be gay. On the other hand they put him in a dress and they threw him in the water. It was a difficulty for the writing staff. Bob was kind of open to doing something different — he was. But what happened in terms of the character was that on the original *Brady Bunch* he was a *Father Knows Best* kind of dad. The only way to make it work in the variety show was to kind of make him a 'boob.' I remember saying to Marty at the time, 'Marty, if you put him in the pool he's a jerk. He's the fall guy.' He said, 'What else are we going to do with him? He can't sing. He can't dance,' which was true. The truth was that the only way to make it work was to 'boobify' him."

With the Brady children, the writers portrayed Greg as being narcissistic with an obsession for music while Marcia didn't appear to have much of an existence outside of sitting around at home looking pretty. Both characters complained about still living with their parents in their twenties and referred to their younger siblings as "kids." Peter was probably the most similar to the original series. He was seen as obsessively girl crazy, the brunt of insults, shy, and self-conscious. Chris Knight notes that he was relieved at not being under a thumb of someone who had a firm idea of who Bradys were and wanted to keep them there. "The Kroffts didn't own that, so they let us evolve," he says.

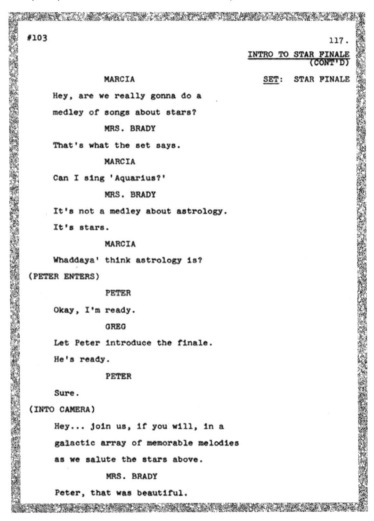

The character of Jan, now portrayed by Geri Reischl, was seemingly mute. She said very little except for declarations about wanting to be dead or wanting to be in a different family. Susan Olsen says, "I didn't like what they did to Jan. I suppose that was the beginning of psychotic Jan. Even though people aren't very aware of the *Variety Hour,* the cliché of Jan now has developed into this neurotic, schizophrenic girl that I was never aware of her being in the original show. So just everything was, 'Oh, I wish I were dead,' overly emotional teen. I use to feel sorry for Geri because she had these one-liners that just came out of nowhere and they weren't funny. It's hard to even remember your lines when they come so out of nowhere. All of the sudden there's Jan saying, 'Oh, I wish I were dead.' Of course I loved it when Marcia said, 'Yeah, why can't Jan be dead?'"

Bonny Dore adds, "Fake Jan was a 'me too!' person, 'Oh, yeah, me too!' That was deliberate and it wasn't because of Geri's talent or lack thereof, but because everybody was so nervous about having a replacement. They put all of the emphasis on the Bradys you knew. Had I been involved early enough, I think I would have objected. I think I would have said there has to be a way to convince Eve to do this because it's either the Bradys or it's not."

The two youngest Brady characters were also minimized, but primarily because Mike Lookinland and Susan Olsen were minors and unable to work long hours. The writers decided to make Bobby a junior producer of the family variety show who at times became somewhat arrogant and condescending with the family and guest stars. He was often seen bickering with Cindy, whom the writers simplified and portrayed as a blonde airhead. "By this time I understood the comedic value of being stupid. Actually, I don't think Cindy was much different than she was on the original show," says Susan Olsen.

The writers did what they could with a challenging set of circumstances. "In a bizarre way it was entertaining but we knew we weren't coming up with something that was going to live for the ages," says Bruce Vilanch. "The Brady family was not the Osmond family and didn't have a tradition of trooping the way the Osmonds did. When the Osmonds came to television, love them or hate them, they were seasoned vets by the time they got to their variety show. The people on *The Brady Bunch Hour* were handed this task, 'Okay, now you are going to be musical comedy stars!' That's not how it's done," Vilanch adds.

Lens Crafters

After several weeks of preparation for the series premiere of *The Brady Bunch Hour*, the show was finally ready to go before the cameras. The camera crew at KTLA was comprised of pioneers from the earliest days of television when the studio first began broadcasting in 1947. There were a minimum of four or five cameras running at one time operated by Dick Watson, Gary Westfall, George Wood, John Gillis, and Ken Dahlquist. "It was definitely a multi-camera production. We had a crane camera, two Norelco PC-70 cameras on the wing, and a TKP-45 portable handheld camera," Dahlquist says. By comparison, the original *Brady Bunch* had been shot primarily with a single camera. The Chapman Company provided KTLA with various sized cranes where the camera operator would sit behind the camera. Dahlquist recalls, "There would have to be a guy driving the crane and then a guy arming the crane as well. The choreographer for that was Gary Westfall."

To shoot the swimming pool numbers the crew mounted one camera up in the rafters looking down. Dahlquist says, "Dick Watson hauled that camera all the way to the top of the stage. He did the majority of those shots, and he would go up high and lay up there in the rafters. They made a platform for him, and a trapdoor they'd open up, and then they would mount the camera on a tilt plate and get the overhead shot. For those times, it was a very ambitious show."

Ted Van Klaveren recalls that camera work on the pool set was exceptionally difficult because they couldn't easily shoot the Bradys directly from the front. "It was hard to do that portion of it. We had the booms up on the pool deck off to the side because it was a raised stage. When they came out to do the openings of the show they had little skits up in there. It was one of the tougher variety shows I did because of the pool, and the swimmers, and everything," Van Klaveren says. There were also six camera aisles built around the perimeter of the pool under the deck. There were two aisles on each side, each with a Plexiglas window, so that they could film underwater. "We encapsulated the camera in the space behind each window of the pool with a black curtain," Dahlquist adds. "The clarity of that camera for way back then was almost unheard of. I am amazed at how clear those shots were."

None of the cameramen was very familiar with the original *Brady Bunch* and did not know the names of the characters nor the actors who played them. Florence and Bob may have been exceptions, but the kids were new to them. During rehearsals for the *Variety Hour* pilot episode, they had the Brady actors wear large, rectangular-shaped cards tied around their neck with yarn. Each card had the corresponding character's name in black letters so that the camera crew would be able to sort them out. Assistant director Rick Locke laughs, "What's a way to make cast members feel important? Hang a sign around

RCA *Broadcast News*, Courtesy David Sarnoff Library

KTLA USES TKP-45
FOR STUDIO AND FIELD CAMERA

KTLA-TV (Golden West Broadcasting) Los Angeles, is making full use of the versatility designed into the TKP-45 Portable Camera. The camera is used for outdoor field productions such as the Rose Parade and sports events, and for a range of indoor studio productions. KTLA designed a special "gyro" mounting for the TKP-45 (photo) which permits the camera to be swung about to achieve unusual video effects. The camera is used as a shoulder-mount portable; or a tripod mount—and with the Minimax adapter—as a studio camera, with 7-inch viewfinder and zoom lens.

their neck, 'My name is Greg.'" Stage manager Steve Dichter says they had used the same method on other shows and it was a coping mechanism for working with director Art Fisher, who was very quick calling cameras. "It was their character names on the name tags. That's how the cameramen learned who it was," Dichter explains. "This was really fast-paced cutting. It was early on during the first show, but after a while they knew who everybody was. I don't think the original *Brady Bunch* show was high on my viewing list when it was on. When I had that many people in a cast, plus the guest stars, I kind of appreciated it if I had to give someone a note that they had their name on their chest. It benefited lots of folks. The cast, I recall, was pretty good natured about it," he concludes.

Dahlquist explains that it could have been a request from some of the older camera operators who were not familiar with the cast, in order for them to know who to shoot. "The guys who did that show were getting up in years and may have requested that," he says. Dahlquist also claims sometimes name tags were used for stand-ins, although Susan Olsen has no recollection of that. "No, we didn't have stand-ins. You need stand-ins for properly lighting a set. I don't think anything was done properly on this production," she quips.

Director Jack Regas choreographed most of the camera angles so that they were synchronized with the music. Because of Regas' experience with movie musicals in the 1940s, he knew exactly how and from what angle the numbers should be filmed. Dahlquist says, "It was all Jack's doing, the timing of the cut, the zooms, and all that." Some of the distinctive camera angles were satirized when *The Simpsons* spoofed the Bradys in the "Simpson Family Smile-Time Variety Hour" episode in 1997. This included what has come to be known as the "seasick cam," where the screen slowly tips sideways and moves back in the other direction. Dahlquist recalls, "It was Dick Watson's idea to slowly tip the camera sideways with the handheld camera, angling it 45 degrees or so, he's cradling it in his arms. Back in 1976 it was pioneering handheld work. There were very few handheld cameras back then."

Watson also had a moving camera that rolled along the floor and stopped so that one of the actors could sing directly down into the lens. "The rolling camera was on a little wheelie cart that Dick made, and they mounted the handheld camera on it, and he would just walk down stage pulling it along for the tracking shot," Dahlquist says. Cameras for videotaping back in the 1970s were quite large and extra equipment was needed to move them around. Dahlquist adds, "We'd move the cameras from stage to stage, they'd take a forklift, and roll them out, and put them onto a platform, and roll them down to the stage, roll them off, put them in the stage, plug them in, and the engineers would have to set them up again because they were bouncing around."

Dahlquist is amused that people are still talking about *The Brady Bunch Hour* and its unusual place in television history. He recalls that the camera crew enjoyed working with

everyone involved with the production. "The Bradys were so busy on that show learning their stuff week in and week out. You just kind of let them have their space. They were pleasant, they'd say hello. I've worked on shows for years where a cast won't even acknowledge your existence. I gave them much credit for what they were trying to do," he says.

Dead on Arrival

Although cast and crew members remained optimistic about *The Brady Bunch Hour*, privately some felt that the show was dead on arrival. "We knew in the beginning it wasn't going to work out. I couldn't believe it worked out as long as it did," says Chris Knight.

Maureen McCormick had mixed feelings. "It was like a dream come true in one way, and in another way it was a nightmare. To think that we were ever thought of as a musical group just blows my mind. But you know, it was really cute and funny," she adds.[28]

Susan Olsen made her friends promise not to watch the show. She recalls, "I was like, 'Please don't watch this, please.' How embarrassing was it for you to have your friends watch? You tell them not to watch the show, but it's like, 'Quick, don't think of an elephant!' and of course they're going to watch the show so they can rip you to pieces."

Barry Williams, on the other hand, was happy to be involved with the production. Barry reflects, "Being involved from the inside out, I tended to stay in the creative buzz of it rather than step back and look at the finished product. I throw myself in 100 percent and I assume it's going to work. So I'm always surprised if it doesn't."

The first real indication that *The Brady Bunch Hour* was in trouble came when the network decided not to have the show on every week and spread out the eight episodes over several months. ABC put the Bradys on a wheel, running opposite *60 Minutes* on Sundays, where it would air once a month alternating with *The Hardy Boys/Nancy Drew.* Those shows really clicked with the audience so ABC ordered more *Hardy Boys* and just left the Bradys hanging. Bonny Dore explains, "They were trying to give them more time to get it right. I think they were just trying to find a better place for *The Brady Bunch Hour.* I think Fred Silverman was very worried at that point. I actually do think the show improved as it went along. I don't think Fred would agree with me. I was there a lot, so I felt that by the third or fourth show they were getting it. But it was a little late. When they started to move shows around that was the death knell."

Eventually *The Brady Bunch Hour* ended up all over the schedule — seemingly whenever ABC had an opening. Sometimes the show would turn up on Mondays, sometimes on Friday nights, and at one point was even

> **It was like a dream come true in one way, and in another way it was a nightmare. To think that we were ever thought of as a musical group just blows my mind.**
> — Maureen McCormick

put up against the Oscars telecast. It was nearly impossible for viewers to find the show or for anyone to know when it would be on. "That absolutely hurt the show," Dore says. "I argued with Fred about it. Before the pilot, Fred didn't want to put it on the wheel. He wanted to put it on every week. After the pilot I think he got nervous. Plus, *Hardy Boys/Nancy Drew* was doing well and I think that was a surprise. Wheels were very big then and they felt it would give them more time to do each of the shows well. It sounded good, but the truth was that a family show like *The Brady Bunch Hour* you need to fall in love with the family and see them every week. It's not like a filmed show where the story line pulls you along."

Nielsen ratings for the series premiere January 23, 1977, were respectable. An estimated 14,254,500 viewers, or 19.5 percent of all households in the country, watched the show. Of all households with a television, 31 percent were tuned in at some point during the hour, and 13,880,000 households were watching per average minute. *The Brady Bunch Hour* wasn't performing poorly by modern standards, but with only three networks in 1977 the expectations for viewers were significantly higher than they are today. "When we started the first week, I think we got great ratings because I remember we got nifty baskets from the network afterwards," says Bruce Vilanch.

Susan Olsen, Robert Reed, Florence Henderson, Lee Majors, and Farrah Fawcett in a final dress rehearsal on January 19, 1977, for the premiere episode of *The Brady Bunch Hour*. Afterwards, Farrah left the set to finish her hair. "At the exact moment she turned on her hair dryer, the lights went out all over the KTLA lot. We weren't sure if it was a power failure or attributed to her," Bruce Vilanch joked.

Director Jack Regas recalls, "I think we all thought it was a good show. It had possibilities. Here was the famous *Brady Bunch*. Not only are they going to act, but they are going to sing and dance. What a great thing. Then, the reviews, how deflating! I felt terrible about it and more than that I felt sorry for the cast, I really did." However, one generally upbeat review appeared in *Daily Variety*, which stated, "In its favor was a continual sense of movement and pace, good choice of musical material, energetic dancing by the Krofftette dancers that helped immeasurably to flesh-out the musical production numbers, and the Kroffts' penchant for colorful costuming. And, of course, the very legitimate singing talents of Florence Henderson… Hardly world-shattering, *Brady Bunch Hour* nevertheless qualified as painless entertainment."[29]

Marty Krofft explains that every effort was made to make *The Brady Bunch Hour* a success, but that ABC never really gave them an opportunity to connect with viewers. "They all worked real hard, everybody gave it their all. Except Maureen, she didn't give it her all, her heart wasn't in it, but everybody else did and wanted it to work. It just was at the wrong time. It was a tough challenge. There were shows that had a lot more problems than ours. If we had lasted a whole season, we probably would have made it. If we had moved beyond the curiosity level, we would have wound up keeping the audience. The network sold us out after the first two weeks."

Birth of the Krofftettes

During the 1970s a core group of dancers made the rounds performing in the chorus lines on many variety shows. They were a very close-knit community who all knew one other from dance classes, auditions, workshops, and competitions. These young girls came from all over America — from small towns, big cities, and the middle of nowhere — to pursue their dreams of being stars in Hollywood. "We were professional dancers, and we worked on a lot of other shows together, but we were always auditioning and it was kind of the same girls who would work all the time, or if you got to know a choreographer they would hire you," recalls Dee Kaye. When *The Brady Bunch Variety Hour* went into production in October of 1976, many of the dancers who showed up for interviews were already seasoned veterans.

Sid and Marty Krofft with their Water Follies

Charkie Phillips had been appointed by choreographer Joe Cassini to make final selections for the Krofftettes and Water Follies troupe because of her extensive experience as a synchronized swimmer growing up in Florida. Chris Wallace, a former competitive swimmer, was selected as her assistant. Charkie's best friend, Linda Hoxit, who was a finalist for the Krofftettes, had a swimming pool at her home with rock legend Al Kooper, so she was asked if she could host some training seminars in synchronized swimming. Linda thought being a Krofftette was a great idea, "I took swimming lessons at the YMCA every summer growing up, because my grandparents made me, so I was a strong swimmer and had a dance background in ballet. It went together quite nicely." Charkie organized a crash course for all the finalists to teach them the basics of synchronized swimming.

Olympic synchronized swimming coach Chris Carver admires what Charkie set out to accomplish. "Good for her! That's really gutsy. To me, I'd rather take a swimmer and make a dancer out of them. A lot of times people don't understand that you can't just do it right away. What a challenge." Linda Hoxit recalls they all just jumped into the water and gave Charkie their undivided attention. "We'd all get into my pool and Charkie would

To me, I'd rather take a swimmer and make a dancer out of them. A lot of times people don't realize you can't just do it right away. What a challenge.
— US Olympic Synchronized Swimming Coach Chris Carver

train us how to 'skull' and how to do the extensions, the 'oyster move,' and 'back dolphins,' and some of the things you still see on water ballet today in the Olympics," Linda says. Charkie and Chris then held a final audition to see who would be able to handle the roles of both dancer and swimmer. In addition to Linda, they selected Susan Buckner, Lynne Latham, and Robyn Blythe. Robyn recalls, "I'd always swum. I had to be taught all the water ballet movements, but I was always very athletic. I also was a diver from a very early age because I was a thrill seeker. I'd get right up on the high dive when I was six years old and I was competing for diving medals. I've always been a fish, always." To round out the group Charkie and Chris cast newcomers Judy Susman, Darine "Dee Kaye" Klega, Laura Steele, and Michelle Horowitz.

What qualifications does a person need to be a synchronized swimmer? Above all, one needs to be exceptionally strong in the water and possess above average upper and lower body strength. Other requirements include a good sense of balance, rhythm, and flexibility. It is also preferable to have a background in dance, music, and competitive swimming. Chris Carver says, "I think it takes far more than anyone can ever imagine. It takes a lot of tenacity because it doesn't happen overnight. You're in it for a long time to reach a world-class level. I've likened it to being a classical musician, it's that kind of a skill building endeavor. Many of the young women today swim hours every day, six days a week, all year round. You have to be passionate about what you're doing."

Meet the Krofftettes

Charkie Phillips — Charlotte "Charkie" Phillips was born in Ohio. She began her dance training at the age of three in Atlanta, Georgia, and was accepted at the age of eight into the Southern Ballet Company. At the age of three she was taught to swim by her father. Her love for the water continued with her first competitive instruction in both swimming and diving under the tutelage of coach John Foster. She performed her first synchronized swimming routine at the Ansley Golf Club at the age of five with her seven-year-old sister, Sheril. When she was nine years old her family moved to Fort Lauderdale, Florida, where she continued her rigorous competitive swimming and diving training with the coaches of the CRYC Swim Club. Her dance study continued as well at the Del Academy School of Dance with "Miss Chris" and she was accepted into the Fort Lauderdale Civic Ballet Company. As a teenager Charkie (pronounced "Sharkie") became a member of the elite Pine Crest Prep School swimming and diving team where she was featured swimming and diving in their annual water show. She also competed yearly in both Jr. Olympics and Jr. Nationals. She came in second in diving at the state championships. In her lifetime of competitive swimming and diving she received 375 medals, 52 trophies, and 550 ribbons. In New York City she studied dance at the Ballet Russes and after moving to California she appeared as a dancer on television programs such as *The Mac Davis Show*, the *Mitzi Gaynor Special*, the *Entertainer of the Year Awards* (in the June Taylor Chorus), and the *Krofft Comedy Hour*. In addition to choreographing water ballet for *The Brady Bunch Hour*, Charkie staged synchronized swimming for NBC's *The Big Show*, *The Great Muppet Caper*, and for a McDonald's commercial in the 1988 Olympics. Onstage she was in the international tour of the *The Ray Anthony Show* as a "Bookend" and *The Happy Side of the Thirties* at the Shubert Theater. Charkie is also remembered as a dancer in the movie *Grease* and was a choreographer for *The Star Wars Holiday Special*. She holds a black belt in karate and was formerly an instructor in Hanakido karate. In the 1970s Charkie did martial arts exhibitions at Universal Studios where she met her husband, Dragan Marjanovic.

Charkie Phillips

Christine Wallace

Christine Wallace — Christine Wallace was born and raised in Los Angeles and worked as a professional dancer and choreographer for over twenty years. She appeared in films such as *Grease, Annie, New York, New York*, and *The Goodbye Girl*. Chris also performed on numerous television series and specials, including many of the Academy Awards shows, American Music Awards, Golden Globes and the Grammy Awards. The highlight of her career was performing for the Queen of England at the Palladium in London. Chris served as choreographer for the movie *The Man in the Iron Mask* and worked with stars Leonardo DiCaprio, Jeremy Irons, and John Malkovich. She is an accomplished swimmer and was the assistant water ballet choreographer on *The Brady Bunch Variety Hour*, *The Big Show*, and *The Great Muppet Caper*.

Susan Buckner

Linda Hoxit

Judy Susman

Susan Buckner — Susan Buckner was born in Burien, Washington, a suburb of Seattle. In 1971 she became Miss Washington and was a top-ten finalist in the Miss America Pageant, winning both the swimsuit and evening gown awards. Susan moved to Los Angeles in 1973 after she won a national audition to become one of Dean Martin's "Golddiggers," who appeared as dancers and singers in his stage act and television variety show. She later became a synchronized swimmer on *The Brady Bunch Hour* and also went on tour as a dancer for Telly Savalas. Her roles acting on television include *The Amazing Howard Hughes* as Jean Harlow, *The Nancy Drew Mysteries*, *When the Whistle Blows*, and she co-starred with Elizabeth Taylor on television in a live theatrical production of *Return Engagement*. Susan also made guest appearances on *Starsky and Hutch*, *The Love Boat*, and *B.J. and the Bear*. She is most frequently recognized for her role as Patty Simcox in the movie musical *Grease* with John Travolta and Olivia Newton-John. Susan also starred in Wes Craven's *Deadly Blessing* with Sharon Stone and Ernest Borgnine.

Linda Hoxit — Linda Hoxit is a native of Eugene, Washington, and a veteran dancer on dozens of 1970s variety shows including *The Smothers Brothers Show*, *The Sonny and Cher Show*, *Tony Orlando and Dawn*, *The Brady Bunch Hour*, and *The Carol Burnett Show*. A member of Actors' Equity, she has appeared in over thirty musicals, including the bride role of Sarah Kines in the national tour and Broadway run of *Seven Brides for Seven Brothers* at the Alvin Theater in New York City. Linda was one of Ray Anthony's "Bookend" dancers, and her film credits include *Grease*; *History of the World, Part I*; and *Movie, Movie*.

Judy Susman — Judy Susman grew up in St. Louis, Missouri, and attended Stephens College and Ohio State University where she majored in dance. After her marriage to actor Todd Susman she moved to Los Angeles and found work as a dancer on many televisions shows, including *Sonny and Cher*, *The Brady Bunch Hour*, the Academy Awards, along with the movies *Grease* and *Sgt. Pepper's Lonely Hearts Club Band*.

Lynne Latham — Lynne Latham was born in Iowa City, and moved to Los Angeles when she was seven. She studied ballet as a young child and then at the age of thirteen she saw a performance of *Giselle* with Margot Fontaine and Rudolf Nureyev and was incurably stricken with a passion for dance. After an ankle injury precluded Lynne from further study of ballet, she turned to jazz and studied with Roland DuPree, Jaime Rogers, and Claude Thompson. Lynne began her dance career on television with *The Dean Martin Show* and also went on tour with Sammy Davis Jr. In the 1970s she returned to Dean Martin as one of the *Ding-a-ling Sisters*, and also appeared as a dancer on *The Donny and Marie Show*. Lynne worked as a synchronized swimmer on television in *The Brady Bunch Hour* and *The Big Show*, and then in the films *History of the World: Part I* and *The Great Muppet Caper*. She also starred opposite Olivia Newton-John as Muse #2 in the cult classic *Xanadu*. In 1983, after many years of experience with wardrobe and costumes onstage and onscreen, Lynne became a fashion designer and designed the handbags for the outrageous English fashion icon, Zandra Rhodes.

Lynne Latham

Dee Kaye — Although best known for her comedic talents, Dee Kaye is also an accomplished, classically trained dancer. Born Darine Klega, she was an original Los Angeles Rams cheerleader. She participated in the Miss California pageant, and has been seen on the fashion runways in Milan, Italy. Dee has appeared on *The Tonight Show*, the Academy Awards, *The Brady Bunch Hour*, *The Big Show*, and in the films *The Great Muppet Caper* and *Annie*. She also has been seen onstage in theaters around the world — from the London Palladium to the Dorothy Chandler Pavilion in Los Angeles. She has been doing improvisational comedy for over fifteen years and has honed her skills working with comedy greats such as Milton Berle and Dick Shawn.

Dee Kaye

Robyn Blythe — Robyn Blythe is a native of Southern California. In nursery school Robyn earned the nickname "Miss Hollywood" from her teachers because she would always wear her sunglasses and sing in the sandbox. While growing up she was a member of the Royal Academy Ballet and the Long Beach Civic Opera. At the age of thirteen Robyn starred onstage as Laurie in the musical *Oklahoma!* Then, at seventeen, she was in the touring company of *Gigi*, which ended its run on Broadway. Calling upon all her talents at age nineteen, Robyn joined rock star Alice Cooper for a six-month national tour and appeared as the lead dancer in his film *Welcome to My Nightmare*. She then won a role in the original *Death Wish* movie. After being a Krofftette in *The Brady Bunch Hour*, Robyn appeared on *Fantasy Island*, *Charlie's Angels*, *Trapper John M.D.*, *General Hospital*, and was a featured model in David Lee Roth's music video "California Girls." Her other stage work includes *Babes in Arms*, *I Love My Wife*, and an appearance with Joe Namath and Bobby Morse in the musical *Sugar*. She is also remembered for her role as Gloria Sternvirgin in Mark Pirro's films *Deathrow Gameshow* and *Rectuma*.

Robyn Blythe

Jumping into Cold Water

All of the girls were excited to become Krofftettes, but the idea of having a swimming pool on a variety show seemed a little ridiculous to some of them. "My first thought was you've got to be kidding me, they're going to make a variety show out of *The Brady Bunch* with swimmers and everything else?" says Lynne Latham. Dee Kaye, who grew up watching *The Brady Bunch* as a child, says, "It was not that long after the series, which was really popular. In those years, they were still doing variety shows. Now it's odd because nobody does them. Especially for the dancers, it was our bread and butter. With the swimming pool, that was odd. It was the first time I'd heard about it, we were the very first ones to do it. Nobody else had that. I think it was a novelty and probably why Sid and Marty Krofft wanted something like *Donny and Marie*, which had ice skaters."

One of the original ideas for the Krofftette Water Follies was to develop the group around a "star swimmer" similar to Esther Williams, and then Charkie Phillips would serve as coach and choreographer. "We had to choose between Lynne Latham and Susan Buckner, both tall and with pretty figures." Charkie recalls. After a few rehearsals, Charkie decided she would need to be in the water with the swimmers to lead them through the

Susan Buckner is pulled out of the water on a trapeze for her big splash debut.

routines so that the scenes could be filmed more quickly. But Marty Krofft wanted to continue with the "star swimmer" idea and selected Susan Buckner for the role. Nobody, except Susan, knew of her intense fear of heights. She became very nervous about having to free fall from the top of the soundstage. "You did anything anyone asked you to do. You didn't say no to anything," Susan explains. "If they said, 'Can you roller skate on a tightrope with your eyes closed?' you'd say, 'I do it all the time.' We were professionals and we would do whatever we were asked to do."

When the time came for Susan to rise out of the water on the trapeze, she was completely terrified. She was pulled up slowly, higher and higher into the rafters. "All eyes were on me to let go of my white knuckle grip. I gave a big 'Miss America' smile all the way up as I hung from the bar, inside feeling like I was going to the gallows to be executed. Everyone below became a coach at that moment as I tried to choose the best advice for entry into the shallow pool," Susan recalls. Any entry into the water from that height was going to be a hard fall, and Susan found herself panicked and unable to process Charkie's vocal instructions from the ground. "I had to smile the whole time, or was it fear frozen on my face? Art Fisher was the director of that show. I remember looking at him and he was a comforting face at that point because I think he knew I was scared to death. I just remember glancing at him, he didn't tell me what to do, but I knew he was the only one who realized what was going on in my head."

When Susan finally let go, her feet went behind her and upon entry her knees slammed into the bottom of the pool. "I was in such agony, and I smiled because there was an underwater camera aimed right at me. There's still a dent in my kneecap," she laughs. "They wisely let Charkie handle all of the other dives because she was really good at it, and I wasn't going to do anything but let go of a bar and even that was hard for me."

Staging and Planning Swimming Numbers

To plan the intricate swimming numbers, Charkie attended weekly production meetings with the Kroffts and took notes on what they had in mind for the upcoming episode. "They'd basically say, 'Here's what the Bradys are going to be doing, here's basically what we want. We want you to do this.' They set most of it up and then I'd just do choreography," says Charkie. Her new job presented an unusual challenge because she was also supposed to be part of the

In front of their dressing room huts, the Water Follies run through their routine one final time before entering the pool for filming.

ensemble. "Being that I was one of the smaller ones I could put myself on the end or pull myself out totally and put myself where they could see me," she says. The swimmers had to work together as a team without a choreographer on the surface counting aloud to keep them in time during rehearsal. Charkie did her best to play both roles, but sometimes Joe Cassini would help out by calling out commands over the microphone or tap the pool window with a coin while they were shooting underwater. "I was in the pool with them most of the time, unless I could pull out and watch it through the glass window downstairs. Then I'd be able to just drop myself in somewhere. It was all new to me too. Most choreographers won't be in the number because they can't control what's happening. I'd just try to be creative and do something different, that I knew they could do, that would make them look good because they were all such pretty girls and very talented," she says.

Charkie would open each swimming number with some kind of "deck work" to set the mood on the surface before entering the water. It involved a variety of techniques from week to week, and included dives, cartwheels, backflips, and the traditional "peel" technique in which the swimmers would line up along the edge of the pool and dive in rapidly one after the other. The next sequence was usually underwater and revealed the girls sitting on the bottom of the pool, in some kind of formation, smiling for the camera. Sometimes they would move their arms in rhythm with the music, or wave silk streamers under the water as Charkie elegantly swam by.

The swimmers prepare for their opening water entrance with Hula Hoops.

Lynne Latham recalls, "They had props in the pool that were weighted to the bottom. You'd get tangled in the props all the time. There was all kinds of stuff to deal with. It was always a bit of a mad dash getting everything right. It was a very difficult job, it really was."

The final part of each swimming segment involved choreography on top of the water, which included overhead kaleidoscopic shapes like those used by choreographer Busby Berkeley in his films of the 1930s. The grand finale each week was Charkie rising dramatically out of the water on a trapeze to perform her signature dive. Stage manager Steve Dichter recalls that KTLA would have to bring in special effects people because there was not anyone on the crew that they would trust with rigging trapezes, and the like, to carry weight and do it safely. Charkie explains, "It was a hand pulley, a man was pulling the trapeze up by hand on the side and he'd try to lock it off. You only got one or two tries and towards the end you just didn't get to practice, which is tricky," says Charkie. "If you look at some of the shows, I'm doing a backflip towards the stage. I don't always know exactly how close I am to hitting the stage as I'm coming down. The one where I swung out on a star, I think I only got one practice. Most of time it was hit and miss, try, and do the best you could," she adds.

Putting together the swimming numbers in only a few days, in addition to their other duties as dancers on land, presented significant difficulties for everyone involved with the production — from the swimmers, to the cast, crew, cameramen, to the director. "We definitely had to have a plan. We would try it onstage, up on top, before getting in the water," explains Chris Wallace.

Susan Buckner recalls, "Out of the water we would sit in chairs and go through it in our heads and think 'open, close, open, close' where the beat was. Definitely we would do that, like you would run anything through your head if you were doing a dance, and count it out to try and remember it and share it with each other together."

Rehearsal was always limited for the Krofftettes, and they were expected to shoot the swimming sequences each week quickly and efficiently. "You have to kind of talk it through before and then go in the water because otherwise nobody can hear, you're underwater, and you can't give directions," explains Dee Kaye. "We would always mark the moves outside the pool," adds Robyn Blythe, "because if we did all the rehearsing inside the pool we'd all be a bunch of raisins!"

Krofftette Linda Hoxit

The Show Must Go On

A few days before shooting the pilot episode, Linda Hoxit became violently ill and was forced to take a medical leave. Charkie suddenly had a major crisis on her hands. Linda recalls, "I woke up in the middle of the night and was having horrible cramps and couldn't stand up. I got myself to the doctor, he took some tests. He deducted I had peritonitis in my uterus. You can get peritonitis in any organ of your body — your liver, kidneys, or uterus. It's a bacterial infection that can make the organ explode. It was really serious. He asked what I had been doing that's not normal, and I said, 'Well, I'm swimming every day in a pool and I'm doing a TV show where I have to do that. He said, 'You've got some unusual bacteria up there and I think it might be from the pool. That was his deduction, he wasn't conclusive. Obviously he couldn't go down to the studio and take a water sample."

Charkie scrambled to find a replacement, and went to her list of synchronized swimming friends which included Michele Adler, Valerie-Jean Miller, and Susie Guest. Valerie remembers getting a call, rushing to KTLA, and literally jumping right in the pool for a quick run-through. "I was working at CBS doing *Sonny and Cher*, *Tony Orlando*, *Carol Burnette*, and *Jackson 5* and was switching from rehearsal hall to rehearsal hall doing all those shows. Every three or four weeks we'd have a week off. Charkie called me and said, 'Can you get here quickly?' She remembered I did water ballet, but not since high school, so I wasn't right on top of it like everyone else, but I made it through it. It was kind of odd, I didn't quite get the connection, but, hey, it's a job," Valerie says.

Throughout filming of *The Brady Bunch Hour* everyone struggled with problems and unexpected issues because of the swimming pool. The crew tried taping swim numbers in the morning, which later conflicted with rehearsal time for the *Brady Bunch* cast. Then they tried doing swimming in the afternoon, "because once we got in the pool it was too much of a hassle to get us out, and dry us off, and do the dancing. On shoot days, the

dance portions weren't that bad, maybe two or three hours, but then we were in the pool forever," says Linda Hoxit. Then swimming sequences were moved to evenings, and filmed very late, until one, two, or three o'clock in the morning. Several of the girls vividly remember leaving work before sunrise and returning home in the dark. "Sometimes they would put us in a hotel overnight, very close on Sunset there, because we'd have a six or seven o'clock call the next morning. They had to finish things. That stuff takes a long time — swimming. It could take a couple days to shoot just two or three minutes," says Dee Kaye.

Robyn Blythe recalls, "We were exhausted because of the rehearsal hours and it was so physically demanding. They were lucky they found such talent, they were very lucky." Several of the Krofftettes found the job more difficult than they expected and left the production. Although Linda Hoxit came back as a Krofftette for the series, Laura Steele and Michelle Horowitz did not return after the pilot episode and were not replaced. Only eight Krofftettes remained. "They weren't swimmers," explains Charkie. "They were doing great to do what they did, because most people would say, 'Oh, that doesn't look hard,' but it is hard. They all did extremely well for not being trained swimmers."

Making a Splash

The beautiful Krofftette Water Follies made quite a splash with everyone on the KTLA studio lot, and curiosity seekers from the offices and various productions were stopping by Stage 2 to check out the new tenants. Some dancers remember that Marty Krofft especially enjoyed having gorgeous girls around him on the set, and was rather happy about working in that kind of an environment. Costume designer Madeline Graneto recalls, "When all the skaters on *Donny and Marie* were four-leaf clovers, what they wore was four-leaf clovers. What more can I say? Marty always wanted more skin, more sex. But it was Mormons and the family hour. Then Sid always wanted crazy. It's hard to please everybody. You just can't do it all the time. You pick your alliances, and I was Sid's man. Marty came down from the office one time and said, 'You and that brother of mine!' If Marty had it his way the ice skaters would have been dressed in bikinis. It's four-leaf clovers, what do you want?"

Some of the *Brady Bunch* cast and crew stood by watching the synchronized swimming in amazement. "Those girls were gorgeous, they were gorgeous! They all had great bodies and I was jealous. They were just to die for," recalls Maureen McCormick.

Writer Bruce Vilanch says, "I remember Chris Knight and Ronny Graham, our head writer, staring in the portholes and trying to look at all the beaver swimming by. I don't know who was more interested, Ronny or Chris, but it was pointed out to Ronny that what he was doing was probably a bad influence, and Ronny said, 'He's past being influenced already!'"

Marty always wanted more skin, more sex... If Marty had it his way the ice skaters would have been dressed in bikinis.
— Costume Designer Madeline Graneto

Lynne Latham recalls the incident and says, "Some of those guys always had their faces plastered to the porthole windows to try to see anything underwater!" However, Mike Lookinland was ambivalent about what he saw, "I thought it was all complete insanity and craziness…that this is what passes for American entertainment? The pool thing, it's not sexy, or alluring, or romantic, it's just this big pain in the ass. It was plastic and metal, and it was leaking, and it was just crappy. You get the girls in there, and dump them underwater and it just looks weird. Their eyes were bulging. I just remember thinking, 'Man, this is crazy.'"

Barry Williams, of course, took the opportunity to introduce himself to the girls. Chris Knight recalls, "They were very dedicated, and very capable, and very cute. There was some interaction there. I'm sure Barry probably really interacted, although I have no evidence of that. You can only look back and imagine how much interaction they must have had with Barry!" Linda Hoxit remembers Barry as a very nice guy who was close to

Hypoxia Hell

My personal heroes (or heroines) of *The Brady Bunch Variety Hour* would have to be the Krofftettes and Water Follies, which were one in the same — our dancers did double duty. While *Donny and Marie*'s kick line had to skate as well as dance, our ladies had to endure a form of Brady water boarding all in the name of entertainment.

It's always been clear to me that some of the hardest working people in show business are dancers. I see a lot of romance in their dedication. Few dancers ever become wealthy. Their commitment comes from a love for the art and a passion that drives them beyond the pain of their bodies balking at the unnatural demands. There is something so timeless about these smiling ladies who make every move seem effortless. It's so easy to be completely unaware of the tremendous effort that is taking place beneath those smiles.

I was naturally envious of them all because they were in great shape. I loved seeing them in their costumes every day and marveled at their self discipline. These ladies were not only lovely to look at (and really nice), but professional to an extreme. There was no margin for error with them because the only room for error had to be reserved for those of us who were not very good at this stuff. They had to be perfect because one never knew when one of us "stars" might flub a lyric, miss a dance step, or just fall over for no apparent reason.

The underwater sequences were filmed late at night so I don't think I ever got to witness that first hand but I did learn about what they had to go through to create those sequences. In order to

her and all of the dancers. "He did a dance number where he jumped off a platform, we were all whooping it up for him, we were all like, 'Go, Barry, go!' It was fun to watch him do that because of all the Bradys he was the only one who did a real dance solo," Linda says. While Barry was known to be a ladies' man with girls on the set, some of the dancers were also known to be a little flirty. "Robyn Blythe was kind of a wild chick. Actually, she was a big flirt, that's

Krofftette Judy Susman and Chris Knight share a lighthearted moment between takes

what I remember about her. We were shooting with the Hudson Brothers and I remember she was hitting on the oldest one," Linda adds.

In spite of all the raging hormones being generated on the set, it was Krofftette Dee Kaye and Chris Knight who had the most unique connection of all. She was a former classmate and they were in the same classes at Enadia Way School. "I have a picture of us in the fifth grade, and then Chris left for a while doing *The Brady Bunch*. Our fathers were working actors at the time so we had that in common as well," says Dee.

Krofftette Dee Kaye and Chris Knight were in the same class at Enadia Way School in Canoga Park, CA

Paul Shaffer and others working on the KTLA lot for Chevy Chase enjoyed stopping by Stage 2 for a little eye candy. "Not to mention the fact that swimming is the best exercise, these synchronized swimmers had bodies on them that were fantastic," Paul says. "The pool was constructed as such with windows in it so that they could

perform underwater, you have to be able to stay underwater. While it looks easy, try sitting on the bottom of a pool. Divers use weights. But these swimmers were scantily clad and there was no place for weights. (The Krofftettes assured us that there were no lead suppositories being used.) The only way to do this is to expel every bit of air from your lungs and have a fairly low body fat percentage. When you think about holding your breath, you are doing just that, taking a breath and holding it in until the oxygen in it is depleted and you feel the intense need to breathe again. There was no breath to be held for these women so they were "out of breath" before the director even yelled "Action!"

Another reason for getting all the air out of the lungs is to avoid an unsightly air bubble escaping through a nostril. Who wants to be the one to ruin a take for that? To flash a toothy grin, it's necessary to have one's mouth entirely filled with the pool water. These women performed in a state of hypoxia and had to look happy about it. At the end of their work days they had to walk through a bad neighborhood in the dead of night to their cars because they weren't allowed to park on the lot. Nowadays that would be unthinkable without all of them being escorted.

Our Krofftettes were living definitions of the word "trooper." They deserve a great deal of credit and respect.   — Susan

shoot underwater and we could look in there too and see the dancers performing underwater ballet." Linda Hoxit recalls that Chevy's crew members were also quite fond of the girls. "The Kroffttettes were walking through the KTLA lot and we had to go past several soundstages to get to ours. To our right was the open door of the loading dock

Charkie Phillips

door at Chevy Chase's soundstage and some guy was staring us down. As we passed he yelled out, 'You sure are a bunch of good lookin' foxy ladies! Why don't you come visit me up here on my show?' We laughed and replied something like, 'Thanks, but we have to go back to work now,' as we were returning from lunch. It was fun and flirtatious but we never saw him again after that, and frankly Scarlett, I don't think most of us gave a damn," Linda laughs.

Amidst all of the philandering and sexual innuendo, true love was finally found in the strangest and most unexpected circumstances. The late night rehearsals and tapings for water ballet in *The Brady Bunch Hour* presented personal safety concerns for the young women involved. "Sometimes we'd finish a shoot really late, two or three in the morning, and then we'd still have on stage makeup. We'd have to go to a third parking lot, and there wasn't always a guard left to watch us and sometimes we were walking by ourselves," recalls Charkie Phillips. For her own protection, she enrolled in martial arts classes at Eternal Champions Karate in Los Angeles where she earned a black belt and adopted the sport as one of her life-long passions. Through her new interest she met the handsome Master Dragan Marjanovic, a Hollywood fight choreographer, and over thirty years and two children later they are still married.

Treading Water

Linda Hoxit, Paul Williams, Charkie Phillips

The swimmers faced increasing challenges on the job as production continued and they were never offered hazard pay despite obvious risks to their safety. The network refused to officially acknowledge that the swimming pool was a risk to the performers. Assistant director Rick Locke recalls, "At one point we had canisters of gas underneath the water and we actually opened the gas valves and lit them on fire." When Charkie

Phillips brought back swimmers for *The Big Show* on NBC in 1980, she said, "From now on, the girls have to get hazard pay. This is not dancing on the surface. People could drown. It's dangerous."

Another unpleasant reality was the radical change in temperature they experienced getting in and out of the pool with wet swimsuits. "We were right next door to *Donny and Marie*, where it was an ice-skating show. So we had an ice rink adjacent to the pool, and we were always soaking wet in our bathing suits, it was freezing, FREEZING!" screams Susan Buckner. Lynne Latham points out that the swimmers were the only ones on the KTLA lot at that hour, "It was so early in the morning, the place was deserted, and cold,

it was always cold! The pool would be around 80 degrees, so it was quite a shock to our systems when we got out. I remember we always would run for the showers because it would be out of hot water in no time. We would swim all night and then have to jump into a cold shower!"

The production team was sensitive to what was obviously becoming a unique and unpleasant situation for the girls and did their best to make some changes. The crew kept the water warm, and each of the Krofftettes was draped in a thick robe and given heated towels when they came out of the pool. In addition, small dressing room huts were built inside the front of the soundstage so that they would no longer have to leave the building to change clothes. Another modification made after the pilot episode was the installation of underwater speakers so that the swimmers could hear the music they were synchronizing to. Charkie had complained to the production staff that there was no way they could stay together if they didn't have the music being played. Dee Kaye recalls what a big difference it made, "They put a speaker underwater so they could give us direction like, 'now!' or 'turn!' Somebody would talk to us, or you would hear the music. You have to communicate, otherwise the whole thing is not coordinated."

One of the biggest struggles the swimmers faced was learning to hold their breath for long periods of time and to sit on the bottom of the pool with no air in their lungs. "You have to blow your air out before you go down. Otherwise, you float back up to the surface. You're always just gasping for air," explains Lynne Latham. Sid Krofft insisted that no bubbles be seen coming out of the girls' mouths. Some of the swimmers had trouble with that. The ones who weren't as experienced would start rising up, or have to do a couple takes. Sid had additional complaints. "Sid didn't think we could hold our breath long enough," recalls Susan Buckner. "But Sid's brilliant, Sid's just out there with his ideas. He used to want to put all kinds of things in the pool, like dolphins. Someone said, 'Oh Sid, they'll die,' and he replied, 'Well, *how long would they live*?' He didn't care, he had a vision!" Susan laughs.

Judy Susman recalls that at first things didn't seem so bad, "I remember at the beginning of the filming of the underwater numbers, everybody was always really anxious

and volunteered. 'Who wants to go sit on the bottom of the pool and smile?' and everybody would say, 'I do! I do!' but then by the end we'd all try to hide. You couldn't tell who anybody was anyway, so we figured, why bother? It was hard. It was uncomfortable to sit down there without any breath in you, smiling. I was in the front on a lot of those. It must have taken me a while not to volunteer! The only way you could get down there was to blow all your air out so you sink. It was pure effort."

The girls literally spent hours trying to get the underwater poses correct. "We'd do our pose, and if somebody messed up, it's like 'Ugh!'" says Dee Kaye. "Then they would give us the sign to come back up and we would have to do it all over again. Somebody through the window would say 'Up! We didn't get it,' and then we would get mad at the person who messed up because that meant we had to do it yet again. It had to be very precise," she adds.

Robyn Blythe adds, "It was incredibly hard work. Boy, did we all get into shape real quick for those of us who were not as in shape as others. I remember it being very hard work but enjoying it so much."

Charkie Phillips reports that the Krofftettes were performing "old school" synchronized swimming, which meant no nose clips. Nose clips are now a requirement for the sport in the Olympic Games and allow the athletes to do much more in their routines. Olympic coach Chris Carver marvels that the Krofftettes were able to function without them. "It's like asking a football player to go without wearing a helmet," Chris says. The Krofftettes were also forbidden to use goggles. "We did not use goggles [in rehearsals] because if we got used to them we couldn't see one another the way it was, so our eyes hurt pretty bad. That's how it used to be," says Charkie. Linda Hoxit adds, "They didn't want us to because they wanted us to look pretty."

In addition to red and irritated eyes, many of the Krofftettes suffered from horrible sinus infections and earaches. "You blow your air out, and then you always do all these back spins. Well, as soon as you do that the whole pool goes up your nose. It's just the way it works. You can't do anything about that. You try and hold it as much as you can but at some point you're totally out of air. I just remember getting so much chlorinated water up my nose," says Lynne Latham. "There aren't a whole lot of pleasant memories in that respect. It was probably one of the more uncomfortable jobs I've done," she adds.

Although everyone survived *The Brady Bunch Hour,* some incidents the Krofftettes endured will never be forgotten. One of the biggest problems in the pilot episode was that wardrobe did not know what to do with the swimmers' hair. Costume designer Madeline Graneto says, "I remember in the opening number it was dancing costumes and then they literally dove into the pool from the dance number and they had to swim now. Everybody came in and gave their 'expert advice' about Esther Williams and how they used to do that stuff." The stylists were told to glue everyone's hair back but as soon as they went in the water the hair would start to float around. Then they decided to have everyone put a wig on. The wigs became swollen with water, lost shape, and fell apart. Next they tried helmets and shellacked a hard shape of hair to the swimmers' heads. "As soon as we dove in the pool, the things would fill up with water and sink to the ground they were so heavy. So, that didn't work," says Dee Kaye. In a last desperate attempt to solve the problem, the stylists smeared Vaseline in everyone's scalp, and to get it out the swimmers had to wash their hair with Spic and Span and Joy liquid detergent.

"I couldn't get it out no matter what I did!" cries Lynne Latham. "I washed my hair, washed my hair, washed my hair. Oh God, it just ruined my hair! At the time, my hair was colored and it turned green. It started breaking off. I remember this hairdresser took one look at me and he said, 'Darling, you really should take better care of your hair!' He didn't know that we were underwater all the time, and putting in all these bobby pins to hold pieces in place. It was really hard on our scalp and our skin and everything." The production team went back to look at the Esther Williams films again and noticed the swimmers wore turbans, which were light and easy to use. Dee Kaye says, "We're dancers, we were very tough. There were no cry babies. You just do what you're told. We had to do tests

because nobody had ever done this before on television."

Another memorable day on the set was when Pete Menefee took over as costume designer and decided to augment the girls' bust lines with a larger endowment. He made a startling discovery. Sid had asked for a shot where the swimmers would boost themselves

out of the water. Pete padded the swimsuits with falsies made of foam rubber. He recalls the embarrassment that followed. "When the swimmers burst to the surface these falsies were just sodden with water and they looked like very old women. Their breasts were about six inches longer. I found out about Polyfill that week, which does not absorb water and retain it," he laughs. In addition to the traditional swimsuits, Pete also experimented with using fabric in the water. "The first week I tried having the girls dolphin with about forty feet of red China silk, which looked amazing. When Sid saw forty feet of red China silk in back of all these swimmers, he just freaked out. We couldn't get him away from the monitor. He was staring at it, and saying, 'Oh, wow, oh, wow, oh, yeah…' over and over."

Wardrobe mistress Mari Grimaud clearly remembers the big rush to get the swimmers ready, "When they finally started doing the number then all you had to do was stand by and watch and wait for problems. But mostly you could just watch unless something burst, split or something." Mari adds, "We would gasp because half the time their suits were see-through. You couldn't tell in the fitting, but as soon as they would get wet we would say, 'Oh my God!' You can't see it in the finished show, because, truly, they would never let it go if it was," she says.

One thing the audience was not allowed to see was how the swimmers got out of the pool. They were seen diving in, but never getting out. It was as

Lisa Pharren and Charkie Phillips

if they were imprisoned in the water, and there were times the girls felt that way. "I remember one good thing about that situation," says Lynne Latham. "My thought was if I'm ever shipwrecked I can tread water for days. I won't have to worry about it." For some reason the swimming pool had no steps or indentations on the side. The swimmers were forced to keep sculling for hours to stay afloat, or hold on to the edges, which were slippery. "I remember us doing that, and we'd get kind of delirious and start making whatever kind of jokes we could come up with just to keep us going. That was difficult," says Linda Hoxit. After a few episodes Susan Buckner and Chris Wallace made up a little song that the Krofftettes would sing in the water to pass the time, which Charkie Phillips wrote down and saved in a scrapbook:

"Krofftette Theme Song"
Words by Chris Wallace and Susan Buckner
(Based on the tune of "Consider Yourself"
by Lionel Bart from *Oliver!*)

Of all the Krofftettes, Dee Kaye had some of the most unforgettable experiences on the set. On her birthday in 1977 — Tuesday, January 18 — the swimmers were still at work long after midnight, filming one of their synchronized routines. Dee had brought a cake to share and they had been celebrating together between takes. She thought everything was fine until later when they finished for the night and she wasn't feeling well. "When you're swimming in a pool you don't realize that you are perspiring and they keep the pool water very warm. It has to be the same

```
          KROFFTETTE THEME SONG
CONSIDER YOURSELF A PROP
CONSIDER YOURSELF PART OF THE SCENARY
WE'VE TAKEN THIS JOB TO DANCE
IT'S CLEAR  WE NEVER WILL GET THE CHANCE
I'VE BEEN A RAG A BRUSH A BUBBLE AND A WIRE HEART
I GUESS I HAVE GOT MY START
I TOLD MY MOMMY AND MY DADDY WATCH ME ON T.V.
THEN THEY TOOK AWAY MY PART

CONSIDER YOUR ALL WET
CONSIDER YOU LOOK JUST LIKE A DROWNING RAT
WE'VE BEEN IN THIS POOL ALL DAY
DID ESTHER REALLY DO IT THIS WAY?
WE THOUGHT THIS WAS REALLY KEEN
TILL THE CLORINE AND VASALINE
MY HAIR IS GREEN MY EYES ARE RED
I'VE TURNED A PRUNE
I HOPE I'M A STAR .......REAL SOON
```

temperature as the soundstage because otherwise you see steam coming up. It's very tiring to swim like that and you may be perspiring and not know it," Dee says. She stumbled to her dressing room hut in her wet swimsuit and because she felt dizzy, she decided to lie down for a minute. "So I just covered myself and before I knew it, I must have fallen asleep," Dee recalls.

At that late hour everyone was in a big rush to get home and nobody realized she had been left behind passed out on the floor. Around four in the morning she woke up and the soundstage was completely dark. "I had birthday cake next to me that was all smashed because I was holding it in a box just to make sure that I didn't leave it there. They said don't leave food. It was very tight in the dressing rooms. I must have leaned on it. I woke up and said, 'Oh my gosh, it's so dark!' So I changed my clothes, because I was in this wet bathing suit, and I walked out onto the stage and I said, 'Hello? Hello?' and nobody was there," Dee says. She found her way to the door, but it was locked from the outside, and she couldn't get out. "It was four in the morning and we had a six or seven o'clock call, so I just waited. Then a guard came and said, 'You're so early!' and I said, 'I never left! I fell asleep and everybody just left me in this little cubicle!'"

A few weeks later, Dee broke her finger on the set. "We were changing our clothes and somebody opened the door. There were grips outside and someone screamed, 'Close the door!' because we were changing. It was such a tiny little room. We all started to move back, and I grabbed the door," Dee says. Someone slammed it and her finger got stuck in the hinge. Her finger started bleeding and began to swell, so the assistant director rushed Dee to the Emergency Room with just her bathrobe on. "It must have been two in the morning with gunshot wound victims, druggies, and I'm sitting there with a turban on, full makeup and a bathrobe with the assistant director! He waited with me and we finally went in to see the doctor and he said it's broken. He had to pull it, and it was very painful, and set it," Dee recalls. Dee was a trooper and continued to come to rehearsal every day but was not allowed back in the water for a week.

> It was four in the morning and we had a six or seven o'clock call, so I just waited. Then a guard came and said, "You're so early!" and I said, "I never left! I fell asleep and everybody just left me in this little cubicle!"
> — Dee Kaye

Another series of memorable incidents took place while filming the swimming for the opening number in episode five. Writer Mike Kagen remembers, "Sid loved balloons. He was nuts for balloons! Anything that involved less than 500 balloons he was not interested in. They had these machines that would blow up twenty at a time." Sid decided the swimmers were going to release these balloons underwater, and the balloons would float to the top and continue into the air. The production spent quite a bit of money setting up the underwater shot and lighting the pool. One thing they neglected to do was run a test to make sure it would actually work.

Assistant director Rick Locke recalls, "They spent all this time blowing up balloons and attaching them to the bottom of the pool. We had a bunch of divers under the water who were going to cut the strings and release them, and when the cue came they were going to let them go so some of the balloons would go down and some of them would come up. We hadn't thought it out too well. So when I cued the balloon drop the balloons came down, but nothing went up. The ones full of helium were stuck to the water because of surface tension. But when the balloons from the top hit the ones on the bottom they released the surface tension, so then a bunch of balloons went up. People were swimming around trying to knock the balloons to release the surface tension. It didn't work. The pool was a nightmare. Craziest thing you've ever seen."

It cost the Kroffts a fortune because they had to rerig the lighting and reshoot the shot faking it. When the balloons still wouldn't rise, the crew improvised and rigged balloons hanging down from the trapeze on fishing string. Charkie was slightly injured when she became entangled in the string during her dive, which can still be seen in the final print. "I caught myself on the way down and it made a razor burn all the way up my leg. It hurt bad!" she says.

Land Lovers

As if the swimming numbers weren't enough for the Krofftettes to deal with, they had responsibilities as dancers on land too, but they were happy to be out of the water. They were dressed in many ridiculous outfits throughout the production, including Krofft puppet characters, forest animals, hearts, sponges, waterfalls, music notes, and even bubbles. In a number entitled "Comedy Water Circus" Sid Krofft had the girls outfitted as circus clowns, and zooming down waterslides into the pool where they thrashed around as the Bradys cavorted in a row boat. Then in the same show, the girls were asked to tap-dance on roller skates with Donny and Marie Osmond. "The wheels didn't move," Susan Buckner says. "Again, there we are. Do you think we've ever done that before? No! But we had to do it, and we did it. I clearly remember bragging that I can tap on roller skates. I still have them to this day," she adds.

Dee Kaye recalls an odd number with Ann B. Davis featuring the familiar John Denver song "Thank God I'm a Country Boy." It included Dee as a farmer, Judy Susman as his wife, Susan Buckner as a farmer holding a pig (animated by her own arm), and Linda Hoxit as a Daisy Duke redneck. "I had to dance in this huge costume, and I could not see out of the mouth," Dee says. "I kept putting my head up and the director kept coming up and pushing it down. My eyes were where the mouth was, so for me to see out, the puppet appeared to have his head back. So I had to do the whole dance with my chin basically on my chest to make the puppet look like he was looking straight ahead. That was really uncomfortable and I'll never forget that!"

Linda Hoxit was one of the few who enjoyed being a puppet. "They tried some other people, but they got claustrophobic. I'd rather have that thing on than the bubbles or the headdresses because it didn't hurt. It was just kind of stuffy. I kind of had fun doing that," she says.

Charkie Phillips remembers being dressed as a wolf in a musical number with Tony Randall. She recalls, "I had a wolf mask on. I threw the thing off, I got so claustrophobic. We were moving pretty fast and I couldn't breathe! That was showbiz. They always put things on our heads." It was such a tight schedule for the dancers, and at times it was a miracle that they were able to make it through the chaos of a typical day at work. "We had to really pay attention, they didn't want us talking, or stepping off the stage. You always had to be in place," says Dee Kaye.

One number that seems to stand out in everyone's mind is the "Car Wash" production where Ann B., Maureen, Barry, Chris, and Rip Taylor performed the disco song at the "Emerald City Car Wash" as characters from *The Wizard of Oz*. The Krofftettes were Chris and Judy as "Rags," Robyn and Susan as "Brushes," Dee and Linda as "Bubbles," and Lynne and Charkie as "Water." While filming the segment, Charkie Phillips burst out in tears, but bravely continued with the dancing. "At the end, we took off our hats, the hat was digging into her head so tight that it was bleeding. Dancers are tough, they just keep going, but the hat was so huge. I'll never forget it. We took her hat off and there was a huge hole in her head from this cap, because it was heavy and digging into her head. She was on the verge of tears, but did the number anyway," recalls Dee Kaye.

"Sid really liked all of those headdresses," adds Linda Hoxit. Charkie Phillips says, "We'd have the pin curls all around our heads, and some kind of apparatus on, and anything you did as a dancer — your head hurt, your feet hurt, and most of the time you felt like crying, but, hey, the show goes on."

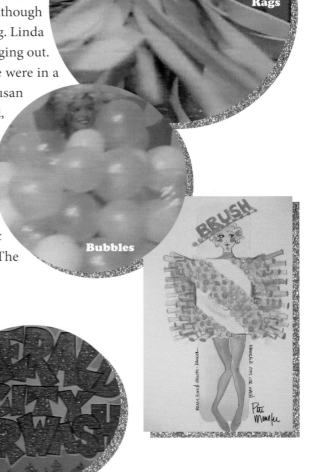

Through it all, the Krofftettes maintained a positive attitude and a sense of humor. That was evident one afternoon when a production delay allowed the girls some time to take a break out in the KTLA parking lot. They were preparing to film a skit with Charo entitled "Cindy Ella," in which they were playing dance hall girls in an Old West saloon. "We had on these frocks, weird costumes, and these weird wigs that were literally nailed to our heads — nailed!" says Susan Buckner. "They had to stay on, and they don't care how much pain you go through. They're not moving, because that means someone as petty as a dancer is going to ruin the whole shot and it's a big production, that's a big shot to ruin with your wig coming off." Although the wigs were on, a very important part of wardrobe was missing. Linda Hoxit recalls, "We didn't have trunks on and our butts were hanging out. We had tights, but they had forgotten to give us trunks, and we were in a holding pattern until they found us some trunks. Then Susan Buckner, she's so crazy, she got someone to take a picture and said, 'Let's moon now!' and we all said 'Okay,' and we're outside at KTLA in the sun. We thought we were pretty cool doing that."

Susan adds, "We were comfortable enough with each other that we had no problem mooning the camera. It wasn't really any attitude behind it, it was just a dare." Pictures speak a thousand words, and fortunately for *Brady Bunch* fans that classic image has survived and is presented for the very first time as 'The End' on the final page of this chapter.

Backstrokes

Looking back on being a Krofftette inspires a wide variety of reactions from the women who lived through the experience. At one point or another Linda Hoxit has been in touch with all of the dancers and has enjoyed many years of friendship. She attended the wedding of Robyn Blythe and continues to exchange letters with Chris Wallace and Susan Buckner. Dee Kaye and Lynne

Latham have remained close, and Lynne reports that Dee can still bring a room full of people to uncontrollable laughter with her birthday cake story from *The Brady Bunch Hour*. Charkie and Linda continued to be friends for a while as well. "I used to sing with Linda," Charkie says. "Linda's an alto, she has this little baby face and you would expect this higher voice. But she had this very low voice! It was so cute."

Judy Susman retired from show business and claims to have very few memories of working on *The Brady Bunch*. "It's funny, I called my daughter, who's over thirty now, and I told her I got the DVD. She said, 'Mom, I didn't even know you were in that!' I said, 'Oh, you must have.' She said, 'No, I don't remember you ever telling me about it.'"

Robyn Blythe is amused by her experience as a Krofftette but prefers to hear what the other dancers have been up to since the old days. "It is interesting to look at what we were doing then and what we're ending up doing now," Robyn says. "What a journey! Here I was a Krofftette and now I am a psychotherapist," she adds. Robyn's friend Mark Pirro recalls that when he purchased a DVD of *The Brady Bunch Variety Hour* from a local video store, he had no idea Robyn was in it. "I remember when I saw the show in the '70s it was bizarre and I hadn't seen it since then. I was watching it and later mentioned to Robyn that I had picked up some new DVDs, including the *Brady Bunch* and she said, 'You're kidding. Why would you get that?' I collect a lot of quirky films and she said, 'Well, you know I'm in that.' I said, 'What?!' She said, 'Yeah, I'm one of the dancing girls in there.' I watched it again, trying to identify which one she was, and it wasn't an easy thing to do."

"Things were corny back then," laughs Charkie Phillips. "But you know what? They were clean, it was wholesome. That's why people are still interested in the Bradys," she adds. Charkie notes that it was a different world during the 1970s and that the dancers were always excited to have work. "It was not as hard for me physically because I was a swimmer. But the other girls, they were taxed to the limit, they were awesome, they tried everything. I don't think anybody was a party pooper. They always seemed like they were trying

Charkie Phillips on the set

The Kroftettes hanging out with Cuban bandleader Xavier Cugat: (L to R) Dee, Charkie, Linda, Xavier, Robyn, Lynne, and Susan

really hard to me. People don't realize how hard it is. It's very hard."

Chris Wallace agrees that they all had a great time working together but she isn't so sure *The Brady Bunch Hour* best represents her long and noteworthy career as a dancer. "It was just kind of a hoot," she concludes. Dee Kaye adds, "It's such a cult thing now, *The Brady Bunch*, who knew? Nobody knew. I used to tell people I did *The Brady Bunch Variety Hour* and they'd say, 'What? What's that?' I think it's fabulous. I'm very proud, actually."

Charkie, Lynne, Dee, Chris, and Linda all worked again as synchronized swimmers in productions such as NBC's *The Big Show* (1980), with Miss Piggy in *The Great Muppet Caper* (1981), and *History of the World: Part I* (1981). "It was nice because *The Brady Bunch Hour* was a season, so it was a fairly long job and we ended up doing other things, mostly through Charkie, like the Muppets. That was a really fun gig, and that really all came from *The Brady Bunch*," says Lynne Latham. "I never would have spent that much time learning to swim if it hadn't been for that. That was a good experience. It really was a good experience," she adds.

Linda Hoxit eventually left Hollywood and moved home to Washington. "The feedback I got when I moved back up here and people would look at my resume to hire me, they'd see *The Brady Bunch Variety Hour* and they'd ask, 'Is that the one with the swimming?' and I said, 'Yes, I was one of the swimmers, the Krofftettes.' They said, 'Oh wow. That was the worst show we've ever seen.' They thought it was funny, they did, and that's why they liked it."

In spite of everything, the Krofftettes made history as television's first-ever synchronized water ballet troupe. The eight young women shared an incredible adventure together that only they can truly understand. "It was certainly unique. I loved being with the dancers, so there were always these friendships. There's nothing wrong with working with your friends," concludes Susan Buckner.

"The End"

The Krofftettes: Where Are They Now?

Charkie Phillips — Charkie Phillips is retired from show business and lives with her husband Dragan Marjanovic in the coastal area north of San Diego, California. She now spends her time as an artist, songwriter, singer, and plays guitar for worship at her church, Freedom Christian Fellowship, where Dragan is the pastor. They have two grown sons. Charkie and her sister Sheril still love to create synchronized swimming routines whenever they spend time together. Charkie's love of dance, diving, and swimming continues.

Christine Wallace — Chris still lives in the Los Angeles area and is the mother of two grown sons. She enjoys traveling the world and loves her hip-hop and salsa dance classes.

Susan Buckner — Susan Buckner currently lives in southern Florida and has two grown children, Adam and Samantha. While raising her family Susan was active in directing children's theater and devoted herself to being a mom. She also has been a dance instructor and a choreographer. Susan continues to be active with acting and travels frequently.

Linda Hoxit — Linda is retired from dancing, but still swims and has a pool at her home. She works full-time for John Robert Powers in Seattle, Washington, where she teaches and coaches all forms of acting, primarily television commercials. Linda also makes occasional appearances in local theatrical productions. She is a caregiver to her husband, a stroke survivor, and they reside in nearby Edmonds.

Judy Susman — Judy Susman now lives in Colorado where she is an esthetician and owns her own business, J.B. Skincare Face and Body. She is a skin-care consultant and massage therapist. Judy has a grown daughter and two grandchildren.

Lynne Latham — Lynne Latham is now an interior designer specializing in "green" architecture involving alternative building materials and energy systems. She purchased twenty-one acres of land in the Tehachapi Mountains that is now being developed by her company, Lynne Latham Sustainable Design, complete with a design studio, residence, and horse facilities. She also continues working in the fashion industry.

Dee Kaye — Darine "Dee" Klega is now a real estate agent for Coldwell Banker in Calabasas, California. She and her husband reside in the Los Angeles area and Dee continues with acting as a member of Brightside Corporate Improvisational Comedy.

Robyn Blythe — Robyn Blythe left show business in the early 1990s and went back to school to earn advanced degrees in psychology and social work. She now has a career as a clinical therapist in a rehabilitation facility for those struggling with substance abuse. Robyn and her husband, artist Doug Webb, reside in the Los Angeles area.

©1977 Krofft Pictures

Gotta Sing! Gotta Dance?

On the original *Brady Bunch* sitcom some of the most memorable moments were musical ones where the kids sang and danced for a local talent show, school play, or amateur contest. So the idea of having the Bradys sing was not a new idea, but on the *Variety Hour* much of the requirements for dancing were at a different level than any of them were used to — aside from Florence. In retrospect, Mike Lookinland admits, "The one thing I really

have trouble with is dancing. I'm even worse now than I was then. I just don't have that sense of timing and movement dance requires. I was hideously handicapped by dancing."

Every day the Brady cast attended two-hour dance rehearsals with Joe Cassini where he would choreograph, stage, and put together a whole finale or an entire musical number in less than a week. They would slowly build up a routine, but they barely knew everything by the time taping came. "When we started, a dance routine would take us four days to learn," said Robert Reed in 1977. "We were stiff, and sore, and awkward. After those early weeks, we began to get the hang of it, and now I can't get enough."[30]

Assistant choreographer Casey Cole looked at her job as a unique challenge. Her method was to water down dance techniques and combinations to the point where average people could learn them quickly. "From having the experience of teaching Fran Tarkenton and Kenny Stabler on *The Donny and Marie Show* how to do some dance steps — if you can teach NFL football players how to dance, you can teach anybody! I'm sorry, but it's true," Cole says. "I've taken beauty contestants who have trouble walking and talking, walking across the stage in high heels, to looking absolutely fabulous. The Bradys were so open and they were so grateful. Everyone was a trooper. When they felt they couldn't do it, I'd look at them and say, 'Yes you can, because I am modifying this to you, and I want you to be comfortable.' It was them on camera, not me. I would make sure that they looked good. You have to, they're the stars," she adds.

As a former dancer himself, director Jack Regas understood that a choreographer was perhaps the single most important person working on any musical production. "Joe Cassini and Florence Henderson got along very well and had a lot of laughs," Regas says. "The choreographer on a show, a star respects them more than a writer, or a director, or anyone,

**Stage manager Steve Dichter
and Marie Osmond**

because all stars think they can write better than the writers, and they know what they should be doing in the book portion of a show. But if you give any star a sheet of music and say to them, 'Stage a number,' they can't do it. They are really reliant on the choreographer, and therefore they don't give them a lot of trouble."

Because they shared the same production team, comparisons between *Donny and Marie* and *The Brady Bunch Hour* were inevitable. After a short period of time many people working on both shows recognized that something just wasn't connecting with the Bradys and the variety hour format. Stage manager Steve Dichter recalls, "When the Bradys came in, I don't know, you just get a feeling after a lot of years of doing these things that it's either going to work or it's not. We didn't see it happening because, in my own personal observation, the talent was okay, but there were just one or two folks that were outstanding. The rest were just doing the best they could."

Sid and Marty were hoping that lightning would strike again after the Osmonds. They employed the same basic format of skits and sketches with a bunch of big production numbers, and then hoped for a second winner. "That didn't happen," Dichter explains. "I'm not being unkind, but that's the way it was." Sid Krofft, on the other hand, felt completely different about *The Brady Bunch Hour* and believed the problems could be worked out. Sid says, "I just thought it would be a huge, huge hit. In today's standards it would be more than a big hit because the ratings were huge compared to what they are today even for *The Brady Bunch*. It was more camp than it was anything. I knew they couldn't sing and dance, I just thought people would take it as tongue-in-cheek."

> **Chris didn't know what he was doing. They'd hit the beat and he'd be half a step off, or a whole step off.**
> — Bonny Dore

Mike Lookinland and Chris Knight found the choreography to be a continual challenge. Writer Steve Bluestein explains, "The other two guys, Chris and Mike, were just sort of in the Robert Reed category, they were out there trying, they were out there doing everything they could." Chris Knight began to take it personally when he couldn't keep up with everyone else. Chris complains, "Joe Cassini couldn't stand someone who couldn't dance. It was very tough. He didn't get it. He didn't understand how someone did not dance." Bonny Dore remembers that the musical numbers could be quite difficult for Chris to learn. "When we had a run-through or rehearsal, Chris didn't know what he was doing. They'd hit the beat and he'd be half a step off, or a whole step off. They worked him to death."

The Bradys' former choreographer from 1972–74, Joe Seiter, had always known that the kids were somewhat lacking in dance expertise, but fortunately for him it was no longer his responsibility. While he was visiting with Donny Osmond on the KTLA lot he checked in with the Bradys to see how they were holding up on their new variety show. Susan Olsen recalls, "It was kind of funny, Seiter was always ribbing us, because we were terrible. He'd always infer we sucked and ask, 'Have you improved any?' No."

Not everyone in *The Brady Bunch Hour* cast was struggling with the dancing. Dore remembers that Barry Williams was an outstanding musician, and was the only one of the kids who had natural gifts in performing: "He was always charming, he was always ready. He was always nice. Barry was perfect. He was never a problem. He was a lot of fun in rehearsal, and he and Florence got along fabulously. He was picking up everything fast. He was watching Florence like a hawk to see what she was doing. He's very talented and could do a lot. I saw Barry get better very quickly by watching her. It was easy for him."

Maureen Mccormick adds, "I definitely think Barry was the most into it."

Dore believes that Barry's positive attitude and cheerful demeanor helped him cope with the pressure much better than his costars on the show. "He was bemused more than anything. I think he thought some of it was kind of silly, and some of it was kind of funny. He just didn't want to get in the line of fire. I don't blame him. It was a very wise choice on his part," Dore adds.

Rip Taylor fondly recalls that Barry Williams still carried a flame for Florence Henderson during the *Variety Hour* although now, as an adult, he had a different perspective about his feelings towards his television mother. "We all knew he liked Florence in more ways than one," Taylor laughs. "Barry had that eye for her, he did, and she knew it too. But how do you control that when you're growing up? He never forced anything that we knew of, but it was always: 'Can I get you anything Florence?' 'No, dear,'" he mimics.

©1976 American Broadcasting Companies, Inc.

(L to R) Lynne Latham, Linda Hoxit, Charkie Phillips, Joe Cassini, Chris Wallace, Judy Susman and Robyn Blythe (kneeling)

Bob and Flo go "Sunny Side Up"

Despite being professionally trained dancers, the Krofftettes were not immune from the pressure of a weekly variety show featuring a cast of primarily inexperienced performers. Linda Hoxit is the first to admit that they never really had to do any difficult choreography on *The Brady Bunch Hour* because the episodes were produced on a short time schedule and the Bradys posed limitations on what they could realistically accomplish. "If it was a TV special, you usually did harder dancing, but if it's weekly, every five days, you really didn't kill yourself because they didn't have time to teach us really hard things. It had to be fairly simple so we could get it clean, and get it all together on shoot day," she says.

Robyn Blythe and Susan Buckner remember that things were not always smooth sailing with choreographer Joe Cassini. On occasion he would get angry at them during rehearsals. "I wasn't Joe Cassini's favorite, he was always picking on me," Blythe reveals. At one time Blythe was considered one of the best dancers in Los Angeles because of her featured role in Alice Cooper's *Welcome to My Nightmare*. "Every dancer in L.A. showed up and I was the only one Alice Cooper picked. I'm just trying to say I wasn't a bad dancer for Joe to pick on. After a while he stopped, so I guess I got through the fire on that one!" she adds.

Susan Buckner recalls that during *The Brady Bunch Hour* she was going through a rebellious stage where she was bored of being in the chorus line, and weary of being told what to do. "Dancers aren't always well respected," she says. "It's kind of like, you — stay put, down, stay, wait, quiet. I was getting tired of being told to stay and sit, so I probably was a troublemaker. I was starting to resist. I was just kind of stubborn with Joe Cassini. Choreographers don't like a dancer who is tired of being told what to do," Buckner says.

Blythe believes that the main reason *The Brady Bunch Hour* was so exhausting and frustrating is because everyone had to do things over and over again to get it right for the cameras. "I think that's when Joe Cassini backed off on always riding Susan Buckner and me — because he had to concentrate that much more on them. He probably appreciated us more," she says.

If Cassini didn't like a dancer they would have known about

it immediately. "I never had a problem with dancers, and I never fired a dancer. I knew how hard it was, I knew how hard it was to get work. I always respected that. If I hired them, then I thought they were good. Your choreography is only as good as the dancers, so a choreographer is always going to try to get on the best side of the dancer. It's tough. When you have eight people and you try to do the same thing with everyone it's very hard. It's harder to be in the chorus than to be a soloist. There were many times when things got on my nerves, and I had to deal with Sid and Marty," he admits. "I was trying to please everybody."

Two Left Feet

Of all the Bradys, Bob Reed struggled the most with his singing and dancing ability, but he approached the challenge with intensity and determination. Bonny Dore says, "Trying

to teach Robert Reed to move was the single funniest thing in the world and of course it was just a disaster. I can still see him on the big staircase from the pilot episode. He was doing his best. Art Fisher is on the speaker yelling, 'What the hell are you doing, Bob?!' It was terrible. Then Bob would get pissed because he couldn't dance at all, he could barely walk down the stairs."

Marty Krofft had enormous respect for Bob and defends him, saying, "Robert Reed worked the hardest. He had trouble walking in rhythm so he had trouble dancing in rhythm, but Robert Reed worked harder than anyone." The cast and crew alike were inspired by Bob's passion but wondered why he wanted to put himself through that kind of embarrassment. "When I heard he agreed to do the *Variety Hour*, it surprised the hell out of me," is how creator Sherwood Schwartz tells it. "He hated *The Brady Bunch*. I think he thought he was just going to have fun on the show. He looked, I thought, ridiculous, trying to dance, but who knows what's inside the brain of an actor," Schwartz adds.

Some of the others who had known Bob for years had a few ideas as to why he wanted to be there so badly. "The reason that Bob did it is because he thought, 'You're kidding, someone's going to pay me to just goof around?'" explains Chris Knight. Writer Steve Bluestein was having similar thoughts. "We always used to think, 'How much money could they be paying him?' because, you know, he couldn't dance from here to there, couldn't sing, but he was out there giving it his all, and we really appreciated that. Florence, on the other hand, was a seasoned professional. She was a singer, she was a dancer. She could do everything. She picked up the slack and she was wonderful," Bluestein says. Rip Taylor adds, "He felt terribly clumsy, I believe, and he was clumsy. That's what made it so entertaining! He didn't do it on purpose, he was just not mobile."

After a few weeks of wrangling with the choreography Bob did make significant improvements, although he still did not look relaxed. Camera operator Ken Dahlquist wasn't sure how long Bob could continue in such circumstances. "He didn't look comfortable in the clothes he was wearing, or the things he was singing, or the things he was dancing. He just didn't seem comfortable. It is painful watching this poor guy having to do it over, and over, and over to get it right," Dahlquist says. ABC network programming executive Fred Silverman just couldn't believe that with Bob's illustrious resume he couldn't be taught to dance. "They were just disappointed because Florence was fabulous," recalls Bonny Dore. "I kept saying to everybody, you're forgetting that Bob was a dramatic actor, and Florence has been a song and dance girl since she was a child. It takes a lifetime to be good at this. Fred Silverman was throwing money at it, and they were trying to get him help. Fred would get frustrated and scream at me, 'Get him extra dance lessons!'"

Krofftette Linda Hoxit says she used to get the biggest kick out of watching Robert Reed during tapings, adding, "Oh wow, he was horrible! Everyone else would go right and he'd go left, some of it was pretty funny, and they had to go with it because the hours of the day were up, and they'd do whatever they could to get the best take of him." Wardrobe mistress Mari Grimaud recalls the clerk at the fabric store that they used for costumes would tease her about Robert Reed every time she came up to the counter. "He would laugh, because he would watch the show, and he'd say, 'Who makes that man drink cement?!' because he just couldn't move. Bob Reed was so gracious, so dignified. He was a serious actor…and then he got hooked up with *The Brady Bunch*," Grimaud says.

Falling in Love with Fake Jan

Everyone seemed pleased with how Geri Reischl flourished and excelled in her new role as Jan Brady. Her exceptional talent and charismatic personality quickly won over the hearts of cast and crew alike. From the point of view of assistant director Rick Locke, recasting the role of Jan really wasn't such a bad development. "It gave us an advantage because we could then go after someone who was more adept musically," he says. Costume designer Pete Menefee agrees that Geri was a welcome addition because she was a strong singer. "I don't know how well the original Jan would have sung, or if she could," Menefee recalls, "but this one sang very, very well, and they looked alike. It was like *Bewitched* — which Darrin are you looking at? It didn't seem to be a problem for anybody. She fit right in and was a terrific gal to work with."

The original Bradys easily accepted Geri, largely because she added a lot to their group as a performer. Mike Lookinland saw her presence as a business decision and wasn't bothered at all. "I was pretty free and easygoing about the whole thing. Who's playing Jan? You? Okay, great, let's be friends, and she was fine. Geri was a lot of fun. I didn't get too worked up about any of that," Mike says.

Robert Reed made a special point to make sure Geri felt welcome and accepted. Geri says, "I just remember Bob giving me a great big hug, and he told me, 'Welcome to our family,' and I remember him telling me it was like I'd always been a part of them, like I fit in, and I had always been a Brady. He made me feel very loved."

> **I just remember Bob giving me a great big hug, and he told me, "Welcome to our family."**
> — Geri Reischl

Barry Williams recognized the reality that, no matter how much they all liked her, the viewing public would have difficulty embracing Geri as Jan Brady. "Whereas they would have fully accepted her as Geri Reischl, she was playing a role, and the role wasn't made famous by her," Barry says. While Susan Olsen was hesitant when she first heard someone else would be playing Jan, she never thought of Geri as being a replacement for Eve. "We definitely missed Eve. I certainly missed her, because out of the cast Eve and Michael were my best friends. I never could grasp the idea of Geri being Jan, but she was the best fake Jan that could possibly be. Don't be fooled, Geri's little but she's mighty. You know, I really grew to respect her. Geri was the only Brady that was actually hired for talent," Susan says.

Geri Reischl's addition to the cast unexpectedly brought back haunting memories of Robbie Rist, who played cousin Oliver in the final six episodes of the original *Brady Bunch*. Ironically, in the script Oliver complained he was bad luck, which proved prophetic when the sitcom was cancelled shortly thereafter. "The sad thing is Robbie Rist — I'm the only Brady who loves him — when he joined our show he was a little spitfire and a pistol," Susan Olsen recalls. "When Geri came along, she was the complete opposite. She stood

back. Geri knew her place, she didn't want to overstep, and all we could do was try to encourage her to be herself and be with us more. There was nothing we could have ever disliked about Geri. Then her cute little weirdness started to come out, and we thought she was adorable. I know every guy on that set lusted after her. Barry and Chris were talking about Geri, and Barry said, 'Geri just exudes sex,' and I said, 'What?! My little Geri?' and Chris replied, 'She's one of the sexiest women I've ever seen.' Then I remember Mike Lookinland said something like, 'Geri? Oh yeah!' and wiggled his eyebrows, and I was like, 'Oh man, you're hot for her too?'" Susan adds.

Over three decades later, Geri maintains a healthy sense of humor about her lust appeal. "I probably would have let Barry or Chris have me. I would have lost my virginity to either one of them," she quips.

Geri did have an on-set romance with Jerry Ketchum, a young production assistant and "gofer" on *The Brady Bunch Hour*. Everyone thought they were cute because as a couple they became "Jerry and Geri." The Kroffts had Ketchum running around doing all kinds of random things, and if anyone needed something he would take care of it while they were on the set. Even though he was six years older than Geri, they shared an instant connection with one another and became inseparable. Geri recalls, "We'd hang out, joke around, and laugh. He was really nice. We ended up dating for about a year until I met my future husband, John. He asked me out while I was with Jerry, but I told John no three times because I'm so loyal. Then I said the heck with it, and went out with John, and broke up with Jerry over the phone, and I never saw him again. He was very upset, but I was married to John for thirty years."

Another Geri admirer was an independent agent and promoter who worked briefly on *The Brady Bunch Hour* but left to accept another job early in the production. During his short time on the set the two became friends, so he invited the country singer to appear on *Pop! Goes the Country* in Nashville at the Grand Ole Opry with Ralph Emery. Geri recalls, "My mom said yes, but made sure she went with me to do this job. He chose the song I was going to sing, and picked the dress I was going to wear, so we filmed that with Marty Robbins and Jody Miller." Geri's mother, Wanda, was less than comfortable about the trip because she felt the promoter had ulterior motives concerning her seventeen-year-old daughter. "He was constantly asking for Geri and I didn't like it. Marty Krofft warned me to be sure I never let him be alone with Geri when we went to Nashville. He took me aside and said, 'Now Mrs. Reischl, I know how you feel about Geri, and how you try to protect her, I just want to tell you don't let her go anywhere with him.' I said, 'Don't you worry, wherever she goes I go,'" Wanda says.

Not intimidated by his excessive attention, Geri became attracted to the much older man who was twenty years her senior. After they finished taping the show, the promoter asked Geri if she would like to go down to the restaurant at the hotel, have something to eat, and then go dancing. Geri recalls, "My mother wasn't too happy about us going off alone but I told her it would be okay. We went downstairs and after dinner we danced for a while. It got a little hot, so we decided to get some fresh air and stepped outside. We then went to his car in the parking lot at the hotel and got busy. I can only say it was a steamy make out session, with a lot of heavy petting, and a happy ending. After we had been there for an hour we then went back inside to the elevator where we made out some more. He pushed himself up against me in the elevator and touched all the right places…but in the end I left Nashville a virgin," Geri laughs. "It was perfectly fine with me. I wouldn't have done it if I didn't want to. I knew he had pursued me for a very long time, and I thought that was the perfect opportunity. My mom was pretty upset when I got back because I was very late, and then she asked me what was going on, and I said, 'Oh nothing, we just went dancing.' Everything was fine, and that was it."

Puffing Stuff

Behind the scenes, the writers were always in search of a coping mechanism to help them get through another week of writing scripts for the Bradys. Take-out food was common at the office, or Ronny Graham would entertain everyone by playing piano and singing songs. All the while, Bruce Vilanch would sit at his desk daydreaming about Donny Osmond. "For a while I shared an office with Bruce Vilanch who was in love with Donny Osmond," recalls Mike Kagan. "Whenever Donny Osmond walked past I had to keep Bruce from jumping out the window after him, and said, 'Bruce, if you go after him we're going to get kicked off the lot. Stay away from Donny!'"

Writers Steve Bluestein and Bruce Vilanch partying in 1977

Then there was marijuana. Drugs were not unusual in 1970s Hollywood, and few in the entertainment industry took much notice of them. Steve Bluestein recalls one afternoon when Carl Kleinschmitt asked Mike Kagan and him to go up to the office and finish the last scene of the script. "We were all basically of the same ilk," Bluestein says of Kagan. "Mike was smoking grass in his office twelve hours a day. So we went upstairs, and Mike says to me, 'Do you wanna smoke?' and I said, 'Sure, why not?' I've never had grass that good in my life! I was completely ripped, and then they needed me for rehearsal, so I went down to the set, and Jack Regas said, 'Look, Bobby's not here, just stand in for him and do his lines.' Milton Berle is on the set and Milton's first line is 'Hello, I'm Milton Berle,' and I was supposed to say, 'Hello, I'm Bobby,' but I said 'Hello, I'm Steve Bluestein, it's really a pleasure to meet you, I've been a fan for a long time!' He said, 'Look at this! I'm such a great actor the kid thinks I'm talking to him!' I lifted up my sunglasses, and looked over at Carl Kleinschmitt, who saw my eyes, suddenly realized what was going on, and fell off his chair he was laughing so hard," Bluestein says.

Assistant director Rick Locke recalls that pot use at KTLA was no secret. "Every time you'd walk past the writers' office you'd get a contact high. It would start early and go on until the wee hours. That was back in the days when pretty much everybody drank and used some kind of drug. Those of us who have survived it say that is a dumb way of living. If we found anybody drunk or using drugs I immediately got into it because the stage can be a dangerous place," Locke states.

Susan Olsen, Geri Reischl, and Mike Lookinland

Head writer Carl Kleinschmitt denies any of the writers were using marijuana. "I don't remember anyone smoking pot, there may have been a little cocaine use at the time, but I don't remember the pot business. I don't share that memory. There were plenty of drugs around, but what happens when you smoke pot is that you forget things, so what do I know?"

Susan Olsen was never involved with drug use on the set but admits to getting high with friends for the first time while *The Brady Bunch Hour* was in production. "Geri sent me an Easter card and on the inside she wrote, 'I would have sent you an Easter basket but somebody smoked all my grass.' I was like...she knows!" Susan exclaims.

Although Florence Henderson did not share the writers' affinity for smoking, she had a great sense of humor and loved to play along with their practical jokes. Steve Bluestein recalls, "We were all in the writers' room, it was on the ground level with four windows, and outside was a staircase that went to the second floor. The staircase went across and past one of the windows. Florence was walking up the stairs, looked in the room, saw all the writers there, and flashed us. I got hysterical! She didn't show her boobs, she showed us her tummy. It was so out of character for Mrs. Brady that I knew we were going to have a wonderful time together. The reason she's lasted so long is because people love her."

On top of everything else going on in the writers' office at KTLA, Steve Bluestein decided he was going to get a nose job. "My manager, Bill Sammeth, said to me, 'You really need to get your nose fixed.' My good friend Liz Tores, who's an actress, had done all the research and she said, 'I'm getting my nose fixed' and I said, 'Okay, good, I'm getting mine done too. We'll do it together.' I asked the doctor if it was going to be bad, and he said, 'No, you'll do it on a Wednesday and be back at work on Monday.' I said 'Fine,' I was that naive. I went in to Carl Kleinschmitt and I said, 'I won't be in on Wednesday, Thursday, Friday, is that okay?' and he said, 'Yeah, don't worry, we'll cover for you, what's the matter?' and I said, 'Oh, I'm having my nose fixed,' and he laughed because he thought I was joking," Bluestein says. On Monday, Bluestein had to have a friend drive him to the studio. He showed up for work with his face black and blue. He had told everyone in advance that he was going to have his nose fixed, and it was the big joke on the set. "I came in, because what was I hiding? I was just walking around, and across my forehead was a piece of bandage where I had penciled in 'Under Construction.' Florence, still, to this day, remembers it. In retrospect, it was insane when I think about actually working on a television show, and in the middle of the run having your nose fixed. It just shows how young I was at the time. I would never do it now. I figured I would just get my nose done and come to work."

Geri Reischl adds, "It was just hilarious. They were just so funny, you never knew what the writers were going do."

Elise Ganz, seen here work-ing with a student at Uni-versal, began her career as a studio teacher with shows such as *The Brady Bunch Variety Hour*

A Minor Concern

While the rest of the cast was working fourteen-hour days on *The Brady Bunch Hour*, Susan Olsen, Geri Reischl, and Mike Lookinland were all under the age of eighteen, and subject to child labor laws. They were limited to an eight-hour workday with three hours devoted exclusively to school on the set. Susan Olsen says, "This production did not know how to deal with minors and the minor labor laws. As a result we ended up having to be cut from a lot of numbers because we would be going home and they would still be rehearsing." Elise Ganz, who worked in the classroom with Susan, Michael, and Geri during several episodes of the *Variety Hour,* explains that the purpose of a studio teacher extends far beyond the classroom. "The role of a studio teacher is to teach and protect child actors from working overtime, anything that could be an affront to their morals, and even their life. They serve as the child's advocate."

Bonny Dore says that as the network representative she was always concerned with the hours the kids could work. "The teacher has the right to call it in if they feel we are working the kids too many hours. Sometimes the teachers were willing to be reasonable, and sometimes they weren't. There was a lot of trouble with the studio teachers. In a sitcom, the minors rehearse, then go back to school. When you can only have kids four hours a day, that includes rehearsal, and you've got so many of them on *The*

Studio teacher Peggy Cobb on the set of *The Love Boat* with child actor Jill Whelan

Mommies Dearest

People often speculate why the Bradys are rarely seen in scandalous situations of child stars gone bad. We didn't grow up to rob dry cleaners, sell drugs, or do porn. Even if you've heard rumors to that effect, they're not true. The credit here goes largely to our parents. None of us had those kinds of stage moms you read about. All of us had parents who were mindful of the fact that we were kids first and performers second. If a work situation were to compromise our happiness and well being, our parents stopped it. The almighty paycheck did not override their parenting sensibilities. On the set, they probably kept each other in check as well. I remember the first season of the original *Brady Bunch* had our six moms hanging out together in the tiniest dressing rooms imaginable. They all got along pretty well, in fact, amazingly well considering their cramped quarters.

That being said, there's still something a little strange about the whole practice of having a kid in the business, taking them on auditions,

Brady Bunch Hour, and they're so integral to the story, it's tough. In a variety show, they've got to dance, they've got to sing, they've got to rehearse, they've got to prerecord, and you're looking at your watch every two seconds to make sure you're not going over. It's really hard," Dore reiterates.

Producer Lee Miller explains that in order to get anything done, a production has to learn to live with a studio teacher, and must remain friends with them at all costs. "They have a job to do and the state laws are very strict," Miller says. "After a while you learn to interpret them so you know what you can and can't do. It scared the daylights out of me. The amount of time you're allowed to work a child is greatly reduced from the time you work an adult under the California State Law. So that meant we had to find ways to write things so that every kid could appear in every episode, and still find time to teach them the music and dance numbers. That was one of the great problems we had, we were always running out of time with the kids," Miller says. At the end of the day, the production frequently ended up with the director tugging on one arm and the teacher on the other.

Susan, Mike, and Geri went through numerous studio teachers during the six months they were in production on *The Brady Bunch Hour*. The teachers included Jeff Zandberg, Elise Ganz, and Peggy Cobb, all of whom came and went rather quickly. "It's like the family that can't keep a babysitter," observes Susan Olsen. Geri adds, "We also had a kind of weird, gross-looking guy who sat there picking scabs on his face that were bleeding."

Mike Lookinland's mother recalls that she almost pulled her son from the production because she felt the Kroffts were putting their personal interests ahead of her child's education. "Sid and Marty Krofft were really ornery. I had a bad experience with them. At the time, Michael was taking physics and chemistry, and they wouldn't hire another teacher. I said, 'We can't do this then. We can't do this if you don't hire another teacher because his education is the most important thing,' and they said, 'Well, you have to make sacrifices if you want your kid in this business.' My agent was with me in the meeting with them, and I said, 'Education is something we're not sacrificing.' So the next day they had the second teacher there, and it all worked out," Karen Lookinland remembers.

For a few days the Bradys ended up with one teacher they would never forget. Susan Olsen recalls, "This woman was just out to get whoever she could. Apparently she didn't want to teach anymore. She was brunette, and sort of not too slender. She would wear three support hose to try to hold herself in. But she was very pretty, and Rick Dees was our musical guest. Of course she took one look at him and said, 'I've got to have that!' because he was adorable." At the time Dees was a pop-star sensation with his chart-topping hit "Disco Duck." He was appearing on *The Brady Bunch Hour* to debut his new song "Dis-Gorilla" on a set complete with enormous ape-like arms swinging down in front of the Brady swimming pool. The studio teacher decided she was going to write Dees a song that she called "Funky Farm." Susan Olsen remembers what happened next. "Mike and I were on the set. We see her corner him. Poor Rick Dees kind of backed up against the wall with this woman flailing her arms about. We were at enough of a distance where we can't hear anything, but her back is to us, and all we can see is Rick Dees' face, and this woman is singing this whole song to him. He's just trying to be very polite, looking like 'Will somebody please shoot me?' or 'Get me out of here!' He's trying to make eye contact with us like, 'Help, help, get me away from this woman,' and we just sat there, and watched her do her little song for him, and never rescued him at all."

and taking them to work. I don't think it's wrong per se, but I don't think I could do it.

In the *Variety Hour* three of us "kids" were grown up enough that they didn't need the mothers on the set anymore. The size of the mothers' coffee klatch was cut in half. In addition to Eve Plumb being replaced by Geri Reischl, her mother, Flora Plumb, was replaced by Wanda Reischl in the dressing room. Wanda was, and is, another good example of a great mom. My mom and Karen Lookinland, Mike's mom, had been best friends for years. Now Karen was going through a divorce and had fallen in love with a new man. This made Karen scarcer, which drew Mom and Wanda closer; they became very good friends.

The thing that strikes me most is the difference between the relationships of my mom and me, and Geri and her mom. Geri just wasn't rebellious at all. She politely went along with everything her mother told her to do. I don't think that what her mother wanted was very different from

Dee Olsen

what Geri wanted. For me, I had spent my life being thought of as a character that I wasn't. My mother was very controlling, and kept me "in character" even when I wasn't working. I wore my hair in those darned pigtails even when we weren't filming — but that's the only thing I find fault with my mother for. I think it was very unhealthy to not let me be myself when I didn't have to be Cindy. Being on TV made the situation worse, but it would have been there anyway. My mother was very feminine and very into exteriors. How a person looked was, in my opinion, entirely too important to her. Because she dressed me, I looked like a very feminine, rather prissy, little girl. This was the type of girl I didn't like. I was a tomboy and if left to my own devices, a slob. My mother had a hard time with this, and we were always butting heads over it. I went along with her wishes but felt resentment, which I showed in how I spoke to her. I was always itching to break out and rebel, no wonder I was drawn to punk rock. But at the same time, I adored my mother and didn't really have the guts to rebel too much. This was a constant internal conflict that I'm afraid I didn't resolve until I was in my thirties.

I really believe that an essential part of our show's success was due to the fact that we were all kids that came from good homes. I believe Sherwood Schwartz made sure of that when he was casting us. I think the industry should take the time to audition the parents as well as the kids before hiring any child for a high-profile role like one has as a regular character in a TV series — but what a disappointment for the tabloids who feed on kid stars gone bad!

— Susan

Rick Dees remembers that moment all too well: "She went through the song demonstrating what sound each animal makes. I didn't want to become the Marlin Perkins of disco."

Many years later Mike Lookinland was surprised to see the same teacher on CNN's *Larry King Live* promoting a new book. Susan Olsen also recognized her on yet another show. "I saw her on *Phil Donahue* and the topic was 'How to have a successful affair with a married man,' and she was an expert at this topic," Susan says.

Finally a teacher arrived on the set of the *Variety Hour* who was a familiar face. Beth Clopton assisted the Brady's primary teacher, Frances Whitfield, starting in 1970. Clopton continued in that capacity for the remainder of the series until the last episode was filmed in December 1973. Susan Olsen explains, "Frances was less qualified to teach above elementary school, so a second teacher was hired to cover junior high and high school subjects." Mrs. Clopton, as she was called, was a legend in the entertainment industry, having worked as a studio teacher for over forty years. She began her career with classic series such as *Our Gang* and *The Dead End Kids* in the 1930s, and retired after working on *Eight Is Enough* and *Mork and Mindy* in the early 1980s.

Her son, Chuck Clopton, says, "I know that she heard from many of her studio pupils for years, including Joan Leslie whom she taught in the 1940s while she worked on films with Humphrey Bogart and James Cagney. I don't know whether it would be more accurate to say they were like mother–daughter or older sister–younger sister, but I suspect that if I'd had a sister she would have been named Joan."

Elise Ganz remembers Mrs. Clopton as a very sweet woman who took her job very seriously. "Beth and I were held up by two guys outside the original Screen Actors Guild building on Sunset. She ran down the street screaming, 'FIRE!' What a reaction!"

Ganz recalls. Geri Reischl says, "Beth Clopton was the strict one, she was an older lady. We couldn't talk that much in class. You would figure out which teachers would let you get away with stuff, or if they didn't care as long as you got your work done by the end of the day. When we were filming we would go back to class and get our three hours done."

When Mrs. Clopton arrived at KTLA she began imposing breaks involuntarily on the kids even if they weren't tired. Susan Olsen remembers, "All of a sudden Beth Clopton, God bless her, would show up with a chair and say, 'Come on, Susan, come sit down.' We thought it was ridiculous that the child labor laws were no different for a five-year-old than they were for a seventeen-year-old. The only differences were for babies."

Assistant stage manager Steve Dichter recalls a constant struggle between himself, head stage manager Sandy Prudden, and Mrs. Clopton. One of them would try to distract her when the clock started to tick down so she wouldn't pull the plug on everything. "She was sometimes forgiving if we were in the middle of a really complex number and needed just one more take. Hopefully nobody would blow something," Dichter says.

Studio teacher Beth Clopton first began working with the Brady kids in 1970 and returned for the *Variety Hour* in 1977

Beth Clopton's son, Chuck, explains that sometimes his mother earned a reputation as an intimidating figure among cast and crew. Chuck recalls visiting Paramount Studios in the mid-'70s where he had an interesting encounter with Henry Winkler, who played Fonzie on the ABC sitcom *Happy Days*. "I was standing off to one side trying to be inconspicuous and Henry walked up to me. He held out his hand and asked if I was 'Beth's son.' When I said that I was, he smiled and said, 'Your mom is one tough broad.' I later found out that Mom had shut down the set one day after several warnings to Henry about his language. She was strict, but she was as tough on herself as on others and was a very loving mother," Chuck explains.

Beth Clopton and her husband, Mort

Producer Lee Miller remembers that Mrs. Clopton made sure he knew she was in charge of the children. "We were shooting in the pool, and we weren't scheduled to come back to it for ten days, and Jack Regas said to me, 'I need one shot of Susan swimming the length of the pool into the camera, towards Rich Little.' It was two minutes until five, and we had to release the kids at five o'clock. I said, 'I'll go throw myself on the sword and see if I can convince the teacher,'" Miller says. "I went over to Beth Clopton and said, 'I've got a problem. We missed a shot. We had a camera problem, I need one shot. It will take five minutes. I explained to her what the shot was, and I said, 'She'll be out of here at five after five.' Mrs. Clopton said, 'Then who else is involved?' and I said, 'Just her, just Susan and one camera.' Mrs. Clopton replied, 'Okay, you can do it.' So we did it, and in fact we did it

Rich Little loses his memory after bumping heads in the pool with Cindy Brady

in three minutes because she did it on the first take. Three minutes after five, Jack looked at me and said, 'We got it, thank you.' We thanked the teacher, we went home, and the next day I received a fine from the state. I went to Mrs. Clopton and said, 'What's that for?' and she said, 'Well, you kept her four minutes past five o'clock.' I said, 'Wait a minute, didn't I come to you and ask you if I could do that?' and she said, 'Yes, and I said you could, and I gave you my permission, but you went past five o'clock so you were fined.' I just looked at her and walked away because there was no argument. I knew she was right, but I assumed that when she said we could do it that she would look the other way for five minutes. She was there. It wasn't like we were doing it behind her back," Miller says.

Susan Olsen adds, "I remember doing it quickly, and our moms talking about how Beth was getting out of control. She had the right to get us in trouble if we worked too many hours, but to give permission for something and still fine them, that's unfair."

Not only were the imposed breaks frustrating for the three young actors, but when they were available and in rehearsal they would often be just sitting around doing nothing. "There were plenty, plenty of times where Geri, Michael, and I would be sitting around saying, 'They could be using us now, they could be working with us now. But they're not! Instead they're blocking a number that we aren't in.' If they had really sat down and dealt with their schedule they wouldn't have had to cut us out of so many things. They just didn't know how to manage their time," Susan emphasizes.

Growing tired of the restrictions, and aggravated about being cut from musical numbers after learning the dance steps, the three kids and their parents hatched a plan. "We tried to pull a fast one," Susan confesses. "We would leave the set and say goodbye to Mrs. Clopton, and then we'd sneak back in the studio lot and go to rehearsal. Well, she stayed one evening, I guess she was suspicious, and she stayed, and she caught us, and threatened to have our work permits taken away. So we had to be good and play by the rules after that. It meant getting cut from more musical numbers," Susan concludes.

Geri adds, "It had to be Marty's idea for us to come back. He would do that every now and then. He'd say, 'Just come back and finish this taping, we've got to get these shots done, I've got to get them in today. We were running slow, so just come back in.' Sometimes the teacher would be gone and it didn't matter. Usually they were supposed to make sure we left, but not all of them did."

Ditching School

One afternoon Geri and Susan were walking back to the office where they went to school at KTLA when they decided to take a little detour. Geri recalls, "After lunch we just wouldn't go back. Michael went to class and he usually wasn't with us. Susan and I did most of the ditching. We were the bad ones and we would get in trouble." They turned the corner and ran into Chevy Chase. Having recently left *Saturday Night Live*, he was working on a television special at KTLA. Susan says, "For some reason I had a hold of Geri's hand and I think I squeezed it really hard. I was just like, 'Oh! Hello!' and he replied, 'What are you doing here?' and Geri said, 'Well, we're part of *The Brady Bunch*,' and started telling him what we were doing. She didn't know who he was." Chevy got to be friends with the two girls and invited them to visit his office. There they found Paul Shaffer, who played the piano while Geri sang and Chevy did the jitterbug with his secretary. "We would always measure our hands to their hands. Of course their hands were so much bigger than ours," Geri says.

> We would leave the set and say goodbye to Mrs. Clopton, and then we'd sneak back in the studio lot and go to rehearsal...she caught us, and threatened to have our work permits taken away.
> — Susan Olsen

Paul Shaffer recalls that during his time working for Chevy on the KTLA lot he and friend Tom Leopold constantly pulled pranks on everyone. "Also on the lot was *Liar's Club*, some short-lived quiz show. We interacted with them a lot too," Shaffer says. "One time the *Liar's Club* audience was coming in for a taping. Tom diverted the lines. 'Do you want to meet Chevy Chase, right through here, this way if you want to meet Chevy Chase!' The whole line turned and went right through our office, and forced Chevy to greet and shake hands with all of them. And then they went out the back door of our office and onto *Liar's Club*. These are the kinds of things we were doing," Shaffer says. Shaffer had already visited the Brady set on several occasions to watch the swimmers perform, so he got to know the kids. "They were worried about these numbers. In a very charming way they were worried about their performances, so I said, 'Well, hey, come on over and let's run the songs. I'll run the material with you and we'll have our own

little rehearsal.' We sang 'I Got the Music in Me,' which was going to be their song that week that they had to perform, and it was just a funny thing to do. We were very interested in the goings-on at *The Brady Bunch Hour*. We would always check in there every day and it made our job, Chevy's special, even more fun than it already was," Shaffer adds.

According to Susan, Chase was one of those comedians who couldn't stop being funny, and was seen walking around the KTLA lot carrying a fake hand. Susan says, "It was made of this really gross, gelatinous-feeling material. He'd have his hands in his pocket and he'd go to shake hands with somebody and give you this horribly gross hand. Of course I loved that. This hand, I asked to borrow it, we'd play catch with it. I decided to put it in the blender of the Brady kitchen set, just so I would have something, one little detail in the background to point out to my friends. Darn if some eagle-eyed grip didn't spot it and remove it before cameras rolled, 'Somebody remove…CUT… somebody remove the hand from the blender please.' Foiled again!"

Chevy Chase was also working at KTLA while *The Brady Bunch Variety Hour* was in production

Geri and Susan started to make regular visits to Chase's office and brought Mike Lookinland along, who also played the piano while they sang. Paul Shaffer explains, "We were having a lot of fun, that's all I can tell you. There certainly was an interaction and certainly a maternal relationship between our two shows. We were there all the time, and Chevy's working situation was loose enough that we could go over there, unlike the kids, who should have been in school. We didn't have to go to school."

The kids began to wonder how long they could get away with ditching class and when the studio teacher would find them. At the time, Geri was supposed to be working on her ceramics project. Finally her mother ended up having to do it for her so she wouldn't fail art. Geri says, "During my junior year I just happened to take art. All of my classes came from my high school and I had to do them at the studio. I took clay making, and had to make a clay box with a lid and an ashtray. I was horrible at art of any type and could never do anything right. I would try and try. It was hard because I didn't have the spinning wheel, and I didn't have a sink for water to make the clay moist and the right texture. My mom didn't want me to get a failing grade, so she just ended up doing my art project for me. She's very creative, and for the handle of the lid on the box she sculpted a little bird. I got a B on it I think. My teacher thought it was really good!"

When Geri happened to glance out the window of Chevy Chase's office she spotted their teacher below walking around everywhere looking for them. Susan recalls,

"I thought, 'This is so cool,' because that's the one thing you just don't ever get to do at the studio — you don't get to ditch class."

Geri adds, "My mother was looking for us also. She got really mad when she realized I was not in class, but it was fun." Wanda Reischl was very upset with the girls. "I really busted Geri, and threatened her on the way home several times about it. I told her, 'Geri, you cannot afford to just do that sort of thing.' I didn't want Geri to feel she had the privilege to do whatever Susan was doing. I felt that I had Geri trained enough to where she wouldn't go and do what she knew she shouldn't be doing. Dee Olsen and I had no idea what the girls were up to. When we left them after lunch, they were to go to school. They would head in that direction, and we would go in our direction. Evidently they didn't go back," she says.

Geri and Wanda Reischl

Wanda Reischl became concerned about Susan's defiant attitude, especially when she began arguing with Dee Olsen, who was trying to talk some sense into her daughter about ditching school. Wanda explains, "I was very shocked Susan talked to her mother the way that she did sometimes. I was not raised that way. I felt sorry for Dee because it was embarrassing for her. I was a little bit ashamed that Susan would talk that way because I loved her. All of Geri's friends would not talk to their parents that way. Susan was running around with some of the kids I was not used to seeing. Susan would invite some of her school friends to come visit the set, but they didn't dress the way that Geri's friends did back home. That's what made me worried there might be some influence there, and the fact that I had seen Susan talk back to her mother a lot. I felt like that was not an influence I wanted for Geri."

Susan agrees reluctantly, saying she trusts Wanda Reischl's memory. Susan recalls, "Remember, this is when I was starting to hang out with the stoners. I don't think they looked bad, and I don't remember really talking back to my mom. I remember, as do most of my friends, that my mother was rather controlling and was even cool enough to acknowledge that, but not change it. I suppose years of being told what to do by everybody took their toll, and I was a smart mouth. I find this a bit hard to believe since my recollection of my mom is as a very strict person who wouldn't stand for such things. It's possible that it's a matter of perspective. Geri was rather perfect, and agreed with pretty much everything Wanda said. I used to wonder if Geri would ever have her own voice, or were they just that much alike? Mom and I were very open with each other even in conflict. I suppose that, in comparison, I must have looked very unruly. Of course in my circle, I was considered the Goody Two-shoes who did everything her mother said. I would love to see hidden video of me then, especially as I am now dealing with how my son talks to me!"

Go With the Flo

Behind closed doors the Bradys finally began to show the first hints of cracking under pressure. Florence Henderson was losing patience with her costars, who floundered and lacked motivation with the musical numbers. Producer Lee Miller explains, "Florence is a perfectionist and a highly skilled performer. She wanted these kids to look good and she wanted them to sound good. She was very much concerned about how the kids appeared because they were loved universally out of the sitcom." Florence was stern with the kids because she didn't want them to appear sloppy. Miller adds, "She was a mother hen taking care of her brood. She was very professional and worked hard to make them look professional. For them to look bad was going to make her look bad."

The cast members were a little surprised when Florence began to snap at them in rehearsal even though they knew that she had their best interests at heart. Chris Knight has his own hypothesis on why she was feeling annoyed. "Florence performed very well, and the idiocy and the incompetence of all the people around her is like working with remedial talent. It's like a school production," he says. "Unfortunately she wasn't the star of this thing and she could so easily be upstaged by Bob not knowing what he was doing. It was a terrible compromise for her to be in. She's not used to being part of an ensemble, or part of a chorus. It was a very strange position. There was almost no gain for her in it," Chris adds.

Susan Olsen shares her costar's sentiment, "Florence would have been into it, but we were all taking a dump in her church. She's the one with the experience in this field and she's got to lug our sorry asses along with her."

In 1977, Florence Henderson told reporter Jean Lewis, "The kids have never done variety and they're just getting used to moving quickly…I'm pleased to give them any help I can, and there are times I find myself yelling 'pay attention — if you'd paid attention you wouldn't have missed that step again!' — as if they were my kids, and they take it because they understand! We have a very special relationship."[31]

Director Jack Regas recalls that Florence was outspoken in rehearsal. He explains, "She is a very disciplined person, and regardless of whatever you think of her when she was given a period of time to rehearse that is all she wanted to do. Her concentration was strictly at that. Florence had high expectations and definite ideas. She was very determined to do it her way. Because of our long relationship — we had done car commercials together years before — Florence would turn to me to ask if they looked good. She knew I was a choreographer before I became a director. Mainly it would be with her eyes, she'd look at me when they'd do something, she'd look over at me and raise her eyebrows. If I shook my head, or shrugged my shoulders, then Florence, she does have a mouth, said, 'Well, I don't think this is what we should be doing. This is not right for us.' That's the way it would go in the rehearsal hall."

Mike Lookinland, in particular, experienced considerable conflict with Florence as a result of his sporadic absences. It first began when the cast had time off: he skipped their dance classes to go on a skiing trip that his family had been planning for months. Mike intended to be at formal rehearsals when they resumed, but on the first day back he didn't show up. Florence was furious. Susan Olsen recalls, "Florence complained about that all during the rehearsal. I think maybe Mike just got there late, and when he walked in she said to him, 'I guess skiing is more important than being a star?' Mike kind of looked at me like, 'Yeah.' He might want to work, but he doesn't give a darn about fame. It was only an embarrassment for us. After Mike came back and learned the numbers, he asked, 'Why did Florence blow up at me? I learned everything, I'm not behind,'" Susan says.

Mike asserts than he was doing the best he could in an uncomfortable situation. "At least I showed up for work even though Florence Henderson complained about my attitude. I was there," he says.

On another occasion, Susan was late to a rehearsal because she was getting a facial. "Michael and I had bad acne and Florence said, 'Well, who cares what you look like if you don't know the dance numbers?' I'm like, 'I do,'" Susan recalls.

Writer Steve Bluestein saw the daily conflict from a different point of view, "Those kids needed a good kick in the pants. Florence was doing exactly what was needed at that moment. Kids think they can get away with things and no one's noticing. Florence let them know someone did notice."

Geri and Susan finally decided they were going to do something about Florence yelling at them during rehearsals. Defiantly, they went up to the producers' offices where they complained vehemently to the Kroffts. "I absolutely have a memory of Geri and me going to Marty and getting shot down," Susan recalls. Geri's mother Wanda says that she was furious when she found out what the girls had done. "I know that she and Susan both knew better than to go up there to complain about something. I really balled Geri out about that because Sid came to me and said, 'Mrs. Reischl, did you know that Geri and Susan had the nerve to go up to the office and complain?' Sid and Marty were really nice to me and I liked them. They knew I would get on Geri, and they wanted me to tell her you don't do that. They were complaining about what Florence had said to them. I told Geri, 'You don't do that. You just don't do that! You're just a child and whatever they say is what goes.' I could not imagine she and Susan had the nerve to do such a thing," Wanda Reischl exclaims.

Susan is amused as Florence makes an "adjustment" between takes

Ultimately all the hostility between Florence and the kids led to what Mike Lookinland firmly believes taught him one of the most important and personal lessons of his life. Mike recalls, "There was a number that the rehearsal time allotted to it didn't seem adequate. Florence arranged for all of us to come in early or during lunch to polish up this one number. I shrugged and didn't show up for that one rehearsal, which was an hour earlier than our regular call. At some point during that day, we were done with the day's work, I was going back to my car and Florence pinned me against the car in the parking lot. She cornered me, and said, 'Look, Mike, here's the deal… if your heart is not in this then neither should you be!' and she walked away. One of my problems was that I didn't want to be there, but it was a good lesson for me to learn that I am there, and I'm going to make the best of it, and do the best I can. It was very strong. She presented it to me very succinctly and pointedly. There was no misunderstanding. It was funny coming from my TV mother, a life lesson like that being handed to me from her, the consummate entertainment professional. She knew what she was talking about, and, you know what, she's right. She was right."

Florence's frustration with everyone had compromised her usually jovial demeanor. For the first time, she was actually starting to get testy. Susan Olsen says, "I remember that every now and then little flurries of dissing Eve would flare up. Mike said, 'She's not here, don't talk about her.' This was in a rehearsal, I said, 'Well, come on, let's get real, don't we all wish we, like Eve, had something better to do?' Florence shot me a look. I'm surprised I didn't turn into a pillar of salt! Probably it was that strong because in the back of her brain, she was thinking, 'Susan's probably right, this probably does suck.' It's strange to me because that is so not like Florence. I don't know if it was because we were doing music and that's her forte. Probably whatever suggestions she had were right. It was just a different side of her that I never saw before and I've never seen since."

Florence with Bonny Dore

ABC network representative Bonny Dore finally had to sit down with Florence to discuss her concerns. "I talked to her about it. Florence and I became very good friends. I liked Florence very much and I respected her. She was frustrated, and I said to her, 'You know, I appreciate that you're frustrated, but remember they don't have any training.' She said, 'I know, I know, I just want them to be better.' Florence was a total professional and when she was a kid you worked all night if you didn't get the steps right," Dore says.

The tension reached a boiling point when Bob Reed could no longer tolerate Florence nit-picking at the kids in rehearsal. He suddenly snapped. After some harsh words with Florence, he stormed out of the dance studio, slammed the door and left for the day, threatening to never come back. Wanda Reischl recalls that dramatic moment vividly, "Bob stuck up for the kids against Florence. Here she had lessons all her life and the kids hadn't, especially Susan and Michael. One day Bob really got mad. In fact, he threatened that that was the last time he would ever do another show with Florence, and if the show came back he wasn't going to do it again because of her. We could hear it through the door. Dee Olsen and I were sitting outside on a bench in the waiting room of the dance hall. You could hear Florence getting really mad about what they were doing and we had no idea which one she was yelling at. You could tell she was really bitching at them. Bob would then come out into the waiting room where we were sitting and be really irritated."

Susan Olsen recalls that day as well, "My mom said, 'That's how much he loves these kids, he walked out. He didn't like the way Florence was treating them.' But, it's understandable. We were on her turf."

Assistant choreographer Casey Cole recalls Bob and Florence fighting, but didn't take the situation too seriously. "I'd just look at Florence and say, 'Okay, she's stressed,' and just relax. If you mess up, you keep going, you keep pushing through it. You just keep smiling and enjoy it for the time you have the spotlight because someday it isn't going to be there. Florence was such a perfectionist, she thought this was a Broadway show, and she took it so seriously that it would make her nuts. You'd sit there and say, 'Oh, that's Florence, she'll get over it,'" Cole says. "Joe Cassini was the perfect antidote for Florence's temper because he knew exactly how to work with her. He knew how to settle her down and he knew what to say to calm her nerves," she adds.

Anxiety on the set trickled down to Marty Krofft when Florence decided she was going to stop the cameras during tapings because she couldn't see herself in the monitor or because she had made a misstep. She would hold up her hands and refuse to continue. Geri Reischl says, "I remember Florence getting upset when we'd film because the camera wouldn't be on her, or she would make a mistake, and we'd have to do it all over again. Marty would get mad, I heard him yell, 'There goes thousands of dollars!'"

Assistant director Rick Locke shared Marty's frustration. "Florence wanted it to look as good as it could look, and she knew when it didn't. She would stop things. If it's not good for Flo, it's not going to happen. What Florence didn't realize, or trust us to do, is that we would do multiple takes and if there was a misstep by Florence it wouldn't be in the final cut. Sometimes she would stop a take that was good for somebody and it had never been good for them before. Bob would get his steps right and then Florence would stop it, and he never got his steps right again, and we had to use a take that was inferior for him. That was frustrating for us. If she did that when we were on overtime it could cost the production thousands and thousands of dollars, especially if you're right at the edge of overtime. You have to regroup and figure out where you were, or if you can't do that then you have to go back to the top all over again. Then maybe you have to do it a couple more times to get it just as good as it was when she stopped it. Those are things that sometimes cast members don't get."

In an effort to reduce dance blunders during tapings, Casey Cole suggested that while shooting she would stand right beside the camera as the Brady cast was dancing so that they could watch and copy her movements. Then everyone would feel more secure, make fewer mistakes, and Florence would keep her cool. Stage manager Steve Dichter recalls, "Casey had to be looking downstage in the same position as them, she couldn't be facing them because then she'd be opposite, so she had to have her back to them. The Bradys absolutely had to have Casey there, which isn't unusual — I've seen this in other production shows — but she especially had to do it for *The Brady Bunch*."

©1976 American Broadcasting Companies

Here comes the Easter Brady...

What About Bob?

No one who knew Robert Reed would deny that he was a very complex man who lived life in the shadow of his public image. While there were many sides to Bob's personality, he remained a beloved father figure and friend to *The Brady Bunch* cast. "He couldn't care more about children, and young minds, and wanting to be respectful, and loving, and a good role model," says Susan. This may provide some explanation for why he could never walk away from the role of Mike Brady, and the undeniable emotional attachment he developed with his on-screen family.

Maureen McCormick clearly remembers how pleased Bob was to be a part of *The Brady Bunch Hour*. "The thing that shocks me most about the show is how much Bob was into it. He was on cloud nine," she says. "One day, as I stood next to Florence in rehearsal, I leaned in and asked how I could not have seen he was gay. Suddenly it was obvious. We joked that it was the first time any of us could remember him wanting to do something Brady-related. But he sang and danced without caring that he was lousy and the show itself was even worse," Maureen concludes.[32]

In retrospect, Susan Olsen wishes there could have been more opportunities for Bob to do broad comedy on *The Brady Bunch Hour* because that was something he truly enjoyed. "That Christopher Columbus sketch, Bob is having the time of his life. He loved doing the *Variety Hour,* which is amazing because he had been so miserable on *The Brady Bunch*. Now, here he is on this train wreck, and he's having the time of his life. He was like a pig in mud!" she exclaims.

Director Jack Regas also found Bob to be in good spirits on the set. "Robert Reed was a jewel. I really enjoyed him, and he worked so hard. As difficult a job as it was I believe he enjoyed having to learn to dance. It was a challenge. Now some may say he hated it, I say no, he enjoyed it." In a 1977 interview, Bob explained, "I'm not supposed to be any good. After all,

I'm a father. But I'll tell you one thing, I haven't had this much fun in a long time."[33]

But when the stage lights went down and the cameras were turned off, Bob would tend to gravitate into his own private world. Rip Taylor remembers him as distant, but never rude or unfriendly. "He would be in his little dressing room, and when they'd call, 'Bob…' 'Yes?' he'd come out, do it, and go back in, back in the cocoon. I always figured he was a loner, and that's fine, and he was, until you broke the ice. I think he was ill put-upon, but never said anything. He is from the old money, a little aloof at home, brought up that way. I don't know any of this to be true, but that's what I felt. I felt he was put-upon by having to do *The Brady Bunch Hour*. Tony Randall would say to me, 'You're given shit material, but you'll make it work.' I said, 'You're absolutely right.' I think that's what Bob went through, they gave him stuff he did not want to do, and after bitching so much he gave up because he wanted to perform and work," Taylor says.

As the variety series progressed, Bob got more frustrated. He improved, but then became anxious. Bonny Dore recalls, "Sid was very good at talking to him. When things got really rough we'd call for Sid. Bob was a professional. It was when the camera went off that there was a problem. When we got deeper into the show, and the ratings weren't good, and they were feeling that maybe this wasn't going to work, Bob would say, 'Why are you making me do this? Why are you making me dance so much? I can't do it.' It wasn't that he was wrong. I don't blame him. I understood. What are they going to do with him? I used to call it, 'What about Bob.' It wasn't Bob the person. It was the character of Mike Brady, and trying to transition him to a variety landscape. It was almost impossible. Florence wanted Bob to try harder. I said to her, 'He is trying…' She wanted this to work. This was a perfect vehicle for Florence. She had every reason to want it to work. I begged the powers that be, as we were developing the scripts, to pull Bob back a little bit and have him do more in the house. I suggested early on that they pull Bob out of the performing

Bob is attended to by hair and makeup crew on the *Variety Hour* set

part. He's at home, and it's Mom and the kids off to perform. I got shot down by the network. I was told he was to be in everything. My bosses and I didn't agree on it. He's Dad Brady. What were they going to do? Kill him?"

Florence Henderson believes that Bob was frustrated during the years they worked together by not having enough time to get a scene right or to master something correctly before cameras began to roll. "We didn't have the luxury of taking the time to really build the scene. But you're forced to make selections quickly and to make them effective. So, it becomes a tremendous challenge, and I think sometimes that's what would be some of the things that would make Bob just absolutely balk and have such a tough time," Florence has said.[34] To make matters worse, cast and crew alike were making fun of Bob behind his back and making jokes at his expense. "I always felt he was so uncomfortable in the rehearsals that it was unbearable for him. I always felt badly because people laughed so much. The crew would make a lot of comments about how he looked, in the control booth. I felt sorry for him," says director Jack Regas.

After taping would finish for the evening Bob could often be seen across the street from KTLA at a little bar called VJ's. Rick Locke recalls, "It was just outrageous. It was filthy, the floors were greasy. The pool table in the backroom, sometimes fights would break out in there. Stage manager Sandy Prudden was a big contributor to VJ's, and in those days I was too. You finish rehearsal, there might be a lot of traffic and you figure, 'I'll go have a beer and wait for traffic to die down.'" Steve Dichter would also sometimes stop in with the rest of the crew. "Robert Reed would be in there having one for the road and we would chat in general terms about the day's shooting. He was, I recall, not terribly negative. But I sensed he was not a happy guy. Robert was a little moody, sometimes, and not particularly thrilled with doing the job, but he did it. We would chat just briefly at the bar over there and he wouldn't complain particularly, just kind of shake his head. It just was my impression, 'What am I doing here,' you know, at that stage in his career when he wanted to do Shakespeare," Dichter says.

Susan Olsen insists that Bob never drank around the kids while they were growing up and kept that part of his life completely separate from work. "I never saw Bob having problems. Every now and then we'd go into a restaurant, and we would see he was at the bar getting hammered. He did not do that in front of us," she says.

One of Bob's happiest memories from *The Brady Bunch Hour* was dressing in drag as Carmen Miranda for a comedy skit with Milton Berle. The costume was unforgettable — a full-length gown with bright red sequins and saggy breasts that hung down to his waist. "I remember making the baggy tits for that dress. They were full of bird seed," says designer Pete Menefee. To top it off, Bob wore a basket of fruit on his head and hoop earrings.

Bruce Vilanch recalls, "He was just generally so uptight, but I guess when he actually had these moments he allowed himself to get free. I just remember he was in the actor's dilemma. He was playing the dad, he was handed this situation. The father of the Bradys on the old show would never have been in a situation like that. I think he was always conflicted because I'm sure if he had his way he would have done forty-five minutes in that dress." Susan Olsen recalls that Bob was having so much fun at that unique moment in time. "I just remember him pointing out the fact that the fake breasts on the dress were sand bags so he was kind of juggling them and flopping them around. Bob told me the fact that he wasn't very good at singing and dancing was how he used to play Mike Brady in a variety show. It's so funny because he refused to be in an episode of the original *Brady Bunch* where we all win a trip to Hollywood and we're in a pie fight. He refused to be in that because he did not want Father Brady to look silly. But he'll put a dress on?! He wasn't going to do anything Sherwood Schwartz asked him to do, but I think he liked Sid and Marty," she says.

Very few people at that time realized that Robert Reed was gay. Head writer Carl Kleinschmitt explains, "He was the most closeted guy you'd ever meet in your life. He was very nice, he was very sweet and he tried his damnedest to do stuff for which he had no talent. Here was a great dramatic actor who became famous for playing in a show I think he hated. Then he was asked to tromp around on a stage like a clown, and he did it all with extremely good humor and grace. His sexual orientation was of no interest to anyone."

J. Paul Higgins was a twenty-year-old production assistant on his very first job in Hollywood. He recalls feeling that Bob was paying extra attention to him on the set. "When I was hanging out in the audience bleachers, Bob came over and sat down next to me and started chatting in such a way that I knew he was trying to pick me up. He wasn't overt about it whatsoever, but I knew what he was doing at the time. It was well-known [on the set] that he was gay. I was just coming out at the time, I was still with girls. He must have picked up that I might be gay. It was just one of those things where I felt it and I'm sure I was right," Higgins asserts.

©1976 American Broadcasting Companies

People working on the set of *The Brady Bunch Hour* remember that cast members were not affected by Bob's orientation and it wasn't a concern. However, Florence was known to openly tease and ridicule him, which was not well-received. Costume designer Pete Menefee elaborates, "Anytime someone would compliment Florence on her clothes she'd reply, 'Oh, Bob would love to wear it.' I just didn't understand her. There's a time and a place for that, and you don't do it in front of a whole crew you don't know. I would never do that to anyone. It was always a reference to Bob trying the dress on. But they were very good friends, and they had a whole different relationship."

Alice Doesn't Live Here Anymore

Ann B. Davis also became unhappy and frustrated during *The Brady Bunch Hour*, so much so that even decades later her feelings about the show have not changed. Ann explains, "I will not talk about the *Variety Hour*. I loved the people, but it was an unmitigated disaster as far as I am concerned." Among the complaints was her disapproval of costar Rip Taylor. The two actors rarely spoke, and worked together only because they had to. Writer Mike Kagan says, "They didn't get along at all. Rip Taylor is a salty guy, he's got a dirty sense of humor and Ann B. Davis is a born-again Christian. She can quote chapter and verse from the Bible, and Rip Taylor is standing there cracking the dirtiest jokes you ever heard in your life. Those two were supposed to be some kind of love interest in the show? He couldn't be friends with her, there's no way."

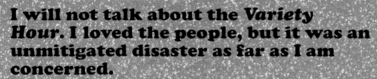

I will not talk about the *Variety Hour*. I loved the people, but it was an unmitigated disaster as far as I am concerned.
— Ann B. Davis

Geri Reischl recalls that Ann would distance herself from Rip Taylor the whole time they were working, as if she didn't want to be near him. "She would do the scenes and act like they were an item on the show, but afterwards she would go and be by herself and stay away. It was the buzz around the set that she didn't care for him that much. I don't think she was as crazy, nutty, wild, and goofy as Rip was, and she probably thought he was too much slapstick, too silly for her taste. I don't think she liked being paired with him or even letting people think on the show that they had a little romantic thing together," Geri says.

Bonny Dore emphasizes that Ann wasn't horrible about the situation and was very professional about it. Dore explains, "Following his lines or hitting his mark is not something that was as important to Rip. Rip is used to being Rip, he's more variety than sitcom. In a sitcom

Ann B. Davis with choreographer Joe Cassini

you write it, you rehearse it, you block it, and you shoot it. In variety there's a lot more looseness. Rip was more used to variety where he could just go. That didn't make Ann very happy. *The Brady Bunch* was a family, and they had been together for years, and they knew exactly how to make those scenes work. I think Ann was worried it was not the best it could be." Director Jack Regas also feels that Ann did her best with an uncomfortable set of circumstances, "As far as hate, I doubt she hated him. I don't think she respected him. He was a show-off and when he was around there wasn't much for her to do because it was always him."

Ann was inspired by her belief in God, and experienced a great feeling of fulfillment far more significant to her than anything she ever experienced in show business. The Kroffts had reached a compromise with Ann that allowed her to be on *The Brady Bunch* set only a few days each week while she commuted back and forth to Denver, Colorado, so she could also fulfill her responsibilities to the church. Bonny Dore says, "The network wanted her so badly that we agreed to it. Our joke was she could stroll on the stage, get her makeup done while she was walking in, look at the page once, and do it perfectly. She had been doing it for a long time. We didn't see her very much. Ann had a special deal where she could come in and out because we needed her presence on the show. She could hit her mark, and she wasn't doing the singing and dancing, it was just a vignette." Anyone that knew Ann couldn't help but admire and respect her firm commitment to what she believed in. "She always wore the same shirt every day embroidered with 'Jesus is Lord' on it," Susan Olsen recalls. "Usually she drives a little red sports car, she loves her bourbon. I'd have to say when she showed up for the *Variety Hour*, I was like, 'Oh no, she's joined a cult, she's a Moonie now,' but there was a light in her eyes that really hadn't been there before. Whatever she was doing, it worked for her," she adds.

Geri Reischl finds it unusual that during the entire six months of production she never once had a conversation with Ann B. Davis. "She was always off doing something else and she wasn't always on the set. She didn't have as big a part on the show as the rest of us did. She had to have introduced herself, but I don't remember sitting and talking to her. A lot of the time she just sat by herself."

Geri's mother, Wanda, remembers Ann was sometimes on edge and short-tempered on occasion. Ann was sitting behind them in the studio audience during a taping when she overheard chatter in the crowd about the character of Alice and suddenly lashed out at the unsuspecting fans. "Somebody's mother nearby us said she would have loved to have been an actress, but would rather do something like Ann does," Wanda Reischl explains. "Boy, it made Ann mad when she heard it. I didn't see anything wrong with what was said, she just meant she didn't want to be the big star, you know, to have to have the lines and everything. She knew that Ann was sitting back there. But Ann told her off, 'I want you to know it takes a lot more acting than you think it does to play my part. You couldn't play it!' The mother was really embarrassed. Whatever was said wasn't meant to be anything bad about Ann. That person was just saying that Alice would be the type of part they would like to play."

Ann B. Davis felt it was completely bizarre when Rip Taylor was cast as her love interest, and could not figure out why the Kroffts thought Alice would be interested in him. "I knew that she was uncomfortable with it, but she's a trooper," Susan Olsen says. "There's nothing at all subtle about the Kroffts, and there's nothing subtle about Rip. Rip was like an element — like Charles Nelson Reilly in *Lidsville* — Rip Taylor was the Krofft element in the show. Over the top, in your face," says Susan Olsen.

Rip Taylor explains that when he first met Ann B. Davis she barely said two words to him, and later rarely acknowledged his presence. He found her demeanor towards him not only unjustified and inexplicable, but also personally insulting. "We did the scenes… 'Cut'… and she'd walk. You couldn't get close to this woman no matter how hard you tried, that's all because she was looking for God, probably. I hope she's found him by now. I think she was very rude for no reason. I don't think I was a threat because she was on *The Brady Bunch* for years. I am trying to figure why a person would have to do that, to go out of their way to hurt somebody. Don't give me, 'I didn't know I was doing it.' I don't believe it. We're adults. I haven't seen her since, needless to say," Taylor says. He continues, "She was not friendly at all. I almost said to her, 'I didn't book me, they did.' I was really offended by it because I figured it was me. No, it wasn't, it was her, not letting anybody in, she owned the place, and that's fine. 'Go be in the corner and I won't come near your area.' I didn't say that, but I wanted to. The people on the set had dealt with it because they had to, and they probably broke the ice. I didn't have the patience. Eight weeks was enough to try and get in there, and I said, 'The hell with it. You don't have to play.'"

Best of Times, Worst of Times

Some who worked on *The Brady Bunch Hour* remember it as a time when unpleasant personal events came into their lives. An ominous tone began to set in when producer Toby Martin's two-year-old daughter drowned at home in his backyard swimming pool. Sid Krofft recalls, "It was devastating. That was before people put fences up around their swimming pools." Then Ann B. Davis lost her mother, Marguerite. "To Ann, the *Variety Hour* is not a very happy memory. She didn't enjoy working with Rip and she was going through a lot with her mom," Susan Olsen says.

Between takes, the exhaustion of cast members is revealed

Susan and her family didn't have it easy either. Her grandmother, Elsie, became terminally ill in December 1976 and because of rehearsals her mother, Dee, was not able to be at the hospital. Susan recalls, "It was terrible. These mothers spent so much time sitting in cars, reading, or going to coffee shops. Since my mom's mom was dying, she would sit in the car. My grandmother died around the time of the first show. It happened very suddenly. There's my poor mom just grieving, and having plenty of time to sit in the car and think how bad she feels, and we're doing our dance lessons."

In addition to her family problems, Susan had a broken toe and was called into the director's booth by Marty because he said she looked like she was in pain during the dance numbers. "I was in pain because I was dancing on a broken toe. Prior to working on the *Variety Hour*, I was engaged in a lifelong dream of being an equestrian. Shortly before we began production, I'd had an accident, a horse stepped on my foot, squashing my little toe like a ripe grape. I never liked that horse anyway, her name was Cherry Bomb. Marty wanted me to go to the doctor, which I did, but as my mother already knew, there's nothing you can do about it. The fun just goes on and on. I'm sure the disco music made the pain far worse."

There was other unhappiness on the set not directly known to everyone. Geri and Susan began to notice that Mike Lookinland's mother, Karen, was increasingly absent from the studio, and either Wanda Reischl or Dee Olsen was asked to be her son's guardian for the day. "We had a room that was ours at the studio," Wanda Reischl recalls. "That's where we mostly sat and stayed. If one of us was not there, we had to sign a paper giving another mother the responsibility of the child," she says. At that time it was Karen's younger son Todd, who had also started in show business, with whom she traveled. He went to Russia and was playing Elizabeth Taylor's son in *The Blue Bird*. What many did not know was that the Lookinland family was in turmoil at home.

Mike's parents, Paul and Karen, were going through a divorce and Karen was worried about being excommunicated from the Mormon Church. She had a lot going on in her personal life and on some days Mike drove himself to work. Wanda Reischl explains, "Karen was talking about getting a divorce, but Dee and I weren't sure that was going to happen or not. But she was telling us her problems. Paul, her husband, seemed to be crazy about her from what I could tell. I know it was a very unhappy time for Paul because he was in love with Karen, and he was trying to make her come back to him. Karen was very cute and had a real cute personality." Susan and her mother had known the Lookinland family for years and they were both confused by what was going on. Susan recalls, "Paul, Mike's father, came to the studio one day, and I just remember my mom being so sad, on the

Karen Lookinland and Dee Olsen

verge of tears. I said, 'Mom, what's wrong?' and she said, 'Oh Susan, did you see Paul?' I said, 'Yeah, I saw him.' She said, 'Well, you wouldn't see what I saw. I'm seeing a broken man. It's so hard for me because I've loved Karen all my life, we've been great friends. I understand it, but I can't get happy for her.'"

Brady Got Back

In yet another unexpected turn of events, Marty Krofft requested a meeting with Dee Olsen and delivered the startling news that Susan had to lose some weight. "I was big and fat, Marty's the one who went to my mom and said, 'Susan's overweight — do something

The Whole Tea Set

Costume fittings were always a very trying time for me. I was fighting my weight and I have literally been engaged in this battle all of my life. I have home movies of me at the age of three refusing an ice cream cone because I wanted to shed some ugly fat. Even then, I wanted to have thinner legs like my cousin, Bethany. How sick is that? I couldn't even say Bethany (I called her "Befunny"), but I knew she was superior to me because she was thin. My brother used to make fun of my chubbiness when I was eating, so I figured out that food had something to do with it, but I have never really figured out how to control

about it,'" Susan says. The order to get thin or get out came from network chief Fred Silverman who was very anxious about the show's future. Bonny Dore recalls, "There were four or five guys in the room, and it came up that they thought Susan was overweight. I defended her and said they were being too hard on Susan, plus she's fifteen and still growing. They said, 'Well, see if you can do something about that,' and I said, 'Like what? Lose ten pounds by Tuesday? What do you want her to do?' I was worried about it and told Marty, 'I really think hair, makeup, a little wardrobe, and it will be fine.'"

Director Jack Regas says the entertainment industry always felt that all of the girls had to look like fashion models. "It's sad. I remember Marty harping on the young one, that she was too chubby. It was not unusual for that to happen, not at all. They always claimed that television made girls look heavier anyhow, whether it be true or not," Regas says.

Concerns about weight were nothing new in Hollywood, but up until this time Susan had just been a cute little girl with no restrictions on what she could eat. It came as a bit of shock to be put on a diet by the network. Susan and Geri had already seen what Marie Osmond was going through trying to stay thin. Geri says, "I remember Marie pacing around backstage and always worrying about being overweight. She'd be walking around our set saying, 'Oh, I've got to lose weight.' I'd be getting my makeup on and I could see all she was eating was salad because she was trying to stay thin. I thought it was crazy. She was distressed and didn't like it at all."

Producer Lee Miller believed that there was no logical comparison between Susan Olsen and Marie Osmond, and that Fred Silverman might have had unrealistic expectations. "Marie, at the time, was the epitome of what the network wanted a young girl to look like. Susan was never going to look like that, she was just chubby. It's not her. The image of Marie Osmond was a musical performer. The image of Susan Olsen was as one of the Brady kids. They wanted to make Susan into Marie Osmond, and that's not going to happen. That's apples and oranges," Miller says.

Susan was suddenly lonely, depressed, and embarrassed about being the "big fat girl" in the *Brady Bunch* cast. "I was jealous of Maureen and Geri's bodies. I was jealous of Marie's body. Mom would say, 'See, Marie only eats salad.' That's why I was eating those salads at Denny's, but I was eating chef salads with blue cheese dressing. I could have had a burger and had fewer calories," Susan says.

Wanda Reischl explains that the situation became somewhat uncomfortable for everyone involved and that it did more harm than good: "I would get embarrassed for Dee and Susan because I would overhear Sid and Marty, they would say, 'The young one's definitely got to be getting some of that weight off, she's way too heavy.' Dee and I could hear it quite often, and I felt sure Susan had to be hearing it some too. I couldn't help but feel sorry."

Susan recalls that even at public appearances for the *Variety Hour* some fans would heckle her about her weight. "When Geri and I rode in the Pan American parade, I remember us walking past a couple of really good-looking guys, and the one guy said, 'Oh, they're cute!' and the other guy says, 'Yeah, but Susan's a bit chunky.' Then the other guy goes, 'Oh shit, I think she heard you.' I was like, 'Yep, I sure did.' They're just being guys, being pals, and they're checking out the girls," Susan says. "As much as I loved doing the *Variety Hour*, I was really embarrassed. I felt fat… and I wanted to be a rock star," she adds.

my profound love for eating. Food is still my kryptonite. Quitting smoking after twenty years of a pack a day habit was nothing compared to dieting.

At the time of the *Variety Hour*, I was five foot two and weighed 115 pounds. I was hardly fat but I was bigger than the other girls. I wanted to lose fifteen pounds and would have looked a lot better if I did. That was easier to wish for than to do. Even if I had gotten down to a hundred pounds I would still have been bigger than the others. Florence, Maureen, and Geri are wee folk. I felt like I was in *Gulliver's Travels*. I remember looking in the mirror and thinking, "This is impossible, even my head is way bigger than any of theirs."

So fittings were like weekly weigh-ins at Weight Watchers, my moment of truth, and another opportunity to feel crappy about myself. I definitely got firmer from all the dancing. There was no flab on me, but I didn't get any smaller. While costumes were always a source of fascination for me and should have been a fun experience, my physical self-loathing turned them into a nightmare. However, I must say that even if I had the perfect body (and in my eyes both Maureen McCormick and Geri Reischl did) the look in the mirror would still not have been much fun. With so many cast members our budget was limited, and the lion's share went towards the wardrobes of Florence and our guest stars.

Pete Menefee's creativity was evident in his ability to reconstruct items. For our opening numbers we had basic jumpsuits made in several colors, and often what had been appliquéd to one set of costumes was removed and replaced with more embellishments for "new" recycled attire. I loved seeing what our dancers were wearing each week, especially their swimsuits. They were so much more interesting than our costumes, but I dare say that ours were equally waterproof. I'm sure the fabric used had a similar molecular structure to that of the AstroTurf lawn in the original *Brady Bunch* backyard. How this fabric felt under the hot lights conjured fears of it actually melting and fusing to our skin. Asking anyone's body to look good in this stuff was an extreme request. No roll of fat or ripple of cellulite was concealed, nor was the anatomical correctness of our Brady males. I remember Robert Reed looking in a mirror and making a comment to Florence about the tight pants not leaving much to the imagination. Then he exclaimed, "You can see the whole tea set!" He went on to say this was a visual analogy that Noël Coward used. It is a visual analogy that will never leave my mind.

— Susan

Marcia, Marcia...Marcia?

The Brady Bunch Variety Hour marked a significant turning point in the life of Maureen McCormick. After surviving an unhappy childhood, she began to experience strong feelings of ambivalence for the character of Marcia Brady. Maureen desperately sought ways to remove herself from the pain of her real life, and the stigma of being known only as a character on television. For the first time she was living on her own terms, and fled suburban Woodland Hills for a new life of excitement in Los Angeles. Then Maureen had the misfortune of encountering recreational drugs. "I had a boyfriend and he introduced me to his group of friends, and they were drug dealers," Maureen remembers.[35]

According to writer Mike Kagan, Maureen didn't think the *Variety Hour* was going to go past two or three episodes. Of all the cast members, she was the one who wanted to be a serious actress, do films, and segue into that from the sitcom world. Kagan recalls, "As she was trying to launch that aspect of her career

Maureen in 1977 with boyfriend Chris Mancini

here comes her agent saying, 'Alright, it's Brady time. You're going to do an ABC variety show with a swimming pool, singing, and dancing.' It was not what she wanted to be doing. I think that was a contributing factor. She was less than enthusiastic about the whole thing."

Maureen says that the origins of her personal problems went back several years earlier to high school when she learned about bulimia from some of her friends. "It was really more peer pressure. I was with a bunch of girls, and we were eating a bunch of ice cream and a ton of cookies, and they said, hey, you know what you can do? And I was like, you're kidding me? I mean, I had no idea," Maureen explains.[36]

Chris Knight remembers that when they all got back together to begin work on *The Brady Bunch Variety Hour* Maureen had become someone he hardly knew. "Maureen was a pain in the ass. She had a drug problem. This was the first time I had actually seen that. She had changed quite a bit. It was 1976, and we were off the air in early 1974. Over those two years there was a ton of difference. Maureen would go to her dressing room, pull the star number and stuff. She wouldn't come out. There were rumors that she got into drugs, and apparently what was going on in her dressing room was that she wasn't ready to come out because she was still, sort of, in a drug stupor or something," Chris says.

Susan Olsen adds, "I was aware Maureen was on drugs, because I was just looking into them myself. I had my two friends come to the set — they were the girls who introduced me to smoking pot. They took one look at Maureen and said, 'Oh… she's all coked up.' They knew 'the look.' It's funny because they weren't really doing it, but they knew other people that did. It was sort of a little drug society they lived in that I got introduced to, which wasn't the seedy little thing it sounds like because it was more of an offshoot of the whole hippie era."

Others in the cast and crew weren't immediately aware of anything out of the ordinary, but as the show progressed Maureen's behavior became increasingly erratic. Geri

Maureen McCormick on the set — November 23, 1976

Reischl recalls, "Maureen was a little casual and felt like she could come in whenever she wanted, that 'I'm Marcia Brady, and they can't do anything to me' kind of thing. If she was on something you don't think clearly anyway so Maureen probably wasn't thinking rationally or she would have been at work every day because I know she has a strong work ethic. Most of the time she was there. In the beginning she would be late, but Marty let her know, 'Hey, you'd better straighten up, get here on time, and come to work every day, or you're out of here.' She just needed to be reminded, I guess."

The Brady kids had become somewhat cloistered during the *Variety Hour* with Barry and Chris hanging out with Maureen, while Geri, Mike, and Susan were usually off in another group with their studio teacher or parents. But Geri remembers that on some days Maureen barely spoke to anyone on the set: "We never knew for sure that she had a drug problem, but a lot of people assumed she did. Occasionally she appeared disoriented. You could see it in her eyes, like she was buzzed or something. But all of her performances were perfect. She would always remember her lines and her dance steps, and her singing. If she was on anything she hid it quite well."

Writer Bruce Vilanch believes that Maureen was experiencing a delayed teenage rebellion. He says, "She was going through her Lindsay Lohan and Britney Spears period, and she was lusting heavily after some of the guest stars on the show." Assistant director Rick Locke adds that Maureen was also flirting with members of the stage crew and letting them know she was interested in them. "I think being twenty had everything to do with it, and being very successful, and it was a high visibility show. That's a pretty heavy thing," Locke says.

One of the first real indications of a drug problem began when Maureen allegedly showed up to work with a lot of bruises on her legs. "I didn't see it at first, but Geri did," recalls Susan. "She said, 'Susan, Maureen has bruises all over her legs.' I remember her being bruised, and I couldn't figure out why," Susan adds.

Geri says that everybody began to notice them in rehearsals, "They would be on her legs, upper thighs, and lower parts of her legs, a few on her arms. We would just always wonder how she was getting those bruises? We knew she was coming in late to work, or not showing up, but we couldn't understand why she had the bruises on her." Wanda Reischl clearly remembers waiting hours sometimes for Maureen to show up. "It was from drugs. She was really messed up, and was definitely a user at that time. She had marks on her arms and legs. They were telling her if she dared to come in with any marks on her again that they would fire her. You could tell she was upset about it and was promising that she wouldn't," Wanda Reischl recalls.

Costume designer Pete Menefee explains that Maureen's erratic behavior sometimes made her unpleasant to work with, "You don't have to become best buddies with everybody. But of all of the kids she was the one that was kind of a problem. It wasn't too bad. You never know if somebody's having a bad day, or if they're really rotten on the set. You don't know what their problems are. Everything going on around them could be a terrible imposition."

Maureen recently admitted to using drugs such as cocaine and quaaludes in her 2008 memoir, *Here's The Story*. She also revealed that her problems became especially intense during the time of the *Variety Hour*. Maureen explains, "I did coke throughout those shows. It was the first time I'd showed up for work high. I never should have crossed that line, because once past it, I kept going. One day I showed up strung out after three straight days without sleeping."[37]

The wardrobe crew for *The Brady Bunch Hour* was one of the main victims of Maureen's anxiety during production. Wardrobe mistress Mari Grimaud recalls that Maureen

Maureen poses with a visitor backstage — March 29, 1977

had some mood swings that she thought were inexplicable, "I didn't know about drugs when I was twenty-seven, and so somebody had to explain to me, 'It's called cocaine.' Alright, now I get it. To my own self, she was never unpleasant. Maureen was just a little unpredictable. Sometimes we'd come for a fitting, and we couldn't get Maureen to stand up, and other times she'd be so cooperative and happy. That's why I talk about mood swings, so I thought, 'What is going on with her?'"

"It Was the '70s, Man"

That's what I find myself saying when it comes to talk of drug use having an influence on *The Brady Bunch Variety Hour*, and the whole decade in general. Certainly in Los Angeles drug use was fairly normal. I think that saying that you did cocaine in the '70s is no big admission. Drugs had yet to play themselves out. In time people would see all the great talents get literally wasted. Reliability and good work ethics would return to being in vogue, but for a while things were very loose as long as the job got done. While I had yet to really begin my tasting of all the mind-altering substances life had to offer, Maureen McCormick was obviously having a problem with substances.

Bear in mind that if Maureen had not revealed that she had a drug problem in her own book, I would not be talking about this at all. We Bradys are fiercely protective of each other. There's been a feeling of, "Wow, she got away with it, nobody has 'told on her' and we certainly won't." I'll admit that I'm glad she told on herself because it would be difficult to tell the story of the *Variety Hour* without including our trouble with Maureen.

As anyone who has had a family member with a substance problem knows, it's a tough road that goes from fear and compassion for the person to anger at them. This production had enough

When they all realized that somebody needed to stay on top of Maureen, Mari Grimaud appointed assistant costumer Donovan Sage to be her shadow. Sage recalls, "I was responsible for babysitting Maureen McCormick, corralling her, making sure she was where she was supposed to be, and in the right clothes. She was the one I dealt with. Maureen needed a full-time person to help her. Irene Soto was her personal assistant. She was certainly responsible and she had a handful. Irene was very, very professional. I was delegated to deal with the clothing end of it. Maureen was a piece of work. It was tremendously difficult. I think she was having some personal issues. Maureen was locking me out of her dressing room on a regular basis, and Irene took a lot of crap — a lot. I was responsible for getting her clothing in the dressing room, and getting it set up. I knew exactly what her changes were. She could be pleasant, but you never knew what you would be getting. I would ask Irene, 'Is the coast clear?' and she'd say either yes or no."

Mari Grimaud clearly remembers everyone's frustration with Maureen on shooting days when she became uncooperative, and their intense panic wondering what would happen if they could not get Maureen onto the stage in time. "There's always a big push right before tape rolls — 'Okay, is everybody ready?! Are the dressing rooms set?' Donovan rolled down the rack to set up Maureen's dressing room, and sometimes she wouldn't let anyone in, and she would have only a half hour to get it done. It was ridiculous," Mari says. However, Sage had a lot of compassion for Maureen and believes that her difficulty may have come from the fact that she was just not a happy person. "I truly do not think Maureen was happy. Thinking back on it, you just don't act that way if you are a happy person and not taking the situation into consideration as far as how you impact people by your actions. I think she was probably coupled with unhappiness and immaturity. There were a lot of meltdowns," Sage says.

Maureen was aware of the havoc her drug use was creating, but couldn't find a reason or a motivation to stop. "It got really bad. It was awful, it took over my life and it was an awful time. There were a lot of rock bottoms. But one was just knowing that if I was to go on, that I could die," Maureen says.[38]

In the beginning of the *Variety Hour,* the cast was patient with Maureen's unpredictable behavior because she had never caused any problems before. Also due to Eve Plumb's absence from the show they couldn't afford to lose another Brady, leaving them no other choice except to put up with the situation. Sid Krofft says, "How could we replace her? One was enough. She was a popular character and we needed to have her there." Krofftette Susan Buckner sensed that people weren't very happy with the choices Maureen was making, "She was quite the princess. But Maureen probably was always the princess, and was doing what she always does. She has always been such a star in the show." Both Sid and Marty remember that on more than one occasion they had to send someone in a car to go look for Maureen, and according to Marty one time he finally found her laying out at the beach. Sid explains, "We knew she was doing drugs. When she didn't show up we'd send a car for her. Someone would have to go pick her up and we'd be waiting on the set. She was a huge problem."

Maureen's lack of enthusiasm for *The Brady Bunch Hour* and her personal problems finally began to put her future as Marcia Brady in serious jeopardy. On Monday, March 7, 1977, Maureen was present for a morning run-through of episode five, with guest star Rich Little. That afternoon she prerecorded her vocals along with the rest of the

difficulties. Never knowing when or even if Maureen would show up for work added a lethal straw to the camel's back on a few occasions. While I now understand that hiding behind a fake persona of perfection was a protective measure Maureen took to shield herself from the pain of her real life, the result was a personality that seemed less than sincere. There were times when it was difficult to relate to her because it didn't seem like there was anyone real in there. Mo often seemed to have her head in the clouds so making her the brunt of practical jokes was so easy it could not be resisted. If Maureen seemed high on drugs or out of it, so what? She'd been acting that way since she was thirteen. Those of us who knew her found her phoniness less than becoming. I can't really say that we saw through Maureen because if we did, we might have seen what was going on inside her. I think her "Let them eat cake" attitude along with being blessed with an unfair amount of good looks and talent kept us from really looking.

So when we were all left waiting hours for her to show up for work during the *Variety Hour,* our reaction was less sympathetic than it would have been for somebody else. It just seemed like Maureen was getting away with not caring how much she put other people out. She gets away with it because she's beautiful, talented, and popular — Maureen, Maureen, Maureen! (Sorry, I had to.)

But there came a point where she could not get away with it. Finally Marty Krofft had had enough and he took a stand. Right in front of all of us, he let Maureen have it with both barrels. He gave her a tongue-lashing that was truly scary. Physically, Marty is a presence: big and tall with a booming voice. When Marty began his rant I think we all were in his corner. I know I was. How dare she? Who does she think she is? You tell her,

Marty! But then it was like watching an elephant stomp on a fly. It was frightening. When he was done yelling, I experienced a dichotomy of emotions I will never forget. Maureen looked wounded. Fighting tears, she looked to all of us. She looked at us with these gigantic, sad and beautiful eyes. I felt awful, I wanted to hug her. I know she wanted to be hugged. I know she wanted us to say, "It's okay, we still love you." She was looking for that from us, but we couldn't give it to her. Our hands were tied. Marty was right. He had given her what she deserved. To take away the sting of his verbal spanking would have disrespected him. It also would have done Maureen no good.

Still, it was a terrible feeling and I'll never get that image of her out of my head.

Unfortunately nobody was very savvy about drugs at the time. These were the days of indulgence; the days of interventions being fashionable were yet to come. After the Marty smackdown, Maureen always showed up to work. I think she was on time too. However, she often seemed high as a kite and sometimes refused to open her dressing room door.

Mo was also very into health food. This was common back then for drug abusers. I found it funny that these folks would get high, but never touch a head of lettuce that had pesticides on it. I assumed this practice was to make up for the damage they were doing to their bodies with drugs. I guess when you do enough coke to send an elephant into cardiac arrest, it might be a good idea to cut out caffeine.

One day we encountered Maureen in the parking lot at KTLA arriving to work on a happy high. She was hugging my mom, and loving the world, and saying how fabulous she felt. She went on about how amazing lecithin is, and how healthy

cast. Then on Tuesday, March 8, she failed to show up for taping and nobody had any idea where she was. When interviewed, Maureen reflects, "It was just a hard time in my life. I was in a bad relationship, so that was really, really difficult. It was a dark time, actually. Then I realized at a certain point how ridiculous the show was. This wasn't what I signed up for."

Bonny Dore recalls that Maureen became increasingly withdrawn, "She wasn't being difficult, but she wasn't helping out. I knew something was wrong but I couldn't be sure what it was. The week before, she wasn't happy. I could tell that, but it was hard to know what the problem was. There was so much going on. Things got worse, and things got worse, and one day she just didn't show up."

Maureen's absence was a major issue because the day she ditched was a very big shooting day for the production. All anyone could do was sit patiently. Susan Olsen says, "I remember us waiting around, and waiting around, and Florence was livid. It was a drag. You do get angry when you're waiting around and somebody hasn't shown up," Susan concludes.

Dore says they called Maureen repeatedly but there was no answer. "Marty then sent a driver to

During happier times: Mike, Susan, and Maureen in 1969

the house and while he was on his way there Maureen called in and said, 'I'm sick, I've got the flu,' and Marty went crazy. I was in the booth with him when we got the phone call that morning, and I thought he was going to have a complete meltdown right in front of me, and rightfully so, because we couldn't shoot. I remember that whole morning was a shut down. Sid and Marty couldn't handle that because it's very expensive. I had to call the network, and you have no idea when this happens what goes down because hundreds of thousands of dollars are in play. There are hundreds of people on the payroll. Remember — the Kroffts were financing the production. Any money that they spent above what the network gave them, it was their dime."

Sid Krofft explains it was cost prohibitive to have the crew sit there doing nothing, "I remember Maureen was a beautiful girl, but she had many problems and we knew there were drug problems. When Marty sees the cash register going he freaks out."

The Kroffts had no other choice but go on "insurance" when Maureen didn't show up for the taping. For an insurance claim to be approved Maureen was required to submit to an examination by the studio physician. Her personal physician had no jurisdiction over the matter. "There is a whole procedure when the show shuts down. It has to be guaranteed that indeed she is ill with what she says she is because then, and only then, does the insurance kick in. Marty was having a heart attack. I think Marty had his doubts about what was really wrong with Maureen," Dore says. The Kroffts had to go into motion immediately and everyone had to be notified. Marty had to get the studio physician to Maureen's home quickly to document her illness, and then the insurance

she felt now that she was taking it. She floated away, and I looked at my mom and sarcastically said, "Well there you have it, she's just on lecithin." Mom said, "She must be smoking it."

I'm sorry we didn't know any better. I'm even more sorry that when we reunited for the next Brady reunion (*The Brady Girls Get Married*, which led to *The Brady Brides*) Maureen was not any better, in fact she was worse. It's easy to feel guilty for not doing anything, but it's also so rare for doing anything to be of any help. I really doubt that any of us would have had that much influence on her then. All we could do was love her and protect her privacy.

I might also add with amazement that Maureen NEVER looked bad. Just like she never went through an awkward age, she went from being a beautiful baby to being a beautiful woman; she was also a beautiful coke addict. There is an inner glow to her; even drugs couldn't snuff it out. While I'm happy that Maureen survived substance abuse, I am mostly glad that she is letting down the act and able to be herself. She is comfortable in her own skin and in my eyes, she's never been prettier.

— Susan

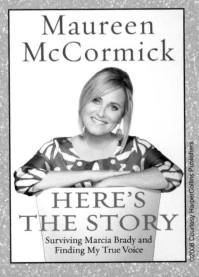

Maureen McCormick
HERE'S THE STORY
Surviving Marcia Brady and Finding My True Voice

©2008 Courtesy HarperCollins Publishers

company had to meet with the physician. Dore recalls, "I had to call the network, and it was a mess. It was very difficult and we were scrambling every minute because she's in everything. We were prepped for the day, and we had hundreds of people ready to hit their marks. They've been working all night to get ready for the day for the specific things in sequence. It's not that easy. It's not like a sitcom where you say, 'Well, we'll just shoot the kitchen.' It doesn't work like that. They were able to make a case for the insurance. It was by the skin of their teeth as I recall. Marty had to really hustle. I remember I was very, very worried because I thought if she doesn't show up today, will she show up tomorrow? If she's gone two or three days then we're done."

Marty decided to work around Maureen and do anything he could to salvage the day. Geri recalls, "We were waiting on the stage, but then Marty said, 'We can't sit around, so

let's just go.' He said, 'You do this, you do this,' and he delegated Maureen's part and her words to other people. We divided up her lines." Choreographer Joe Cassini was asked to restage the musical numbers without Maureen, and Susan Olsen was elected to take her place up front and lip-synch Maureen's vocal solos to the prerecorded soundtrack.

Cassini recalls, "I knew she was going through a lot. I understand it now. I remember it explicitly because I had to change things. They stood around in their costumes waiting for her for an hour or two, I think even more than that. More than once they asked me to figure out a way to do it without her. It didn't bother me, I was the one who could change things right on the spot. It was tough on the kids. I would plan the number, and when she didn't show up I'd have to change it."

Because Marty was not sure if Maureen would be back for the next day of taping, Geri Reischl was asked to cover her part in an upcoming comedy sketch and musical number. "I had to learn 'Ease on Down the Road' and everything else because Maureen wasn't showing up. I had to learn it like that, just the night before. That was tough, and then she showed up and I didn't have to do it, but I had to learn it anyways, and all the words, really quick," Geri complains.

The next morning, things were a little tense on the set. "We had enough pressure and we didn't need this. Everybody was working around the clock," says Bonny Dore. The Brady cast was in a dress rehearsal for the second day of taping when Maureen unexpectedly walked in. Everyone stopped what they were doing and just stood there, in complete silence, not knowing what to say. "It was uncomfortable and there were some crew members who were very annoyed, as well they should have been," Dore says. "They were staying up all night just to keep up. When Maureen came back, Marty was just beside himself. You have to understand, in those days Sid and Marty were the studio. They didn't have Warner Bros. backing them up, it was their company and they were paying for everything. The network sometimes gave you enough money and sometimes they didn't. They had debts to finance. It was their livelihood she was screwing with. She didn't stroll back into work, she was very nervous that day, because I was there. I had to be there, and it was very tense. She was trying to pretend everything was okay, but it was clear to me she was nervous."

Marty Krofft informed Dore he was going to confront Maureen about her behavior upon her return, and he requested that she be present to witness it and back him up. She declined. "It was inappropriate for me as the network to be there when he had his discussion with her. I said, 'I can't Marty, this has to be between you and your stars. If I'm involved it goes to a whole different level. You don't want me there.' But I heard all about it, of course. Marty really had to make Maureen understand this was neither a movie nor was it a sitcom. He was pretty scared because they were on the hook financially pretty deep. Everyone was gathering for the day… and I went out to get coffee," Dore says.

The room grew uncomfortably quiet as Marty made his entrance. Susan Olsen recalls, "Then Marty just reamed Maureen, and I don't blame him for doing it. He had every right to, and I'm sure he was hoping that he'd talk some sense into her. To me it was a pretty strong statement, and it was done loud enough for everyone to be aware of it. I think it was done with the intention to humiliate." After Marty stormed out, Maureen was left standing on the stage alone. According to Susan, she looked over at everyone trying to find a friendly face where there wasn't one. "Florence was furious and Bob was heartbroken. But none of us could break the silence. Looking at her green eyes full of tears just ate at me. You couldn't really go to her because she had made all of us mad. Poor Geri, she had to learn songs, she had to stay late, and to learn stuff, and cover for her. We all were completely put out by it, and we couldn't very well go, 'There, there, Maureen, it's okay,' because it wasn't okay. We all knew Marty was right. It was awful watching Marty rip her to shreds, and then Maureen looking at us all. That was our worst moment ever. That speech had to have hurt him, he's a dad. He was shaking, he was so mad," Susan says.

Looking back at that fateful moment in her life, Maureen is philosophical, "I remember it was harsh but I don't think he was being unfair because I had been out partying too much the night before. That was the beginning of the *Variety Hour* being unpleasant, definitely."

Bonny Dore had originally suggested to Marty Krofft that he reprimand Maureen in private, but he was afraid her "I can't do it" attitude would spread to the other cast members. "I didn't think he should have done it because Maureen freaked out, you have

no idea," Dore says. "No one had much sympathy for her because she had ruined the whole show, and they all knew something was wrong. We all knew. You don't want to accuse someone of using drugs unless you know for sure, and as a network person I couldn't even let those words out of my mouth unless I was 100 percent positive, but I wasn't. I knew she wasn't doing very well. She was pretty shaken by Marty getting mad at her. They had all signed up for the run of the show and there comes a moment where you have to say, 'everybody get on the boat and let's go.'"

Susan Olsen comments that considering the severity of Marty's outburst, she is shocked that Florence didn't yell at Maureen as well. "Florence is very intolerant of anything like that. She would chew Mike out for going on a skiing trip, but not Maureen for not showing up?" Susan ponders.

Costumer Donovan Sage adds that she never actually witnessed Maureen's alleged drug use. "Let me emphasize that nothing was ever done in front of me. I was never visually involved, and did not hear anything to that fact. But there was some strange behavior. I absolutely had some sympathy for Maureen. That can be an overwhelming scenario, being put in that position at the age that she was. As you can see, many of our young actresses, or actors, are going down the drain on a regular basis on *Entertainment Tonight*, or whatever horrific tabloid thing that is on television."

Susan Olsen says that at the time Maureen never wanted to discuss her problems nor did she seek any advice from her fellow cast members. "She never opened up to me, never. We knew obviously something was wrong. We speculated that it was drugs, but we were all kind of naive then, so we weren't that sure. It wasn't until 1980 when we were doing *The Brady Girls Get Married*, they were having all kinds of trouble again with Maureen not showing up, that Eve Plumb's mother Flora speculated it was either drugs or alcohol, or probably both. Eve would tell her mother what was going on, and how many hours they had waited for Maureen that day. She said one time Maureen kept everybody waiting on Christmas Eve."

Maureen McCormick continued to struggle with drug addiction until the early 1980s when she finally found the courage to overcome her demons. "I think what's helped me most in my life, is just I am really celebrating me, all of me, who I am. And, you know, I don't feel like hiding it anymore. This is who I am, and I think every person has to find that for themselves," Maureen says.[39] "My feet are squarely on the ground, that's for sure. I definitely feel like I've turned a page in my life, and that I'm doing good and positive things now. I think that once you're an addictive personality that you will always be one. So I think that you have to be careful," she adds.[40]

Bye Bye Bradys

The cast wrapped production on the final episode of *The Brady Bunch Hour* at KTLA on the evening of April 6, 1977. Although they completed the network's order for eight episodes the future of the show was still up in the air. "I suppose we should have believed we would be cancelled because the show stank so much, but I thought *Donny and Marie* was pretty bad too," says Susan. "Not because Donny and Marie stank, it was the show, but it was such a hit. So we had every reason to think ours might be a hit too. I sure got a lot of fan mail. I got, like, 3,000 letters at the KTLA mailroom. We were just taking our stuff home, and leaving after filming the last episode, and not all of them had aired yet. My guess is that we didn't know, but we had every reason to think it was going to be cancelled." The *Brady* cast was relieved to have the hard work behind them. They went to celebrate with a wrap party hosted at the Old Spaghetti Factory on Sunset Boulevard. There, everyone enjoyed one last time together drinking wine and eating oodles of pasta.

The Bradys celebrate the last day of shooting by throwing choreographer Joe Cassini into the swimming pool

Geri Reischl, however, was having other thoughts: "You know what I wanted to do in the worst way? I wanted to leave there with Chris Knight, go in his car somewhere, and make out. We were at that big, long table. We were eating our spaghetti and I thought, I swear to God, I could so go and do Chris right now!"

Susan adds, "Geri and I both got buzzed!"

The main challenge the Kroffts had faced throughout production was that ABC refused to give *The Brady Bunch Hour* a regular time slot. "I know when you change time slots it's bad. When you change weekly airings it's bad and the people can't find it. That was a problem," Marty says. After the pilot, ABC committed itself for eight shows, every fifth week, and then planned to take the show through the summer. Following the first two episodes, the network decided to give the Bradys a stronger test to see how well they would hold up in prime time as a weekly show on Mondays from 8 to 9 p.m.

Writer Bruce Vilanch recalls the frustration that they experienced. "It never really caught on because it wasn't there every week. They do those wheels because they couldn't decide what they wanted to put on. As a result, it never really developed any momentum. So, we kept doing them, and we never knew when they were going to air because they kept changing the schedule on us. We were having a good time and when it was over we had all these shows in the can, but they decided that they weren't going to pick up any more of them because the ratings on the ones they had aired were not that great. So everybody was sad and felt like we had kind of been screwed, that we really didn't have a chance. Of course, television was different in those days. It was just those three networks. We didn't feel like we got a fair shake. On the other hand, we weren't creating deathless art."

Bonny Dore says that Fred Silverman didn't believe in the show at all and that ABC was very disappointed by how things turned out. "They were screaming at me every week. I was the one who took the heat," she says. "I think they were so devastated by the pilot because it was so not what they thought they were getting. When it didn't happen right away, especially in those times — when there were only three networks and the competition was so fierce for every single eyeball — they were taken aback. They thought it was bulletproof, that it didn't matter what you did with the Bradys, it would work. It's not true. You have to do what the Bradys know how to do. I think we were pushed too hard and too fast. I certainly spoke up about that, whether anyone wanted to hear me or not. I felt that we needed more time to develop the show. Just about the time they were getting good at it they got cancelled. We should have taken a little more breathing space between the pilot and the series, and given the kids some real backup in terms of singing and dancing, because they were picking it up slowly, but then they did," Dore says.

The Kroffts were shooting one or two weeks ahead of the air date and they weren't happy when the numbers came in from Nielsen. "I recall there were some times they would come in with the ratings, Marty and Sid, and they would chat, and it wasn't good," Steve Dichter says. "So, Marty would even get more frustrated. They'd try more elaborate dance numbers, or more elaborate effects to try and juice it up a little."

Susan recalls that their episode with guest star Rich Little was given a suicide time slot against the Oscars telecast. "Maybe two people watched it. But nowadays you have shows that are hits that probably have no better ratings than we had," she says.

The official cancellation of *The Brady Bunch Hour* came on April 27, 1977, in an article from the *Los Angeles Times* announcing ABC's fall television schedule. ABC programming chief Fred Silverman stated that "The Brady Bunch Musical Hour" [sic] would be back as occasional specials next season. That call back never came. The Bradys were in good company however — other shows axed that day included classic series such as *The Bionic Woman* and *The Streets of San Francisco*. Ironically, the Bradys had been beat yet again by their old rival Redd Foxx, who also led them into cancellation back in 1974 when *The Brady Bunch* was trampled by *Sanford and Son* in the ratings. Even though it would last only a few episodes, it was his new show, *The Redd Foxx Comedy Hour*, which replaced *The Brady Bunch Hour* as ABC's newest variety series.

Nielsen Ratings for *The Brady Bunch Hour*

Date	Household Rating	Household Share	Household Projection (0,000)
November 28, 1976	21.6	31	1538
January 23, 1977	19.5	31	1388
February 27, 1977	15	23	1068
March 4, 1977	19.3	31	1374
March 21, 1977	18.5	29	1317
March 28, 1977	19.3	32	1374
April 4, 1977	16.2	25	1153
April 25, 1977	16.9	29	1203
May 25, 1977	11.3	24	805

Understanding the Nielsen Ratings System in 1977

Household Rating: A rating is a percent of the total universe, most commonly referred to as a percent of total television households. A rating is always quantifiable, assuming you know the universal estimate. For instance, the total number of households in the U.S. for the 1976–77 broadcast season is 73,100,000. Hence a household rating of 1 is equal to approximately 731,000. For example, for the pilot episode that aired November 28, 1976, the total number of households tuned in was 15,789,600 (21.6 x 731,000) or 21.6% of all households in the country.

Household Share: The term means the percent of households using televisions that are tuned in to a specific program or station at a specified time. A share does not immediately tie back to an actual number, because it is a percent of a constantly changing number of TV sets in use. Shares can be useful as a gauge of competitive standing. For example, for the pilot episode that aired November 28, 1976, 31% of all households watching television were tuned in to the show at any given time during the hour.

Courtesy Nielson Media Research

Most of the Brady cast was relieved by the news that they had been given the boot, although perhaps no one more than Chris Knight. "This was the incarceration that was way too long. It should have been axed earlier. The fact that it even got decent ratings once is amazing. At first the viewers were very curious and then after, when they were duly horrified, the ratings continued to drop off," he says.

Maureen couldn't have been happier, and exclaims, "I felt relieved, thrilled, and relieved! I had a feeling that it wasn't going to go on forever, definitely not."

Mike Lookinland's mother, Karen, adds, "I don't think there were any tears shed when it didn't go on."

However, others in the production, such as choreographer Joe Cassini, were bitterly disappointed by the news. "I thought it should have been picked up. It was very entertaining and it was the first of its kind. I thought it was as good as *Donny and Marie* or any other show," he says.

Geri Reischl was unhappy because she had so much fun working with the original Brady cast and made so many wonderful friends. "They just ended up saying that it wasn't

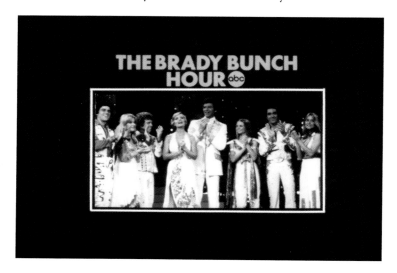

picked up, that we weren't going to be doing it anymore. I was sad about it," Geri admits. "I was sad because that's what I loved to do — the singing and the dancing. I loved that much more than the acting. I just loved to perform in front of anybody, anywhere, any time. That was really heartbreaking. Then I knew I wouldn't be seeing Susan and Mike, and you become like a family, and it becomes your life. You do it every day and that's all you do, and it changes your whole world. Of course I have my family and school to go back to, but I felt empty," Geri continues.

Geri explains that she was basically unaware of how *The Brady Bunch Hour* was faring in the ratings: "Being a kid, I didn't really see it because I was just going to work every day to have fun. That was my whole thing. I probably had a feeling, just because of the show, that it wasn't going to go a real long time. I was more concentrating on learning my lines, my dance steps, and my songs every day because we only had a couple of days to practice." Wanda Reischl adds, "They just happened to have one of those years where they had quite a few really good shows going. They had no place to put them. I wasn't really surprised when it didn't go forward. It would have had a better chance if it had more sitcom to the show rather than all singing and dancing."

Florence Henderson believes she was fortunate to work with some really terrific people on *The Brady Bunch Hour*. "I got to do a lot of wonderful musical numbers and so therefore I enjoyed it. But rehearsing with the kids sometimes could be really difficult because they weren't professional in that aspect of the business. But they worked very, very hard. We were asked to do some pretty unbelievable things. We didn't get picked up, which didn't surprise me."[41]

Assistant choreographer Casey Cole had known the end was near for several weeks when she didn't see anyone jumping around after the Nielsen numbers were released. "I would overhear conversations, like Jack Regas, all the guys out of the director's area, they would sit and they would talk about it. They would say, 'Oh maybe, oh maybe not,' 'Well, if we do this…' 'If we're not in competition with another show we might have a better shot at it,' and that sort of thing. You'd hear them talk about it," Cole remembers. She continues candidly, "You know what? I was so busy running back and forth, doing the show, and taking classes, looking for the next job that I didn't really put a whole lot of hope into it. Because for me, a job was a job, and at that time in my life I was taking every bit of pennies that I had and was putting them away in a bank to make sure I had myself protected on the next dry spell. You just never know. At least *Donny and Marie* had the same time slot."

Krofftette Susan Buckner was perfectly fine when the show ended. She went on to infamy, starring as Patty Simcox in the 1978 movie musical *Grease*. "I wasn't attaching my hopes and dreams on this show. I was just taking off. Right after that I started guest starring on television shows, and I was doing a lot of commercials. So, you get this attitude, this is so beneath me, and you have to, or you're not going to make it," Buckner says.

According to producer Lee Miller, musical variety shows are very fragile animals and don't survive well unless there is a central star towards whom the audience can gravitate. Miller explains, "Ensemble shows don't really catch the excitement of an audience. I was hired to make it work, not ask, 'Why are we doing this?' I think that some of the things the Kroffts did were very much off-the-wall and so far afield from the natural talents of these people that they had trouble keeping up. They were a gifted cast, these kids were very good. It was a stunt show, in the sense that when you take someone who's never been on a trapeze before and you put them on a trapeze, that's a stunt. It's a stunt designed to make the audience tune in. To say, 'Okay, guys, tomorrow you're singers and dancers, you're going to wear different costumes. And to have to look, act, and feel differently was a stress on some of these kids. I thought they did a heroic job. It's one thing to take a kid who desperately wants to sing and dance, and make them into a dancer. It's another to take a kid who never, in their wildest dreams, thought they were going to be singing and dancing. Suddenly, a whole lot was demanded and expected of them in areas where they had no experience and no background," Miller emphasizes. "In the end they absolutely did get it. I think that it was a growing thing, and if ABC had stuck with the show they would have surprised a lot of people."

Bonny Dore feels strongly that it would be unjust to suggest *The Brady Bunch Hour* was mismanaged. "Marty and Lee were as sophisticated and experienced in doing variety as anyone on earth. So that would be unfair. It was a collision. I really think the network expected too much out of the kids too quickly. Their attitude was, they're talented, they'll figure it out. No, they won't, it takes time and experience. In their heads, Michael Eisner and Fred Silverman were thinking that *The Brady Bunch* could be converted into *Donny and Marie*, 'How tough can it be?' You just can't, it's not possible. Not even Sid and Marty could do it, and they came darn close. You can't take thirty-five years of Florence's experience and tell Susan Olsen to learn it in a week. You can't do that. We almost got there, but it was too late."

The Bradys say "goodbye" for now

THE BRADY BUNCH HOUR

TONY RANDALL

DONNY AND MARIE

LEE MAJORS

FARRAH FAWCETT-MAJORS

KAPTAIN KOOL AND THE KONGS

MILTON BERLE

TINA TURNER

VINCENT PRICE

H. R. PUFNSTUF

KIKI BIRD

CHARO

THE HUDSON BROTHERS

EDGAR BERGEN

MELANIE

RICH LITTLE

REDD FOXX

OHIO PLAYERS

ROBERT HEGYES

RICK DEES

PATTY MALONEY

"WHAT'S HAPPENING" KIDS

LYNN ANDERSON

PAUL WILLIAMS

Tony Randall

Birth: February 20, 1920, in Tulsa, Oklahoma

Death: May 17, 2004, buried at Westchester Hills Cemetery in Hastings-on-Hudson, New York

Brady Bunch Variety Hour Guest Star: November 28, 1976

Career Highlights:

- Tony Randall served in the United States Army Signal Corps during the Second World War.
- Randall made his television debut as the gym teacher Harvey Weskitt in *Mister Peepers* (1952–1955).
- He starred on Broadway in *Inherit the Wind* (1955).
- His films include *Will Success Spoil Rock Hunter?* (1957), *Pillow Talk* (1959), *Let's Make Love* (1960), and *Boys' Night Out* (1962). He also played the title roles in the cult classic *7 Faces of Dr. Lao* (1964).
- He returned to television in 1970 as Felix Unger in *The Odd Couple*, opposite Jack Klugman. The show ran successfully for five years. He also starred in *The Tony Randall Show* and *Love, Sidney* during the 1980s.
- Randall was nominated for five Golden Globe Awards and two Emmys, winning one Emmy in 1975 for *The Odd Couple*. He also received an honorary degree, Doctor of Fine Arts, from Pace University in 2003.

Memories from *The Brady Bunch Variety Hour:*

"Tony Randall was great, I love Tony. He was one of the few showbiz 'professionals.' He didn't cause any problems, just a real pro, just like Milton Berle, another pro. Sometimes you get stars that demand so many things, and they actually end up not having that much talent when they act that way." — Sid Krofft

"Tony Randall was a serious, Shakespearean type guy that would stick right to the script and wouldn't sway one way or another." — Casey Cole, choreographer

Donny and Marie Osmond

Birth: **Donny** — December 9, 1957; **Marie** — October 13, 1959, both in Ogden, Utah

Brady Bunch Variety Hour Guest Star: November 28, 1976

Career Highlights — Donny:

● Donny Osmond became a teen idol in the early 1970s with his trademark song, "Puppy Love," which propelled him into international fame.

● From 1976–1979 he starred in his own variety show on ABC with sister Marie.

● In 1989 he appeared once again on the pop charts with the songs "Soldier Of Love" and "Sacred Emotion."

● He starred on Broadway in *Joseph and the Amazing Technicolor Dreamcoat* for over 2,000 performances.

● He reunited in 1998 with sister Marie for their own syndicated talk show.

Career Highlights — Marie:

● In 1973, at the age of thirteen, she gained success with her country pop ballad "Paper Roses."

● She teamed up with her brother Donny in 1976 to become one of the youngest performers to ever host their own network variety show.

● Her other country music hits are "Meet Me in Montana," "There's No Stopping Your Heart," and "Read My Lips."

● Along with actor John Schneider, Marie is the co-founder of the Children's Miracle Network.

● Onstage she garnered rave reviews in *The King and I* (as Anna) and *The Sound of Music* (as Maria).

● Marie also portrayed her mother, Olive, in the TV movie *Side By Side: The True Story Of The Osmond Family,* and starred in two additional telefilms, *The Gift of Love* and *I Married Wyatt Earp.*

● She has also started her own successful doll company called Marie Osmond Fine Porcelain Collection Dolls. She was recently a judge on the short-lived television show *Celebrity Duets* and she competed on *Dancing with the Stars.*

Memories from *The Brady Bunch Variety Hour:*
"They were wonderful, and they were the best of the Osmonds. There was always that religious thing where you had to be careful about what you said or what you talked about in hearing distance of them. It was wonderful to have them there because they knew everybody. The Bradys might have not been as comfortable because they were overshadowing them."
— Steve Dichter, stage manager

"Donny would get thrown in the pool regularly. It would be his production staff. All of the sudden around the corner here'd come some people carrying Donny. They brought him in on the first day. He'd be laughing, pretending to protest. Now, he's such a sweet guy… always good natured, always fun to run into him… so hard to believe he and Marie would think we're all going to hell." — Susan Olsen

Lee Majors and Farrah Fawcett

Lee — Birth: April 23, 1939, in Wyandotte, Michigan;
Farrah — Birth: February 2, 1947, in Corpus Cristi, Texas
Death: June 25, 2009, in Santa Monica, California

Brady Bunch Variety Hour Guest Star: January 23, 1977

Career Highlights — Lee:
● While growing up in Kentucky he excelled in sports from track to football at Middlesboro High School.
● At the age of twenty-five, Majors won his first role in the film *Strait-Jacket* (1964), starring Joan Crawford.
● His television roles include Heath Barkley on *The Big Valley* (1965), to *The Virginian* (1970–1971), to *Owen Marshall Counselor At Law* (1971), to *The Fall Guy* (1981–1986), and *Raven* (1992–1993). It was through his starring role as Steve Austin on the overwhelmingly popular *The Six Million Dollar Man* (1974–1978) that Majors became an icon and a part of the American culture.

- In recent years he has appeared on television shows such as *Will and Grace* and *Son of the Beach.*
- Majors received critical acclaim for his understated yet riveting performance in the short film *Here* (2001).

Career Highlights — Farrah Fawcett:
- She attended the University of Texas.
- In 1976, Fawcett played the character of Jill Munroe for one season on *Charlie's Angels.* That same year, her swimsuit poster sold a record 12 million copies.
- Fawcett achieved critical praise and her first of three Emmy Award nominations for her role as a battered wife in the 1984 television movie *The Burning Bed.* She also won acclaim in the stage and movie version of *Extremities* (1986), and the miniseries *Small Sacrifices* (1989), receiving a second Emmy nomination. Her third Emmy nomination came in 2004 for her work in *The Guardian.*
- She caused a major stir by posing nude in the December 1995 issue of *Playboy*, with over 4 million copies sold worldwide. She later posed for the July 1997 issue, which also became a top seller.
- Her May 15, 2009 documentary *Farrah's Story*, about her battle against cancer, was seen by over 9 million viewers.

Memories from *The Brady Bunch Variety Hour:*
"They were huge at that time. That's for ratings, you know you're going to go five points higher. That's why you have those guest stars, just to push your ratings up. It was great, I remember there was no problem. The two of them were huge, and they liked each other at that time." — Sid Krofft

"I remember them like it was yesterday. Farrah Fawcett was absolutely breathtaking to look at. She was breathtaking at that time in her life. When they came on the show there was such excitement in the air. Because it was Farrah Fawcett and Lee Majors — and they were hot, they were the number one couple in America — people were coming to visit on the set. We had to keep paparazzi away, and I remember just sitting there, I was watching the sitcom part of the show. It's funny how you remember some things all your life. I was just sitting there and saying, my god, she's the most gorgeous woman I've ever seen." — Steve Bluestein, writer

"I was just shocked that Farrah really was as pretty as she was. I remember somebody saying, 'Well, yeah, but look at her, I mean, take away all the hair and what do you have — a gorgeous bald woman.' She was just really pretty and very sweet. She seemed very like her character on *Charlie's Angels*, soft spoken, and kind of innocent. Just sweet, very sweet. Lee was kind of quiet. I don't remember much of anything about him other than thinking, oh you know, the kids at school will be impressed or jealous that we're doing this with him because he was a cutie." — Susan Olsen

Kaptain Kool and the Kongs

Cast: **Debra Clinger** — born June 8, 1952; **Michael Lembeck** — born June 25, 1948;
Louise DuArt — born October 30, 1950; **Mickey McMeel** — November 28, 1948

Brady Bunch Variety Hour Guest Star:
January 23, 1977

Career Highlights:

● Kaptain Kool and Kongs made their debut as a live fantasy rock band on *The Krofft Supershow* in 1976, a Saturday morning television program for children. They would perform skits and songs and introduce the other live action segments. Much of their music was written by the Osmonds.

● Kaptain Kool and the Kongs released two albums of songs from the show, both in 1978: the self-titled *Kaptain Kool and the Kongs*, and *Stories From the Krofft TV Supershow*. In addition, they released one single, "And I Never Dreamed."

● The cast included Michael Lembeck as Kaptain Kool, Debra Clinger as Superchick, Mickey McMeel as Turkey, and Louise DuArt as Nashville. Bert Sommer as Flatbush appeared only during the first season.

● Michael Lembeck appeared on dozens of TV shows, and is probably best remembered for his regular role as Max, Mackenzie Phillips' husband on *One Day At a Time*. He went on to greater success as a director with credits including *Friends, Everybody Loves Raymond* and *Californication*.

● Debra Clinger came from a musical performing family, and is remembered for performing in the pop group "The Clingers" with her sisters Peggy, Patsy, and Melody. She was later part of the fabricated girl group "Rockflowers" (based on the Mattel dolls of the same name). In the '90s, Debra became part of a Christian vocal group, "The Clinger Sisters," again with her siblings.

● Louise DuArt is one of the most revered impressionists today, with a range of over 100 famous imitations. Her voice has been heard on *The Family Guy* and *Tiny Toon Adventures* among others. She also toured with Tim Conway and Harvey Korman in the hit stage show *Together Again* (recreating acts from *The Carol Burnett Show)* as well as appearing as host of the ABC family morning show *Living the Life*.

● Before joining Kaptain Kool, Mickey McMeel played drums for the band Three Dog Night. He was later seen as the accountant in the cult classic *Xanadu* and later turned up as a cop in the Steven Segal movie *Hard to Kill*.

Milton Berle

Birth: July 12, 1908, in New York City

Death: March 27, 2002, buried at Hillside Memorial Park Cemetery, Culver City, California

Brady Bunch Variety Hour Guest Star: February 27, 1977

Career Highlights:

● Milton Berle's acting career began at the age of five when he won a Charlie Chaplin look-alike contest. The following year he made his film debut in *The Perils of Pauline* (1914) and commenced a career as a child star in silent movies. In 1916, Berle made his stage debut in *Florodora* in Atlantic City and the show eventually moved to Broadway.

● During the early 1930s Berle performed on programs such as *The Rudy Vallée Hour* and *Stop Me If You've Heard This One*. He continued his radio career in the 1940s with shows such as *Three Ring Time, Kiss and Make Up,* and *Let Yourself Go.*

● Berle's biggest hit came with *The Texaco Star Theater,* which began on radio in 1948 and that same year was one of the very first programs ever broadcast on a new medium known as television. Berle is credited with doubling the sales of television sets in 1949 which garnered him the title of "Mr. Television."

● The first charity telethon (for the Damon Runyan Cancer Fund) was hosted by Berle in 1949. A permanent fixture at benefits in the Hollywood area, he was instrumental in raising millions for charitable causes.

● He was nominated for an Emmy as a dramatic actor in the episode "Doyle Against the House" on *The Dick Powell Show* in 1961.

● In later years, Berle made guest appearances in television shows such as *Batman*; *Get Smart*; *Ironside*; *The Brady Bunch Hour*; *The Love Boat*; *CHiPs*; *Fantasy Island*; *Diff'rent Strokes*; *Murder, She Wrote*; *Beverly Hills 90210*; *The Fresh Prince of Bel-Air*; *The Nanny*; and *Roseanne.*

● Berle was named to the *Guinness Book of World Records* for the greatest number of charity performances made by a show business performer.

● As "Mr. Television," Berle was one of the first seven people to be inducted into the Television Academy Hall of Fame in 1984.

Memories from *The Brady Bunch Variety Hour:*
"Oh, please! He takes a glass, puts his lips all around the whole thing and walks around with the glass in his lips. That's an old burlesque trick. He never got over it, he never stopped. Sit down, Milton! We know you're funny, we know you're the King of Comedy, we know you're the King of Television, sit down! Take a breath! How much can we laugh?"
— Rip Taylor

"Over the years we had done a bunch of things with Milton Berle, like appearances here and there. I picture myself being onstage with him, and there was a curtain and everything but it wasn't in the *Variety Hour*. I distinctly remember Milton Berle being the timing-is-everything guy. In comedy, timing is everything. I don't know if he actually said that to me or if I just applied it to him because I had heard he said that. But that was definitely his MO, 'Look kid, you've gotta hit this cue, timing is everything!' He totally took over our variety show. He wasn't going to let us languish and he wasn't going to play by our rules. He came in and took over." — Mike Lookinland

Tina Turner

Birth: November 26, 1939, as Anna May Bullock in Nutbush, Tennessee

Brady Bunch Variety Hour Guest Star: February 27, 1977

Career Highlights:
● Tina Turner is known worldwide for her identifiable voice, energetic stage presence and her long, well-proportioned legs.
● She is an eleven-time Grammy Award-winning singer, songwriter, and actress, and has been acclaimed as one of the most popular and biggest-selling music artists of all time. With album sales of over 180 million she has sold more concert tickets than any other solo performer in history.
● In 1956, Anna Mae Bullock met Ike Turner, an established rock and roll recording star. After much persistence he allowed her to perform with his group and renamed her Tina Turner. Within a few years she became the spotlight of a popular soul revue led by Ike Turner and his Kings of Rhythm.
● Throughout the 1960s and into the 1970s, Ike and Tina rose to superstardom. Their 1968 hit "Proud Mary" was their greatest success and won a Grammy for Best R&B Vocal Performance by a Duo or Group.

- In 1975 Tina achieved critical acclaim for her role as the Acid Queen in the rock opera *Tommy*.
- Her autobiography *I, Tina* was later made into the film *What's Love Got to Do With It?*
- In the spring of 1984, Turner released her fifth solo album, *Private Dancer*. The album was a huge success and established Turner as a credible solo artist. Her album included the

number-one hit "What's Love Got to Do With It," which won Record of the Year, Song of the Year, and Best Female Pop Vocal Performance at the 1985 Grammy Awards. Turner also contributed her voice to the multi-Grammy Award winning number-one charity song "We Are the World."

- Turner returned to the big screen in 1985 as Aunty Entity in *Mad Max Beyond Thunderdome* and scored an additional hit with the song "We Don't Need Another Hero."

- In 1990 Turner released one of her most enduring hits "The Best," originally a song recorded by Bonnie Tyler, and, in 1995, she recorded the title theme of the James Bond movie *GoldenEye*. After a long career, she retired from major concert tours in 2000 but continues to make public appearances.

Memories from *The Brady Bunch Variety Hour:*
"Tina Turner was really sweet. I was amazed to see what great shape she was in. Back then, people weren't in the kind of shape they are now and she had the best-looking legs! That was an inspiration to me."
— Charkie Phillips, Krofftette

"I remember Tina Turner coming on and being extremely frail, quiet and demure, and not demanding. She was such a star and such a legend. I was reading her book twenty-five years later and thinking she was doing *The Brady Bunch* because she just walked out on Ike, was broke, had no money, and was living in friend's houses. It's one of those amazing show business stories. You think that everybody has everything and you realize they don't."
— Steve Bluestein, writer

"I remember Tina being certainly very cordial, and staring at her legs, and going, 'oh my gosh those are perfect!'" — Susan Olsen

"That was when her career was kind of in a 'hadn't taken a new direction.' Just for her to be on this show, shows you that her career hadn't come back into full swing yet. I think that was my favorite stuff, the musical artists. To me Tina Turner was the icing on the cake, we got to wear white Afros!" — Susan Buckner, Krofftette

"Ann-Margret has this estate in Benedict Canyon and they have a coach house, which is a garage and above the garage an apartment for the chauffeur. That's where she was living. She walked out on Ike with the wig on her head and the dress on her back. She discovered that she had all of these dates for Ike and Tina Turner that Ike could not play without her. If she didn't make up these dates Ike could sue her for the loss of income. So she had to play these dates and pay him some money because otherwise it was going to be very complicated. She had to put an act together, and he wouldn't give her anything. She had done *Tommy,* the movie, with Ann-Margret. They had gotten friendly in England when they were shooting the picture. She walked out on Ike in Dallas, or some place like that, and wound up coming back to L.A. and moving into Ann-Margret's coach house. In the interim she did all of these nightclub things, she was in Vegas opening for Buddy Hackett, co-headlining with Connie Stevens, this bizarre series of improbable appearances, one of which was a guest shot on *The Brady Bunch Variety Hour.*" — Bruce Vilanch, writer

Vincent Price

Birth: May 27, 1911, in St. Louis, Missouri
Death: October 25, 1993, cremated with ashes scattered at sea

Brady Bunch Variety Hour Guest Star: March 4, 1977

Career Highlights:
● Vincent Price Jr. attended Yale University where he studied art history and began appearing in stage productions.
● He made his film debut in 1938 with *Service de Luxe* and quickly established himself as a diverse actor in drama as well as comedy. His early films include *Brigham Young* (1940), *Laura* (1944), *Leave Her to Heaven* (1945), and *Dragonwyck* (1946).
● Price made a transition to horror films in the 1950s, most notably the 3-D feature *House of Wax* (1953) and *The Fly* (1958). During the 1960s Price starred in many low-budget horror films such as *House of Usher* (1960), *The Pit and Pendulum* (1961), *Tales of Terror* (1962), *The Raven* (1963), *The Masque of the Red Death* (1964), and *The Tomb of Ligeia* (1965).
● One of his favorite roles was playing the evil character, Egghead, on the 1960s television series *Batman*. He is also remembered for his guest appearance on the Hawaii episodes of *The Brady Bunch* in 1972.

● During the 1970s and 1980s Price began to turn more of his attention to narrative and voice-over work. His voice is frequently remembered in Alice Cooper's first solo album, *Welcome to My Nightmare,* and in Michael Jackson's *Thriller.*

● From 1981 to 1989 he hosted the PBS television series *Mystery!* He also was the voice of Professor Ratigan in Disney's *The Great Mouse Detective* (1986) and portrayed the inventor in Tim Burton's *Edward Scissorhands* (1990).

● Price was an art collector. His *Vincent Price Collection of Fine Art* was sponsored by Sears and sold nearly 50,000 pieces of fine art, by artists such as Rembrandt, Pablo Picasso, and Salvador Dalí. The line included original paintings for serious collectors and also more affordable prints.

● Price was a gourmet cook and wrote several cookbooks.

Memories from *The Brady Bunch Variety Hour:*

"He was absolutely, so surprisingly funny. You expect that horrible man, Frankenstein type, to come in. He was funny and friendly, and his wife, Coral Browne… 'Hello, darling, how do you do…' I swear to God it was Talullah Bankhead come back from the dead! 'Vincent, we're going now, stop this silliness, we're going…' She called it 'silliness.' He said, 'But darling, it feeds us.' 'I don't care, we're going…' Very funny, the two of them, oh, so funny!"
— Rip Taylor

"Vincent is a gem. He really impressed me because when he got on the set he came over to me, not only was he nice, he came over — he knew my name. You know, most people didn't bother learning the kids' real names. He'd done the episodes in Hawaii, not in Hawaii but the Hawaiian episode, and he comes over to me: 'Well, Susan, hello, how are you?' It really impressed me, and we talked about cooking and painting. He was just such a nice man. I really liked him." — Susan Olsen

H.R. Pufnstuf and Kiki Bird

Brady Bunch Variety Hour Guest Star: March 4, 1977

Background: *H.R. Pufnstuf* was a Saturday morning children's television program produced by Sid and Marty Krofft, which ran on NBC from 1969 to 1971. The plot revolved
around a boy named Jimmy, played by Jack Wild, who discovered "Living Island" where
everything was alive and could talk. The Island was governed by a friendly dragon, H.R.
Pufnstuf, who took Jimmy under his care and protected him from the evil Witchiepoo. The
series was so popular that it was made into a feature film in 1970, entitled *Pufnstuf.*

Van Snowden as Pufnstuf:

● Van Snowden was born in San Francisco but
grew up in Branson, Missouri. After graduating
from high school he moved to New York City and
eventually took a job moving scenery for the
Kroffts on their puppet show *Les Poupées de Paris.*
● Snowden then directed Six Flags puppet shows for
the Kroffts, and was leading the Texas company when
they started the "Pufnstuf" series in 1969. At that time,
Snowden was more valuable to them in Texas.
● They brought him back for the *Pufnstuf* movie in
1970 and he doubled for Roberto Gamonet, who
played Pufnstuf and did some scenes as Puf. He also
did puppets including all close-ups of talking
Freddie the flute. Roberto died soon after filming
the movie. Snowden then took over the Pufnstuf
character and made appearances for more than
thirty-five years on such shows as *The Dating
Game, CHiPs, The Drew Carey Show,* and *My Name
Is Earl.*
● Snowden is also an Emmy-nominated puppeteer, and has worked on shows such as
Barbara Mandrell and the Mandrell Sisters, Tales from the Crypt, X Files, and the *Child's Play*
movie series. Snowden is retired and currently resides in the Los Angeles area.

Sharon Baird as Kiki Bird:

● Sharon Baird was born in Seattle, Washington. She is an American dancer and actress,
best known for having been a performer on the original *Mickey Mouse Club* television
show from 1955 to 1958.

● Baird began dance lessons at age three and appeared in her first film *Bloodhounds of Broadway* in 1950. At age nine she began regular appearances on *The Colgate Comedy Hour* and did an unbilled song and dance number with Dean Martin in the 1955 film *Artists and Models*.

● During the 1970s and 1980s Baird danced in costume on a number of children's television shows, including *H.R. Pufnstuf, The New Zoo Revue,* and *The Brady Bunch Hour*. She is now retired from show business and lives in Reno, Nevada.

Memories from *The Brady Bunch Variety Hour:*

"We had at least one musical guest cancel. They saw the show on TV and said 'We're not doing that.' It was a kind of half-way decent musical guest. But I figured, well, you know, they realized what they were booked on and went, 'No, no, no, no,' so that week our musical guest was Pufnstuf and I was just mortified. 'This show will never ever be cool.' I wanted us to get real rock bands on." — Susan Olsen

"It's the cross promotion thing. The Kroffts brought in a lot of people from shows they were producing at the time. I don't think the show had any direction because when you go from Vincent Price to H.R. Pufnstuf, where are they headed? They never really pinned it down. I never knew what demographic they were going for." — Steve Dichter, stage manager

Charo

Birth: March 13, 1951 (also given as 1941) under the name María Rosario Pilar Martínez Molina Baeza in Murcia, Spain

Brady Bunch Variety Hour Guest Star: March 21, 1977

Career Highlights:

● Official documents in Spain and the United States recorded her birth as 1941 but in 1977 a United States court ruled that she was born in 1951.

● Charo showed musical talent at a very early age. She studied classical and flamenco guitar with Andrés Segovia beginning at the age of nine. Charo's virtuosic playing ability on the guitar has often been overshadowed by her flamboyant personality and provocative wardrobe.

● Charo was discovered by the famous band leader Xavier Cugat, and they were married on August 7, 1966 at Caesars Palace in Las Vegas when he was sixty-six and she was only fifteen. In 2005 she explained that the marriage was a business arrangement that allowed her to come to the United States legally with her mother and aunt. When Charo was of legal age, Cugat reportedly gave her a Rolls Royce as a parting gift. In her stage performances with Cugat's orchestra she became most famous for her catchphrase "cuchi-cuchi."

● By 1971 she was reportedly being paid as much as Frank Sinatra, Dean Martin, and Ray Charles for her Las Vegas act. As her career progressed, Charo appeared in the films *The Concorde — Airport '79* (1979) and *Moon Over Parador* (1988) with Richard Dreyfuss. She made hundreds of appearances on top-rated comedy television shows such as *The Carol Burnett Show, The Dean Martin Show, Sonny and Cher, Donny and Marie, The Brady Bunch Hour,* and numerous Bob Hope and Sammy Davis Jr. specials. She was also a favorite guest on the talk-show circuit including, *The Tonight Show, The Merv Griffin Show,* and *Late Night with David Letterman.*

● In 1977, she became a naturalized citizen of the United States and on August 11, 1978 she married her manager, Kjell Rasten, in Lake Tahoe. During much of the late 1980s to late 1990s Charo had limited visibility because she moved to Hawaii where she opened and performed at her own dinner theater while she and Rasten raised their son.

● In recent years, Charo headlined a new show in Las Vegas entitled *Bravo.* She appeared in nationwide commercials for Sprint and Geico Insurance, and made regular appearances on *Hollywood Squares* and VH1's *The Surreal Life.* She also donates her talents to Jerry Lewis's annual Muscular Dystrophy Association telethon.

Memories from *The Brady Bunch Variety Hour:*
"She's great. I just did a *Surreal Life* with her too. She's smart, and she's funny, and she's talented, and she recorded 'Malagueña' for the show."
— Barry Williams

"Before *The Brady Bunch Hour* there was a Charo special and she had done very well for the network. It got great ratings, so putting her on the show was not a bad thing. Plus she's a great dancer and a pretty good singer. She could do more than cuchi cuchi." — Bonny Dore, ABC Television Network

"I knew Charo before. I think I had done a special. Actually, we had done a pilot for a series. Fred Silverman had bought Charo for a half-hour series. The series was not picked up but she was doing *The Brady Bunch* and that was one reason I was down (on the stage) a lot because I had known her so well. But yeah, she was fun to be around."
— Bruce Vilanch, writer

"She called me 'Rape Taylor.' Charo was so charming, and funny, funny!" — Rip Taylor

The Hudson Brothers

Birth: **Bill Hudson** — October 17, 1949; **Mark Hudson** — August 23, 1951; **Brett Hudson** — January 18, 1953; all born in Portland, Oregon

Krofftette Dee Kaye with the Hudson Brothers: Brett Hudson, Bill Hudson, Mark Hudson

Brady Bunch Variety Hour Guest Star: March 21, 1977

Career Highlights:

● The Hudson Brothers began their music career in 1964 when Bill, Mark, and their friend, Kent Fillmore, formed a local band called My Sirs in their hometown of Portland, Oregon.

● In 1966 they won a prestigious competition and were able to cut their own demo record. Renamed the New Yorkers, they were offered a contract by Chrysler to travel around the country playing at company events. The band achieved further recognition with their songs "When I'm Gone" and "Mr. Kirby," which were moderate hits. The boys' good fortune came to a crashing halt when their manager allegedly stole over $150,000, leaving them bankrupt. They were dropped by their record company and forced to withdraw from show business.

● The band reformed a year later with Kent being replaced by Bob Haworth. They were picked up by Decca Records which then dropped them unexpectedly after they arrived in New York for a promotional tour. In 1970 they regrouped for a third time — now with only the three brothers — and moved south to Los Angeles where they were known as Hudson. They released their first album in 1972 and in 1973 they were signed to Rocket Records by Bernie Taupin and Elton John.

● After a European tour, television producer Chris Bearde and Allan Blye picked them up for prime time with *The Hudson Brothers Show* and then on Saturday mornings with *The Hudson Brothers Razzle Dazzle Show.* During this time they continued to record for Rocket Records and briefly for Casablanca Records.

● During 1978 the Hudsons were busy in England working on their syndicated television comedy *Bonkers.* They released a new album from Arista Records, appeared in the movie *Zero to Sixty,* and a telefilm, *The Millionaire.* In 1980 they released two more albums, neither of which was a commercial success. After their horror-spoof film *Hysterical* (1983), the brothers decided to go their separate ways professionally. In 1994 they released a CD of the best recordings plus several new tracks.

- Mark Hudson has had continued success in the music business as a producer and songwriter for Ringo Starr, Celine Dion, Aerosmith and Hanson, among others (including his daughter Sarah Hudson and her band Ultraviolet).

- Bill Hudson is the father of actress Kate Hudson and actor Oliver Hudson (both the product of his first marriage to Goldie Hawn). He also had two children with his second wife, Cindy Williams (Zachary and Emily). While still married to Cindy Williams, they started the production company Taylor Made, which produced Steve Martin's *Father of the Bride* films.

- Brett Hudson has served as executive producer for several television programs as well as the 2008 documentary *The Seventh Python*. He also has sung background vocals for Wayne Newton, Alice Cooper, Aaron Neville and Ringo Starr.

Edgar Bergen

Birth: February 16, 1903, Chicago, Illinois
Death: September 30, 1978, buried in Inglewood Park Cemetery, Inglewood, California

Brady Bunch Variety Hour Guest Star: March 28, 1977

Career Highlights:

- Edgar Bergen was born in Chicago and grew up in Decatur, Michigan. At the age of eleven he taught himself the art of ventriloquism from a pamphlet and a few years later he started performing with his lifelong sidekick Charlie McCarthy. The puppet was sculpted by woodcarver Theodore Mack in the likeness of an Irish newspaper boy Bergen knew.

- Bergen returned to Chicago at the age of sixteen to attend Lakeview High School and worked part-time at a silent movie theater. Bergen then attended Northwestern University but never graduated. The school later gave him an honorary degree as "Master of Innuendo and Snappy Comeback."

- Bergen was discovered by Elsa Maxwell when he and Charlie were doing their act at a New York party for Noël Coward. She recommended them for an engagement at the famous Rainbow Room. That appearance was so successful that they secured a spot on Rudy Vallée's radio program and subsequently were given their own show which ran for almost twenty years. During this time Bergen added two new characters, Mortimer Snerd and Effie Klinker.

● As an actor Bergen appeared in the films *I Remember Mama* (1948), *Captain China* (1950), and *Don't Make Waves* (1967). With Charlie McCarthy he appeared in *The Goldwyn Follies* (1938), *You Can't Cheat an Honest Man* (1938), *Look Who's Laughing* (1941), *Here We Go Again* (1942), *Fun and Fancy Free* (1947), and much later in *The Muppet Movie* (1979). Bergen died shortly after completing his scenes, marking it as Bergen's last appearance. The film was dedicated in his memory.

● Bergen also made frequent guest appearances on television shows such as *The Colgate Comedy Hour*, *Do You Trust Your Wife*, *What's My Line?*, and on dozens of variety shows hosted by the likes of Steve Allen, Jack Benny, Andy Williams, Smothers Brothers, The Brady Bunch, and the Muppets. He also originated the role of Grandpa Walton in *The Homecoming: A Christmas Story* (1971).

● Bergen is the father of actress Candace Bergen, who achieved fame in the CBS sitcom *Murphy Brown* (1988-1998)

Memories from *The Brady Bunch Variety Hour:*

"The writers sat in an office with Edgar Bergen one afternoon and he told stories and did jokes. He was tremendously funny in that context. You think of Charlie McCarthy and Mortimer Snerd as dated 1940s characters but Bergen himself was very bright and very funny. I remember being quite impressed with that."
— Carl Kleinschmitt, writer

"I do remember sitting with Edgar Bergen and discussing his ventriloquist act and he gave me — which I still have to this day — a printed off copy of a monologue of him and Charlie McCarthy. I remember thinking, 'god, he's so old!' He was such an old man, but when he got on camera he was young again. But I remember being in awe that I was actually sitting in the same room with Edgar Bergen, whom I had seen all my life."
— Steve Bluestein, writer

"I felt rather honored to work with him and it was one of his last appearances. I thought this was really special. He was very polite. This man had been around for years. I actually got to hold Charlie McCarthy — I wish I had a picture of that — and then I would hand Charlie to him. It was quite an experience for me." — Steve Dichter, stage manager

"I loved Edgar Bergen. We didn't have to rehearse too much because he already knew his material. I was just in awe sitting there. Susan and I could not believe we were doing the scene with him, and then I had to act stupid because I couldn't say 'ventriloquist.' Then we were sticking our fingers in our mouth. How corny is that? Then Michael [Lookinland] became the dummy." — Geri Reischl

Melanie

Birth: February 3, 1947, in Astoria, New York City, as Melanie Anne Safka

Brady Bunch Variety Hour Guest Star: March 28, 1977

Career Highlights:

● She made her public debut at age four on the radio show *Live Like a Millionaire* and the following year she made her first recording, "Gimme a Little Kiss." When Melanie was a student at New York's American Academy of Dramatic Arts she began singing in the folk clubs of Greenwich Village and landed a recording contract with Columbia Records.

● The young singer later signed with Buddah Records and had her first hit in France with her song "Bobo's Party," released in 1969. This was immediately followed by a second hit, this time in the Netherlands, "Beautiful People." The genesis of Melanie's signature song "Lay Down (Candles in the Rain)" came from her appearance at Woodstock when the audience began lighting candles as she sang. It became an international hit in 1970. Later that same year, Melanie performed at the Isle of Wight Festival where she received four standing ovations.

● In 1971, she established her own recording label, Neighborhood Records, with her husband Peter Schekeryk, and had a new hit with "Brand New Key." The song was banned by some radio stations because some interpreted the lyrics as sexually suggestive. The song was quickly followed by two additional hits, "Ring the Living Bell" and "The Nickel Song," thereby setting a record for the first female performer to have three Top 40 hits concurrently.

● Melanie is one of music's most prolific artists and has released almost one album a year since 1969. She has been awarded two gold albums and is also recognized for her musical adaptations of children's songs. Many of her albums have received wide critical acclaim.

● She achieved pop culture status in the 1980s when the Quaker Oats Company used a version of her "Look What They've Done to My Song, Ma" in their commercials for Instant Oatmeal, with the revised lyrics "Look what they've done to my oatmeal."

Memories from *The Brady Bunch Variety Hour:*

"I loved Melanie. I was a big fan of hers, I was always into musicians, I liked that kind of music more. I was trained in more of the dancing/variety show, that's where I worked a lot, but I really loved real musicians, and groups, and artists. Melanie, I remember everything about her. I thought she was so sweet. I was in her number, it was so cool. I thought it was very dynamic. She and her husband, they were traveling in a VW van. I remember that clearly. I thought it was very interesting, and very much still the hippie lifestyle at that time. I would imagine they are still in that space." — Susan Buckner, Krofftette

"We were in the office one day and we heard what sounded like glass breaking — a screech. It was Melanie warming up with her accompanist. She had a very piercing voice. It was just this loud noise." — Carl Kleinschmitt, writer

"Melanie was the Britney Spears of that time." — Sid Krofft

Rich Little

Birth: November 26, 1938, in Ottawa, Ontario, Canada

Brady Bunch Variety Hour Guest Star: March 28, 1977

Career Highlights:

● Rich Little began doing impersonations of his teachers in middle school. He was active in Ottawa's Little Theatre, was a radio disc jockey, and at the age of seventeen he began performing professionally in night clubs where he did impressions.

● In 1963 he was discovered by Mel Tormé and made his television debut on *The Judy Garland Show.* Then from 1966 to 1967 he appeared in ABC-TV's sitcom *Love on a Rooftop* as the eccentric neighbor, Stan Parker.

● Rich was a frequent guest on variety and talk shows during the 1960s and 1970s hosted by Ed Sullivan, Jackie Gleason, Glen Campbell, and Dean Martin, as well as on such series as *Laugh-In, The Julie Andrews Show, The Brady Bunch Hour,* and his own variety show.

● He was well known for his appearances on *The Tonight Show,* which he hosted twelve times, and he later played Johnny Carson in the 1996 HBO TV-movie *The Late Shift.*

● His dramatic television roles include appearances on *Young and the Restless; Santa Barbara; Fantasy Island; CHiPS; Murder, She Wrote; Hawaii Five-O; MacGyver; Police Woman;* and *Mannix.*

- Little has starred in numerous HBO specials including the 1978 one-man production, *Rich Little's Christmas Carol.*
- He has released nine albums.
- One of his best known impressions is of former U.S. President Richard Nixon.
- He is also known for providing voices in movies for actors unable to deliver their lines. When David Niven proved too ill for his voice to be used in his appearance in *Trail of the Pink Panther*, Little provided an overdub. Little also contributed his expertise to the 1991 TV special *Christmas at the Movies* by providing a dub for Gene Kelly.
- Little has been active in several charities including the Juvenile Diabetes Fund and the Children's Miracle Network. He has been named to Miami Children's Hospital International Pediatrics Hall of Fame and been honored by the naming of the Rich Little Special Care Nursery at Ottawa Civic Hospital.
- Little was the host for the 2007 White House Correspondents' Association dinner.

Memories from *The Brady Bunch Variety Hour:*

"Rich Little was a quiet man, didn't really hang out a whole lot with us, probably more with Florence and Bob. He was very funny, I remember everyone cracking up. He did a lot of ad-libbing. I was pretty amazed he could go into character so instantly like he did." — Susan Olsen

"Rich Little was always fun to work with. He was very spontaneous, so he could run with something. We were always struck by the amount of impressions he could do, he was a nice guy and very pleasant. He'd crack everybody up, in stitches, doubled-over in laughter."
— Steve Dichter, stage manager

"Rich Little never turned off, he was always on. He always stayed in whatever character he was doing at the time, like Truman Capote, and he was really good." — Geri Reischl

Redd Foxx

Birth: December 9, 1922, in St. Louis, Missouri, as John Elroy Sanford
Death: October 11, 1991, buried in Palm Memorial Park, Las Vegas

Brady Bunch Variety Hour Guest Star: April 4, 1977

Career Highlights:

● Redd Foxx first began doing "blue humor" stand-up comedy on the infamous "Chitlin' Circuit" in the 1940s and 1950s. Blue humor was very raunchy and considered inappropriate for white audiences. As a result, Foxx's party albums were not sold by white record stores.

● By the 1960s Foxx had a large following and became one of the first black comics to play to white audiences on the Las Vegas Strip. In 1972 NBC gave him his own television show, *Sanford and Son*. The sitcom was a huge success.

● Foxx left the show in 1977 to star in his own variety show on ABC, which was cancelled by the network in less than a year. A few years later he attempted and failed to revive Fred Sanford in the spin-off series *Sanford*. In 1986 he had a brief stint on ABC with *The Redd Foxx Show*.

● In 1989 he starred with Richard Pryor and Eddie Murphy in the hit film *Harlem Nights*, which told the story of three successful black comedians of different generations.

● He was making a comeback in 1991 with a new television series, *The Royal Family* costarring Della Reese, when a fatal heart attack struck Foxx on the set during a rehearsal break.

Memories from *The Brady Bunch Variety Hour*:

"I don't remember Redd being on. He must have brought ALL of his drugs. I had worked with Redd on other occasions and barely remembered but for other reasons because we were so slammed most of the time. He loved to party, he was a major coke whore. This was before it was trendy. I had the impression Redd was doing everything for as long as it could be done." — Bruce Vilanch, writer

"Redd Foxx didn't do one dance step, ever. He would walk in at the very end, throw his arms up, and that was it." — Casey Cole, choreographer

"Redd Foxx was dirty all the time, a lot of bleeping." — Rip Taylor

"I didn't know that I worked with Redd, and there it is, me with my Hermie hair with Redd Foxx. He didn't hang out with us, but I loved him even though *Sanford and Son* was our toughest competition when *The Brady Bunch* was on. We met Redd at a Dodgers game where it was a celebrity baseball game and we took publicity pictures with him to show 'hey, we'll hang out with the enemy.' But I really liked the show, *Sanford and Son*, my dad liked it, and I thought Redd Foxx was very funny. It was an honor to have him around." — Susan Olsen

The Ohio Players

Brady Bunch Variety Hour Guest Star: April 4, 1977

Career Highlights:

● They originated in Dayton, Ohio, and began performing together in 1959 as the Ohio Untouchables.

● In 1967 they became the house band for Compass Records, which was based in New York City.

● The band was reformed several times in the early 1970s. Among their hits during this time were "Pain" (1971), and their number one hit "Funky Worm" (1973). The band had seven more Top 40 hits between 1973 and 1976, including the smashes "Fire" and "Love Rollercoaster." The group's last big hit was "Who'd She Coo."

● The Ohio Players were widely recognized for their unique sound, which has been frequently sampled and copied over the years. Noteworthy examples include The Red Hot Chili Peppers covering "Love Rollercoaster" for the film *Beavis and Butt-head Do America,* and Van Halen's song "Runnin' With the Devil," which was inspired by "Runnin' From the Devil."

● The Ohio Players song "Fopp" was rerecorded in 1990 by Soundgarden. In the UK a chain of music and DVD stores was known as "Fopp."

● The music of the Ohio Players also appeared in the 1997 movie *Boogie Nights* and on television in *The Sopranos.* In 2004, their song "Fire" served as the theme for the Joaquin Phoenix movie *Ladder 49.* That same year the band also appeared on the soundtrack of *The 40-Year-Old Virgin* with "If I Was Your Girlfriend."

Memories from *The Brady Bunch Variety Hour:*

"The only thing that was cool about the guests that comes to mind was seeing the Ohio Players sing 'Fire' and it was very psychedelic and it was really freaky, and thinking, 'Wow, I wish I had gotten to meet them' because we never saw them." — Mike Lookinland

"There was no way they were going to get Emerson, Lake, and Palmer on the *Variety Hour.* We had the Ohio Players and I thought that was cool. They were pretty upset. When they arrived they realized what [kind of show] they were doing, and were like, 'Oh, no…'" — Susan Olsen

"I'll never forget the Ohio Players. The Ohio Players had 'Fire' out at that time, a big R&B and crossover hit. They were performing it poolside and the dancers were swimming with batons that were on fire, real flames. They were holding up big wands that were on fire as they were swimming. The whole thing was way over the top." — Paul Shaffer

Robert Hegyes

Birth: May 7, 1951, in Perth Amboy, New Jersey

Brady Bunch Variety Hour Guest Star: April 4, 1977

Career Highlights:

● Robert Hegyes showed interest in theater from an early age and began acting in high school under the direction of drama teacher Dr. Barton Shepard. Hegyes then attended Rowan University of New Jersey and graduated with a Bachelor's degree in Speech/Theater and Secondary Education.

● After moving to New York City, he performed educational theater with a Greenwich Village children's theater group known as Theater in a Trunk.

During this time he also was a performer at Washington Square, the Provincetown Playhouse, and in the political improvisational troupe Jack LaRumpa's Flying Drum & Kazoo Band.

● Hegyes had his big break as an actor when he costarred off-Broadway in the drama *Naomi Court,* which was then followed by his Broadway debut in *Don't Call Back.* During his run on Broadway he auditioned for producer James Komack, and was cast as Juan Epstein, in a new ABC sitcom entitled *Welcome Back, Kotter,* which ran from 1975 to 1979.

● In the early 1980s, Hegyes received critical acclaim onstage in Los Angeles as Chico Marx in *An Evening with Groucho.* Following this success, Hegyes was then cast to star as undercover detective Manny Esposito, in the CBS Emmy Award-winning drama, *Cagney and Lacey.*

● During the course of his career, Hegyes has guest starred in dozens of television shows, including, *Saturday Night Live, Diagnosis Murder, The Drew Carey Show, The Brady Bunch Hour,* and *Streets of San Francisco.* His screen credits include: *Underground Aces,* and *Bob Roberts,* among others.

● Hegyes has served as an artist-in-residence at his alma mater, Rowan University, teaching acting for camera, public speaking, and screenplay writing. He was also an adjunct instructor at Brooks College in Long Beach, California, where he taught essay writing and public speaking. A California-certified secondary education teacher, Hegyes has worked regularly in recent years at Venice High School in Venice, California.

● Hegyes has also collaborated with writer/producer Craig Titley on the internet series, *The Venice Walk.*

Memories from *The Brady Bunch Variety Hour:*
"One of the miracles that I was granted over the years in my blessed career was working with Susan, and her legendary television family, *The Brady Bunch.* Going to work for that week I kept pinching myself. After watching the series for years, suddenly I was one of them." — Robert Hegyes

"We were friends during that time period. He use to come down to the Comedy Store and we did a show called *Make Me Laugh* together. He had just gotten a divorce and no one could make him laugh. I had them make an announcement that Steve Bluestein was going to show you everything he was left with after his divorce and I ran out in my underwear and a tie, and he started screaming with laughter."
— Steve Bluestein, writer

"I remember him being around the set, and it seemed like he had the hots for Maureen!"
— Geri Reischl

Rick Dees

Birth: March 14, 1950, in Jacksonville, Florida, as Rigdon Ogdon Dees III

Brady Bunch Variety Hour Guest Star: April 25, 1977

Career Highlights:

● Rick Dees first showed interest in radio as a teenager, and at the age of sixteen he landed a job at WGBG, a local station in his hometown.

● In 1976, he recorded "Disco Duck" with his band, Cast of Idiots, while working at WMPS-AM in Memphis, Tennessee. The song never received any airtime because rival stations did not want to promote their competition, and Dees was expressly forbidden from playing it on his show by station management. He was immediately fired for discussing the song on the air one morning.

● Dees then went to WHBQ-AM in Memphis and was able to release "Disco Duck," which sold over two million copies and reached number one on *Billboard* Magazine's Hot 100 chart on October 16, 1976.

● He moved to Los Angeles in 1979 and did a morning show on Top 40 station KHJ for several years until it changed to an all-country format.

● In 1981 Dees began working at KIIS-FM, also in Los Angeles, where he served as host of *Rick Dees in the Morning* and was named *Billboard Magazine's* "Number One Radio Personality in America" for eleven consecutive years. He launched his weekly Top 40 radio program in 1983, which has remained on the air for over twenty-five years. Dees left KIIS in 2004 when he was replaced by Ryan Seacrest after a contract dispute.

● Dees is also an actor and has appeared in the film *La Bamba,* and on television in *The Love Boat, Roseanne, Married with Children, Melrose Place,* and *Burke's Law.*

● In the 1980s he hosted the syndicated television program *Solid Gold,* and in 1990 he hosted his own late night program *Into The Night* on ABC.

● His voice-over work includes the character "Rocket Rick"

Patty Maloney as "Disco Duck" with Rick Dees in *Jetsons: The Movie* and "Rock Dees" on *The Flintstones.*

Memories from *The Brady Bunch Variety Hour:*

"He had a huge hit called 'Disco Duck.' There was a joke around the office that this was the song that killed disco and we were so happy. He was very nice on the set, and years later we became very good friends." — Steve Bluestein

"Rick Dees was such a cutie. I did something else [a show] with Rick Dees, he's the sweetest guy. I swear to God, I saw a picture of him recently and he hardly looks any different than he did then. He was very cool. I really enjoyed working with Rick."
— Lynne Latham, Krofftette

What's Happening Kids
Cast: **Ernest Thomas** — born March 26, 1950; **Haywood Nelson** — born March 25, 1960; **Fred Berry** — March 13, 1951–October 21, 2003; and **Danielle Spencer** — born June 24, 1965

Brady Bunch Variety Hour Guest Star: April 25, 1977

Career Highlights:
- *What's Happening* was a sitcom that ran on ABC from August 5, 1976 to April 28, 1979. It was based on the film *Cooley High* written by Eric Monte. It premiered as a summer series with four episodes that received good ratings. It was then added to the prime-time schedule in November of 1976.
- *What's Happening* depicted the lives of three African-American teens living in the Watts area of Los Angeles. It starred Ernest Thomas, as Roger "Raj" Thomas, Haywood Nelson as Dwayne Nelson, and Fred Berry as Fred "Rerun" Stubbs. Costarring were Danielle Spencer as Roger's younger sister, Dee, Mabel King as Roger and Dee's mother, Mabel, and Shirley Hemphill as Shirley Wilson, the waitress at Rob's Place, a local diner.
- Ernest Lee Thomas was born in Gary, Indiana. In addition to his most famous role as Raj on *What's Happening,* he has been featured in *Everybody Hates Chris* (2005–2009), the film *Malcolm X* (1992), and had a cameo in *Dickie Roberts: Former Child Star* (2003). His guest appearances on television include *The Jeffersons, Baretta, Roots, The Parent 'Hood, The Steve Harvey Show, Soul Food,* and the Nickelodeon series, *Just Jordan.*
- Haywood Nelson was born in New York City. In 1974, at the age of fourteen, he made his film debut in *Mixed Company* and appeared opposite Marlo Thomas on Broadway in *Thieves.* On television Haywood played the role of Jerry Smith on *As the World Turns,* and a guest appearance on *Sanford and Son* led to a short-lived sitcom, *Grady.* He then won the part of Dwayne Nelson on *What's Happening,* which ran for three seasons on ABC, and reprised his role in the follow-up series *What's Happening Now.* Since playing the role of Dwayne, Haywood has continued to work in show business behind the scenes as a cameraman, director, and writer.

● Fred "Rerun" Berry was born in St. Louis, Missouri. Berry was a former *Soul Train* dancer and a member of the Los Angeles based dance troupe The Lockers when he was cast as Rerun on *What's Happening* in 1976. The show was cancelled in 1979 when Berry organized a walkout by the cast who demanded a salary increase. After years of being type-cast, he ultimately embraced the Rerun character and was often seen wearing his trademark red beret and suspenders in public. He reprised his role as Rerun in *What's Happening Now* but left the show after one season in another salary dispute. Berry struggled with personal problems, drug addiction, and alcoholism throughout the 1980s. In the 1990s he lost over 100 pounds when he was diagnosed with diabetes. Berry also became a Baptist minister. He returned to show business in 1998 with the film *In the Hood*, and appeared in several other movies including *Big Money Hustlas* (2000), *Dickie Roberts: Former Child Star* (2003), and *In the Land of the Merry Misfits* (2007), released after his death. Berry also made many guest appearances on television shows such as *Saturday Night Live, The Howard Stern Show, Scrubs, Weakest Link*, and *Star Dates*. He was married six times to four different women and is the father of two daughters and one son. Berry died on October 21, 2003 in Los Angeles at the age of fifty-two where he was recovering at home from a stroke.

● At the age of eleven Danielle Spencer quickly rose to stardom playing the sarcastic character Dee Thomas on *What's Happening* from 1976 to 1979. She also appeared as Dee in eleven episodes of the sequel series *What's Happening Now*. In 1996 she became a Doctor of Veterinary Medicine. She also portrayed a veterinarian in the movies *As Good As It Gets* (1997) and *Peter Rabbit and the Crucifix* (2001). She married Garry Fields in 1999.

Memories from *The Brady Bunch Variety Hour*:

"I love *The Brady Bunch* television show and I had a surreal and great time doing their *Variety Hour*. It was surreal because I was a fan of the show way before becoming a television star. I had also had a crush on Florence Henderson as a young kid from the Dorie Miller projects in Gary, Indiana. But then when I saw Geri Reischl it was like seeing 'an angel' in person. I was honored that they included me and my cast mates from *What's Happening* to be a part of their glorious history." — Ernest Thomas

"It was really fun to have the kids from *What's Happening* on the set with us because Danielle and Haywood went to school with us. It was neat to have a couple of other kids. They were really, really nice. Haywood was such a sweetheart and Danielle was very funny. She's a nice lady now." — Susan Olsen

"We were really cool with each other because they did a lot with us on that show. We all clicked really well. Danielle was a lot like her character in real life and Fred was really cool. Poor Ernest couldn't get the rhythm down or the dance steps but he was sweet. Haywood was slick, suave, and he was cool with the girls. He was Haywood." — Geri Reischl

Patty Maloney

Birth: March 17, 1936, in Perkinsville, New York

Brady Bunch Variety Hour Guest Star: November 28, 1976 (uncredited, as Dancing Bear), April 25, 1977

Career Highlights:

- Patty Maloney grew up with dwarfism but was never treated any differently from her brother or sisters. Her mother always told young Patty, "You can attain any goal you wish to." Maloney began her show business career at age three, performing on Broadway, and moved to Winter Park, Florida with her family at the age of seven where she continued her interest in dance and theater.

- While in high school she spent one summer traveling with a carnival and, later, one year with Ringling Bros. Circus, followed by another year with the Nate Eagle Troupe.
- Her mother insisted that even if she became successful, she should have another profession. So Maloney attended the University of Florida and became a key punch operator.
- Maloney then returned to New York where she obtained a position with National Airlines and met her future husband: Joseph Vitek, a printer from Chicago who was four feet eight inches tall. After several years of correspondence they were married at the Actors' Chapel in New York and moved to Chicago, where she resided happily with her husband until his untimely death.
- She returned to show business and met Sid and Marty Krofft, who were putting together a new show, *Far Out Space*

Nuts. They promptly hired her. Maloney moved to Los Angeles where she has been working ever since, much sought after for entertaining skills. She was often a guest on the 1970s variety series *Donny and Marie.*

● Best remembered as Lumpy from *The Star Wars Holiday Special*, Maloney's cartoon voice-over work includes *The Little Rascals, Scooby-Doo,* and *New Batman Adventures.* She operated the crypt keeper puppet on *Tales from the Crypt,* and has appeared in many other television shows such as *My Name Is Earl, Nash Bridges, Star Trek Voyager, Married with Children, Little House on the Prairie, The Love Boat,* and *Charlie's Angels.*

● Other roles include playing Tom Thumb in the telefilm *Barnum* (1986) and Lois in the feature film version of *The Addams Family* (1991).

Lynn Anderson

Birth: September 26, 1947, in Grand Forks, North Dakota

Brady Bunch Variety Hour Guest Star: May 25, 1977

Career Highlights:

● At a young age Lynn Anderson won horse show competitions statewide.

● She was inspired to music by her mother, a successful country singer and songwriter, and as a teenager Anderson was discovered when she entered a singing contest sponsored by the Country Corners radio program in Sacramento.

● In 1966 she was signed to a recording contract by Chart Records. Anderson's debut single "Ride, Ride, Ride" (written by her mother) made the Top 40 on the country music charts in 1967 and was followed by "If I Kiss You (Will You Go Away)," which became her first top five hit.

● Anderson first achieved national recognition when she began appearing on *The Lawrence Welk Show* in 1967.

● In 1968, she married her first husband, legendary songwriter and producer Glen Sutton. Together they had a daughter, Lisa.

● In 1970 Lynn signed a contract with Columbia Records and moved to Nashville, Tennessee, where she recorded the smash single "I Never Promised You a Rose Garden." The song unexpectedly rose to number one on the country charts and reached number three on the pop charts, something that was almost unheard of at the time. "Rose Garden" was also a

hit in fifteen countries around the world. Anderson won a Grammy Award in 1971 for Best Female Country Vocal Performance. It then became her signature tune. "Rose Garden" went gold around the world and held the record for the biggest selling country album by a woman for over twenty-five years.

● In 1973, she recorded a song written by Richard Carpenter entitled "Top of the World" which rose to number two on the *Billboard* charts. The song was then released a second time, sung by the Carpenters, which also became a hit.

● Anderson became the first female country performer to win an American Music Award for Favorite Female Vocalist and was the first female country singer to headline and sell out Madison Square Garden in 1974.

● Anderson made a comeback in the 1980s with the singles, "You're Welcome to Tonight" and "What I've Learned from Loving You," which were both hits.

● Anderson has sung for five U.S. presidents and other world leaders, including former President Jimmy Carter on his seventy-fifth birthday, the Queen of England, Charles Prince of Wales, Prince Rainier and Prince Albert of Monaco, and King Hussan.

● She has been featured on *The Tonight Show, The Carol Burnett Show, The Brady Bunch Hour, Solid Gold, Good Morning America,* and three Bob Hope specials. Her acting credits include *Starsky and Hutch, Country Gold,* and an NBC Movie of the Week. Anderson has also starred in her own CBS television special.

● She never lost her love for riding and produced a television special called *American Country Cowboys,* which helped many handicapped groups across the country. She has also worked with the "Special Riders of Animaland," a horseback-riding therapy program for children.

● She released a new album in 2004, *The Bluegrass Sessions,* which resulted in her first Grammy Award nomination in over thirty years.

● In 2006 Anderson released a new CD of original songs entitled *Cowgirl,* all songs composed by her mother, Liz Anderson.

● In a career that spans over four decades, Anderson has racked up eight number-one records, eighteen top-ten hits, fifty Top-40 hits, and seventeen gold albums.

Memories from *The Brady Bunch Variety Hour:*

"It was fun just to watch Geri because she was just a diehard fan of Lynn Anderson. When Lynn came on our show, Geri was completely enamored." — Barry Williams

"Sid and Marty had asked Geri what country star she would like to have as a guest. They had planned for Geri to get to do a duet with her, and she picked Lynn Anderson and Tammy Wynette." — Wanda Reischl

"My agent called me and said, 'Do you want to do *The Brady Bunch?*' and I said, 'Sure.' We had a lot of fun on that show and what was amazing to me is that the other guest was Paul Williams, who is now almost my brother-in-law. I've been dating his brother for twenty-five years. It was really funny to go back and realize that basically that was the one show we did together. Geri Reischl was a big fan and I thought that was so cute because I was a big fan of the show too. I always run around pinching myself that I got to be a part of the business and it was always surprising to me when someone said they were a fan. It always just knocked me out. She looked like she could be my kid or my sister. We looked like we could be family." — Lynn Anderson

"She was my favorite country singer. I was totally starstruck and she was so nice. I remember her saying she loved my voice and how much we looked alike. She brought her daughter to work and she was cute. I thought it was the greatest to pick the guest for a show that was geared around me." — Geri Reischl

Paul Williams

Birth: September 19, 1940, in Bennington, Nebraska

Brady Bunch Variety Hour Guest Star: May 25, 1977

Career Highlights:
- Oscar, Grammy and Golden Globe-winning songwriter Paul Williams is recognized as one of America's most prolific and gifted lyricists and composers.
- A Hall of Fame songwriter and recipient of the 2004 National Music Publishers President's Award, Williams' standards have been recorded by such diverse musical icons as: Elvis Presley, Frank Sinatra, Barbra Streisand, Ella Fitzgerald, Ray Charles, David Bowie, Tony Bennett, R.E.M., Sarah Vaughn, Johnny Mathis, Bing Crosby, the Carpenters, Luther Vandross, Mel Tormé, and Diana Ross. His songs have also found favor with country legends including: Chet Atkins, Garth Brooks, the Dixie Chicks, Kris Kristofferson, Charlie Pride, Crystal Gayle, Anne Murray, Lynn Anderson, The Oak Ridge Boys, Diamond Rio, and Neil McCoy.
- "The Rainbow Connection," from the children's classic *The Muppet Movie,* is one of two Paul Williams songs that grace the American Film Institute's list of the top movie songs of all time. The second, "Evergreen," is from the award-winning 1976 remake of *A Star Is Born.*

- Additional song scores include the cult favorite *Phantom of the Paradise* and *Ishtar,* as well as *The Muppet Christmas Carol,* and *Bugsy Malone.* Williams also penned the lyrics for the blockbuster hit *The Sum of All Fears.* For the season finale of *Ally McBeal,* Williams offered the touching "I Know Him By Heart," recorded by Vonda Shepard.

- Williams recently teamed up with legendary songwriter Carole King to write the title song "Stand Back," sung by Joan Osborne, for the movie *Raising Helen.* He also wrote the music and lyrics for the Garry Marshall musical *Happy Days.*

- Although most people came to know Williams as one of Johnny Carson's recurring favorites on *The Tonight Show,* or as an actor in dozens of films, television comedies, and dramas, it is his musical legacy that continues to inspire. "We've Only Just Begun," "Rainy Days and Mondays," "You and Me Against the World," "(Just An) Old Fashioned Love Song," and "Let Me Be The One" all remain pop classics.

- He is also responsible for writing the theme to the classic television series, *The Love Boat.*

- As a part of America's large recovering community, Paul is very active on the Speakers Circuit. Sharing stories of his own escape from addiction, he quips, "You know you're an alcoholic when you misplace a decade."

Memories from *The Brady Bunch Variety Hour:*

"I remember Paul Williams wouldn't always stay focused and was 'out there' sometimes. They'd stop and he'd get focused again. He was a very, very fun guy. The day we were filming our musical finale he definitely had a few drinks. He was tipsy and swayed a little when he shouldn't have and couldn't get his lip synching right. It was funny in a way. He had to have a couple drinks before we filmed that one." — Geri Reischl

"This was quite a few years ago before I found the camp value to the *Variety Hour.* I said something to Paul about, oh, well, sorry, I hope the experience on the *Variety Hour* wasn't unpleasant, and he's like, 'Are you kidding?! I enjoyed it. I loved it.' This is after he got sober so I was surprised he had any memory of it. I remember us all sighing and being very relieved that he got through the number without falling over. I'd say I think he was partying a little, but he certainly was jovial. He's a nice guy, definitely nice, always cracking jokes." — Susan Olsen

So Good to Be Bad
You Can Run, But You Can't Hide

Unforgettable

More than thirty years later people continue to be fascinated by the absurdity of *The Brady Bunch Variety Hour*. While memories of the award-winning variety shows that topped the Nielsen ratings during the 1970s have faded, those disco Bradys refuse to go away. Marty Krofft says, "They're still talking about that show. I think it's an honor. That means it's unforgettable. We never did the norm, I think we were always ahead of our time, and I think we still are." Susan Olsen, who once kept a low profile about the production, finally made peace with her shame and decided to come out of the closet. "I no longer want to hide. It's one thing to be in something that just sucks. I've been in plenty of those. But when it sucks so bad that it actually makes history that's kind of cool," Susan explains. Maureen McCormick notes that despite how things turned out she believes the *Variety Hour* should be remembered fondly by fans. "I think it's definitely an important part of our history because it was so campy. It was so kitschy, and unbelievably unforgettable!" she laughs.

Krofftette Lynne Latham is especially amused when she sees old photographs of the show or watches it on television. "I feel guilty saying how tacky I thought it was. That whole era was tacky, tacky, tacky: from the costumes, to the makeup, to the hair, eyelashes, falsies, you name it. When I saw myself in *The Brady Bunch Variety Hour* on DVD, I just thought, 'Oh my God, I swear to God! This is my legacy!'" she exclaims.

Barry Williams, however, is among many involved who definitely do not appreciate negative comments about the *Variety Hour*. "I think there's a way to have fun with it, and

be good natured. It's when it gets mean-spirited that I go a little bit south. The way I would look at judging the show is, what was it trying to accomplish and how close did it come to accomplishing what it tried to do? We were presenting a very different kind of a show, and I think we did it well," Barry says.

New Year's Reincarnation

As the 1980s drew to a close *The Brady Bunch* entered a seemingly endless resurgence of nostalgic popularity. *The Brady Bunch Variety Hour*, however, sat collecting dust in a film vault, completely forgotten and disregarded. Reruns of the original sitcom remained

popular, especially during the explosion of cable TV, and a series of new *Brady Bunch* television movies produced by Sherwood and Lloyd Schwartz seemed to successfully quash any memories of the variety show. Then Diane Robina, director of acquisitions for retro cable network Nick at Nite, had an idea to bring back programs that would catch people by surprise. "We had been going through the archives of Paramount to see what they hadn't sold — TV gems that were just sitting on the shelf that everyone kind of forgot about. We definitely loved all things Brady, for sure. The Bradys always did well for us. It was a touch point with the demographic we were going after," Robina recalls.

Nick at Nite decided to feature *The Brady Bunch Variety Hour* pilot episode to ring in the new year at midnight on December 31, 1990. It was the first time it had been shown since 1976. Robina continues, "It was a special on variety shows, because they were the convention of television in the '70s. It was a retrospective of celebrating all things variety and we culminated with *The Brady Bunch Variety Hour* because we thought with our audience that was going to be the best one. Variety shows are really super hard to clear because of the music issues, but the Bradys hit such a sweet spot with our audience, we always did well with that." Nick at Nite

Diane Robina

continued to rerun *The Brady Bunch Variety Hour* pilot throughout 1991 and it was paired on the network with *The Sonny and Cher Comedy Hour* as the "Have a Nice Day Power Hours."

Geri Reischl recalls her reaction: "I was so surprised to see the *Variety Hour* on Nick at Nite. I honestly thought I'd never see it again. I started yelling to my family… 'Hurry, hurry my show is on TV…. Get in here!' I wanted my two kids to see it really bad. They were kind of laughing while they were watching it. My son liked the music, and my daughter started making comments about our very unusual costumes — 'Mommy! What are you wearing?' I had to remind her that it was the '70s. My husband had seen it a few times when it had originally aired."

The Simpson Family Smile-Time Variety Hour

Once Nick at Nite brought back *The Brady Bunch Variety Hour* to a viewing audience, Brady fans quickly became acquainted with the show — many of them for the first time. *The Real Live Brady Bunch* had been a resounding success onstage in Chicago in the early 1990s and people were beginning to recognize the huge potential for parody involving the Bradys, especially on shows such as *Saturday Night Live*. The first pop-culture reference to the *Variety Hour* came in a 1992 episode of *Tiny Toon Adventures* entitled "Grandma's Dead" in which Elmyra's pet hamster, "Jan Brady," dies and her new one is called "a mid-season replacement."

Steve Tompkins

Then in 1997, writers Steve Tompkins and Bill Oakley decided they would dedicate an entire segment of *The Simpsons* to a satire of the Bradys in "The Simpson Family Smile-Time Variety Hour." The parody was a part of episode #4F20, "The Simpson's Spinoff Showcase" (May 11, 1997), which featured possible ideas for other shows involving *Simpsons* characters. This episode later ended up being rated number nineteen in the top twenty-five episodes of *The Simpsons* by *Entertainment Weekly* magazine (February 7, 2003).

Bill Oakley says, "The whole thing is basically a direct parody of *The Brady Bunch Variety Hour* and was intended as such with a few references to *Donny and Marie*, *Sonny and Cher*, and *Laugh-In*, as well as any other '70s variety show we grew up watching. The reason this is there is because I am a gigantic *Brady Bunch* fan. When I was a very little kid, both *Brady Bunch* and *Partridge Family* were on in prime time and I got to stay up to watch them. The only reason I watched *Partridge Family*, which was vastly

Bill Oakley

inferior, was because I got to stay up an extra half hour. Then, in syndication, I watched the Bradys over and over throughout my teens. I am sure I have seen most episodes of *The Brady Bunch* at least five times. I also suspect I was the only freshman at Harvard in 1985 who would rush back from class to watch *Brady Bunch* reruns in the dorm every afternoon. It was a thrill to be able to finally make use of my *Brady* knowledge in this segment." Steve Tompkins adds that while growing up he also shared Oakley's obsession for the Bradys. "The bittersweet truth is I have more memories of *The Brady Bunch* than I do of *The Simpsons*," Tompkins says.

One of their first tasks was to think about how they wanted the Simpsons to look in a variety show landscape and who they would interact with. Tompkins says, "Although it was not unique to *The Brady Bunch Hour*, I remember being slightly unsettled when Robert Reed's curly perm first appeared. I believe I lobbied hard for the animators to give a curly perm to Homer but memory, like Robert Reed's hairstyle, is a little fuzzy." Tompkins also remembers pushing for Rip Taylor to be the guest cameo in the segment, which would have definitely tipped the balance of the homage clearly towards the Bradys. The producers ultimately decided on using Tim Conway.

"The only distinctly remarkable thing I remember from producing the episode was meeting with our musical director Alf Clausen to discuss the songs, telling him we wanted a *Donny and Marie* feel, and him telling me it wouldn't be a problem because he'd been the musical director on their show," Tompkins adds. The animators also obtained a copy of *The Brady Bunch Hour* as a reference for the costumes and camera angles, and created a generic laugh track, which was a staple of variety shows during the '70s.

FAKE JAN   FAKE LISA

The parody would not be complete without a reference to Geri Reischl and Fake Jan. Tompkins says, "I remember being a boy of twelve feeling confused and betrayed by the sudden replacement of Jan on the *Variety Hour,* but I think I carried a little guilt too, because I secretly thought Geri Reischl was really cute. (Blasphemy!)" Oakley and Tompkins came up with an idea. Oakley explains, "The Fake Lisa is 100 percent a reference to the Fake Jan, and the whole joke is that Lisa Simpson would be too smart and have too much integrity to ever appear in such a show, even though the rest of the Simpsons were willing to sell out. Furthermore, it was clear to us at the show that the people at FOX Network never really liked Lisa, and every time we did a Lisa show they wouldn't put Lisa in the ads, but instead would focus on whatever tangential thing Bart or Homer would be doing. It also seemed like the natural cheesy network TV instinct would be to immediately recast Lisa, the smart, introspective prodigy, with a mindless, personality-free 'sophomore prom queen' basically the polar opposite of the real Lisa and much more advertiser friendly! There are some obvious parallels between Lisa and Jan."

Mike Lookinland thought it was hilarious. "We were spoofed so effectively on *The Simpsons*. I can't overstate how great it was for me to see that. They spoofed that Lisa was a pain in the ass and got replaced. Lisa refused to do the show for artistic reasons so she just got replaced with some hot chick that looks just like Geri. She was very energetic, and cute, and smiling all the time. Of course, they only did public domain songs."

Susan Olsen says she also was impressed when she saw the episode. "They had Fake Lisa. It was brilliant, obviously. It's wonderful because they're not encumbered by a network or somebody saying, 'No, no you can't do that joke, that's too much of an art history joke, or that's too much of an inside joke, or it's too obscure.' They can do obscure stuff like that and get away with it," Susan says.

Geri Reischl had no idea about the episode until much later when a friend mentioned seeing it. Geri recalls, "I was shocked. I thought it was awesome. My kids' friends just thought that was the greatest thing, because they said they have the poster with all the characters that have ever been on *The Simpsons* and I am on the top row in the back. My son had to go buy it. Our show didn't last that long, but I put an impression in somebody's head that they would want to use my likeness."

Rebirth and Resurgence

The Simpson's Smile-Time Variety Hour marked a rebirth and resurgence of *The Brady Bunch Variety Hour,* which came as an unexpected surprise to the cast, and gave die-hard *Brady Bunch* fans something new to feast upon. Australian cable network TV1 was quick

to tap into the immense popularity of *The Brady Bunch* with audiences down under, and in 1997 began to rerun all nine episodes of *The Brady Bunch Hour* once a week as part of their "TV1 Cool Summer" programming. This was the first time most of the shows had been seen by viewers in over twenty years and it sparked an intense demand for bootleg copies in the United States. Collector Glenn McLain explains: "For years following the Nick at Nite broadcast, video collectors were searching everywhere for the *Variety Hour*. Other than horrible, multigeneration VHS copies of that airing, there was nothing in circulation. However in 1997, thanks to the internet, a fellow collector discovered that an obscure TV station in Australia was re-airing the series. Somehow he found someone to record it. Despite the fact it was half-a-world away and in a completely different broadcast format, U.S. fans were finally going to be able to see the show. Let's just say some stones are better left unturned. While the quality of the recording was poor by today's standards, I don't think anyone was really prepared for how bad the show was. It was a traffic accident you couldn't pry your eyes away from, which only caused more people to want to see it. Along the way it crossed the line into that realm of being 'so bad, it's good'… falling somewhere between *Pink Lady* and *Plan 9 from Outer Space*."

In 1998 the American cable network TV Land also decided to rerun three episodes of *The Brady Bunch Hour,* although some scenes were heavily edited. Then in late 1999, the website entitled *Complete Guide to The Brady Bunch Hour* was launched by writer Ted Nichelson. It included information on each episode, screen captures, sound files,

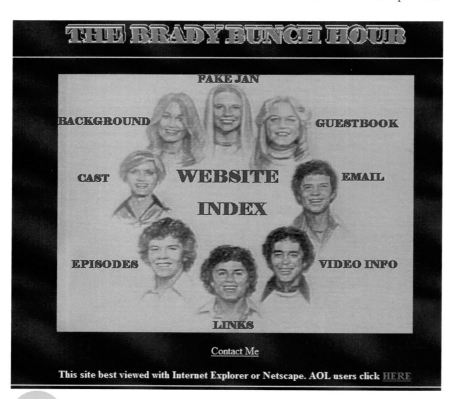

photographs, and contributions from several cast members. Finally in 2000, two episodes of *The Brady Bunch Variety Hour* were made available to American audiences on DVD when they were released by Rhino Video as part of their distribution rights to the library of Sid and Marty Krofft.

On October 10, 2000, the Bradys were satirized yet again on *That '70s Show* with "The Forman Bunch Variety Hour." Bradyologist Lisa Sutton says, "In the name of comedy, *That '70s Show* skewered so many clichés of the '70s. What better way to point out the lowest point in the have-a-nice-decade than by lampooning the acknowledged low point in television history? Many viewers of *That '70s Show* may have been entirely unaware of what they were mocking, since so many of the show's fans were not around to see the *Variety Hour,* and those who were old enough were too busy tuning out to catch it in the first place. But it was a well-researched and hilarious send-up, nevertheless." At the beginning of the spoof the Forman family is seen watching *The Brady Bunch Variety Hour* and eating a Bundt cake. After everyone is quickly repulsed by the show, Kitty is left alone in the living room and daydreams of a family "who gets along, and sings, and dances" in their very own variety show. Their guest stars are '70s icons Shirley Jones, Charo, and Gene Simmons. Debra Jo Rupp, who played Kitty Forman, recalls, "So, we had to watch *The Brady Bunch Variety Hour*, and, I don't know, it was quite possibly one of the worst things I've seen in my life."[42]

"The Forman Bunch Variety Hour" from *That '70s Show*

Jim Zrake, unit manager on the original *Brady Bunch Variety Hour,* found the *'70s Show* parody entertaining. "I think it's probably the greatest compliment, because it sticks in your mind. *The Brady Bunch Hour* is easy fodder for jokes anyway. Do people remember if it was good or bad, or do they remember it was the *Brady Bunch* out of their element doing something completely different? The fact that people still refer to it, I think, is kind of cool. It becomes a part of the fabric of the culture of this country."

The Formans perform their opening number: "I Got the Music in Me"

Susan Olsen adds, "To me, anybody who parodies the *Variety Hour* is just cooler than

Real Love for Fake Jan

What is it about Fake Jan that makes her the greatest replacement character in television history? She certainly wasn't the first to fill in for an actor in a well-known role (Dick Sargent famously became Darrin Stephens back in '69 when Dick York could no longer fulfill his duties) and she certainly won't be the last (I'm still reeling over Fake Becky on "Roseanne" -- death to Sarah Chalke -- you will NEVER be Becky Connor to me!).

An entry from the Kenneth M. Walsh blog,

Kenneth in the (212)

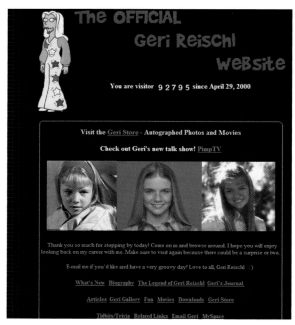

A website devoted to Fake Jan was launched in

January 2000 by Ted Nichelson

cool because in the first place they know about it. Then to see it as being fodder for parody is great. So my opinion of *That '70s Show* went up by 1000 percent when I saw that episode and I realized what a good show it is."

The Many Lives of Fake Jan

Contrary to common belief, "Fake Jan" is not the most hated of the other "fake" Bradys. Bradyologist Lisa Sutton explains, "That honor belongs to cousin Oliver, the jinx. Chalk that up to fifth season 'cute waif' syndrome. Fake Jan, however, serves a much greater purpose in the world of Brady."

As far as Brady culture goes, "Fake Jan" helped to elevate the status of the "Real Jan" to the top of the Brady heap. Although younger fans would cite "Marcia, Marcia, Marcia" as top Brady, those who followed the Bradys from 1969 to the present know it was Jan who was really the most popular girl. Eve Plumb's somewhat exaggerated absence from several Brady reunions has more recently made her the most sought after Brady. The insertion of Geri Reischl into *The Brady Bunch Variety Hour* proved Eve was not easily replaced, and resulted in the lasting moniker of "Fake Jan." The results made Eve Plumb appear more savvy than she really may have been, while raising her value on the Brady stock market. Sutton continues, "It was fortunate timing for Eve, who was never much of a singer. And fortunately for the *Variety Hour's* producers, Geri was. As much as I love the 'Fortune Cookie Song,' Reischl could sing circles around her TV doppelgänger. In retrospect, the camp value of having a replacement for an original Brady helped elevate *The Brady Bunch Variety Hour* to legendary status in terms of the exquisitely bad. 'Fake Jan' serves as the epicenter of the disaster, giving onlookers a landmark to point their fingers at."

According to noted pop-culture addict Don Smith, he and his sister Erin coined the phrase "Fake Jan" during their childhood obsession with *The Brady*

Bunch and then used it for the first time during the late 1980s in their fanzine *Teenage Gang Debs*. Smith explains, "When *The Brady Bunch Variety Hour* began airing on Nick at Nite in 1991 we had many friends working at the network and talked to them all the time. Who didn't want to work there? We regularly sent issues of *Teenage Gang Debs* to their offices." The advertising staff at Nick at Nite was amused by Don and Erin Smith's creative use of "Fake Jan," and recognized the potential of exploiting the term to make viewers more aware of the show. Diane Robina recalls, "To promote the *Variety Hour,* because Eve Plumb wasn't in it, we made promos about it since everyone referred to the 'Fake Jan.'"

Geri Reischl thought it was a fun idea. "I would overhear the promos on Nick at Nite from the TV at home and right before the promo was over I would hear 'and a Fake Jan.' I thought, 'Wow, they are singling me out.' I loved it. I don't mind being called 'Fake Jan.' It gives me my own identity," she explains. Don Smith adds that his sister also made use of the concept when she moved to New York City. "Erin later worked as an intern at *Sassy* magazine, which printed the phrase 'Fake [blank]' to refer to actors and models who looked reasonably like other celebrities. In fashion there are tons and tons of inside jokes like that. But I am pretty surprised there was that much interest in the phrase," he says.

After *The Brady Bunch Hour,* Geri Reischl starred in a series of commercials for breakfast cereal "Crispy Wheats 'n' Raisins" from 1979–1982.

Geri Reischl has remained an intriguing figure to *Brady Bunch* fans. After production ended on *The Brady Bunch Variety Hour*, Geri went back to high school and after graduating held a job in a doctor's office while continuing to audition. She married in 1979 and then landed a series of *Wizard of Oz*-themed commercials for the breakfast cereal Crispy Wheats 'n' Raisins, which ran nationally for four years. Because of her contract with General Mills, she was forced to give up the role of Blair Warner, a role made popular by Lisa Whelchel, in a television pilot entitled *Garrett's Girls,* later known as *The Facts of Life*. When she became pregnant with her first child in 1983 she decided to retire from show business. From that point on Geri showed little interest in her *Brady Bunch* past and eventually her whereabouts became a mystery. Geri explains, "I just decided that that was a wonderful part of my life. I totally enjoyed show business, but that was only one part of my life. When I had my first child I decided that that was going to be my new role. Because

with interviews, you never know when you're going out, you'll be home late, you get a job, you go at four in the morning. You work until maybe ten or eleven at night. I'd never get to see my kids, and I decided that I wanted to be a full-time mom. It's one of the best jobs that I could ever experience. I've never worked outside of the home and I've always been here for my kids. That's why they're so well adjusted!"

Then in 2000 Geri unexpectedly received an invitation to collaborate with the *Brady Hour* website by starting her own home page: FakeJan.com. She had no experience with the internet and was reluctant, but her children begged her to buy a computer and become a part of the new technology. Geri says she was astonished and flattered by the outpouring of messages she received through the website, and enjoyed interacting with *Brady Bunch* fans. "I couldn't believe there was a website dedicated to me on the internet. I was shocked! I didn't own a computer so I didn't get to see it right away. I thought, 'Who would want to start a website dedicated to me?' Now I am quite proud of my website. It has enabled me to interact with my fans. This has changed so many things for me. It's awesome to have someone tell you that they loved your work on a show, and that you might have helped them get through some difficult times in their lives. After reading that, you can't help but get a warm feeling in your heart," Geri explains. She adds that even after all the time that has passed Brady fans remain loyal. "I still get a lot of fan mail. It's usually men that write me who are unbelievably nice. I am plagued by the 'Fake Jan' thing. Sometimes people

Kevin Sinclair and Troy Stone

The 2003 short film *Fake Stacy*, by Sean Blythe and John Chuldenko, was partially inspired by Fake Jan and played at the Sundance Film Festival

will write and say, 'You know, I thought Jan didn't look like herself, but maybe I didn't see right, or she changed a little bit. Then I realized it was another Jan, but that's okay,'" Geri says.

In 2001, in Danville, Illinois, musicians Kevin Sinclair and Troy Stone formed a rock band known as Fake Jan and released a CD called *Love That Feeling*. Stone explains how the band got started. "Kevin and I have been in bands forever, but this was never a group that was out as a five- or four-member piece band. This was a project that we put together ourselves and recorded everything for. He called me up one time — he had a bunch of music written and I had some music written. Since there was no band at that time we needed some kind of name for the project," Stone says.

"We kind of dabbled around and he mentioned how Geri had taken the place of Eve on *The Brady Bunch Hour*. The spotlight was on her coming in and then everybody was kind of making fun of that saying, she's not the real Jan, she's the fake Jan. We said we'll put this project out on the internet, and we'll just glorify that name, and say it's not so bad to step into something. Once we did that, people thought we were slapping her in the face and we're not. Basically we thought it was a really cool-sounding name for the fact that people were poking fun at it and we were not. We had some people who saw our website and were really upset we called our band Fake Jan. I don't understand. These are die-hard fans. It was just crazy with things like, 'How dare you' and such. I thought, 'Get over it.' We just kind of ignored them," Stone explains.

A short film in 2003, written by Sean Blythe and directed by John Chuldenko, was partially inspired by the concept of "Fake Jan" and was entitled *Fake Stacy*. The story gives the audience a glimpse of a grown-up child star that played twins on a television show but was only credited for one role, and everyone talks about her as she walks by. Blythe summarizes the film this way: "When Claire Owen was fourteen, they put her on television… *Fake Stacy* is the life story of an accidental pop culture icon — told to us in the time it takes to drink a cup of coffee and smoke a cigarette — by every single person Claire passes on the street." The film featured

The Brady Bunch Variety Hour References in Pop Culture

Nick at Nite's "Have a Nice Day Power Hours" (1991)

Tiny Toon Adventures, "Grandma's Dead" (November 10, 1992)

The Simpsons, "The Simpsons Spin-Off Showcase," featuring *The Simpson Family Smile-Time Variety Hour* (May 11, 1997)

Complete Guide to *The Brady Bunch Hour*: www.bradyhour.com (January 27, 2000)

Official Geri Reischl Website: www.fakejan.com (January 27, 2000)

That '70s Show, "Red Sees Red," featuring *The Forman Bunch Variety Hour* (October 11, 2000)

The band Fake Jan, CD release, *Love That Feeling* (2001)

Futurama, "Where No Fan Has Gone Before" (April 21, 2002)

TV Guide's "50 Worst Shows of All-Time" Issue (July 20, 2002)

The Gilmore Girls, "Application Anxiety" (October 7, 2002)

Fake Stacy, a short film by Sean Blythe and John Chuldenko (2003)

Live talk-show host Seth Rudetsky, "Deconstructing *The Brady Bunch Variety Hour*," Ars Nova Theater, New York City (2002–2004)

The Family Guy, "Don't Make Me Over" (June 5, 2005)

First official "Fake Jan Day" ("Jan 2," 2008)

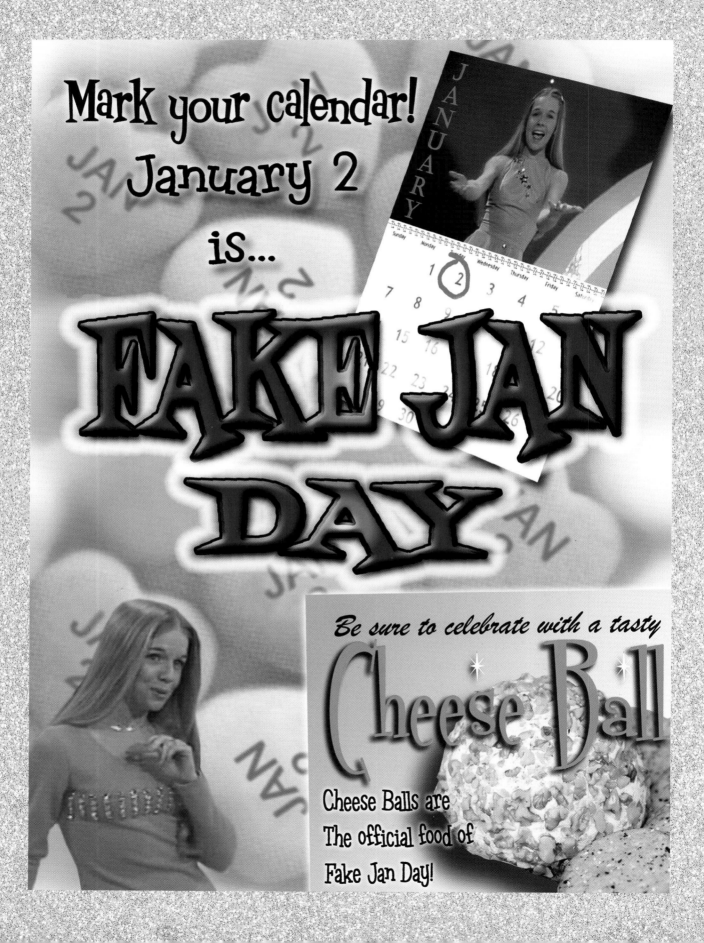

Meagan Mangum as Claire Owen and contained a cameo by CNN's Larry King. It was well-received when it played at the Sundance Film Festival. Sean Blythe explains how he got the idea for the film. "I had this collection of fragmented ideas that never seemed to fit anywhere. I wanted to write a story about paranoia, where everyone is literally talking about a character behind her back. I wanted to write something about Friday night television, and how there are certain shows that I loved as a kid, that my cooler friends who went out on Fridays never even heard of. I always liked Kieslowski's movie *The Double Life of Veronique,* and thought it would be interesting to, you know, rip it off. Anyway, it was all this kind of stuff that didn't make sense in a feature. I didn't really have a central idea that tied all of that together," Blythe admits. "Then, one day, I was watching the *E! True Hollywood Story* about *The Brady Bunch,* and they mentioned that when they did *The Brady Bunch Variety Hour* they replaced Eve Plumb with another actress, and that the fans of the show called the new girl Fake Jan. And then I changed the channel and saw Alan Thicke say, innocently, I'm sure, that he wished he had two Tracey Golds, one he could work with as his daughter on *Growing Pains,* and one he could keep for himself. And I think I literally said out loud: 'Oh!'" Blythe adds.[43]

Brittny Lane Stewart who played Young Claire, recalls, "The film was really exciting to make. I'll never forget reading the script for the first time before my audition and I thought to myself, 'I have to be a part of this!' I think all the cast would agree that when we were making the film we all knew we had something special. I had so much fun playing Young Claire 'cause I had the privilege of doing some green screen work, where I got to be two different people on a split screen. Even still, every time I watch the movie I love it just as much as the first time I saw it."

A dedicated group of *Brady Bunch* fans recently celebrated the first official "Fake Jan Day" on January 2, 2008. Because Geri Reischl was the second actress to play Jan Brady it seemed logical. One enthusiast explains, "It really started a couple years ago when I saw my computer calendar on January 2, but it said 'Jan 2' and I thought, 'Jan 2, is that a reference to the second Jan?' So I sent out MySpace messages wishing people a 'Happy Fake Jan Day' and I got a lot of funny replies. It was even bigger in 2009. Within a couple of years, it should grow into a genuine Brady holiday, or at least another opportunity to break out a cheese ball — the official party food of Fake Jan."

Parodied, Panned, and Patronized

The year 2002 was an interesting one for *The Brady Bunch Variety Hour*. The show was referenced on *Futurama, The Gilmore Girls,* and appeared on the cover of *TV Guide's* "50 Worst Shows of All Time" issue. In addition, comedian Seth Rudetsky launched a live stage show in New York called "Deconstructing *The Brady Bunch Variety Hour.*"

While some fans assert that the cartoon *Futurama* is a parody of *Star Trek,* it was confirmed by the April 21, 2002 episode "Where No Fan Has Gone Before," taken from the

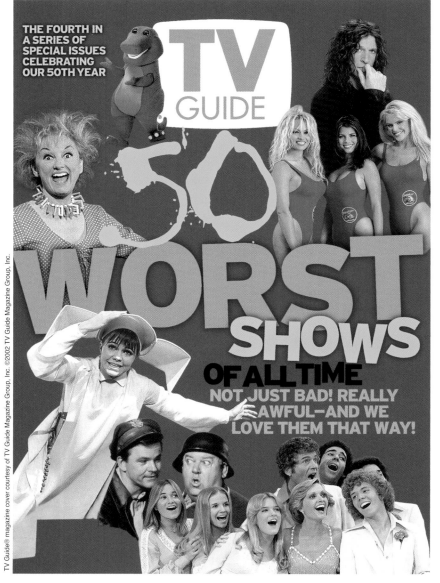

THE BRADY BUNCH HOUR

January 23, 1977–May 25, 1977
The TV family that wouldn't go away starred in two sitcoms, a quasi drama, a cartoon, a TV-movie and this, the most dumbfounding of all: a variety show featuring the original cast (with the exception of Eve Plumb, always the smart one) *in character*. Seems architect dad Mike had reluctantly given up blueprints to join his family in a musical endeavor—which explained actor Robert Reed's profound lack of song-and-dance talent. So what was the kids' excuse? We'll never know.

famous catchphrase, "Where no man has gone before." The episode featured the voice talents of the original *Star Trek* cast, with the exceptions of DeForest Kelley, who had passed away, and James Doohan, who refused to be a part of the show. DeForest was depicted as a character in the episode, but did not speak. However, the character of Scotty was replaced by "Welshy" from "The Star Trek Musical," since Scotty could not yodel. This was a direct reference to Geri Reischl replacing Eve Plumb. When the presence of "Welshy" is questioned by the cast in the episode, Nichelle Nichols explains, "We did some musical reunion specials in the 2200's but the guy who played Scotty had trouble yodeling," to which George Takei adds, "Ever since then, Welshy has been a welcome participant in our escapades."

Then a few months later in July of 2002, *TV Guide* came out with their "50 Worst Shows of All-Time" issue with the subheading "Not just bad! Really awful — and we love them that way!" *The Brady Bunch Variety Hour* was prominently featured on the cover and was rated number four, right behind *Jerry Springer*, the 1965–1966 series *My Mother the Car* (in which an attorney's mother is reincarnated as an antique car), and the short-lived 2001 extreme football show *XFL*. Susan Olsen recalls, "I didn't know we were on the cover of *TV Guide* until a friend of mine, who has his own radio show in another part of the country, called me up to see if I would do an interview with him. I said 'Why?' and he said, 'Well, don't you know you're on the cover of *TV Guide* as the fourth worst show in TV history?' I'm like, 'Alright! We finally got credit.'"

Original *Brady Bunch* creator Sherwood Schwartz is somewhat dismissive of the rating. "Show business is a matter of opinion. Some people hated *Gilligan's Island* when it came on and now it's an icon of TV, it's the same with *The Brady Bunch*. Not everybody loved that show when it came on," he says. Rip Taylor shares this sentiment, "They're wrong, that's the bottom line, they're wrong, just like when *TV Guide* put Oprah's face on Ann-Margaret's body on the cover."

The Brady Bunch Variety Hour was also featured in the October 7, 2002 episode of *The Gilmore Girls* entitled "Application Anxiety." In the opening, Lorelai and Rory are sitting at home watching television, engrossed by the Bradys. Lorelai exclaims, "It was the golden age of television. All the cylinders were fired on this one boy!" Rory asks, "Who knew they had such musical talent?" to which her mother replies, "and such far-out booty-shaking abilities as well!" When the mail is delivered Rory's application to Harvard arrives and they discuss the "heavy importance" of making a decision on where to go to college. Rory says, "I feel dizzy," and Lorelai interjects, "Are you sure it's not the sight of Robert Reed in tight clown pants?" Rory concludes, "Oh jeez. Let the record show when my application to Harvard arrived we were watching *The Brady Bunch Variety Hour*."

Geri Reischl explains, "The *Variety Hour* never goes away. Look…it was part of the storyline for *The Gilmore Girls*. My daughter watches it, so that made me look a little bit 'cooler' in her eyes. *The Gilmore Girls* obviously have good taste when it comes to choosing good television shows!"

Comedian Seth Rudetsky took Brady fans by surprise with his "Deconstructing *The Brady Bunch Variety Hour*," which he performs at the Ars Nova Theater in New York City. In the show, Rudetsky delivers running commentary about the program, scene dissection, and, in his own words, "hilariously harsh judgments." Rudetsky tells how he came up with the idea for his deconstruction, "I got a brilliant compilation tape that somebody made with an image of Mike Brady totally in drag as Carmen Miranda and it immediately segues to Florence Henderson singing, 'It's sad, so sad…' I would have people over to my house and show them clips of the show, and make fun of it, and my friend said, 'You should put that in an actual comedy show.' So that started in 2002."

Seth Rudetsky deconstructs *The Brady Bunch Variety Hour*

Chris Knight was not surprised when he heard about Rudetsky's show. "I discovered something recently. The *Variety Hour* is a giant cult classic, sort of on the level of the *Rocky Horror Picture Show* with the transvestite community. It's a huge hit. They watch it in bars."

Seth Rudetsky begins his show with an introduction to *The Brady Bunch Variety Hour* so the audience has a general understanding of what it was about. Rudetsky says, "I deconstruct the show and people's jaws are agape the whole time. They cannot, *cannot* believe this was ever on the air! Most people don't know it existed, and they're shocked when they see it. I just play different clips from the show and I give them a heads-up of what to watch for. For instance, with Mike Brady, he sort of sounds like a deaf person when he sings. Why can't you just use your actual speaking voice to sing, why do you have to adopt *The Miracle Worker*?" Then Rudetsky explains the subtext of Alice during "Shake Your Booty." "First of all, she's a maid? For some reason she's in a pant suit on a variety show so it's bedazzled! Obviously she had it in her contract, 'I'll just show up the day of taping, just put me in the last sixteen bars of the number.' Then in the comedy bit she pretends, 'I can't dance!' but as soon as the camera turns away she's the most amazing dancer ever. Her 'Shake Your Booty' is unbelievably fierce."

Rudetsky continues with the rest of the cast, "In 'It's Not Where You Start, It's Where You Finish,' Florence is the only one who has a 180-degree split in the air. It's like 'I've still *got it!*' as she kicks. I feel like that's a big subtext of hers. You see Greg blatantly falling in the roller-rink scene and for some reason it's not edited out. Carol goes into head voice on the climax of her duet with Greg, with incestuous overtones, as well as her sassy telling off of Charo. Mike Brady's complete lack of body awareness makes his rendition of the Hustle seizure-like, and then there is Fake Jan's machine-gun vibrato on 'Turn the Beat Around.'"

Rudetsky brags that he had the opportunity to confront Tony Randall about his guest appearance in the pilot. "He was totally not embarrassed. I said, 'Don't you think it's weird you did a poem set to music by William Walton?' He was completely proud of it. Why is he not embarrassed? I was mind-boggled! It's the worst thing I've ever seen, where he's rapping that poem and those creatures dancing in back of him!" One of the highlights of Seth Rudetsky's comedy performance comes at the end when he shows "how unbelievably simple the choreography is" on *The Brady Bunch Variety Hour*. Rudetsky explains, "I say 'It's an hour of all singing and all dancing, but no one can actually sing or dance.' I bring up seven members of the audience and I play Mike Brady. Then we do 'Baby Face,' and I teach them the choreography, and we do it *Rocky Horror* style in front of the video screen. I have two people on the side with water pistols shooting water up in the air."

Embracing the Past

Those involved with *The Brady Bunch Variety Hour* may never fully understand why the show induces such a strong reaction from the viewing public. However, the cast and crew will always be proud to have played a role in creating a unique moment in television history. Writer Mike Kagan reflects, "It's remarkable. None of us there thought this show was going to have any kind of an imprint or an impact on anyone. None of us thought this thing was going to go. Everyone was sort of looking at it as an interim gig. I don't think anyone went onboard thinking, 'Oh, we're going to be here for years.'"

Bruce Vilanch asserts everyone involved tried to do the best they could with it at the time, "Now it's a camp item, it was probably a camp item then. In a bizarre way it was entertaining, but we knew we weren't coming up with something that was going to live for the ages."

Maureen McCormick adds, "The *Variety Hour* was really cute and funny. I look back and say, 'It is what it is.' I can take pleasure in the fact that it was a weird kind of enjoyment."

Bonny Dore believes that in any failure, there's a lesson. "The lesson was that there was a great team of people working on *The Brady Bunch Hour* but they were experimenting with a 'sitvar' format — situation combined with variety. It hadn't really been done before. So instead of giving it more time to ferment and develop they got less time. There's a kind

of arrogance in that for the network to say, 'How tough can it be?' The truth is that Donny and Marie Osmond don't come along every day. When you take the reverse point of view you begin to see the enormity of what these kids walked into. Everybody was depending on Sid and Marty to do yet another miracle, but this time they were asking them to do something different. The Kroffts are rightfully proud of what they did accomplish in no time and on very short money."

Guest star Lynn Anderson adds that we all need more shows like *The Brady Bunch* for families to watch together. "At the time it was so simple, so innocent. Those days in the '70s were before our world was involved in such ugliness. I love looking back at images from then because it was just a kinder time. Those people were people you wanted to be like. The reason why we remember *The Brady Bunch* is because it's something we wish we had. I think we're afraid those times are gone and we won't get them back again. We miss it and we need it," she says.

Lloyd Schwartz explains that even though *The Brady Bunch* is one of his greatest career accomplishments as a producer, he will always have uncomfortable feelings surrounding *The Brady Bunch Variety Hour*. "I'm not saying we've always done the greatest things with the Bradys, but I do know I can stand beside almost all of the other shows and say, 'This is what we wanted to do,' maybe it didn't work, or maybe it did. But I sure don't like being linked to something I had no part of, and read in the magazines it was one of the worst shows in the history of television. We're still responsible in the public's eye."

When *Brady Bunch* creator Sherwood Schwartz was asked what he would like future generations to remember about *The Brady Bunch Variety Hour*, he paused for a moment and said: "I would want for them to know I had nothing to do with it."

©1976 Krofft Pictures

All episodes of *The Brady Bunch Hour* were filmed at KTLA "Golden West" Studios, Hollywood from November 22, 1976, through April 6, 1977. Stage 2 was used for the swimming pool and opening numbers, while Stage 6 was shared with *Donny and Marie*, and housed the Brady living room, comedy sketches, and large production numbers.

Donny and Marie Show: October 8, 1976

Guest Stars: **Ruth Buzzi, Chad Everett, Florence Henderson, Mike Lookinland, Patty Maloney, Maureen McCormick, Susan Olsen, Greg Rice, John Rice**

Taped: September 23–24, 1976

Summary of cameos by Brady Bunch cast:

Florence Henderson tells the audience about her childhood on an Indiana farm. Donny, Marie, and Florence then sing a medley of country songs including favorites such as "Don't Fence Me In," "I'm an Old Cowhand from the Rio Grande," "She'll Be Comin' Round the Mountain," "On Top of Old Smokey," and "You Are My Sunshine."

In a skit satirizing the '70s soap opera *Mary Hartman, Mary Hartman*, "Marie Hartman" (played by Marie Osmond) is chatting on the phone when Chad Everett comes to the door. Marie recognizes him as a doctor on TV. (At the time Everett was on *Medical Center* and in more recent years has held roles on *Melrose Place* and *Mulholland Drive*.) Chad explains that he is no longer working because of a malpractice lawsuit. Instead of taking out a boy's tonsils, he performed a Hammond Organ transplant. He laments that the parents had no sense of humor and leaves. The doorbell rings again, but this time it is "Florence Henderson, and the Brady Bunch." Florence explains to Marie that they can't stay, saying, "We're just passing through the neighborhood collecting old clothes to give to the Waltons." Marie then offers the kids a cold drink, and when Bobby speaks all that comes out of his mouth is the sound of an organ. Florence explains, "He's been that way ever since he had his tonsils out. Some crazy doctor gave him a Hammond Organ transplant." Marcia tells Marie that their brother Greg has left the Brady Bunch and moved to Milwaukee to get a date with Laverne and Shirley. Cindy adds, "We've been trying to find a teenage boy to replace him." Florence then introduces "someone wholesome enough to fit our wholesome image." Donny walks through the door grinning ear-to-ear as the new Greg Brady.

Songs:

● Florence, in Renaissance costume, sings "Have I Spent Too Long at the Fair" (B. Barnes)

● Susan, Michael, and Maureen sing "We Open In Venice" (Cole Porter)

Viewer Alerts:

● Chris Knight was scheduled to appear in this episode but later dropped out.

● Many years later, Susan Olsen made a horrifying discovery when reviewing a video tape of her appearance on *The Donny and Marie Show*. Sid Krofft came up with the idea of having doves released at the very end of the finale, but one of the birds didn't take flight fast enough, crashed into the stage floor, and is clearly seen in the final cut being trampled unknowingly by Florence Henderson! Although Marie tried to swat the bird off stage with a broom, the poor creature is seen a few seconds later staggering out from under Florence's giant hoop skirt dress.

DONNY & MARIE AND TONY RANDALL LAUNCH
THE BRADY BUNCH ON A NEW CAREER!

The whole bunch—Robert Reed, Florence Henderson, and the kids set out to conquer show biz. It's an hour of fun and music as guest stars Donny and Marie Osmond, and Tony Randall help them break into the "big time."

THE BRADY BUNCH VARIETY HOUR
ⓐⓑⓒ **SPECIAL TONIGHT 7:00 PM**

Pilot: November 28, 1976
Guest Stars: **Patty Maloney, Donny Osmond, Marie Osmond, Tony Randall**
Taped: November 22–24, 1976

Summary:

The Brady Bunch opens their new variety show with a medley of disco songs, and Carol updates the audience on what the family has been up to since they last saw them. Behind the scenes, the Brady kids decide to dump their father from the show because, according to Bobby, "he's stinking up the act." (Robert Reed's character will be picked on in episode 4 as well.) Tony Randall happens to stop by the house and Bobby suggests he play the father. When Mike overhears the conversation, the kids begin to feel guilty and welcome their dad back.

Sketches include a retrospective of the 1950s with Donny and Marie at "Ratsie's Rollerama" and the Bradys dressed as clowns in the "Comedy Water Circus." Tony Randall performs poetry set to music and is introduced by Mike in a bunny outfit, Greg in a bear costume, and Peter as a chicken. Patty Maloney appears as a dancing bear.

Alice makes a special guest appearance and talks about the special love amongst the Bradys.

The Bradys' musical finale this week is "Young and Old Songs."

Songs:
● "Baby Face" (Benny Davis/Harry Akst) and "Love to Love You Baby" (Donna Summer) Performed by the Brady cast
● "One" from *A Chorus Line* (Edward Kleban/Marvin Hamlish) Performed by the Brady cast
● "Splish Splash" (Bobby Darin/Murray Kaufman) Performed by Barry, Maureen, Donny and Marie

● "Hot Time in the Old Town" (Theodore Metz/Joe Hayden) Performed by Florence, Barry, Chris, and Clowns
● "Corner of the Sky" (Stephen Schwartz) Performed by Barry
● Poetry: "Façade" by Edith Sitwell (set to music by William Walton) Performed by Tony Randall

● "What I Did for Love" (Edward Kleban/Marvin Hamlisch) and "The Way We Were" (Alan Bergman/Marvin Hamlisch) Performed by Florence
● "Attitude Dancing" (Jacob Brackman/Carly Simon) Performed by Barry
● "Cheek to Cheek" (Irving Berlin) Performed by Robert and Florence

● "Dance With Me" (John Hall/Johanna Hall) Performed by the Brady cast
● "I Could Have Danced All Night" (Alan Jay Lerner/Frederick Lowe) Performed by Florence
● "The Hustle" (Van McCoy) Performed by the Brady cast

● "Shake Your Booty" (Harry Wayne Casey/Robert Finch) Performed by Geri, Ann B., and the Brady cast

Viewer Alerts:
● In the opening number the light bulb behind Florence's head is burnt out.
● During the final kick line of "One" Geri Reischl moves her hat down in the wrong direction.

● Geri trips on her rollerskates in her first entrance to "Ratsie's Rollerama" and then later her hair ribbon slowly slides down her pony tail and falls onto the floor.

⑦ BRADY BUNCH—Variety
Special: Tony Randall, and Donny and Marie Osmond are guests as members of the original TV Brady family re-create their roles in an hour of music and comedy, still in production at press time. Robert Reed and Florence Henderson (Mr. and Mrs. Brady) are joined by TV offspring Barry Williams (Greg), Maureen McCormick (Marcia), Christopher Knight (Peter), Geri Reischl (Jan), Mike Lookinland (Bobby) and Susan Olsen (Cindy) for sketches that spoof both their series and life in the '50s. (60 min.)
Musical Highlights
"One" . . . . .Robert Reed
"What I Did for Love," "The Way We Were" . . . . . . .Florence Henderson
Dance-tune medley . . . .Reed, Randall

New Show! Have the time of your life tonight as Florence Henderson, Robert Reed and The Brady Bunch bring you fresh new comedy, music and variety with guests:
Rip Taylor   Kaptain Kool And The Kongs   The Water Follies
Ann B. Davis   The Krofftette Dancers
THE BRADY BUNCH HOUR
ⓐⓑⓒ **6:00PM**

• Barry completely wipes out on his roller skates in the "Ratsie's Roller-ama" skit and Chris is seen laughing at him.

• There is a giant letter P for "Peter" on Chris Knight's belt buckle in the closing finale.

• Robert Reed becomes exhausted in the finale and just stands there looking disgusted.

• Watch the Krofftettes in green outfits dancing high in the scaffolding at the opening of the grand finale. The scenery is shaking so badly, it looks as if it could collapse at any second.

• In the encore, notice the reaction of the Krofftette (third dancer from the left of center) when she kicks the wrong direction.

Episode 1: January 23, 1977
Guest Stars: **Kaptain Kool and the Kongs, Farrah Fawcett-Majors, Lee Majors**
Taped: January 18–19, 1977

Summary:

The Bradys sing "Yankee Doodle Dandy" in celebration of the American Presidential Inauguration. Carol is excited about moving into the family's new house and then explains that the show is on just once a month.

The Bradys arrive at their new house but find that the furniture is missing. The moving company arrives with some furniture, but it does not belong to them. Mr. Merrill (Rip Taylor) discovers he has moved himself out of his own house and promises to have their furniture delivered the next day.

The next evening, Mike announces that the Bradys are officially moved into their new house and sends the kids to bed. Mike and Carol's romantic evening is interrupted by the doorbell. Mr. Merrill explains that before they bought the house, he rented the property to Lee Majors and his wife, Farrah Fawcett. Mike and Carol learn that the couple has no place to stay and invite them to sleep in the living room.

The next morning, Cindy calls the rest of the Brady kids to get out of bed and the boys swoon over Farrah while the girls kneel speechless over Lee. Farrah wakes up and is startled by the boys looking down at her and calls to Lee for help. Mike and Carol then explain the situation to the kids.

Mike and Carol introduce the finale, "Songs about Hearts."

Songs:
- "Yankee Doodle Dandy" (George M. Cohan) Performed by the Brady cast
- "Razzle Dazzle" (Fred Ebb/John Kander) Performed by the Brady cast
- "Car Wash" (Ramon Whitfield) Performed by Ann B., Maureen, Barry, Chris, and Rip
- "Your Song" (Bernie Taupin/Elton John) Performed by Geri

- "Send in the Clowns" (Stephen Sondheim) Performed by Florence, Robert, Barry, Maureen, and Chris
- "Names" Performed by Kaptain Kool and the Kongs
- "You've Gotta Have Heart" (Richard Adler/Jerry Ross) Performed by Maureen, Geri, and Susan
- "Heart and Soul" (Hoagy Carmichael) Performed by Florence and Robert
- "Happy Heart" (Jackie Rae/Hans Last) Performed by the Brady cast

- "Heart of My Heart" (Andrew Mack) Performed by Florence and Robert
- "Don't Go Breakin' My Heart" (Bernie Taupin/ Elton John) Performed by Kaptain Kool and the Kongs
- "How Can You Mend A Broken Heart" (Gibb Brothers) Performed by Florence
- "Heartbeat, It's A Lovebeat" (William Gregory Hudspeth/Micheal Kennedy) Performed by the Brady cast

- "United We Stand" (Tony Hiller/Peter Simmons) Performed by the Brady cast

38 BRADY BUNCH—Variety
Debut: The Bradys return in a new variety format. Opening guests are Lee Majors, Farrah Fawcett-Majors, Rip Taylor and Kaptain Kool and the Kongs. A running comedy sketch concerns the mix-ups connected with moving into a new beach house. Carol: Florence Henderson. Mike: Robert Reed. Greg: Barry Williams. Jan: Geri Reischl (who replaces Eve Plumb). Marcia: Maureen McCormick. Peter: Chris Knight. (60 min.)
Musical Highlights
"Yankee Doodle Dandy," "Razzle Dazzle," Medley of tunes . . . Bradys
"Send In the Clowns" . . . . . . Florence
[Nancy Drew and Hardy Boys mysteries will share this time slot with the Brady Bunch.]

Viewer Alerts:

● In the opening number as the Bradys sing "Here we go again!" Chris Knight doesn't know which way his arms are supposed to be going and throws them up in the air at the wrong time.

● In the original 1977 airing, sponsored by Oscar Mayer, an animated "Little Oscar" danced across the screen at the end as the Bradys exited the stage.

Episode 2: February 27, 1977
Guest Stars: **Milton Berle, Tina Turner**
Taped: February 17–18, 1977

Summary:

The Bradys sing "Hooray for Hollywood" and Bobby complains that the show's comedy stinks.

Alice and Mr. Merrill are playing with the CB radio when Bobby overhears Milton Berle cracking some jokes. Bobby takes the receiver and asks Berle if he would like to be on their show. The kids wait for Berle to arrive and he agrees to write jokes for the Bradys.

Berle introduces the "All-New Milton Berle Brady Bunch Hour" and the family tells a series of bad jokes. Meanwhile, Jan hits anyone who says "makeup" in the face with a giant powder puff. Mike and Carol tell Bobby that he has to fire Berle. Bobby tells Berle his humor doesn't fit the Bradys.

Peter introduces the finale, "Songs About Stars."

MILTON BERLE AND TINA TURNER JOIN THE BRADYS TONIGHT!

It's sensational entertainment with Florence Henderson, Robert Reed, the Brady Kids and great guests!
THE BRADY BUNCH HOUR
abc NEW SHOW 7:00 PM
Next Sunday: "Hardy Boys Mysteries"

Songs:

● "Hooray for Hollywood" (Johnny Mercer/Richard Whiting) Performed by the Brady cast
● "Make 'Em Laugh" (Arthur Freed/Nacio Herb Brown) Performed by Robert, Florence, Barry, Maureen, and Chris

- "Sing" (Joe Raposo) Performed by Collette the Puppet and Chris
- "Rubber Band Man" (Linda Creed/Thom Bell) Performed by Tina Turner
- "Evergreen" (Paul Williams/Barbara Streisand) Performed by Florence
- "Catch a Falling Star" (Paul Vance/Lee Pockriss) Performed by Robert and Florence
- "You Don't Have to Be a Star" (James Dean/John Glover) Performed by Geri and Barry
- "You Are My Lucky Star" (Nacio Herb Brown/Arthur Freed) Performed by Florence
- "Everybody Is a Star" (Sylvester Stewart) Performed by the Brady cast
- "Don't Let the Stars Get in Your Eyes" (Slim Willet) Performed by Milton Berle, Florence, and Tina Turner
- "Good Morning Starshine" (James Rado/Gerome Ragni/Gault McDermott) Performed by the Brady cast
- "Shining Star" (Maurice White/Philip Bailey/Larry Dunn) Performed by the Brady cast
- "United We Stand" (Tony Hiller/Peter Simmons) Performed by the Brady cast

Viewer Alerts:

- During a scene in the Brady living room, Maureen accidentally knocks a pillow off of the sofa and Milton Berle improvises a sarcastic remark: "You're very alert picking up that pillow!"

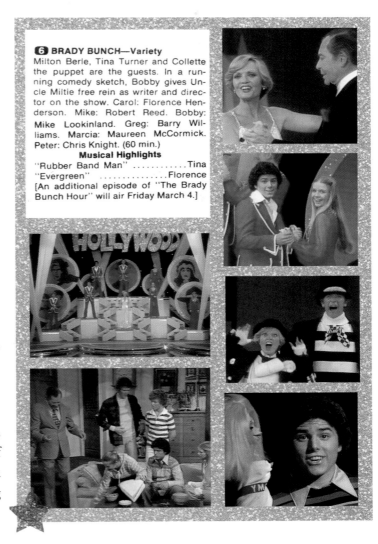

6 BRADY BUNCH—Variety
Milton Berle, Tina Turner and Collette the puppet are the guests. In a running comedy sketch, Bobby gives Uncle Miltie free rein as writer and director on the show. Carol: Florence Henderson. Mike: Robert Reed. Bobby: Mike Lookinland. Greg: Barry Williams. Marcia: Maureen McCormick. Peter: Chris Knight. (60 min.)
Musical Highlights
"Rubber Band Man" . . . . Tina
"Evergreen" . . . . Florence
[An additional episode of "The Brady Bunch Hour" will air Friday March 4.]

Episode 3: March 4, 1977

Guest Stars: **Sharon Baird, Vincent Price, H.R. Pufnstuf, Van Snowden**
Taped: February 8–9, 1977

Summary:

The Bradys open the show by singing "Sunny Side Up," in yolk-yellow jumpsuits.
Greg announces to the family that he's moving out of the house. Carol is caught off guard

and Mike tells Greg he's not going anywhere. Mr. Merrill barges in and announces that he's found the perfect apartment for Greg, which he rents on the spot. Mike and Carol are furious.

Mr. Merrill shows Greg his new studio apartment, which has no bathroom and a sofa with one leg missing. Someone knocks at the door. The visitor claims to be investigating a ghost. Greg recognizes him as Vincent Price. Price insists Greg is a ghost named Binky Beaumont and warns him not to kill any flies.

Carol anxiously waits to hear anything from Greg and grabs the phone when he calls with his new number and hangs up. Later that evening, Greg shows up at the house and says he regrets moving out in such a hurry.

The Bradys organize a surprise party to welcome Greg back. Carol returns with a lock for Greg's room but Mr. Merrill drops the key into the cake. Greg arrives unexpectedly. Bobby runs into Alice with his skateboard and smashes his face into the cake. He does, however, find the key stuck to his cheek.

The Bradys discuss their musical finale about happiness. Greg suggests music as the origin of happiness, while Bobby opts for money, Peter for girls, and Marcia for love.

Songs:
● "Sunny Side Up" (Buddy G. DeSylva/Lew Brown/Ray Henderson) Performed by the Brady cast
● "It's Not Where You Start" (Dorothy Fields/Cy Coleman) Performed by the Brady cast

● "Traces" (Buddy Buie/James Cobb/Emory Gordy) Performed by Florence
● "All by Myself" (Eric Carmen) Performed by Barry
● "Celebration" Performed by Van Snowden and Sharon Baird
● "Time in a Bottle" (Jim Croce) Performed by Maureen
● "I Want to Be Happy" (Irving Caesar/Vincent Youmans) Performed by Robert and Florence

● "You've Made Me So Very Happy" (Berry Gordy Jr./Brenda and Patrice Holloway/Frank Wilson) Performed by Barry
● "Make Someone Happy" (Betty Comden/Adolph Green/Jule Styne) Performed by Florence
● "Happy Together" (Gary Bonner/ Alan Gordon) Performed by Geri

● "Put on a Happy Face" (Lee Adams/Charles Strouse) Performed by Robert, Florence, Ann B., and Rip
● "Happy Days" (Norman Gimbel/Charles Fox) Performed by the Brady cast
● "United We Stand" (Tony Hiller/Peter Simmons) Performed by the Brady cast

Viewer Alerts:
● In the skit with Vincent Price, writer Bruce Vilanch notes the following connections to real-life personalities: "It occurred to me that if Stella was a ghost, we might have chosen that name so that Price could call out 'STELLA!' like Brando in *A Streetcar Named Desire*. Binky

Beaumont was a big, flamboyantly gay London producer, everybody knew him, especially Price's wife, Coral Browne. My mother played Canasta with Zelda Makowsky in Paterson, New Jersey. She had a dog named Pickles, a Dachshund. Kitty Sheehan was a very old, very fat drag queen in Chicago who ran a gay bar from the 1950s to the '70s named after herself. It was a 'wrinkle room,' where old queens picked up young studs, usually hustlers. Kitty looked a lot like Mayor Daley in drag. We used to joke that you never saw them together."

● At the end of the musical finale Michael Lookinland fumbles his dance routine during the intro to "Happy Days," but he keeps dancing with improvised motions until he can get back on with the others.

Get together for non-stop music and comedy with special guests **Charo** and **The Hudson Brothers**…and the liveliest bunch on television. Starring Florence Henderson, Robert Reed and the Brady Kids!

THE BRADY BUNCH HOUR
abc **NEW SHOW 7:00PM**

⑥ ⑨ ⑩ ⑲ **BRADY BUNCH**
—Variety
Charo and the Hudson Brothers are the guests. In a comedy sketch, Charo portrays a Western-style Cinderella transformed into a beautiful cowgirl by a fairy princess (Ann B. Davis). Carol: Florence Henderson. Mike: Robert Reed. Greg: Barry Williams. Marcia: Maureen McCormick. Peter: Chris Knight. Jan: Geri Reischl. Bobby: Mike Lookinland. (60 min.)
Musical Highlights
"Malaguena" . . . . .Charo
"Disco Queen" . . . . .Hudson Brothers
"Sorry Seems to Be the Hardest Word" . . . . .Florence
"I've Grown Accustomed to Her Face" . . . . .Robert
[Now seen at this new day and time.]

Episode 4: March 21, 1977
Guest Stars: **Charo, The Hudson Brothers**
Taped: February 24–25, 1977

Summary:

The Bradys sing "Toot Toot Tootsie" and debate whether or not Mike can sing.

Carol vocalizes while the kids rehearse a dance number. Mike comes home and announces he hired Merrill to help him with his singing. The family is neither convinced nor interested.

Mike goes to the studio to practice his guitar playing and meets up with Charo who complains about her poor English skills. She tells him her method was to marry someone who liked her musical abilities. Mike shows her his guitar work and she offers to help. Carol and Mr. Merrill overhear the conversation and discover Charo being affectionate with Mike. Carol is shocked and upset.

Charo is invited to dinner at the Brady house. The kids are stunned to learn about Mike's flirting with her. After the meal everyone is speechless. Carol politely confronts

Charo and calmly tells her she's not a jealous wife, but suddenly threatens Charo with bodily harm and storms out of the house. Mike tells Charo they'd better cancel their duet and goes to comfort Carol. Mike finds Carol crying on the back porch and they apologize to one another.

Carol narrates "Cindy Ella," a sketch starring Charo (as a western Cinderella) and Peter (as a cowboy at the hoedown). Mr. Merrill plays one of her ugly stepsisters. Alice is the Fairy Godmother.

The Bradys discuss their finale on the theme of "Places." Carol slaps Peter across the face for mimicking her.

Songs:
- "Toot Toot Tootsie" (Gus Kahn/Ernie Erdman/Robert A. King/Dan Russo/Ted Fio Rito) Performed by the Brady cast
- "Malagueña" (Ernesto Lecuona/Marian Banks) Performed by Charo
- "Sorry Seems to be the Hardest Word" (Bernie Taupin/Elton John) Performed by Florence
- "I've Grown Accustomed to Her Face" (Alan Jay Lerner/Frederick Loewe) Performed by Robert
- "Strike Up the Band" (George Gershwin/Ira Gershwin) Performed by Robert, Florence, Barry, Maureen, and Chris
- "Seventy-Six Trombones" (Meredith Wilson) Performed by Robert, Florence, Barry, Maureen, and Chris
- "Disco Queen" (Randall Foote/Hudson Bros/Peter Leinheiser/William Thomas) Performed by the Hudson Brothers
- "Chicago" (Fred Fisher) Performed by Robert and Florence
- "California Dreamin'" (John Phillips/Michelle Gillian Phillips) Performed by Maureen
- "Back Home Again in Indiana" (James Hanley/Ballard MacDonald) Performed by Florence
- "Do You Know the Way to San Jose" (Hal David/Burt Bacharach) Performed by Maureen, Geri, and Susan
- "San Francisco" (Gus Kahn/Walter Jurmann/Bronslaw Kaper) Performed by Robert and Florence
- "Philadelphia Freedom" (Bernie Taupin/Elton John) Performed by Barry and the Hudson Brothers
- "America" (Stephen Sondheim/Leonard Bernstein) Performed by Charo
- "Big D" (Frank Loesser) Performed by Ann B. and Rip
- "America" (Stephen Sondheim/Bernstein) Performed by the Brady cast

- "United We Stand" (Tony Hiller/Peter Simmons) Performed by the Brady cast

Viewer Alerts:

- In the first minute of the opening number, the corner of a cue card appears briefly in the top right of the screen.
- The duo flip from the trapeze into the pool is a rarely performed acrobatic trick that is considered dangerous.

- In the reprise to "Toot Toot Tootsie" the Krofftette standing next to Geri Reischl does a kick out of sequence with the rest of the group.
- In the fade out just before "Sorry Seems to be the Hardest Word" you can see the shadow of a boom microphone on the scenery wall a few feet above Robert Reed's head.

Episode 5: March 28, 1977

Guest Stars: **Edgar Bergen, Rich Little, Melanie Safka, Van Snowden**

Taped: March 8–9, 1977

Summary:

The Brady Bunch opens this episode without Marcia and her absence is not explained. Greg suggests that the family make a movie and everyone bickers over who will play what part.

Following a musical interlude, Jan, Bobby, and Cindy perform a sketch with Edgar Bergen who teaches the kids how to say things without moving their lips. Back at the swimming pool, the Bradys rehearse Rich Little's introduction. He dives into the pool and bumps heads with Cindy under water. He surfaces, stricken with amnesia.

After everyone has gone to bed, Mike and Carol have a talk with Cindy in the den. Cindy feels guilty about the accident. Little barges in but now thinks Mike and Carol are his parents.

Mr. Merrill shows up the next day pretending to be a doctor but Little panics during the examination and jumps into the ocean. During the confusion, Little bumps heads with Mr. Merrill and gets his memory back but now Mr. Merrill is the one who thinks he's a Brady.

Carol narrates a parody of the story of Pinocchio with Alice as Apple Annie and Peter as Pinocchio. In this version, Pinocchio heads to Hollywood. Mr. Merrill plays Stromboli, a famous motion picture director, while Greg and Marcia appear as movie stars Lance Lust and Leena Malemauler.

Peter, Marcia, and Greg introduce the finale "Songs from Movies."

Songs:

- "I've Got the Music in Me" (Tobias Boshell) Performed by the Brady cast
- "Consider Yourself" (Lionel Bart) Performed by the Brady cast
- "Cyclone" (Melanie Safka) Performed by Melanie Safka
- "Beautiful Noise" (Neil Diamond) Performed by Florence
- "Ease on Down the Road" (Charlie Smalls) Performed by Ann B., Barry, Maureen, Chris, and Rip
- "That's Entertainment" (Howard Dietz/Arthur Schwartz) Performed by Robert and Florence
- "Pinball Wizard" (Pete Townshend/Des McAnuff) Performed by Barry
- "Pink Panther Theme" (Henry Mancini) Performed by the Krofftette Dancers
- "For All We Know" (Robb Wilson/Fred Karlin/Arthur James) Performed by Florence
- "Live and Let Die" (Paul and Linda McCartney) Performed by the Brady kids
- "Supercalifragilisticex- pialidocious" (Richard and Robert Sherman) Performed by Ann B., Rip, and Rich Little
- "Over the Rainbow" (E.Y. Harburg/Harold Arlen) Performed by Melanie Safka
- "That's Entertainment" (Arthur Schwartz/Howard Dietz) Performed by the Brady cast
- "United We Stand" (Tony Hiller/Peter Simmons) Performed by the Brady cast

Viewer Alerts:

● Maureen McCormick is absent from the first fifteen minutes of this episode because she did not show up for the taping (see Chapter 7). Susan Olsen is seen lip synching Maureen's prerecorded vocal solos.

● Peter suggests they make the movie "All the President's Bradys." *All the President's Men* had just been released.

● The scarecrow in "Consider Yourself," played by Van Snowden, is a parody of Cher. Sid Krofft called his creation a "Cher Crow."

● In the finale when Melanie sings "Over the Rainbow" her hair is pinned up, but only seconds later she is seen dancing with Barry and her hair is down.

● Ann B. Davis can be seen bending over and spitting confetti out of her mouth in the "Confetti Encore."

Episode 6: April 4, 1977

Guest Stars: **Sharon Baird, Redd Foxx, Robert Hegyes, The Ohio Players**
Taped: March 15–16, 1977

Summary:

The Bradys sing "Celebrate" to usher in the start of spring. Redd Foxx shows up unexpectedly and says he will be observing the show to get ideas for his own variety program on the ABC network.

That evening, the Bradys are settling in for the night when Marcia comes home with a boy named Winston Beaumont (played by Hegyes) and announces they are engaged. When Mike and Carol forbid Marcia to marry Winston, she becomes defiant and says she'll marry him whether they like it or not.

The next morning, Alice and Mr. Merrill encourage Mike and Carol to give Winston a second chance and they agree to meet him again. The other Brady siblings express their dislike for Winston because of his tall tales. Marcia confronts Winston with how he contradicts himself and calls him a fake. Winston admits that he says and does whatever is necessary for people to like him. Marcia gently calls off the engagement and asks him to call her when he figures out who he is.

Redd Foxx explains in an extended monologue why he would never be able to have his own variety show.

Mike, Carol, Greg, Marcia, and Peter introduce the finale about "Spring." They are all holding flowers. Greg complains that he has only one carnation and Marcia has a whole bunch of roses. Peter says all he has is an onion. Carol explains that it's a flower bulb.

Songs:

(7) 21 28 BRADY BUNCH—Variety
Redd Foxx, Robert Hegyes and the Ohio Players are the guests. In a running comedy sketch, the Bradys try to dissuade Marcia (Maureen McCormick) from accepting a marriage proposal from a very unusual fellow (Robert). Carol: Florence Henderson. Mike: Robert Reed. (60 min.)

- "Celebrate" (Alan Gordon/Garry Bonner) Performed by the Brady cast
- "If My Friends Could See Me Now" (Cy Coleman/Dorothy Fields) Performed by the Brady cast
- "Southern Nights" (Allen Toussaint) Performed by Barry, Maureen, and Geri
- "Fire," Performed by the Ohio Players
- "How Lucky Can You Get" (Fred Ebb/John Kander) Performed by Florence and the Krofftette Dancers
- "Singing in the Rain" (Nacio Herb Brown/Arthur Freed) Performed by the Krofftette Dancers
- "April Showers" (Buddy De Sylva/Louis Silvers) Performed by Robert and Florence
- "I Never Promised You a Rose Garden" (Joe South/Barry Harris) Performed by Geri
- "Spring Will Be a Little Late This Year" (Frank Loesser) Performed by Florence
- "Paper Roses" (Fred Spielman/Janice Torre) Performed by Maureen

- "Tip Toe Through the Tulips" (Joe Burke/Al Dubin) Performed by Ann B. and Rip
- "Stop and Smell the Roses" (Mac Davis/Doc Severinsen) Performed by Barry
- "Laughter in the Rain" (Neil Sedaka) Performed by the Brady cast
- "United We Stand" (Tony Hiller/Peter Simmons) Performed by the Brady cast

Viewer Alerts:

- Towards the end of "How Lucky Can You Get," a tussle of Florence's hair becomes lodged in her eyelashes as she swings her head around. She keeps going (although the problem is obvious) and then Florence cleverly throws her arms up in the air and tries to fix the hair when her hands come back near her face.
- The Brady kids wear the exact same costumes in the finale from episode 3 as in the episode 6 finale. You'll also notice the same scenery from the finale of episode 2 turns up in the opening of episode 6.
- As the Bradys begin to sing "Laughter in the Rain" a Krofftette goes running across the back of the stage bent over hoping not to be noticed.

Episode 7: April 25, 1977

Guest Stars: **Fred Berry, Rick Dees, Mike Kagan, Patty Maloney, Haywood Nelson, Danielle Spencer, Ernest Thomas, Bruce Vilanch**

Taped: March 29–30, 1977

Summary:

The Bradys sing "Get Ready" because here they come for another show. They then explain to the audience about the Water Follies and Krofftette Dancers.

Mike and Carol look through her old high school yearbook and wonder how it is different for the Brady kids going to school on the set.

The Brady kids complain how much they dislike school, especially at the studio. Mr. Merrill enters ringing a school bell, he is their substitute teacher. The *What's Happening* kids arrive because their classroom is closed for the week. Peter invites them to be on the show. Bobby says for them to come over to the Brady house to discuss the details.

Peter asks everyone if they have any ideas about what to do on the show. They all try to decide what famous character they want to be and act them out for each other. Mike and Carol come home and are confused by their children's odd behavior. Jan reports

they have asked the *What's Happening* kids to be on the show. Mike becomes nervous and says he'll drive them home because it is getting late. After they leave, Carol tells the Brady kids that their friends can't be on the show this week because the guests have already been booked. She chooses Peter to break the bad news.

Peter, Jan, Bobby, and Cindy are dreading their meeting with the *What's Happening* kids. Peter can't decide how to tell them they won't be on the show. When Ernest, Danielle, Haywood, and Fred arrive and demonstrate some humorous imitations of the Bradys they would like to do on the show, Peter then explains that they won't be able to. Upset at the news, Ernest, Danielle, Haywood, and Fred get up to leave the house. Peter panics and says he'll find a way to get them on the show. Filled with sudden inspiration, and a bright idea, Peter displays an evil smirk.

② ⑥ ㊽ BRADY BUNCH—Variety
Guests are Rick Dees and the "What's Happening!!" kids (Ernest Thomas, Haywood Nelson, Fred Berry and Danielle Spencer), who fantasize about portraying various celebrities. Carol: Florence Henderson. Mike: Robert Reed. Greg: Barry Williams. Marcia: Maureen McCormick. (60 min.)
Musical Highlights
"Dis-Gorilla" . . . . .Rick
"This Masquerade" . . . . .Florence
"Thank God I'm a Country Girl" . .Ann

Greg asks Peter if he wants to be pushed in the pool before or after he introduces Rick Dees. Peter says he is not being pushed in the pool, and calls in the *What's Happening* kids. Peter says they can be on the show by being pushed in the pool instead of him. But they gang up on Peter and push him in.

The Bradys are seen in a skit involving the grand opening of "Merrilino's House of Perfect Pizza". Bobby is working for Mr. Merrill and will be playing the piano for customers. Mr. Merrill introduces "Bobby Pepperoni" the piano player. Two more customers arrive, a very big man and a very tiny woman (Mike Kagan and Patty Maloney). The two customers talk extremely loud and yell insults at Bobby. Mike smashes a pizza over the man's head.

Carol tells Mike that the kids are saving their energy for the finale about "Disco Songs" so it is up to the two of them to make the introduction. Mike insists they do not have more energy than the kids. Carol replies that since they have six children the kids must think they're bionic.

Songs:
- "Get Ready" (Smokey Robinson) Performed by the Brady cast
- "Walk Right In" (Gus Cannon/Hosea Woods) Performed by Robert, Florence, Barry, Maureen, and Chris
- "Thank God I'm A Country Girl" (John Sommers) Ann B. and the Krofftette Dancers
- "Dis-Gorilla" (Rick Dees) Performed by Rick Dees
- "This Masquerade" (Leon Russell) Performed by Florence
- "Turn the Beat Around" (Gerald and Peter Jackson) Performed by Geri and the Brady kids
- "Those Were the Days" (Gene Raskin) Performed by Robert and Florence
- "Enjoy Yourself With Me" (Kenny Gamble/Leon Huff) Performed by Barry and Krofftette Dancers
- "Disco Duck" (Rick Dees) Performed by Rick Dees and Patty Maloney
- "Tangerine" (Johnny Mercer/Victor Schertzinger) Performed by Ann B. and Rip
- "Dancing Machine" (Hal Davis/Don Fletcher/Dean Parks) Performed by the *What's Happening* kids
- "Disco Lucy — 'I Love Lucy Theme'" (Eliot Daniel/Harold Adamson) Performed by the Brady cast
- "You Make Me Feel Like Dancing" (Leo Sayer/Vincent Poncia) Performed by the Brady cast
- "United We Stand" (Tony Hiller/Peter Simmons) Performed by the Brady cast

Viewer Alerts:
- Michael Lookinland is seen playing piano in several episodes. In real life Mike is an accomplished piano player and got to show off this talent.
- Writer Bruce Vilanch and Krofftettes Chris Wallace and Dee Kaye all have cameo appearances in the "Merrilino's House of Perfect Pizza" sketch.
- During the "Confetti Encore," Bob Reed can be seen gagging on confetti for a brief moment.

Episode 8: May 25, 1977

Guest Stars: **Lynn Anderson, Steve Bluestein, Paul Williams**

Taped: April 5–6, 1977

Summary:

The Bradys sing "I Got Love" and debate the impact of love. Back at the house, the Bradys are preparing for a visit from Paul Williams who will be their guest on the show this week. Paul arrives and is awe struck by Carol's beauty. He openly declares his love for her in front of the entire Brady family.

Mike confronts Paul about his love for Carol, and Paul explains that Carol is a "foxy lady." Mike, becoming agitated, says he knew that when he married her. Paul then suggests he and Carol could get married in the swimming pool and offers Carol a piece of jewelry which belonged to his grandmother. After he leaves, Jan rushes in and an-nounces that country music

singer Lynn Anderson has arrived. Lynn tells Mike and Carol that she just met Paul Williams outside and that he told her he loves her. Lynn then shows them a piece of his grandmother's jewelry she received which matches the one given to Carol a few minutes earlier.

Paul Williams introduces a sketch about "The Columbus Bunch," history's answer to *The Brady Bunch*. This Bunch lives in fifteenth century Genoa. Mike sets out to prove the world is round. Mr. Merrill is the king of Spain and Alice plays the queen.

The Bradys perform their musical finale, "Songs About Music." The family says good-night to everyone. Carol imitates Porky Pig and says, "D-D-D-D-D That's All Folks!" As it would turn out, that was goodbye.

Songs:

- "I Got Love" (Gary Geld/Peter Udell) Performed by the Brady cast
- "We Got Us" (Walter Marks) Performed by the Brady cast
- "Me and My Shadow" (Al Jolson/Billy Rose/Dave Dreyer) Performed by Chris and Rip

- "Right Time of the Night" (Peter McCann) Performed by Lynn Anderson
- "The Hell of It" (Paul Williams) Performed by Paul Williams
- "Born to Say Goodbye" (Alan Gordon) Performed by Florence and her disembodied head
- "Music Music Music" (Stephen Weiss/Bernie Baum) Performed by Robert and Florence
- "What Have They Done to My Song, Ma" (Melanie Safka) Performed by Maureen
- "The Sweetest Sounds" (Richard Rodgers) Performed by Florence
- "Music Is My Life" (Alan Gordon) Performed by Barry
- "Hey Mister Melody" (Marvin Yancy/Charles Jackson) Performed by Geri
- "The Music Goes Round and Round" (Red Hodgson/Mike Riley/Edward Farley) Performed by Ann B. and Rip
- "An Old Fashioned Love Song" (Paul Williams) Performed by Paul Williams and Lynn Anderson
- "Piano Man" (Billy Joel) Performed by the Brady kids
- "I Believe in Music" (Mac Davis) Performed by the Brady cast
- "United We Stand" (Tony Hiller/Peter Simmons) Performed by the Brady cast

Viewer Alerts:

- During the song "We Got Us," Maureen McCormick accidentally hits Florence Henderson in the head and her hat falls off on the lyrics "Something that always will be there…"
- Since it was the final show, there are several songs in this episode about saying goodbye.
- Writer Steve Bluestein has a cameo in "The Columbus Bunch" sketch.
- Some on the set recall that Paul Williams had a little too much to drink prior to filming the musical finale. He stumbles at times through the choreography and lip synching.
- At the end of the show, as the cast exits the stage, Susan Olsen reaches out to take Mike Lookinland's hand but then yanks it away.

SPECIAL APPEARANCES

Donny and Marie Show: January 21, 1977

Summary:

The Brady Bunch made a cameo appearance with Fran Tarkenton, Kenny Stabler, Tony Martin, Cyd Charisse, Paul Lynde, and the Osmond Brothers in a satire of All-American football stars announcing their team players, but this time as the "All American Show Business Team."

Mike Douglas Show:

February 9, 1977

Summary:

Robert Reed and the Brady Bunch kids made an afternoon talk show appearance with Doc Severinsen from *The Tonight Show* and David Soul from *Starsky and Hutch*. Douglas asked the cast to wear name tags so that he could remember all of their names. Barry and Maureen also sang a duet — the Carpenters' hit song, "I Won't Last A Day Without You."

Easter Seals Telethon: April 9, 1977

Summary:

The Brady kids made an appearance on the *Easter Seals Telethon* hosted by Michael Landon. Geri sang "Your Song," by Elton John.

All-Star Anything Goes:

October 28, 1977
and March 24, 1978
Summary:

All-Star Anything Goes was a prime-time series hosted by Bill Boggs that aired Fridays on CBS during the 1977–78 season. Judy Abercrombie was the score girl and Jim Healy did the play-by-play. It featured groups of television personalities pitted against one another in a series of strange and wild relay races. The show was filmed in a stadium at Fullerton College in Fullerton, California. The Brady cast (Barry, Chris, Geri, and Susan) battled The DeFranco family in stunts such as crossing a grease pole over a pool of water, catching balls in a device unofficially known as "hoopy pants," and pedal cart races. In the end the DeFrancos beat the Bradys, 48 to 18. The Bradys asked producer Sam Riddle for a rematch because their pedal cart was found to be defective, and won against the DeFrancos the second time around. Susan Olsen recalls, "One of the things involved a cart and our cart was defective, and there were things that happened that we really didn't think were fair so that's why we said we want a rematch."

START

START

THE
BRADY BUNCH
VARIETY HOUR

THE SIMPSON FAMILY SMILE-TIME VARIETY HOUR

The Simpsons: Simpson's Spinoff Showcase

May 11, 1997

Summary:

Troy McClure hosts this special episode of *The Simpsons* featuring three possible spinoffs, including "The Simpson Family Smile-Time Variety Hour." McClure explains: "The Simpson family finally gets the chance to show off the full range of their talents. Unfortunately one family member didn't want that chance and refused to participate. But thanks to some creative casting, you won't even notice." In the parody, Lisa Simpson has been replaced by a caricature of Geri Reischl, and the family performs several musical numbers. Guest star Tim Conway appears at one point in a skunk costume asking, "...and they thought I stunk?"

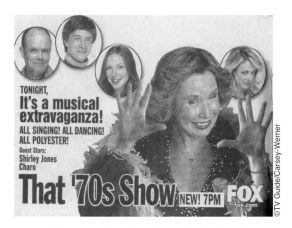

That '70s Show: Red Sees Red

October 10, 2000

Summary:

Amidst family bickering, the Formans settle down together for an evening of television. Kitty suggests they watch *The Brady Bunch Variety Hour* and fantasizes about the Foremans having their very own variety show. The Forman Bunch opens its *Variety Hour* with a rendition of "I Got the Music in Me." Eric and Hyde inform Mrs. Forman that they've decided to run away from home and Red leaves the stage cheering. In the meantime, Laurie is caught making out with Shields and Yarnell. Kitty wants to know who will take care of the boys and Shirley Jones appears. Eric and Hyde reveal their intentions to become part of *The Partridge Family*, and "nail Susan Dey." Shirley Jones explains to Kitty that the boys are leaving because she "chose to be a bad mother." Laurie begs to join too but is rejected by Shirley Jones for being a "whore." Charo then appears and annoys Kitty with her "hoochie coochie." Back in real life, Kitty vows that she won't let the boys leave home, and laments, "This show is crap!"

(Portions of the episode guide are based upon original research by Tony L. Hill)

Epilogue:
When Bad Television Happens to Good People

This book began as an exercise in pointing and laughing. A part of me wanted to say, "Look at this terrible thing we did. I want you to know that I knew it was bad when we did it and it reflects no artistic standards of mine." Writers, directors, and producers all contribute to a production that ends up being a steaming turd, but it's the performers who have to wear that turd. For a few years I resented it when people would come up to me and comment on the *Variety Hour* in an unfavorable way, like it was my fault. I was just doing my job. Hey, I thought it sucked too! The embarrassed fifteen-year-old in me would have liked to shout to the world that I had no artistic say-so in this mess, or better yet, let it remain in obscurity; forget that it ever happened.

©2004 Jan Van Ham

The Bradys reunite for *Still Brady After All These Years* in 2004

Rather quickly people did forget the *Variety Hour* ever existed and that was fine with all of us. I know that some cast members have not been too thrilled that I'm dusting off this skeleton in our closet and exposing it to the world. But it's funny, and it dances the Hustle! I can nearly hear Florence in my head saying, "Susan, put that thing away! It's dirty and it smells bad!" I might have felt that it should remain forgotten were it not so darned amusing in its badness. There were the moments that just had to be shared — the sights of this show that most people have never laid eyes on: Carol Brady ready to catfight Charo for flirting with Mike; Mike Brady wearing a dress; Alice dressed up as a basket of flowers singing "Tiptoe Through the Tulips." These are things that beg a good laugh — maybe not to laugh at us, but to laugh *with us*. In order to do that, I would have to get us laughing. Hopefully this book will have succeeded in that.

What I found out early on was that many people involved with the show did not consider it something to hide. They had a great time and did great work. Look at all the dancers who did double duty as swimmers with every reason to feel proud of an amazing accomplishment. Most of the participants we spoke with had good memories, and in looking at individual contributions, there was some marvelous work done by really talented people.

I have quickly learned that while we may often scoff at our Brady characters, the public does not like it when we do so! I have been quoted as saying that I thought my character Cindy seemed retarded. If you really look at the things she says and does and consider her age, she's not the sharpest tool in the shed, but nobody saw her that way, and for me to insult her like that is a form of blasphemy. I remember an English teacher telling us all, "Sure, everyone loves Lucy, but look at it, Lucy Ricardo is terrible person! She's a horrible wife, a selfish friend, she's dishonest…" I was shocked! Not my Lucy! Over the years I realized how right the teacher had been. (But I still love Lucy — I am a die-hard *I Love Lucy* fan.) I've had people get really mad at me for suggesting that Cindy might not be very intelligent. Just because we played these characters doesn't give us the right to insult them! Poking fun at the Brady family is something to be done very gently. It seems to me that even if we were involved in a show this bad, the public was more than willing to forgive, and might even feel kind of sorry for us that we made such a poor career choice. After all, we were doing this *Variety Hour* as the Bradys. It was Mike, and Carol, and the kids who went into show business. Maybe you can even give us an "E" for effort. (Come on, "E" is right next to "F").

Most of what comes to my mind while I write this now is how *The Brady Bunch Variety Hour* was only the first in so many reincarnations of *The Brady Bunch*. These are the events that kept bringing us back together. These reunions shaped the most richly rewarding and unusual relationship between nine people that I am privileged to be one of. We have come together time and time again. We ARE a family. We are still reuniting for various reasons, some personal, like birthday parties and weddings, some professional. We're not going away just yet. (Will there be a Brady special set in a nursing home? There's a scary thought.) We are not just family with each other, but with an entire generation that we grew up with. Actually, it's several generations. If I weren't me, I would envy myself. It's good to be one of the "Bunch." — Susan

Director Jack Regas (R) and stage manager Sandy Prudden (L) discuss how to clean up the mess the Bradys created.

Costume Sketches

Pete Menefee's dress design for Tina Turner in *The Brady Bunch Hour*

Wizard of Oz costume sketches for Sid Krofft's "Emerald City Car Wash" production number

Costume sketches from the musical number, "Make 'Em Laugh"

Pete Menefee's scarecrow costumes for the number "Consider Yourself" from _Oliver!_

A sketch of Marcia Brady for the number "We Got Us"

Scenic Designs

Art director Bill Bohnert

Early conceptual drafts of scenic designs for the 1976

Brady Bunch Variety Hour **pilot, by Bill Bohnert**

FINALE TALK

FINALE

FAMILY PORTRAIT

WHAT I DID (WAY WE WERE)

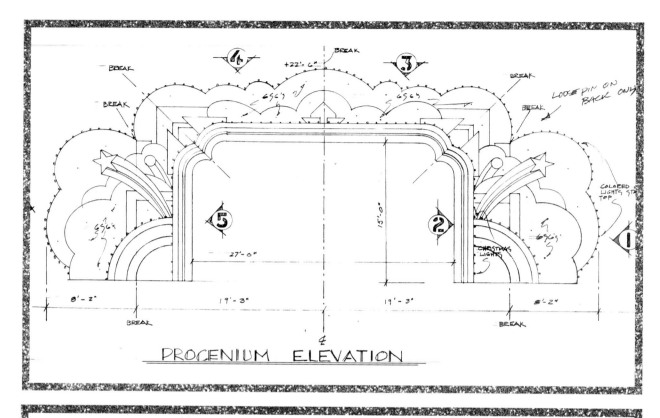

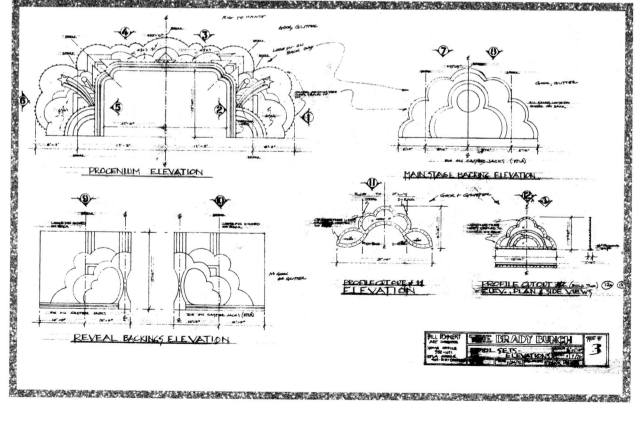

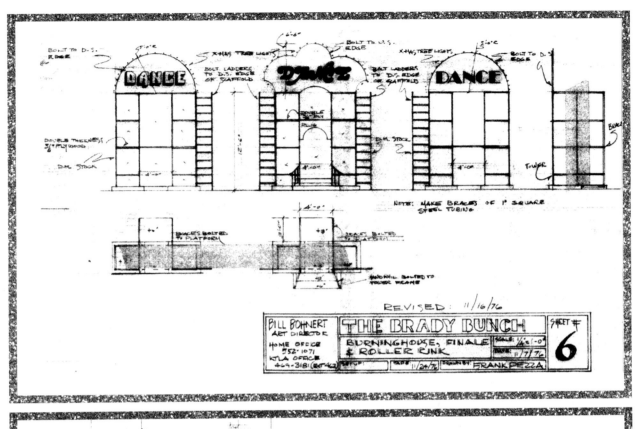

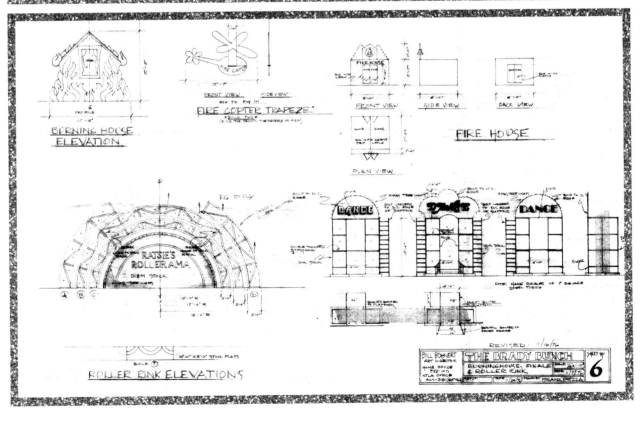

Art director Rene Lagler took over scenic design when *The Brady Bunch Hour* was picked up as a series by ABC in January 1977.

Lagler's first job was to redesign the pool proscenium.

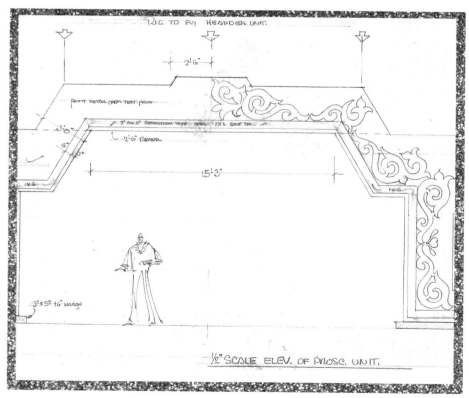

He also designed a stage setting for the weekly "Family Production Number."

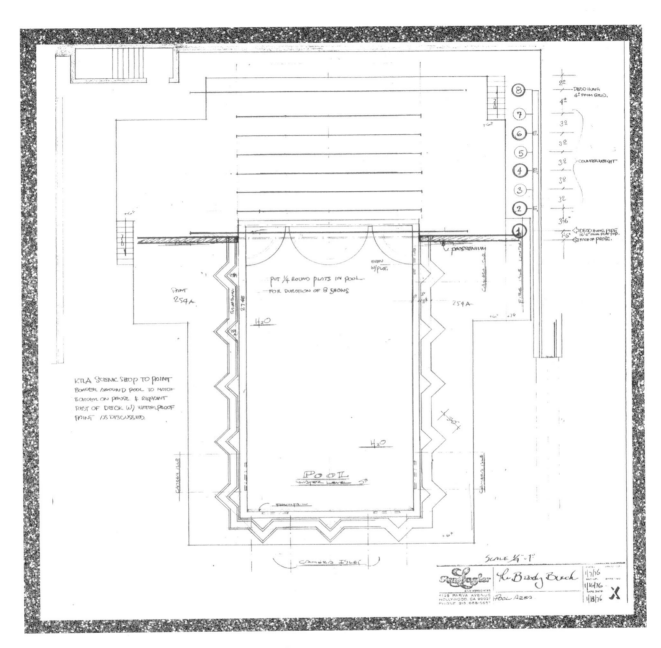

Overhead view of the *Brady Bunch* swimming pool

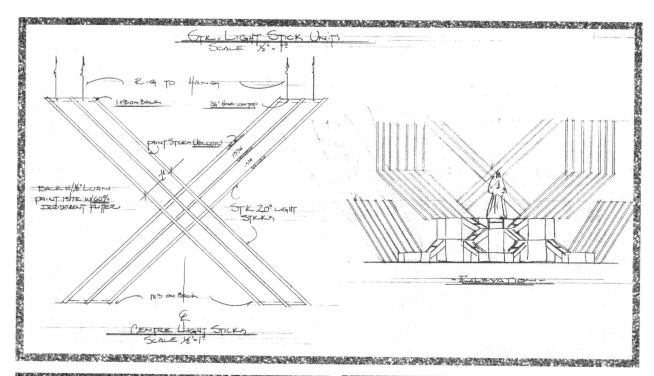

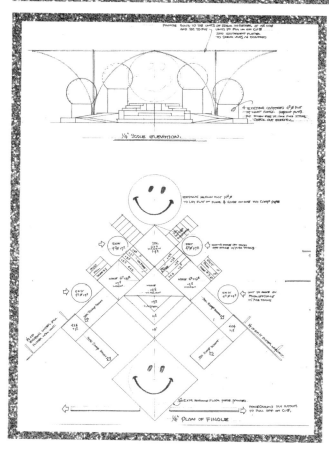

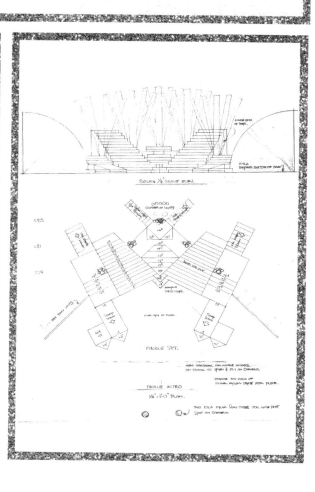

Brady Bunch Hour
Rip Taylor
"Candy"

Pere Menifee

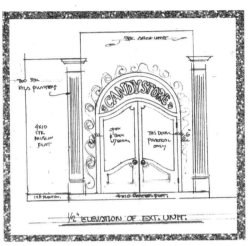

½" ELEVATION OF EXT. UNIT.

A fantasy production number about "Candy" was planned for episode two, but was later cut from the script. Surviving scene designs reveal it was set in a candy shop and a costume sketch shows Rip Taylor as "Tooth Decay."

½" SCALE ELEVATION

APPENDIX

Show Credits

The Brady Bunch Hour (aka *The Brady Bunch Variety Hour*)

First Telecast: November 28, 1976
Last Telecast: May 25, 1977

CAST:

FLORENCE HENDERSON	Carol Brady	ROBERT REED*	Mike Brady
ANN B. DAVIS	Alice Nelson	MAUREEN McCORMICK	Marcia Brady
BARRY WILLIAMS	Greg Brady	GERI REISCHL	Jan Brady
CHRISTOPHER KNIGHT	Peter Brady	SUSAN OLSEN	Cindy Brady
MIKE LOOKINLAND	Bobby Brady	RIP TAYLOR	Jack Merrill

THE KROFFTETTES AND WATER FOLLIES:

Charkie Phillips	Christine Wallace	Robyn Blythe	Susan Buckner
Linda Hoxit	Dee Kaye	Lynne Latham	Judy Susman

ALTERNATES

Michelle Horowitz	Laura Steele	Michele Adler
Valerie-Jean Miller	Susie Guest	Laurie Bartram*

GEORGE WYLE ORCHESTRA:
Directed and conducted by George Wyle*

TRUMPET	TROMBONE	SAXOPHONE/WOODWINDS
Dalton Smith*	Donald Waldrop	Philip Sobel
Albert Aarons	Grover Mitchell	William Collette
Robert Bryant*		Robert Cooper
Charles Findley		Robert Hardaway
Robert Findley		John Setar

PERCUSSION	STRING BASS	REHEARSAL PIANISTS
Earl Palmer*	Mel Pollan	Claude Williamson
Wallace Snow	Jay B. Wolfe*+	Clifford Bryant
Gene Estes*		Bob Bailey
Evan Diner	PIANO	Dick Emmons
Alan Estes	William Mays	
Angelo Mauceri	Russell Freeman*	
	James Drennen*	

GUITAR	ARRANGERS	COPYISTS
Jimmy Wyble	George Wyle*	Albert Ingalls
Daniel Sawyer	Sid Feller*	Bernie Lewis*
Mickhael Kollander	Van Alexander	Emanuel Gershman*
David Doran+	Claude Williamson	Robert Reid
	David Campbell	Gene Bren*
		Barret O'Hara

* Deceased
+ "Melanie" band members — Guest Star, Episode Five

Production Credits

EXECUTIVE PRODUCERS: Sid and Marty Krofft

PRODUCED BY: Lee Miller and Jerry McPhie

DIRECTED BY: Jack Regas (Series),

Art Fisher (Pilot)*

ASSISTANT DIRECTOR: Rick Locke

ASSOCIATE DIRECTOR: Chuck Liotta,

Carol Englehart Scott

WRITING SUPERVISED BY: Carl Kleinschmitt

WRITTEN BY: Ronny Graham,* Terry Hart,

Bruce Vilanch, Steve Bluestein, Mike Kagan

HEAD OF ABC NETWORK VARIETY AND SPECIALS:

Bonny Dore

ASSOCIATE PRODUCER: Tom Swale

COMEDY CONSULTANT: Ronny Graham*

MUSIC SUPERVISED AND CONDUCTED BY:

George Wyle*

MUSIC ARRANGED BY: Sid Feller,* Claude Williamson

MUSIC CONTRACTOR: John Rosenberg

MUSIC CLEARANCE: Mary Williams

MUSIC RESEARCH: Tony Martin Jr. (Pilot)

ART DIRECTOR: Rene Lagler (Series),

Bill Bohnert (Pilot)

ASSISTANT ART DIRECTOR: John Vallone*

CHOREOGRAPHER: Joe Cassini

ASSISTANT CHOREOGRAPHER:

Casey Cole (Series), Mark Hudson (Pilot)

COSTUMES DESIGNED BY: Pete Menefee (Series),

Madeline Graneto (Pilot)

WARDROBE MISTRESS: Mari Grimaud

COSTUME CREW: Larry Lefler,* Gordon Brockway,* Judy

Corbett, Donovan Sage Mervis, Tina Hoyser, Paul Dafel-

mair, Michele Neely Puluti, Paul Lopez, John Patton, Kelly

Kimball

LIGHTING CONSULTANT: Leard Davis, Bill Klages

ASSISTANT TO THE PRODUCER: Susie Kain-Maddux,

Robyn Lewis

ASSISTANTS TO SID AND MARTY KROFFT:

Trudy Bennett,* Shelley Nelbert

ACCOUNTANTS: Karen Gordon, Maureen Holmes,

Cyd Kalb

MAKEUP: Mike Moschella, Fred Williams,

Alex Pollock

HAIRDRESSERS: Christine George, Jan Brandow

UNIT MANAGERS: Jim Zrake, Tom Bruehl

TECHNICAL DIRECTOR: Mike Maloof

STAGE MANAGERS: Sandy Prudden,*

Steve Dichter, Kieth Hopkins,

Ted Vanklaveren

LIGHTING DIRECTOR: Reg Leffler

SCENIC COORDINATOR: Ray Brannigan

PROPS: Dave Cazares

CUE CARDS: Tommy Baldwin

AUDIO: Ken Becker,* Dick Sartor*

VIDEO: Dick Browning

CAMERAS: John Gillis, Dick Watson,*

Gary Westfall,* George Wood,* Ken Dahlquist

VIDEO TAPE EDITOR: Bill Breshears, Pam Marshall

PRODUCTION CONSULTANTS: John Braislin,

Rich Heller

PRODUCTION COORDINATOR: Bud Martin (Pilot)

PRODUCTION EXECUTIVES: Toby Martin (Pilot),

Albert J. Tenzer

PRODUCTION ASSISTANT: Manette Rosen (Pilot), Kerry

Cummings (Series)

GOFOR: Mark Bish (Pilot), Jerry Ketchum (Series)

PRODUCTION COORDINATOR: Pat Davis

PRODUCTION STAFF: Tom Rickard, Paula Mehr, Janet

Smith, J. Paul Higgins, Peter Lauritson, Brooke Forsythe,

Irene Soto

STUDIO TEACHERS: Jeff Zandberg (Pilot);

Elise Ganz, Beth Clopton,* Peggy Cobb* (Series)

AFTRA: Anita Cooper

BUSINESS AFFAIRS: Don Lougherty

MIMEO: Ed Leavitt

* Deceased

(These production staff listings are based upon a very limited
number of surviving records. To anyone who was not included,
please accept our sincere apologies.)

Photo/Image Credits

Acosta, John (Musicians' Union): 94, 95, 96
American Broadcasting Companies: 52, 63, 72, 167, 187, 189, 194, 198, 207, 222
Anderson, Lynn: 232, 252
AP Photos: 132
Bison Archives: 31, 44
Bluestein, Steve: 41, 175
Brown, Kip: 6
Blythe, Robyn: 139
Blythe, Sean: 268
Bohnert, Bill: 42, 45, 50, 314-317
Bongo Entertainment: 260
Buckner, Susan: 138, 140
Carey, Jason: 241
Carsey-Werner: 265, 303
Cassini, Joe: 41, 59, 198, 217, 255
Chuldenko, John: 268
Clopton, Chuck: 181
Cole, Casey: 41
Corbis: 71
Corbett, Judy: 56, 69
Daily Variety: 44
David Sarnoff Library: 128
Davis, Ann B: 23
Dees, Rick: 248
Dichter, Steve: 168
Dore, Bonny: 33, 39, 192
Everett Collection: 34, 135, 167
Feller, Bill: 93
Ganz, Elise: 177
Getty Images/Michael Ochs: 126, 148, 191, 206
Glassman, Debbie: 97, 99
Globe Photos: 26, 65, 77
Gordon, Elisa: 117
Grimaud, Mari: 90
Groening, Matt: 260, 302
HarperCollins: 213
Hart, Terry: 40
Hollywood Reporter: 67, 69

Hoxit, Linda: 86, 89, 138, 142, 143, 145, 158, 163
Kagan, Mike: 121
Klega, Darine: 85, 91, 120, 139, 142, 149, 154, 156, 238, 248
Kleinschmitt, Carl: 40
Kozlowski, Madeline: 42, 54, 55
Krofft Pictures: IV, 4, 5, 7, 8, 9, 33, 58, 60, 66, 73, 103. 111, 123, 130, 133, 136, 140. 142, 143, 144, 147, 150, 157, 160, 161, 162, 165, 168, 170, 171, 176, 196, 257, 275, 277
Lagler, Rene: 80, 81, 82, 107, 113, 116, 202, 318-321
Latham, Lynne: 139
Laufer Media, Inc.: 21, 22, 63, 74, 172, 204, 299
Lipscomb, Karen: 1, 6, 8, 9, 94, 95, 96, 106, 203
Lookinland, Mike: 12, 110
Maloney, Patty: 251
McPhie, Jerry: 16
Menefee, Pete: 82, 84, 85, 86, 87, 88, 90, 91, 159, 309-313, 321
Miller, Lee: 16
Music Theatre International: 19
Nichelson, Ted: 35, 78, 264, 266
Nickelson, Kevin: 114, 115
Oakley, Bill: 259
Olsen, Susan: 22, 178, 179, 270
Phillips, Charkie: 44, 83, 90, 104, 105, 137, 141, 142, 143, 146, 150, 151, 152, 154, 155, 161, 170, 195, 200, 209, 295
Photofest: III, 3, 10, 11, 17, 43, 45, 106, 124, 185, 210, 212, 227
Press Telegram: 28
Regas, Jack: 78
Reischl, Geri: 24, 25, 26, 61, 110, 172, 173, 186, 267, 300, 301
Resnick, Linda: 177

Robina, Diane: 258
Rodgers and Hammerstein Organization: 18
Rudetsky, Seth: 273
Sattefield, Joel: 300
Scholastic Publications: 101, 104
Sinclair, Kevin: 268
Snowden, Van: 32, 34, 36, 235
Spencer, Danielle: 250
Stone, Troy: 268
Stringer, Ronald: 40, 122
Susman, Judy Brandt: 138
Taylor, Rip: 76, 77, 200
Tjaden, Karen: 9, 17, 299
Tompkins, Steve: 259
TV1: 263
TV Guide: 272, 279, 280, 282, 284, 286, 288, 291, 297, 300, 303
TV Land: 304, 306
Twentieth Century Fox: 260, 302
Van Ham, Janet: 304, 306
Viacom: 258
Vilanch, Bruce: 40
Wallace, Christine Gow: 84, 137, 142
Walsh, Kenneth: 266
Weissman, Jerry: 42
Winans, Wendy: 214

Interview Record

A total of 99 original interviews were conducted for this book

Anderson, Lynn: 8/12/06
Bluestein, Steve: 5/8/06; 7/26/07
Blythe, Robyn: 5/20/07
Bohnert, Bill: 2/13/06
Buckner, Susan: 3/27/06
Carver, Chris: 8/20/07
Cassini, Joe: 8/31/05
Clausen, Alf: 8/21/06
Clopton, Chuck: 10/26/08
Cole, Casey: 11/20/05; 7/25/07
Corbett, Judy: 8/30/06
Dahlquist, Ken: 7/28/06; 8/9/07
Davis, Ann B.: 7/2/08
Davis, Pat: 10/28/07
DeCaro, Frank: 8/30/06
Dees, Rick: 8/10/05
Dichter, Steve: 4/8/06
Doolman, Deborah: 8/17/06
Dore, Bonny: 8/23/07; 9/4/07
Evanier, Mark: 5/29/07
Evans, Barbara: 10/24/07
Ganz, Elise: 8/20/07
Graneto, Madeline: 9/24/06; 3/18/07
Grimaud, Mari: 8/30/06
Guest, Susie Casey: 10/23/07
Haney, Sonja: 9/10/07
Hart, Terry: 10/8/06
Higgins, J. Paul: 9/29/08
Hegyes, Robert: 9/21/07
Hoxit, Linda: 3/18/06; 7/22/07
Hylkema, Brittny: 8/2/07
Kagan, Mike: 8/18/06
Kimball, Kelly: 8/17/06
Klega, Darine: 4/19/06
Kleinschmitt, Carl: 8/5/07
Knight, Christopher: 4/14/05
Krofft, Marty: 5/16/06
Krofft, Sid: 1/17/06; 8/16/07
Lagler, Rene: 2/26/06
Latham, Lynne: 4/11/06; 7/10/07
Lembeck, Michael 7/2/08
Lipscomb, Karen: 9/30/07
Locke, Rick: 2/17/06; 7/17/07

Lookinland, Michael: 2/12/06
Lovitt, Chip: 7/25/06
Maloney, Patty: 7/29/06
McCormick, Maureen: 6/5/08
McLain, Glenn: 11/02/07
McPhie, Jerry: 8/4/07; 7/27/08
Menefee, Pete: 4/28/06; 8/27/06
Miller, Lee: 7/20/07; 10/4/07
Miller, Valerie-Jean: 9/5/07; 10/8/07
Oakley, Bill: 8/2/07
Olsen, Susan: 4/10/05
Phillips, Charkie: 5/15/06
Pirro, Mark: 8/21/06
Redutsky, Seth: 9/23/07; 10/23/07
Regas, Jack: 2/17/06; 7/17/07
Reischl, Geri: 5/3/06; 8/5/07
Reischl, Wanda: 10/2/06; 8/22/07
Robina, Diane: 9/5/07
Rosenberg, John: 8/21/06
Sage, Donovan: 8/31/06; 8/21/07
Schwartz, Lloyd: 8/21/07
Schwartz, Sherwood: 7/11/06
Seiter, Joe: 9/11/06
Shaffer, Paul: 8/23/07
Smith, Don: 10/30/07
Snowden, Van: 8/7/05
Soebel, Phil: 9/23/07
Stone, Troy: 8/8/07
Susman, Judy: 4/12/06; 7/8/07
Sutton, Lisa: 10/28/07
Taylor, Rip: 4/20/06
Thomas, Ernest: 9/22/07
Tompkins, Steve: 8/8/07
Turner, Rett: 8/21/06
Vanklaveren, Ted: 8/27/07
Vilanch, Bruce: 1/11/06
Wallace, Christine: 5/22/06; 3/18/07
Williams, Barry: 4/12/06
Williams, Paul: 4/19/07
Williamson, Claude: 3/27/06; 8/13/07
Zrake, Jim: 4/13/06

Acknowledgments

Thanks to the following individuals for their help with this book:

Jeff Androsky, Helen Ashford, Blanket, Steve Bluestein, Robyn Blythe, Bill Bohnert, Janet Bonifer, Howard Bragman, Lynne Braiman, Judy Brandt, Kip Brown, Susan Buckner, Tony Carbajol, Gloria Cardenas, Jason Carey, David Caron, Chris Carver, Joe Cassini, Paul Chesne, Maria Ciaravino, Alf Clausen, Chuck Clopton, Jill Clopton, Casey Cole, Judy Corbett, Erin Creasey, Michael Cummings, Jared Curry, Ken Dahlquist, Kagey Dahlquist, Neil T. Daniels, Jack David, Ann B. Davis, Pat Davis, Frank DeCaro, Rick Dees, Steve Dichter, Henry Diltz, Deborah Doolman, Bonny Dore, Louise DuArt, Ron Elberger, Mark Evanier, Babara Evans, Carmen Fanzone, Susie Fellows, Jordan Fields, Sophia Fields, Elise Ganz, Michael Gaylord, Winston Gieseke, Debbie Glassman, Paul Goebel, Mari Grimaud, Susan Guest Casey, Todd Guhlstorf, Sonja Haney, Kerry Hanson, Terry Hart, Robert Hegyes, Tony L. Hill, Linda Hoxit Smith, Whami Hwang, Jonathan Hyams, Chad Irvin, Mike Kagan, Sara Kaufman, Kelly Kimball, Darine Klega, Carl Kleinschmitt, Christopher Knight, Madeline Kozlowski, Marty Krofft, Sid Krofft, Rene Lagler, Fannie LaGreca, Lynne Latham, Annik Lejeune, Arjen van der Lely, Michael Lembeck, Jim Lichnerowitz, Karen Lipscomb, Rick Locke, Michael Lookinland, Frank Lovece, Chip Lovitt, Alexander B. Magoun, Patty Maloney, Judy Mandler, Dragon Marjanovic, Margaret Marr, David Martindale, Maureen McCormick, Michael McMeel, Jerry McPhie, Lee Miller, Valerie-Jean Miller, Jerry Moreno, George Nejame, Kevin Nickelson, Erin Nimmons, JJ Nimmons, Bill Oakley, Charkie Phillips, Mark Pirro, Deanna Pope, Vinnie Rattolle, Jack Regas, Wanda Reischl, Linda Resnick, Diane Robina, John Rosenberg, Matt Roush, Seth Rudetsky, Donovan Sage Mervis, Susan Salerno, Tina Salmon, Joel Satterfield, Leo Savalas, Sue Schneider, Emily Schultz, Lloyd Schwartz, Sherwood Schwartz, Joe Seiter, Paul Shaffer, Denise Silberman, Don Smith, Erin Smith, Van Snowden, Phil Soebel, Mitchell Squires, Wesley Staples, Cassandra Taylor, Rip Taylor, Ernest Thomas, Karen Tjaden, Sam Toles, Steve Tompkins, Bill Tracey, Rett Turner, Ted Vanklaveren, Eddie Velasquez, Byron Villagran, Christine Wallace, Simon Ware, Jerry Weissman, Barry Williams, Claude Williamson, Jim Zrake.

Special Thanks:

Richard F. Brophy, Ruth Cobb, Arthur Corra, James Cummins, Sara Hanlon, Laurent Langlais, Chris Mann, Irene McCormick, Glenn McLain, Robert Mycroft, Erik Morris, Carmen Nichelson, Dave and Janice Nichelson, Lynn and Sharon Nichelson, Mike and Rene Nichelson, Nick and Jeanette Nichelson, John Nimmons, Diane Olsen, Lawrence and DeLoice Olsen, Lennon Parker, Brett Pearce, Robrt Pela, David Pires, Geri Reischl, Andrew Sandoval, Cynthia Sharvelle, Eric and Gladys Sharvelle, Michael Skelly, Gary Strobl, L. Jane Thomley, Wendy Winans.

Endnotes

[1] Andrew J. Edelstein and Frank Lovece, The Brady Bunch Book (New York: Warner Books, 1990) 16.

[2] David Martindale, Pufnstuf and Other Stuff (Los Angeles: Renaissance Books, 1998) 224.

[3] David Martindale, Pufnstuf and Other Stuff (Los Angeles: Renaissance Books, 1998) 225.

[4] David Martindale, Pufnstuf and Other Stuff (Los Angeles: Renaissance Books, 1998) 223.

[5] Jean Lewis, "Florence Henderson Has Two Families," Chicago Tribune TV Week 3–9
       April 1977: Section 10, page 3.

[6] David Martindale, Pufnstuf and Other Stuff (Los Angeles: Renaissance Books, 1998) 228.

[7] Academy of Television Arts and Sciences Foundation, "Interview with Florence Henderson."
       22 October 1999, 27 August 2007 < http://www.youtube.com/watch?v=xjJtZiGWMN0 >.

[8] Academy of Television Arts and Sciences Foundation, "Interview with Florence Henderson."
       22 October 1999, 27 August 2007 < http://www.youtube.com/watch?v=xjJtZiGWMN0 >.

[9] Richard Hack, "Tele-Visions," Hollywood Reporter 16 November 1976: 6.

[10] Academy of Television Arts and Sciences Foundation, "Interview with Florence Henderson."
       22 October 1999, 27 August 2007 < http://www.youtube.com/watch?v=xjJtZiGWMN0 >.

[11] "Singing and Dancing Bradys," Sunday Record 20 March 1977.

[12] Charles Witibeck, " 'The Brady Bunch,' Whooping It Up Again," York Sunday News April 1977.

[13] Barry Williams and Chris Kreski, Growing Up Brady (Los Angeles: Good Guy Entertainment, 1999) 151.

[14] Bill Kauffman, "The Bunch that Bounced Back," Newsday's Weekly Guide to Television 17–23
       April 1977: 4–6.

[15] "Second Chance for the Bradys," LA Times 19 April 1977: F12.

[16] "Eve Plumb: Why She Left the Brady Bunch," Teen Beat Magazine May 1977: 27.

[17] News Citizen, December 1976.

[18] Richard Hack, "Tele-Visions," Hollywood Reporter 16 November 1976: 6.

[19] E! True Hollywood Story: The Brady Bunch, E!, Los Angeles, 6 June 1999.

[20] "Spirit," People Magazine 15 August, 1977: 71.

[21] Internet Movie Database, "Biography for Ann B. Davis," 25 October 2007
           <http://www.imdb.com/name/nm0002036/bio>.

[22] Andrew J. Edelstein and Frank Lovece, The Brady Bunch Book (New York: Warner Books, 1990) 90–91.

[23] "Spirit," People Magazine 15 August, 1977: 71.

[24] Late Night With Conan O'Brien, NBC, Burbank, 20 January 1994.

[25] Richard Hack, "Tele-Visions," Hollywood Reporter 16 November 1976: 6.

[26] Academy of Television Arts and Sciences Foundation, "Interview with Florence Henderson."
       22 October 1999, 27 August 2007 < http://www.youtube.com/watch?v=xjJtZiGWMN0 >.

[27] "Second Chance for the Bradys," LA Times 19 April 1977: F12.

[28] Chris Mann, " 'Marcia Brady' Gets Her Life — and Self — in Shape," TV Guide 3 April 2007.

[29] "The Brady Bunch Hour," Variety, 26 January 1977: 66.

[30] Charles Witibeck, " 'The Brady Bunch,' Whooping It Up Again," York Sunday News April 1977.

[31] Jean Lewis, "Florence Henderson Has Two Families," Chicago Tribune TV Week 3–9
       April, 1977: Section 10, page 3.

[32] Maureen McCormick, Here's the Story (New York: HarperCollins, 2008), 104.

[33] Charles Witibeck, " 'The Brady Bunch,' Whooping It Up Again." York Sunday News, April 1977.

[34] Academy of Television Arts and Sciences Foundation, "Interview with Florence Henderson."
       22 October 1999, 27 August 2007 < http://www.youtube.com/watch?v=xjJtZiGWMN0 >.

[35] Carol Glines, "How I Got Thin at 50!" OK Weekly 14 May 2007: 77.

[36] Larry King Live, CNN, Los Angeles, 5 April 2007.

[37] Maureen McCormick, Here's the Story (New York: HarperCollins, 2008), 105.

[38] Showbiz Tonight, CNN, Los Angeles, 5 April 2007.

[39] Showbiz Tonight, CNN, Los Angeles, 5 April 2007.

[40] Larry King Live, CNN, Los Angeles, 5 April 2007.

[41] Academy of Television Arts and Sciences Foundation, "Interview with Florence Henderson."
       22 October, 1999, 27 August 2007 < http://www.youtube.com/watch?v=xjJtZiGWMN0 >.

[42] Biography: The Brady Bunch, A&E Network, Los Angeles, 24 June 2005.

[43] "Underground Interview; Fake Stacy," Underground, 30 October 2007
           <http://www.ugtv.org/fakestacy.php>

Index

About the Authors

Ted Nichelson

Ted Nichelson is a writer, musician, business entrepreneur, and pop-culture historian. He is an avid collector of *Brady Bunch* memorabilia, and is the author of the award winning website *Complete Guide to the Brady Bunch Hour* and designed the *Official Geri Reischl Website*. These interests were sparked by his friendship with Susan Olsen, who played Cindy Brady.

He earned a Doctor of Arts degree in harp performance and music education from Ball State University, and a Master of Music degree in harp from the University of Michigan. He also received a Bachelor of Music in harp from Illinois Wesleyan University and is a member of Pi Kappa Lambda, national music honorary society. Currently, he works full-time as a freelance harpist in Hollywood, California, and serves Los Angeles County and surrounding areas.

Nichelson's skills in academic research were developed while studying music history at Illinois State University for a degree in musicology. Portions of his work have been published in the *American Harp Journal*, a scholarly publication. He has also served as editor and author on dozens of student publications and research projects.

He is also employed part-time as a property manager in Los Angeles, and works as a teacher in the Beverly Hills Unified School District.

Susan Olsen

Susan Olsen is internationally recognized for her role as Cindy Brady on *The Brady Bunch*. She is an actress, writer, artist, producer, radio personality and, most important, the mother of a wonderful teenage son.

She began her career as an entertainer in 1962 at the age of fourteen months, retiring from the business at the age of three. She returned to show business a couple years later when a talent scout picked her out of her kindergarten class to sing a song on *The Pat Boone Show.* She also appeared singing in an Elvis Presley movie. Various jobs finally led her to the role of Cindy on *The Brady Bunch* — a show that has been on the air for over forty years around the world. In fact, as you read this, it is probably on the air somewhere.

After *The Brady Bunch* ended, she became a successful graphic artist. Olsen worked for fashion designers and served as art director for a Malibu-based clothing company. She left there to start her own firm called Man In Space, and developed a line of glow in the dark sneakers for Converse Shoes.

Olsen has been a favorite guest on all the major talk shows including CNN's *Larry King Live* and *The Howard Stern Show*. The huge response led to her own daily radio show following Stern on KLSX-Radio in Los Angeles with Ken Ober. In the middle of all this, Olsen created and was executive producer for *The Brady Bunch Home Movies,* a CBS prime time special. She most recently toured the country for three years as the national spokesperson for Migraine Awareness and serves as Director of Media and Special Projects for Precious Paws animal rescue.

Lisa Sutton

Lisa Sutton began her professional career as a graphic designer and art director in the music business. She has designed hundreds of CD packages with artists ranging from George Lopez and the Dead Kennedys to the Monkees and David Cassidy. A pop-culture expert and officially credited "Bradyologist," Sutton also produced and wrote liner notes for many historical music packages, including the Grammy-nominated *Have A Nice Decade* box set for Rhino Entertainment and *It's A Sunshine Day: The Best of the Brady Bunch* for MCA.

Sutton served as segment producer on the RLTV daily talk show *The Florence Henderson Show*, and has been involved with several high-profile projects including *A&E Biography*, the Emmy-nominated *Star Wars: The Legacy Revealed, Look Up In the Sky: The Story of Superman* and the Emmy-winning *TV Land Back-Stage Pass.* 2008 marked the debut of her weekly "Collectiblog" for TVLand.com, a column dedicated to TV and pop culture memorabilia collecting. She is also the author of five chapters in the collaborative book *Bubblegum Music is the Naked Truth (The Dark History of Prepubescent Pop, from the Banana Splits to Britney Spears).*